MORE PRAISE FOR *DRAYTON HALL STORIES*

"We appreciate the work and thought devoted to the preservation of Drayton Hall and hope that our contributions to this book's stories will enhance the understanding of our history and of our shared heritage."
— **Molly Drayton Osteen, Anne Drayton Nelson, Charles (Chad) H. Drayton, and Frank B. Drayton Jr.**

"As African American descendants of Drayton Hall, we respect the spirits of our ancestors and believe this book honors their values and work and illuminates our memories and hopes. May we all come to the table."
— **Catherine Braxton and Rebecca Campbell**

"George McDaniel continues to inspire with his broad vision for historic preservation. Decades of oral history research have produced a landmark publication reminding us that descendants' and other stakeholders' experiences are deeply embedded in historic places. By bringing them to light, we can present a new and more complete and compelling interpretation of sites' recent histories."
— **Carol B. Cadou**, Executive Director, The National Society of The Colonial Dames of America (NSCDA) and National Headquarters, Dumbarton House

"Hear in these interviews the voice of a healer. Blacks made easy to talk about a painful past. Whites persuaded that everybody's history makes better history. George McDaniel finds common ground at Drayton Hall, a place for all."
—**Cary Carson**, retired Vice President, Research Division, Colonial Williamsburg Foundation

"By assembling a collection of Drayton Hall's voices, both Black and White, George McDaniel has given us a powerful glimpse of our past. Their stories illustrate the power of place in America's history."
— **John E. Fleming**, Ph.D., Past Chair, American Association for State and Local History

"George McDaniel has created a remarkable narrative of Drayton Hall, one of America's most significant historic places. He has the singular perspective as a scholar, public historian, and community leader to present multiple voices that tell an inspiring story of family histories, historic preservation, and racial reconciliation."
— **Brent D. Glass**, Director Emeritus, National Museum of American History, Smithsonian Institution, Author, *50 Great American Places, Essential Historic Sites Across the U.S*

"We interpret our history through the buildings we choose to preserve, but that history is far more than architecture alone. *Drayton Hall Stories* shows why and is compelling in doing so."
— **Joseph McGill Jr.**, Founder and Executive Director, The Slave Dwelling Project

"Sometimes we become so focused on sharing facts and details at museums and historic sites that we miss the magic of the story. This book conveys Drayton Hall's magic—and that is what visitors remember and why they come back."
— **Helen Hill**, CEO, Explore Charleston

Drayton Hall Site Map*

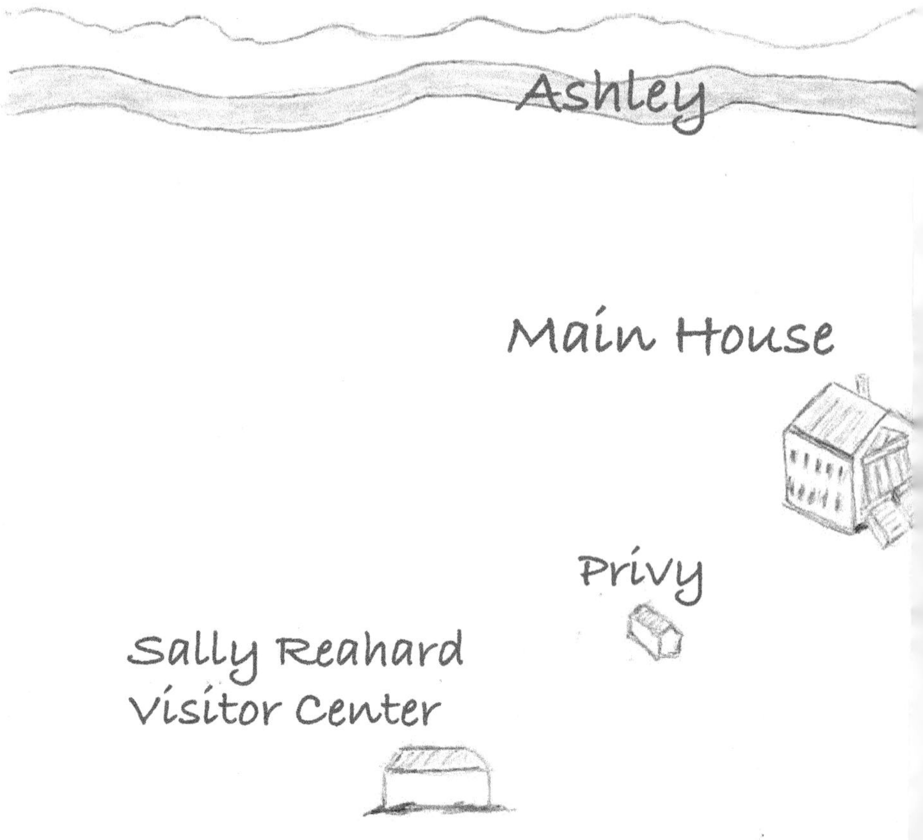

Ashley

Main House

Privy

Sally Reahard
Visitor Center

*Not to scale

River

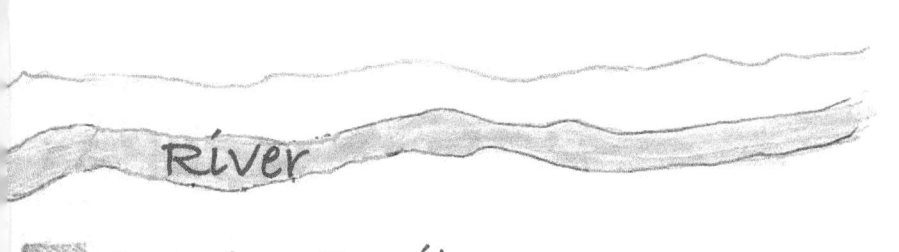

Drayton Family Memorial

Reflecting Pond

Live Oak

African American Cemetery

Entrance Lane

Pond

Richmond Bowens' House Site

Ashley River Road

DRAYTON HALL STORIES:
A Place And Its People

George W. McDaniel

Published by
Evening Post Books
Charleston, South Carolina

Copyright © 2022 George W. McDaniel
All rights reserved.
First edition

Author: George W. McDaniel
Editor: John M. Burbage
Designer: Gill Guerry

Cover Photographs:
  Drayton Hall Landscape - ©tonysweet.com
  Drayton Hall Descendants - Charleston Snapped Photography
    Foreground: Catherine Braxton, granddaughter of Catherine Bowens, enslaved at Drayton Hall, and Charlie Drayton, last owner of Drayton Hall and whose grandfather Charles H. Drayton "owned" Catherine Bowens. Background: Shelby Nelson, Charlie's grandson, speaking to Rebecca Campbell, sister of Catherine Braxton; and Charles H. Drayton, grandson of Charlie Drayton, and Frank B. Drayton Jr., his nephew.

Images are courtesy of the Drayton Hall Preservation Trust and the author unless otherwise noted. Interviewees provided their personal photos; any accompanying photo credits are noted.

No part of this book may be reproduced or transmitted in any form or by any means, electronic or mechanical, including photocopying, recording or by information storage and retrieval system – except by a reviewer who may quote brief passages in a review to be printed in a magazine, newspaper, or on the web – without permission in writing from the publisher. For information, please contact the publisher.

First printing 2022
Printed in the United States of America

A CIP catalog record for this book has been applied
for from the Library of Congress.

ISBN: 978-1-929647-67-5

Dedicated to

Mary Sue Nunn McDaniel, George Hodnett McDaniel,

James Nunn McDaniel, Allen Stuart McDaniel

and to all those who aspire to make a more humane world a reality.

TABLE OF CONTENTS

Foreword: Recent history deserves preservation viii
Preface: A mosaic of the mainstream and marginalized x

Interviews – Family
   Descendants of Drayton Hall: "It's time to heal" 1
   Richmond Bowens: "I'd like to see what's down there" 7
   Charlie Drayton, Anne Drayton Nelson: "When I was young" 13
   Molly Drayton Osteen, Monty Osteen:
      "The many stories about the people" 19
   Charlie Drayton, Rebecca Campbell:
      "Drayton Hall could help bridge the racial divide" 25
   Annie Brown Meyers: "Values my mother and father taught me" 32
   Lucille Blunt: "Just a regular life" 38
   Joann Bowens Huger, Catherine Smith: "Community" 43
   Rebecca Campbell, Catherine Braxton: "I could feel the spirits of my ancestors" . . 48
   Four generations of Draytons: "Memories and hopes" 56
   Alison Rea: "The personal is always most interesting" 61
   Johnny Leach, Isaac Leach, Johnnie Mae Leach: "Hand come. Hand go" . . . 65
   Frank Drayton Jr., Thomas Drayton:
      "Helping people link the 1700s to the present day" 70
   Greg Osteen Howard: "Our families have come full circle" 76
   The Rev. Roosevelt Geddis, Lorraine White:
      "No matter what happens in life" 80
   Rebecca Campbell, Catherine Braxton: "Let us come to the table" . . 85

Interviews – Friends
   Peter McGee, Patti McGee: "A two-word answer" 91
   Charles Duell: "I've known Drayton Hall all my life" 96
   Gene Wilkins: "She cared" 101
   Ralph (Bo) Reahard, Stanley Reahard: "Drayton Hall was one of her projects" . . 107
   Bill Weeks: "An extraordinary person" 112
   Donald Willing, Katherine Willing: "A gift" 115
   Paul Wenker: "She was happy she did it" 119

 Esther Beaumont: "Drayton Hall speaks to me" 123
 Steve Gates: "A focal point for the sweep of history" 127
 Jenny Sanford McKay: "Integrity. Respect. " 133
 Anthony C. Wood: "Transformative" 136

Interviews – Professionals
 Lonnie Bunch III: "The sunshine of remembering" 145
 Bob Barker and Nancy Huggins: "Those early days" 148
 Letitia Galbraith Machado: "Philosophy, interpretation, education, and security" . 155
 Carter C. Hudgins: "A national, indeed an international, treasure" 161
 Sarah Stroud Clarke: "The human spirit across all people" 165
 Damon Fordham: "Tell the truth" 171
 Shelia Harrell-Roye: "Using a story to tell a truth" 177
 Thompson (Tom) Mayes: "A different sense of time" 183
 Helen Hill: "There's magic in telling the story but give visitors options" 189
 Matt Webster: "This privy was advanced for its day" 194
 Susan Buck: "The most magical place" 197
 Craig Bennett: "Every time I go, I understand something new" 204
 Richard Marks: "A time machine" 211
 Glenn F. Keyes: "As an architect" 219
 Jim Thomas: "Significant for the modernist architect and the traditionalist" . . . 224
 Trish Lowe Smith: "Being the best steward I can possibly be" 227
 Sheila Wertimer: "As you walk the landscape" 233
 Toni Carrier: "A sustaining force" 237
 Bernard Powers: "Challenging issues of race" 241
 Marvin Dulaney: "Tell the full story" 246
 Ken Seeger, Jennifer Howard: "The reasons why" 250
 Eric Emerson: "There have to be tangible examples of the past" 256
 Max van Balgooy: "This challenging profession" 261
 Peter H. Wood: "To think and imagine differently" 267
 Joseph McGill Jr.: "To right a wrong" 274
 Michelle McCollum: "A compelling story is not enough" 280
 Elizabeth (Liz) Alston: "Plantations teach us" 285
 Stephanie Meeks: "A leader among house and history museums" 290

Acknowledgments 296
An Initial How-To Guide 299
End Notes 302
About the Author 304
Index 305

FOREWORD

Recent History of Historic Sites Deserves Preservation

Stories most frequently told at historic sites recount who built them, who lived there, what's inside, and what happened there. Often missing is the site's "recent history" — the why and how a place was saved and the stewardship that followed. This is no surprise since those interested in historic sites, whether members of the visiting public or historians, tend to be motivated by the history that made the site worth preserving in the first place, not the history of its actual preservation or of 20th-century residents. However, when its recent history is lost, we lose the history of preservation and the story of those people. A telling example is that Drayton Hall likely would be a club house for a private golf course, not a historic site, if not for the dedication, passion, and vision of the people and organizations who saved it. That and more is what you'll read about in the pages that follow.

Drayton Hall is the real deal. Since the mid-18th century, the Drayton family did not alter its basic architectural style and made only modest changes in keeping with their times, but did not cover its walls with layers upon layers of paint or add electricity, heating, and plumbing. Because it had survived virtually intact, the decision was made, when acquired by the National Trust for Historic Preservation, that it be preserved in that unspoiled condition. That once radical decision is now widely applauded, and has generated fascinating challenges to those entrusted with its care, which this book describes.

Author George McDaniel shares these stories through the voices of Drayton Hall's many people. In his final years as executive director of Drayton Hall, he conducted the majority of these interviews, augmenting them with several more soon after his retirement. After spending 26 years at Drayton Hall, no one is better positioned than George to gather all these voices together into a compelling narrative, which reveals the multiple ways Drayton Hall can be experienced. Appropriately, they include the perspectives of professional preservationists, historians, architects, and engineers. Particularly novel in approach, this book conveys the thoughts and experiences of multi-generational members of the Drayton family, descendants of the African American community of Drayton Hall, board members, staff, preservationists, donors, architects, historians, contractors, docents, and tourism leaders. These narratives put people into the story of this place and its preservation. They make it come alive. All are important in the telling of the stories of this place and can be told because Drayton Hall has been preserved. It can provide the common ground, the safe authentic space, where questions, some painful, can be asked and contemplated.

Drayton Hall is important to me for highly personal reasons. Working to save historic places and capturing the history of their preservation have long been my passion. The physical work of taking care of historic sites was a passion of my older brother — preservation craftsman Stephen J. Wood. His voice is not among those expressed in this book. On August 5, 1980, at the age of 27, he died as a result of a preservation accident while working at Drayton Hall. My decades-long involvement with Drayton Hall is a direct result of Stephen's commitment to the site. This book is in honor of him and of all who have worked to save and steward Drayton Hall. Their contributions are as much a part of its history as the events that led to its preservation in the first place.

The "recent history" of Drayton Hall continues to be made. This book is published with the hope that it will help inform and inspire those who will steward Drayton Hall in the years ahead and in doing so, write the future chapters of Drayton Hall's still evolving story.

– Anthony C. Wood
New York City, New York
Board of Trustees
Drayton Hall Preservation Trust

PREFACE

A Mosaic of the Mainstream and the Marginalized

Like historic sites across the nation, Drayton Hall's long history enables it to tell the story of both the mainstream and the marginalized. If we seek, the story of both remains in the landscape, the buildings, the documents, artifacts, photographs, and oral histories. This book provides a model of how to do so. It demonstrates how one place can serve as a focal point about which a range of people can share perspectives and in so doing, inform us about a new way of preserving and interpreting history and of building understanding and empathy. Like pieces of a mosaic, each perspective is different — intentionally so — but if seen together, they give us a more complete picture of the whole.

Established by John Drayton as a plantation in 1738 about 15 miles up the Ashley River from Charleston, South Carolina, Drayton Hall is now a National Historic Landmark, owned as a historic site by the National Trust for Historic Preservation and operated by the Drayton Hall Preservation Trust. It is open to the public. Completed in the early 1750s, the main house is considered an icon of colonial American architecture and is recognized as the first fully executed Palladian building in America. Interviews in this book describe the many skills and tasks involved both in its construction and preservation.

Unfortunately, no records have been found that name its original architect or its many builders. Although suspicions point to John Drayton as the architect, conclusive evidence remains elusive. We do know that John Drayton and his descendants were leaders in the Carolina colony and later in the state and nation, but who produced the wealth that made their fortunes and political life possible? Who grew the rice and processed the indigo? Who took care of the animals? Who cooked the food? Who tended the gardens? What values and ways of life were passed on? While historical records do list names and provide occasional references to jobs, duties, or even punishments, none describe these diverse people as the sentient human beings they were.

Such questions persist into recent times, but today we can ask them of actual participants and record their answers as evidence for the future. Such questions include: What were the work and values of African American descendants? What might we learn from a plantation? What were the interviewees' first impressions of this place, and how did they evolve? What are the childhood memories of African American residents and Drayton descendants? Why did the Draytons choose not to modernize the house in the 20th century or to sell it to become a golf club for far greater profit? Once open to the public, why was Drayton Hall "preserved" and not restored to earlier periods? What have archaeology, oral history, and architectural investigations revealed? Why care? These questions and more provide structure for this book.

When I became Drayton Hall's executive director in 1989, I stood on the shoulders of a dedicated staff and advisory site council who had done exceptional work with minimal capital support. Although most of Drayton Hall's forest lands were owned by the State of South Carolina and the main house and its surrounding landscape by the National Trust, both the State and the Trust were short of funds due to many competing priorities, and historic sites like Drayton Hall did not rank as high on their lists as other needs. After my first year on the job and our careful clean-up from Hurricane Hugo, I was told by the National Trust that Drayton Hall would continue to receive administrative and technical support but would receive no more annual cash subventions and must become self-sufficient. We could apply for grants, but our needs remained plentiful as did unfunded "good ideas." Faced with this all-too-common situation, how were we to choose between the mainstream and the marginalized and still tell a more complete history?

It is my belief and that of other professionals that good site management requires both. We must resist the either/or choice. In order to grow, we must change and continue, just as we must both work and rest. In strategic corporate planning, this "both/and" approach is known as "polarity thinking." By applying it to historic sites, we see how perspectives of both the mainstream and the marginalized complement one another like mosaics. Together, they enable us to see and understand this one place more completely. As a historical Southern plantation, Drayton Hall's historical people were principally its White owners and African American workers, enslaved and later free, who constituted the majority. After Drayton Hall became a historic site in the 1970s, the range of its people expanded to encompass many professionals featured in this book. Since this range is commonplace among today's historic sites and historical organizations, this approach to preserving the recent history of both the mainstream and the marginalized could be used elsewhere. To provide some basic structure for such efforts, please see the resources and guide at this book's conclusion and on my website, www.mcdanielconsulting.net.

A Brief History of Drayton Hall

In the 18th century, Drayton Hall was the home seat of a plantation empire. In 1738, this tract of over 600 acres on both sides of the Ashley River Road was purchased by John Drayton, who had been born in 1715 on the adjacent upstream plantation, Magnolia. His grandfather had arrived from Barbados in the 1670s to the new colony of Carolina. He had been accompanied, according to the oral history of Richmond Bowens' family, by their enslaved ancestors, who were "here before the house was built." In many ways, they shaped Drayton Hall's construction and success.

Becoming a prosperous planter, John Drayton owned hundreds, if not thousands, of enslaved workers, as well as some 76,000 acres along the Carolina coast and south of Savannah, a portion of which he shared with his brother. From 1761 to 1775, he served on His Majesty's Privy Council for the South Carolina colony. Beginning in 1738 and through the course of his life, he successively married four women — Sarah Cattell, Charlotta Bull, Margaret Glen, and Rebecca Perry — who were well positioned financially and politically. When the American Revolution erupted, his efforts to remain neutral failed, and he died "fleeing the British" in 1779 on the banks of the Cooper River.

His oldest surviving son, William Henry Drayton, became a leader in the American Revolution. In February 1776, he became the first prominent Carolinian to openly call for the establishment of a new government and separation from Great Britain. Elected to the Continental Congress in Philadelphia in 1778, he earned the esteem of his peers and won the heated debate in Congress about whether to celebrate July 4th with prayer and fasting or with celebrations and fireworks. His victory has become a tradition we continue today. Struck by typhus, he died in Philadelphia in 1779. His son, John Drayton, named for his grandfather, became governor of South Carolina and was a founder of the University of South Carolina in Columbia. Their direct descendant, Alison Rea, is interviewed in this book.

William's younger brother, Charles Drayton, studied at Oxford, as had William, and earned his medical degree from the highly respected medical school at the University of Edinburgh, where he studied cutting-edge medicine, surgery, anatomy, and materia medica (pharmacology). Marrying Hester Middleton of Middleton Place, he acquired Drayton Hall from his father's widow and added new Adamesque or Federal-style changes to the interior and made both structural and decorative changes to the exterior, such as replacing the original columns on the first-floor portico in the early 19th century with the limestone ones seen today.

Like many of his Charleston peers, he was a prominent member of the intellectual and cultural elite of the early nation. Nine of his descendants appear in this book, including four namesakes.

Decades later, when the Civil War tore the nation apart, the Draytons chose both sides. In fact, two Drayton brothers, cousins of Drayton Hall's owners, fired on one another in 1861 in the Battle at Port Royal off the coast of Beaufort, South Carolina. Drayton Hall's Draytons sided with the Confederacy. While plantations along the Ashley River were torched, Drayton Hall was spared, perhaps because it had served as a hospital, but no conclusive explanation has been found. After the war, thanks to the mining of calcium phosphate, a marine deposit used as fertilizer for cotton and corn fields across the South, its new owner, Charles Henry Drayton, a direct descendant of the first John Drayton, was able to make substantial repairs to the house, added landscape features like the pond and the mound in front of the house, and ensured its longevity into the 20th century.

Scores of emancipated African Americans left Drayton Hall, seeking freedom's promise elsewhere, but some remained and worked the fields and in the phosphate mining operations or as house servants for the Drayton family. Among those who remained were three siblings, Caesar, Catherine, and John, who assumed the surname "Bowens" for reasons unknown. Earlier records of their ancestors have not been found. Four descendants of Caesar and Catherine share their thoughts in this book. Catherine Bowens' namesake, Catherine Braxton, now serves on the Drayton Hall Preservation Trust's board of trustees, whose current bylaws call for both a Drayton descendant and an African American descendant to be voting members.

The 20th century saw transformation of the site, for phosphate mining and farming gradually ceased, and homes of African Americans, once an integral part of the site as shown by Richmond Bowens' memory map, were abandoned, leaving only the caretaker's house, now part of the Reahard visitor center. Two of Charles Henry Drayton's children, Charles Henry Drayton V and Charlotta Drayton, inherited Drayton Hall. A U.S. Army captain and World War I veteran, Charles died in 1941, leaving two sons, Charlie and Frank. A spinster, his sister Charlotta lived in her parents' home on East Bay St., looking out towards Charleston Harbor, and cherished her weeks at Drayton Hall in the spring and fall. She chose not to modernize and refused to sell the 18th-century wall paneling to Henry Francis du Pont for his Winterthur museum. Becoming elderly, she was unable to stop thefts of antiques, one item being an old trunk, filled with papers of unknown age, documents that may have described the design and construction of the house or provided information about the mainstream and the marginalized – a crime against history.

After Charlotta's death in 1969, the two sons of Charles Drayton — Charlie and Frank B. Drayton Sr. — inherited the estate and had to decide its fate. They knew that repairs, taxes, security, and the site's overall well-being required more money than they could muster. What to do? Interviews with Charlie Drayton, with his and Frank's children, and with Charleston attorney Peter McGee and Middleton Place's CEO emeritus, Charles Duell, shed light on their decisions. The effects have been far-reaching, because since its sale in 1974, Drayton Hall has been toured by hundreds of thousands and has touched the life of each interviewee. While this is their story, in a sense it is also our story because the story of Drayton Hall, as two descendants, Thomas Drayton and Greg Howard explain, is our country's history.

The reader is encouraged to visit Drayton Hall and its website, www.draytonhall.org or to read its numerous blogs, studies, and publications, such as Drayton Hall: The Creation and Preservation of an American Icon. *Please see also the family lines of descent and maps in this book, while my website, www.mcdanielconsulting.net, offers blogs, photographs, and other resources.*

The Back Story

This book is a compilation of transcribed videos of programs and interviews I recorded during my last decade at Drayton Hall for its archives. They were not conceptualized to become a cohesive book but were to be used as resources for different projects. In the winter of 2020, Anthony C. Wood, a member of the board of the new Drayton Hall Preservation Trust, suggested I turn them into a book. Too often, he explained, historic sites devote more attention to their earlier periods than to their recent history. So thanks to Drayton Hall's generosity, I was given access to the transcriptions and photographs and to fill voids, conducted a few more interviews. To achieve brevity and clarity, these are not word-for-word transcriptions, but to the extent possible, retain the interviewee's words.

Two goals guided my editing: 1) to convey the interviewee's main thoughts (not mine or anyone else's); 2) to shape the interview into an interesting and informative story. These two goals I come by naturally and educationally. As a Southerner, I grew up listening to stories. My family was one of story-tellers, as were my friends, teachers, and professors. Stories teach. They teach of values, choices, memories, and beliefs. They use clear language, understood by "all sorts and conditions" of people. When interviewee Peter H. Wood recently eulogized Larry Goodwyn, his friend and colleague and my professor at Duke, he explained:

Now that I live in the West, I have a greater appreciation than ever for the South's rich storytelling habit, which you (Larry) helped me appreciate. Am I being too optimistic to hope that this venerable tradition, so long used to disguise the region's tangled heritage, is now being used to look the real past and future more clearly in the eye? I can't answer that, but the deep well of Southern history still contains an endless supply of surprising, meaningful, and revealing moments." [1]

It is in that tradition that these stories are told. It is also in that more democratic and teachable spirit that I as a historian have tried to get out of the way and let the story-teller speak. Sometimes one may wish the interviewee would say more or "look the real past and future more clearly in the eye," but it is their story, not mine or yours. The hope is that one day, if we keep trying, they or their descendants will build upon this new foundation.

The cover photograph of Charlie Drayton and Catherine Braxton illustrates that hope. Charlie Drayton, the last owner of Drayton Hall, is the descendant of slaveowners, and Catherine Braxton, a descendant of the enslaved. His grandfather "owned" her great grandparents, including the enslaved Catherine for whom she is named. For reasons we may guess but not know, they greeted each other with heartfelt gladness. They did not pose. As Larry Goodwyn used to say, "we've been round the barn too many times" to believe that the wall of racism is down, but that wall does have cracks, which lets the light through, and in that light, at least for the moment, is where Charlie and Catherine were. If they can find light, why can't we? With many cracks, that wall will topple. If historic sites, especially in the South, could create more cracks and transform the challenges of their "tangled heritage" into opportunities, why could they not lead the way in toppling that wall?

To hasten progress toward that end, Drayton Hall's archives contain all of the interviews and transcriptions. For this book, each interview had to be trimmed from sometimes 12,000 words to an average of 3,000. Questions were left in place as a guide for a quick read. To living interviewees, I sent my edits and asked them to read them, make changes, and give their approval. If they are to continue to share their stories, they have to trust. My purpose was not to embarrass them and their family or to display my ideological purity, so if readers think of questions that should be asked, please proceed. Since a book format does limit the number of photographs, the reader is encouraged to visit my website, www.mcdanielconsulting.net, for more

---

1 Peter H. Wood, "Nell's Kitchen, Larry's War Room," in *People Power: History, Organizing, and Larry Goodwyn's Democratic Vision in the Twenty-First Century*, ed. Wesley C. Hogan and Paul Ortiz (Gainesville: University Press of Florida, 2021), 87.

photographs of each interviewee and of the places and people described.

This book deliberately seeks to reveal personal feelings. Too often, a historic site or museum sees a person only as a donor, board member, consultant, or tourism leader and neglects that they too have personal feelings. As donors, for example, they are not just "moneybags," as one donor phrased a stereotype of herself. By featuring people across the spectrum and by my interview questions, it is my hope that we see how all of us blend the professional and the personal. Since social identity shapes perceptions, this book features a mix of race, gender, age, sexual orientation, profession, and connection to the site. I make no claim that this mix is exhaustive. Indeed, it is my hope that its limits will serve as inspiration for more efforts to be made in documenting the recent history of Drayton Hall and other historic places.

Prompting and enabling me to interview such a range of people has been my love of stories and my lived experiences, different from those of most historians. When I went to college at Sewanee, Father William Ralston and Andrew Lytle inspired me to teach. During my junior year in Paris, new fields of study like art and architecture opened before me, and upon graduation, I had the pleasure of incorporating them into my teaching at Atlanta's Lovett School. Serving in the Peace Corps in a rural, rather isolated village in Togo, West Africa, I spoke French all the time, as did most villagers, and gained a new appreciation for hard reality, traditional medicine and religion, and life without electricity, running water, telephones, or other modern amenities like wire screens or window glass. Double-crossed by my draft board, I was drafted out of the Peace Corps and fought with the First Infantry Division between Saigon and Cambodia. I saw enough combat to see what war does to people and got blown up twice, once when a friend, who was walking point ahead of me, stepped on a booby-trapped mortar round. I can still touch the shrapnel in my chin.

Upon return, I went to Brown University for a Master of Arts in Teaching (History), for which I taught at Providence's Hope High School and learned from John Glasheen and my students that new ways of teaching history had to be created. Going for my PhD in history from Duke University, I participated in its oral history program. Thanks to professors like Larry Goodwyn, Sydney Nathans, and Peter H. Wood and to friends like Aylene Cook, I found new ways of doing history and practicing historic preservation, and I began using historic buildings, objects, landscapes, music, art, and oral histories as resources. A fellowship with the Smithsonian Institution and work with the Maryland Historical Trust led me to forge a career with museums and historic sites. Through public history I could implement effective ways to engage both young and old. I found that no book conveyed the recent history of historic sites from multiple points of view, even though my lived experiences had taught me the need for such. Those experiences have shown how we benefit by seeing life from both the top down and the bottom up and influenced by things seen and unseen. Such experiences have shaped the formation of *Drayton Hall Stories*.

What separates history from fiction is evidence. Yet too often the recent history of our historic places is missing. Don't we need both the long-ago and the recent? By failing to record recent history, we marginalize it or see it only from the perspectives and interpretations of others, or worse, leave it blank. We may try to get buildings, artifacts, and landscapes to speak, but what dowe lose without the people who knew them? Prior to this project, many of the accounts in this book had not been recorded, but are they not important to the understanding of this place? They enable us to see these individuals not as stereotypes but as the real people they were – or are. Weunderstand more clearly why Drayton Hall, or any historic place, is as we see it today and how life was lived in the very places where we walk.

While offering recollections of recent history, this book is also about the future. I ask interviewees about the future of historic preservation and sites, for historic preservation is about the past, to be sure, but also about the future. What kind of future do we want? Will there be a presence of the past? And if so, what will those places and things communicate? All of us should ask such questions because the best historic sites and museums help us to understand the past, of course, but also inform us about issues of the future and inspire us to act. That is one reason why this book concludes with a guide.

As I look back on this book's development, I am reminded of my teaching experience when in order to engage my high school students in European history, I took a risk and assigned a big, strong football player Beethoven's Fifth Symphony as an essay topic. I thought the stirring music, especially the strength of its opening motif, might resonate. Later, his mother told of how he came home groaning and complaining about "Mr. McDaniel," but he did listen to the music. A week later, she overheard him inviting his friends, "Come up to my room. I want you to listen to some Beethoven with me!" I hope that these stories will have a similar effect on you.

– **George W. McDaniel**

If you wish to preserve history and use the process to enhance community, my interviews, endnotes, website, www.mcdanielconsulting.net, and workshops might help.

INTERVIEWS

Family

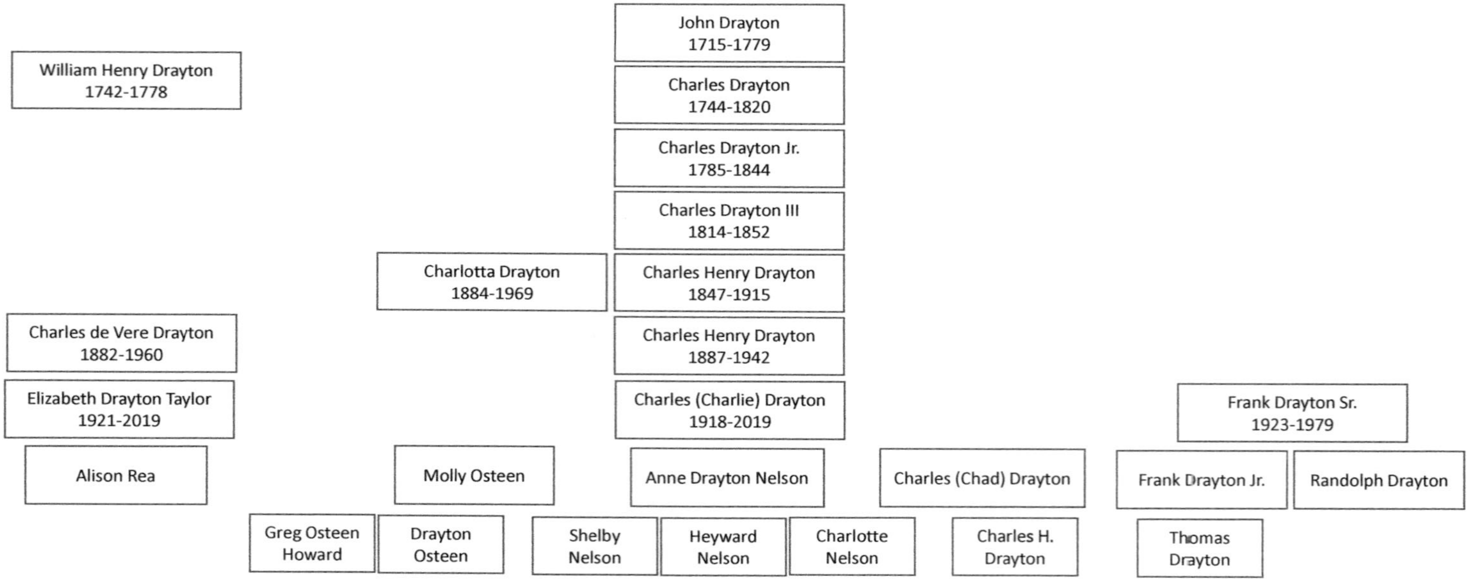

Drayton Family Line of Descent

- John Drayton
  1715-1779
  - Charles Drayton
    1744-1820
    - Charles Drayton Jr.
      1785-1844
      - Charles Drayton III
        1814-1852
        - Charles Henry Drayton
          1847-1915
          - Charles Henry Drayton
            1887-1942
            - Charlotta Drayton
              1884-1969
            - Charles (Charlie) Drayton
              1918-2019
              - Anne Drayton Nelson
                - Shelby Nelson
                - Heyward Nelson
                - Charlotte Nelson
              - Charles (Chad) Drayton
                - Charles H. Drayton
              - Frank Drayton Sr.
                1923-1979
                - Frank Drayton Jr.
                  - Thomas Drayton
                - Randolph Drayton
              - Molly Osteen
                - Drayton Osteen
                  - Greg Osteen Howard

- William Henry Drayton
  1742-1778
  - Charles de Vere Drayton
    1882-1960
    - Elizabeth Drayton Taylor
      1921-2019
      - Alison Rea

Note: These lines of descent show only those featured in the book, not the entire family. For more information and resources, please see: https://www.mcdanielconsulting.net/drayton-hall-book/

xx

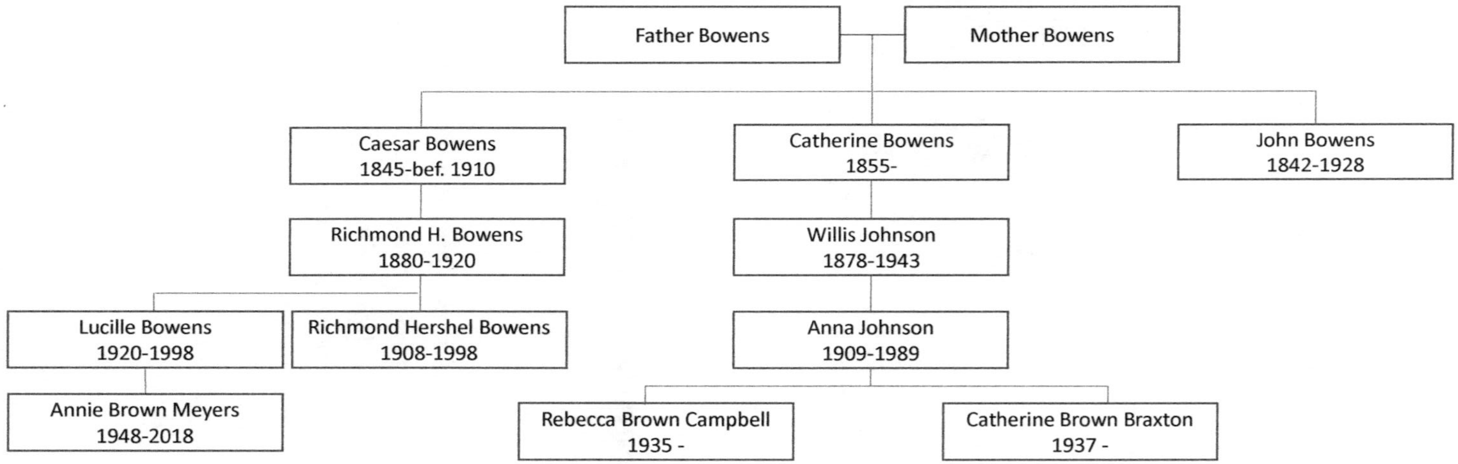

Bowens Family Line of Descent

- Father Bowens
- Mother Bowens
  - John Bowens 1842-1928
  - Catherine Bowens 1855-
    - Willis Johnson 1878-1943
      - Anna Johnson 1909-1989
        - Rebecca Brown Campbell 1935 -
        - Catherine Brown Braxton 1937 -
  - Caesar Bowens 1845-bef. 1910
    - Richmond H. Bowens 1880-1920
      - Richmond Hershel Bowens 1908-1998
        - Lucille Bowens 1920-1998
          - Annie Brown Meyers 1948-2018

Note: These lines of descent show only those featured in the book, not the entire family. For more information and resources, please see: https://www.mcdanielconsulting.net/drayton-hall-book/

Front row (L-R): Annie Brown Meyers, Charles Heyward Drayton, Charles (Charlie) H. Drayton III, Shelby Nelson, Catherine Brown Braxton. Back row (l-r): Rebecca Brown Campbell, Frank B. Drayton Jr., George W. McDaniel.

A Drayton Hall Descendants Program
"It is now time to heal"

A public program by Drayton Hall descendants was presented February 19, 2015 at South Carolina Society Hall in Charleston and was presented to a standing-room only audience. These descendants of Drayton and African American families represented more than three centuries of our nation's history. It marked the first time a cross-racial descendants' program was produced in Charleston for the public, and the positive response from the audience underscores the potential for historic sites to use similar programs to nurture understanding and healing in today's turbulent times. Charlie Drayton and Annie Brown Meyers have since passed away.

Participants:
Annie Brown Meyers: Descendant of Caesar Bowens, who had been enslaved at Drayton Hall, and cousin of Rebecca Campbell and Catherine Braxton.

Charles Heyward Drayton: Grandson of Charles H. Drayton III, born in 1977.
Charles (Charlie) H. Drayton III: Last family owner of Drayton Hall who was age 96 at the time, and seventh-generation titleholder of the property.
Shelby Nelson: Grandson of Charlie H. Drayton III and son of Anne Drayton Nelson.
Catherine Brown Braxton: Descendant of the Bowens family and named after her great-grandmother, Catherine Bowens, who had been enslaved at Drayton Hall.
Rebecca Brown Campbell: Sister of Catherine Braxton.
Frank B. Drayton Jr.: Son of Frank Drayton, who with his brother Charlie sold Drayton Hall to the National Trust for Historic Preservation and State of South Carolina in 1974.
George McDaniel: Executive director of Drayton Hall.
Not pictured: Charles (Chad) H. Drayton Jr.: Son of Charles H. Drayton III, born in 1948 and father of Charles Heyward Drayton.

Introduction by George McDaniel

Tonight marks a special moment in the ongoing preservation of Drayton Hall's history. Descendants of the Drayton family and descendants of its African American community have decided to step up on behalf of preserving history. Since just a few are participating in this panel, I salute all descendants of Drayton Hall — so please stand up and be recognized. [Applause]

We began this process of healing with descendants of Drayton Hall at a South Carolina Department of Archives and History's preservation conference in Columbia and repeated it at the National Trust for Historic Preservation's Conference in Savannah. It's the first time either organization featured such a program with descendants. Let's hope it's a harbinger of things to come from other sites in America and beyond.

Panel Discussion:

George: *Charlie, please describe your decision to sell Drayton Hall after seven succeeding generations. Were there alternatives?*

Charlie: The only choice was to sell it outright. Although we never put it on the market, it obviously was available. I got phone calls and was offered a sum considerably more than what we got from the National Trust. I asked, "What are your plans?" They said Drayton Hall would be the clubhouse for a golf course. No way! We made the right decision. [Applause] The National Trust has done a superb job.

Frank: I was away at the time, but talked a lot about it with my parents. We had had vandalism out there and knew it would continue. It was a hard decision but a wise one.

What does returning to Drayton Hall feel like after all these years?

Frank: People ask me, "Why do you return? Don't you hate going back?" No. I'm still moved driving down the allée of live oaks. I see something interesting every time and get a great feeling of childhood memories. I have no regrets.

Catherine, what does Drayton Hall mean to you today?

Catherine: Drayton Hall means my ancestors. Drayton Hall is where I have roots. Our ancestors stayed at Drayton Hall, worked there, died there, are buried there, so we have to maintain this contact.

Charles: Drayton Hall is an anchor for me and my family too. It represents who we are as people. The why of that is hard to grasp, but it matters somewhere deep in my core.

Chad: Drayton Hall means a lot to me in different ways and at different times. When I was a kid, it was a country place. I'd go there with my family or be dropped off and run loose. When I was 17, my sister had a party there. I have a friend, Chipper Allen, who happens to be in the audience. Nobody paid any attention to us. We got a little bourbon and were standing outside having a drink. Actually, I couldn't stand it. I remember looking at the house with the candlelight and exclaiming, "Wow! This is unbelievable." That's what Drayton Hall meant to me then.

I was angry and upset when it was sold, and it took years before I got over it. I want to thank George for reconnecting me and my family with Drayton Hall, with Catherine and Rebecca, and with you, the audience. Drayton Hall is about bringing people back together, and I think that's the most important thing I've learned in the latter part of my life — the connections. We learn new things almost daily out there, and it's a really special place now.

Rebecca: I'm very spiritual. When I first stepped on that plantation, I felt the spirit of my ancestors running through my body as if we'd made contact. It was like I had been there with them over the centuries. Having never visited a plantation before, I said, "Hey, this is a plantation, and I'm here!" I talked with my cousin Richmond Bowens, who was working as Drayton Hall's gatekeeper and oral history source, and he told stories about our family. Today we appreciate being here with Drayton descendants. We have networked together. Traveled together. Eaten together. Being with this younger Drayton generation, like in Savannah, means having a great time. They take care of me.

Annie: I had negative thoughts about Drayton Hall because it was a plantation where my ancestors were slaves. I remember going near the house where my grandfather, my mother, uncle, and aunts had lived, and I didn't have a good feeling. The change came after my uncle Richmond Bowens returned to Charleston, and I visited Drayton with him. I talked with him and walked with him, and he spoke about the many things that they did there. He often talked about Charlie Drayton: "I have to go and visit Charlie Drayton," and, "I remember doing this with Charlie Drayton."

The strength and love he had for Drayton Hall gradually changed my perception of what the plantation was all about. It was about love. It was about companionship. It was about making each other happy. Now I have an appreciation of Drayton Hall, knowing that my ancestors were there. They came up there. They were strong people. They were religious people, and that has traveled down through the generations.

My goal is to have a Drayton Hall descendants' reunion. We can be working right next to each other and not even know we are a Drayton or a Bowens. If we get that reunion, we can have fellowship and share ideas, and perhaps have a bond that my uncle had with Charlie Drayton. I would like to have that bond with Shelby, Charles, Frank, and all the rest of them, and their children. Drayton Hall is where it started off with a bad situation, but today it has changed. It's a loving situation now where we can gather and be grateful.

Shelby: I'm comforted, Annie, because ultimately, we're all going to be there. It makes me happy to know that no matter what I do in this life, I'm going to be in the family cemetery at Drayton Hall by the river. In 1974 that wasn't the case. It was I who actually handed the keys over to the Trust. Later, I had mixed thoughts. "Maybe we shouldn't have done that sale" came through my mind, but Chad had a poignant observation. Drayton Hall means different things at different times in your life. Today, I am wholly thankful for what George and the Trust have done and couldn't be happier that this is the path it's on. Getting with Annie, Rebecca, and Catherine has been a huge coming together.

My favorite moment came during an archaeological dig. As we dug on the front right corner, we found a brick and another brick. We found 12 courses, and I said, "What the heck is this?" We'd found the original building before Drayton Hall. It had been sitting for 300-plus years right under our feet, and we didn't even know.

That's what Drayton Hall is. It's bigger than our family, bigger than Charleston. It's a treasure to be honored in perpetuity. So, for that, I am forever grateful to my grandfather for making the tough choice to sell, clearly the only choice. I definitely think we need a reunion with everybody and to make that a tradition.

Let's open the discussion to the audience now:

Audience member: *Mrs. Campbell, when you came to Drayton, could you explain your spiritual feeling?*

Rebecca: I remember my grandfather and my granduncle talking about Drayton Hall and how they used to play with their cousins like Richmond Bowens. But we didn't get a chance to mingle around Drayton Hall until the '70s when Richmond came back from Chicago and invited me to visit Drayton Hall. I said, "Drayton Hall? I've heard about it. Okay." When I went, it was grown over and needed landscaping. Like Annie said, I thought, "I feel something strange here. My ancestors are here. My body is beginning to tell me something. I am spiritually a person who belongs here." I began to get on board and met George, and we took off. I forgave the Drayton families for enslaving my ancestors. If I cannot forgive, then God will not forgive me, so I moved on.

Audience member: *Could you, Mr. Drayton Sr. give us two or three of your favorite vignettes about Drayton Hall?*

Charlie: Growing up in Charleston, I went out there not frequently but enough. It didn't mean much to me. It was just a place. After I went in the Navy, my father passed away and my Aunt Charley took over, and that meant a different situation. Five years after she died, we sold it to the National Trust. I don't think there's any way that the Drayton family could have preserved it monetarily or any other way. I hate using the word "money," but the money put into Drayton Hall since the National Trust took over is fantastic. I applaud the National Trust.

Audience member: *How does the panel feel about preservation versus restoration at Drayton Hall?*

Charles: By preserving it, you encompass the entirety of the history, whereas if you restored it, you would have to pick one time. Preservation allows all these centuries to be promoted and learned about.

Audience member: *My name is Jeffrey Bowens. I'm originally from the Hollywood area of South Carolina and a lot of Bowenses live there. I would love to find out more about my history.*

Rebecca: Mr. Bowens, I suggest that you take one of my cards. We'll set up a meeting and discuss it with you and your family.

George: *Why are programs like this important? What do you hope are the take-away messages?*

Catherine: I consider what we're doing tonight to be part of the healing process. The history of slavery and the punishment of our ancestors who worked from sunrise to sunset leaves bitterness. I've heard people describe it as hatred, and this has got to stop. Now we've got this going. Let's heal. Let's sit and talk about this. We have to come together and put this hatred and bitterness behind us! It is now time to heal, and that's what we're doing.

Charles: I hope this becomes an example that other places with divergent histories can find ground to build upon. We've become friends, and that's good. That's the goal of this. I hope we can express it to others who pass it on and help heal this nation.

Chad: Drayton Hall connects those of us from each side. It connects young people through education programs. It's a place that connects people, and tonight is an example of that.

Rebecca: I'm leaving you with two words: "Love" and "Forgive."

Frank: As Catherine said, we've got to go back to the past and come to the future — this is really living history. We have age 96 (Charlie Drayton) down to whatever year the youngest is at the table. We have a good representation of oral history that will be passed on for generations.

Annie: I hope those here who have not yet visited Drayton Hall will do so, and that they'll feel what we feel when we go there. They'll get a better understanding when they walk the grounds, and some will say, "I remember listening to Catherine, Rebecca, or Frank, and now I have a better understanding about what Drayton Hall is about."

Shelby: I'm here only for the reunion. That's why I'm here.

George: *Charlie, why are you here tonight? What messages would you like the audience to take with them?*

Charlie: You're ready for my five-hour speech? [Laughter] It has been well said by those here on the panel. I concur with the message, and let everybody figure out what it is.

[Standing ovation]

Richmond Bowens:
"I'd like to see what's down there ..."

1994 – Drayton Hall

The video, I'd Like to See What's Down There: Archaeology and Oral History at Drayton Hall, *was produced in 1994 and features the archaeological excavation of the boyhood tenant house of Drayton Hall staff member Richmond Bowens. According to his family's oral history, his enslaved ancestors came from Barbados in the 1700s with the Draytons. No detailed documents have been found that track his family's history, but given his exacting accounts about life at Drayton Hall, it's reasonable to assume he has accurately related what he was told. Plantation records do list his grandfather Caesar and grandmother Helen, born in 1855. They and Richmond's parents lived in small wooden houses that were pulled down in the 1930s or '40s. The homesite was unmarked so Richmond showed archaeologists where to dig. As artifacts were unearthed, his oral histories were confirmed. When we asked him about slavery, he made it apparent that he did not wish to discuss it. So out of respect for his wishes, we did not press.*

The video was produced in 1994 by historian Charles Joyner and the author, filmed by the media department of Coastal Carolina University and aired on The History Channel. After viewing it, Roger Kennedy, then director of the National Park Service, declared, "This is the real buried treasure of Drayton Hall."

Participants:
Richmond Bowens: Born in 1908 at Drayton Hall and raised there. His grandfather, Caesar Bowens, was an enslaved person on the plantation. His father, also named Richmond, was born after freedom at Drayton Hall and lived there until his death in 1918.
George McDaniel: Executive Director of Drayton Hall
Lynne Lewis: Chief Archaeologist, National Trust for Historic Preservation
Laurie Paonessa: Archaeologist, National Trust for Historic Preservation

Scott Parker: Archaeologist, National Trust for Historic Preservation
Marguerite DeLaine: Teacher, Alston Middle School and researcher
Warren Ellem: Australian historian, invited to Drayton Hall
Graham White: Australian historian, invited to Drayton Hall

Video begins:

Richmond Bowens: I was born Sept. 2, 1908, and raised here. My father's people came with the Draytons from Barbados before the house was built. My grandfather took care of this place, and my father was born and raised here too. I'd like to see what's down there. If you want to learn, this is the only way you are going to find out.

My father had seven sisters and eight brothers. He was a Christian man and a leader among the people of the plantation. Everybody respected him. He was a barber, too, and some of his barbering things were put on his grave. That's the way they did it. Something the person liked to use or was a favorite thing, they put on their graves. That's how they used to do.

The men would make the coffin and markers out of wood — like crosses or boards with the name and other information on it. We had no local rock, and gravestones cost money. Since all those markers have rotted away and the coffins too, dips in the ground now show where they were. All the graves were directed east and west. The body faced the rising sun. Those were rules and regulations here. One time they made a mistake and buried a man facing west. They had to dig him up and turn him around!

My mother was Anna Bowens. She was a good mother. I was brought up and taught everything that should be taught to a child.

After slavery, the Draytons tore down the slave barracks and built houses for the people. Mine was originally a two-room frame house facing Highway 61 with its chimney on the north end. In later years, my father added two rooms on the back. A kitchen sat off from the front of the house. There were seven tenant houses in this area at Drayton Hall.

Marguerite DeLaine: The census manuscript of 1910 showed 10 members of the Bowens' extended family living in this one small house with Richmond Bowens' widowed grandmother Helen Bowens, born in 1855, as head of the household. The Bowens' family name was misspelled as B-O-N-E-S. Richmond's uncles, Allen and Isaac, are listed in this household, but Richmond tells us that they lived on Magnolia (an adjoining plantation) with their sisters Ida and Lizzy. Richmond, whose birth name was Hersal [*sic*], lived with his father, also Richmond, and his mother Anna. Richmond clearly remembers his grandmother Helen living nearby at Drayton Hall in a separate house, as did his uncle Samuel a little farther away. Contrary to what the census shows, all of these people were not stacked up in this one house together. If you went by these written records alone, the result would be an erroneous picture of family and community life. That's why oral history is so important, especially in African American history.

Lynne Lewis: One of the most important things about this project is the synthesis of disciplines. What we learn by archaeology alone, we could take to any other house site, but when we have the information from somebody who was born here, lived here, and has vivid memories, we can combine the written evidence, oral history, and the archaeology. Between those plus anything else we happen to pull in, we understand the site in greater totality. For example, Mr. Bowens told us the front door had a hole so their cat could go in and out. That's something we would not see archaeologically. It adds something to the site. It puts people in the site. It puts life in the site.

Richmond Bowens (answering questions about trash and garbage disposal, a mother lode for archaeologists):

You won't find a whole lot around the house because in those days, you keep the yard clean. You rake it. You sweep it. You burn up the leaves. Then you put that in your garden for fertilizer. You take the bones and the food from the kitchen and throw it in the hog pen. We didn't have no junky, trashy yard!

Warren Ellem: It's exciting to see the historical person himself, Mr. Bowens, along with the archaeologists, historians, and videographer working together to recreate the past. It's possibly unique.

Scott Parker: Archaeology is a destructive process. We can't put this layer of earth back in the ground the way it was when it came out. That's why we do such detailed recording.

Richmond Bowens: (examining artifacts unearthed by archaeologists, see www.mcdanielconsulting.net/drayton-hall-book/ for more photographs of these artifacts):

This piece is from what you call a firebrick. It's very hard, like a piece of iron. They called it a firebrick because heat won't damage it, not one bit. It lined our chimney. After you go to bed and the fire goes down, that brick stays hot all night. These firebricks hold heat.

The medicine in this bottle was prescribed by the doctor, and you got it from the drugstore. Castoria was the name. It's a baby medicine. If the baby is restless and has stomach trouble, you give the child half a teaspoon. This would quiet him down so he could rest comfortably the rest of the night.

This looks like a castor oil bottle. I don't know if you've ever tasted castor oil, but it was one of the nastiest tasting things ever put in your mouth!

This is a top for a glass dish for either candy or fruit. They used to have what they called a sideboard. It had a mirror and shelves on the top and drawers beneath. My mother had one. On the top were different kinds of dishes used to put fruit in. The drawers kept doilies and tablecloths and so on. At Christmas time, when we had fruits and candies and things like that in the house, and when we had company, you put your candies and stuff in that dish and serve it to people. That's at Christmas time. The only story I know about it is that you better not break one of them! No! No!

This is a part of a clay pipe. The old people used to smoke a clay pipe. They'd put the stem in here, and the stem would be made of wild cane, not sugar cane. Not as many men smoked pipes as women did in those days. Men chewed tobacco and smoked cigarettes. In the bottom of this pipe, nicotine would accumulate, and this thing would get hot. Keep smoking it, and it would get hotter. I used to hear them back then when they drew in and that pipe got hot, and that thing was frying in the bottom. Right over there, my grandmother lived. She went to sleep one day, and I took that pipe, and I pull on it and pull on it, and draw and draw and draw until I got it hot enough to hear it fry. By that time, I was almost dead! I never have been as sick as I was that day. I was so sick that I had to tell my parents about it. [Laughing].

Graham White: Historians are always interested in finding new ways of recovering the past and in getting the most meaning out of the tiniest scraps of evidence. This is a perfect example: The archaeologist discovers a tiny bit of a pipe, and the oral history source spins out a meaningful story based on it. What struck me as innovative about this project is that it addresses two areas: New ways of getting at the past and how to get the maximum meaning out of tiny traces.

Scott Parker: We've found both structural and domestic evidence about the Bowens house. It tells us that Mr. Bowens' account of this being a post-Civil War house, not a re-used slave house, is correct. A pin flag indicates where Mr. Bowens said one of the front corners of the house would have been. We found the (brick) foundation pier about four feet away. Almost 75 years later, Mr. Bowens remembered within five feet.

Marguerite DeLaine: This research is important. As a teacher, we use textbooks that do not provide this type of information. It's important that students know this kind of history. Doing this research has inspired me to help students research their own families, talk to grandparents, uncles, and others, and get that information together. That history needs to be passed down from generation to generation.

Richmond Bowens: A lot of things went on in those days you never would learn about otherwise.

Richmond Bowens (excerpt from a tour by DVD of the Drayton Hall landscape by The History Channel): This whole place is where my father and my ancestors grew up. A lot of people grew up places, and they don't want to see them no more. They don't want to hear the name called. That's different with me. This is like my own home.

When Richmond Bowens died, his family asked Charlie Drayton and me to speak at his funeral. Charlie wept. I said that Richmond Bowens had high standards and that due to segregation and other factors, he had come up, in the words of that gospel hymn, "On the Rough Side of the Mountain." However, knowing Richmond's high standards, I would only recite a verse of that hymn in tribute, not sing it. Later, Charlie and I joined others in shoveling dirt to fill his grave site in Drayton Hall's African American cemetery.

Dating at least to 1800, it is the oldest documented African American cemetery still in use in the nation. With the advice of his widow Velma, we purchased a gravestone and inscribed on it what Richmond told me was his favorite Bible verse: "The Lord Is My Shepherd." Velma now lies next to him in the cemetery Richmond characterized as "sacred space." He had directed us to keep the cemetery cleared but not to landscape it. Since his ancestors had done so much hard work on this earth, now was the time "to leave 'em rest." Those words are inscribed over the cemetery's memorial arch, designed by Charleston's renowned blacksmith, Philip Simmons, a friend of Richmond Bowens and his family.

Please see www.mcdanielconsulting.net/DraytonHallBookProject for more text and photographs of people, places, artifacts, and documents.

Memory Map – The "memory map" of Richmond Bowens (at right) as he recalled Drayton Hall from about 1920. Born in 1908 and growing up in house #10, Richmond remembered a landscape of houses and fields with uncles and aunts living nearby. Ruins of some places remain evident. The cemetery, #7, is still in use. By showing how Richmond grew up in a landscape of kin and community, instead of the forested place seen today, this map helps us understand Richmond's point of view when he referred to Drayton Hall as "home." It also demonstrates the value of talking to elders and of recording oral history. Courtesy Drayton Hall Preservation Trust.

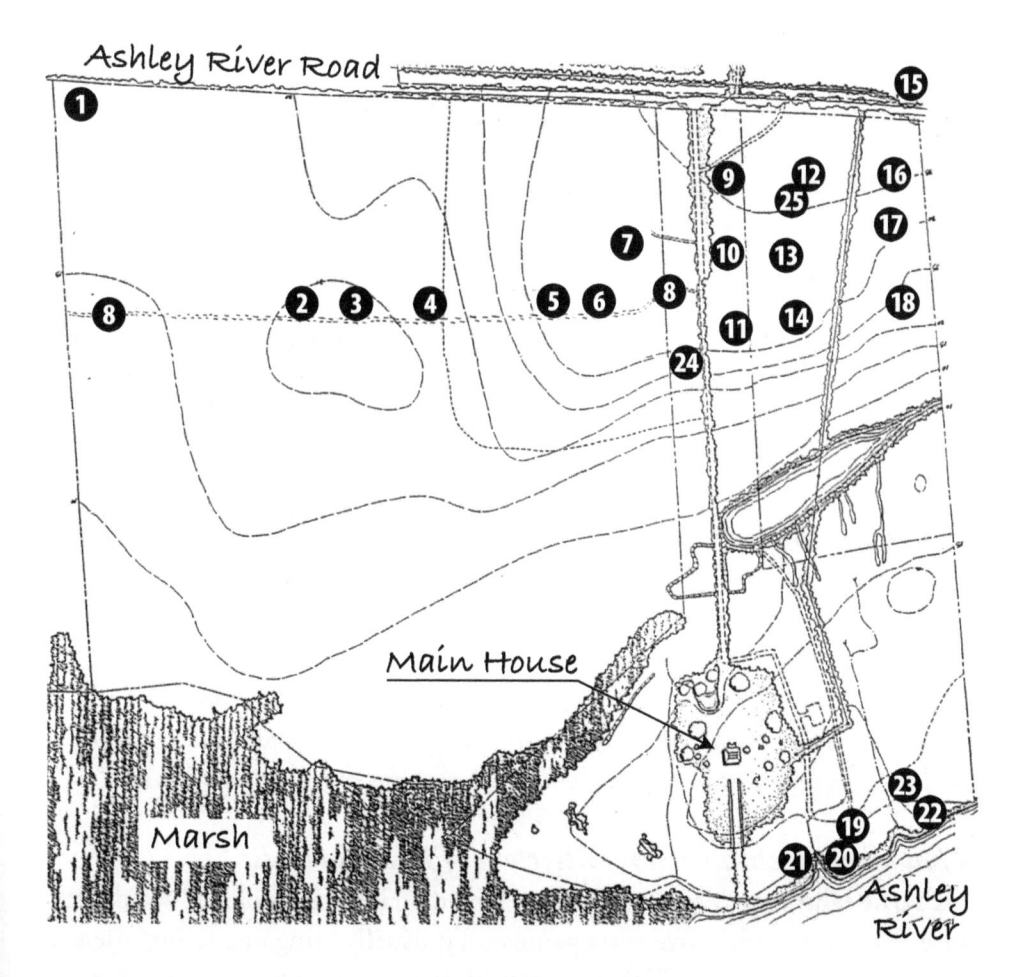

Drayton Hall site map from Richmond Bowens' memory, c. 1920

- **1** Store & house*
- **2** Dennis house
- **3** Washington house
- **4** Nanny Notes house*
- **5** Roberts/McKeever house #2
- **6** Johnson house*
- **7** Graveyard
- **8** MacBeth Road
- **9** (Former house)*
- **10** Bowens house*
- **11** McKeever house*
- **12** Uncle Sammy's house*
- **13** Smalls house*
- **14** (Former house)*
- **15** Store & house*
- **16** Hallman house*
- **17** Hazel house*
- **18** (Former house)*
- **19** Barn
- **20** Blacksmith shop*
- **21** Orangerie
- **22** Store*
- **23** Storekeeper's house
- **24** Spring site
- **25** Old well (open)

* No trace remains

Charlie Drayton, Anne Drayton Nelson:
"When I was young ..."

2005 – Drayton Hall

This is an edited combination of two interviews from 2005. In the early 1970s upon the death of their Aunt Charlotta ("Aunt Charley") Drayton, Charlie Drayton and his brother Frank became owners of Drayton Hall and soon decided to sell it. For reasons he describes, Charlie wanted it preserved and not developed commercially, a decision which his daughter, Anne Drayton Nelson, endorses. She describes her childhood memories, including those about "Aunt Charley" and an ancient live oak, which has been cited in other interviews. Father and daughter share their feelings about Drayton Hall, including the cemetery where he is now buried, and their thoughts about the site's future.

What are your childhood recollections of Drayton Hall?

Charlie Drayton: When I was young, Drayton Hall was absolutely wonderful. Since Frank was almost five years younger, I'd usually bring one or two friends whenever I came out here. With no electricity, it was early to bed and early to rise. My father blew an old cow horn to call us in for lunch, and as soon as lunch was over, we were back out again — climbing trees, hunting, fishing, playing games, just having a lot of fun. I fished in the pond, catching small bream, and later, in the river. We fished the dredge cuts that had filled with water and which had been cut from when my grandfather started strip mining for calcium phosphate after the Civil War. My father loved to set off fireworks, particularly at Christmastime. He'd light a Roman candle, throw it into the pond, and it would go "phfft, phfft, phfft," putting out different colors. Quite magnificent.

One thing we loved was to start right at the top of the mound in front of the house and roll all the way to the bottom, and get up as giddy as could be. The last time I did that was about three Thanksgivings ago, and I swore I'd never do it again.

How has the Ashley River changed over time?

Charlie: Before World War II, we came almost every weekend and shot cans from the riverbank. At that time, where the two oak trees are at the end of the allée from the house to the river, you could walk 20, 30 feet beyond them to the river. Now, the bank is gone. Why? Because after World War II, boating became a big hobby, and lots of boats sped by, and the wakes eroded the bank. It wasn't until the National Trust became owners that stabilization with rock revetment took place. Staff won passage of "No Boat Wake" signs, and the public, in general, does pay attention.

What was your "Aunt Charley" like?
Charlie: She was the epitome of a Southern lady. I never, ever heard her say a mean word about anybody. She loved to travel, especially touring Europe with friends. She lived by herself in my grandparents' house at 25 East Battery, where I spent nights from time to time. I'd stay a week or two out here with her. She let us do whatever we wanted. She never approved of hunting, but we did hunt. She never felt the same way about fishing. Mostly we just roamed, collecting red bugs, ticks, gnats, and everything else. [Laughing]

Why didn't she modernize the house, at least put in electricity or running water?
I'm not sure but think it was two things. One is that she never got married. Two is that she owned it, remembered it, and knew it for what it was. I never knew how much money she had — none of our business to begin with — but I think she had enough because she traveled a lot. She simply didn't want the house changed, so it was never modernized.

Was it unusual to come here, using privies and having no electricity and modern amenities?
We brought amenities with us. If we came out for a weekend, we brought a grill and cooked hamburgers and hot dogs, and everybody had a good time. One of the "modern facilities" was an outhouse to the east of the main house, and that's where we went.

Was the rustic nature of the experience part of the charm of the house?
I'm not sure I understood the charm of it until I was much older and understood the value of the house and the property. I don't know it made any difference.

How do you think your relatives in heaven will respond to you about the decision to sell Drayton Hall after seven generations of family ownership?

My brother and I decided that neither of us could buy out the other, and we couldn't jointly operate it, so we would have to dispose of it. Word got around, and I got a phone call from a fellow who wanted to buy it.

I said, "What are you going to do with it?" He said, "We'll make it into a clubhouse, put in a golf course or two." I said, "No. No way!"

Fortunately, the National Trust for Historic Preservation had its annual meeting in Charleston about 1970, and I knew one of the trustees. I asked him about purchasing it, and he said, "Absolutely!"

So, with the interest that the state, the National Trust, and Historic Charleston Foundation showed, we decided to sell. I want to live for quite some time because I fear that having broken seven generations of ownership, I might not be welcomed upstairs. Generations of Draytons have loved this place, and my brother and I loved it just as much. I'm hoping they've forgiven me by now because it was the move that had to be made at that time.

Charlie Drayton and Anne D. Nelson at Drayton Family Memorial

Charlie Drayton, his daughter Anne, and I were at the Drayton Family Memorial when the interview began. The idea for the Memorial arose when his daughter Molly Drayton Osteen, who lives in Augusta, Georgia, called me to say that, although Draytons had been laid to rest elsewhere, she wanted to be buried at Drayton Hall. I agreed, stipulated the cemetery must be for cremated remains only, and formed a committee of Charlie and his son Chad, architects Jim Thomas and Sandy Logan (a Drayton descendant and member of our site council), landscape architect Sheila Wertimer, former Director of Preservation Matt Webster, former Director of Interpretation Craig Tuminaro, and me.

We chose a quiet corner of the property overlooking the river and devised a low-profile circular design of symbolic materials with plants low to the ground, requiring little maintenance. When the contractor was building the vault for the cremains, I asked him to leave voids in the mortar between the cinder blocks to allow a small amount of groundwater to enter and mix with the cremains. Upon receding, the water would carry the ashes into the marsh, the Ashley River, Charleston Harbor, and the ocean beyond.

Charlie Drayton: I thought about having a cemetery but never pursued it. However, my elder daughter (Molly) called and declared, "I want to cross the river!"

I asked, "What are you talking about?" She said, "I'm talking about when I die! I want to return to South Carolina. That's where I started, and that's where I want to end up. I want to be buried at Drayton Hall!"

Charlie, looking down at a limestone shaft with his late-wife's inscription on it, continued: "Mary Jervey Drayton was my wife for 64-plus years. She was very stylish, a little bit opinionated, and a wonderful, wonderful gal."

Pointing to Anne, he said: "And this is one of the reasons. I have two other major reasons (son Chad and elder daughter Molly) and several minor ones (their grandchildren). This gravestone is for Garnett Nelson, Anne's wonderful husband, one of the finest men I have ever met."

Anne, could you describe "Aunt Charley?"

Anne: "Aunt Charley" — I never knew her as Charlotta — was well-read and well-traveled and she had a studious, inquisitive mind. She lived alone. During the summers, she'd go to Flat Rock, North Carolina, where our family had a house, and attended St. John's in the Wilderness Episcopal Church, where she's buried. She had single female friends, like spinsters or widows, who sometimes accompanied her when she came out to Drayton Hall or traveled. She loved dogs. One was named Nipper, whose height she measured on the door-jamb opposite the one where Drayton children were measured. She buried Nipper here and marked the spot with a gravestone — the only dog so honored over the course of centuries.

She didn't particularly respond to young children. On my mother's side of the family, you could hardly walk past my maternal grandfather that he didn't grab and smother you in kisses. Aunt Charley was not like that. I do remember a story about her and me. When I was little, Mother and I visited Aunt Charley at her house on East Bay. I didn't say a word, and on the way home, Mother scolded me for just sitting there "like a bump on a log." Next time we visited, I had thought and thought, so when I felt the moment came, I asked, "Aunt Charley, why didn't you ever get married?"

What was it like to visit here when you were a child, with no electricity?

Anne: It was exciting. Aunt Charley used to come in the spring and fall for six weeks max. I don't remember staying here with my sister or my brother, so I guess Aunt Charley could only take one of us at a time. It was exciting to have an outhouse that we used during the day. Absolutely beautiful ewers, bowls, and chamber pots were in each of the bedrooms. The chamber pots lived under the bed and were used at night.

I was never much for camping out. Drayton Hall was like camping in. We didn't lack for anything. We had access to water from the hand pump outside the basement door. Aunt Charley did have an electrical extension cord to the basement from caretaker Tom's cabin, which the Trust converted into a gift shop (now the Richard and Jill Almeida Gallery). She plugged in the refrigerator in the basement for eggs, milk, and such. She had a portable kerosene burner with one eye and a handle, so she could move it from room to room. At four o'clock in the afternoon, she moved it into the front room on the northwest side (the same room where my paternal great-grandfather had died), fired it up, on went the teapot, and we'd have a cup of tea.

At lunchtime, the kerosene burner was again fired up. A pot went on the eye, and eggs were dropped in water for hardboiled eggs, sliced on bread with mayonnaise from the refrigerator. There was no cooking. Aunt Charley introduced me to an easy way of living, and it was fun. It was adventuresome to be outside. We'd climb the live oak, explore the barn, and walk the woods. I have no recollection of being bothered by chiggers, gnats, or mosquitoes, but as a child maybe it was accepted as what comes with the farm. I don't remember candles at night, but maybe we used them. For supper, perhaps we had boiled eggs, but I don't remember, and when it got dark, we must have gone to bed.

Could you describe Aunt Charley's bedroom in Drayton Hall?

Anne: Her bedroom was on the second floor, northeast side looking toward the river. In it was Aunt Charley's big, puffy-feather, four-poster bed. The room had been partitioned, creating a large room and two smaller ones, each with a cot and dressing table. Aunt Charley's cot was made by African Americans at Drayton Hall after the Civil War. They also made three "three-quarter beds" for each of the three Drayton sisters, one of whom was Aunt Charley. I slept in one when growing up. Although the big bed in Aunt Charley's bedroom was beautiful, she normally slept on the little cot in her dressing room. Why? Maybe security. I don't know. Even at 25 East Battery, she seldom slept in her large bedroom in the 18th-century four-poster bed. Instead, she chose to sleep in a small room on a cot.

What was her position on this house remaining the way it was?

Anne: I was too young to have a conversation about it, but her basic attitude was to keep Drayton Hall as it is. I believe her concept was, "If I can pass it on the way I inherited it, then I have fulfilled my responsibility. I've done my duty. This was good enough for my parents and it's good enough for me, so it's good enough to pass on."

Could you describe your childhood memories of the ancient live oak in front of Drayton Hall by the curve in the entrance lane?

Anne: The live oak tree was much bigger when I was younger. It was thicker at the top. Huge limbs have since been blown off by storms or cut by saws. Branches swooped to the ground, with one limb that was U-shaped. We used to straddle that and bounce up and down like riding a horse. We'd shimmy up to the center of the tree, which was so big we could lie down in it. When we were pre-teenagers, my second cousin Catherine and I would play "Mr. and Mrs. Squirrel," collect nuts and little snacks, and take them up into our tree house, which nature built.

I always loved the Spanish moss. The tree was like a huge tent because you could get inside the curtain of leaves and moss, have open space around the base, but hardly be seen. You could play tag or whatever you wanted down there. It wasn't bare as it is today.

When coming out on Sundays after church, we never knew who would visit. It was an open invitation for friends or family, and we'd cook hamburgers or hot dogs on the grill. Anybody could bring in-laws and "outlaws." Children played football, tramped through the woods, went out to the barn, and climbed through the trees. I don't remember doing anything in a boat or going out on the pond. I guess the boys did that. The girls played "squirrel tree," ran through the gardens, and went down to the river. Recycling wasn't in fashion then, so we threw bottles into the river and would shoot at them. We roamed the property. You were together as a family and with friends. It was a wonderful experience of freedom.

What is special about the grounds at Drayton Hall?

Anne: When I left South Carolina and moved to Virginia, I missed my family, but maybe even more, I missed the trees. Live oaks aren't the same in Virginia, and Spanish moss doesn't grow where I live now. I miss the trees the most.

What are your recollections about Richmond Bowens?

Anne: Richmond Bowens worked in Chicago when I was growing up. I didn't know him until later when he became the gatekeeper here. But Daddy always spoke fondly of him. Whenever Richmond saw us, he treated us as the children of a dear old friend. When he was sick, Daddy took us to see him and his wife Velma. They had a good relationship. It was Richmond who approached Daddy after the

Trust owned the place and said, "I want to be buried at Drayton Hall. Can you make that happen?" Daddy did. Later, both you and Daddy spoke at his funeral.

Do you think Aunt Charley would be pleased with what's happened to Drayton Hall since its sale?

Anne: Aunt Charley would be more than thrilled with the stewardship the National Trust has provided. She'd be pleased with how thorough they have been with their research in search of knowledge of things we didn't know about.

How did you feel about the decision to sell Drayton Hall to the National Trust?

Anne: I'm eternally grateful to my father and his brother for turning over Drayton Hall to the National Trust. It was a decision of the head, not the heart. If it had come to my generation, there would have been five of us to agree on what to do. I don't think you could get five people to agree. I might have been the most difficult because I tend to live by my heart, not my head.

Absolutely, it was the right decision. I will always appreciate that the very difficult decision was not laid on my shoulders. The house is where it needs to be. It is being preserved. It is being cared for. No amount of money could be poured into this house and save it the way is has been and have it open to the public and shared.

Monty and Molly Osteen:
"Tell the many stories about the people …"

2021 – Drayton Hall

Molly Drayton Osteen, oldest daughter of Charlie Drayton, grew up enjoying Drayton Hall with family and friends. Her wedding reception was there, and she retains strong affection for the place. She and husband Monty live in Augusta, Georgia. He is treasurer of the Drayton Hall Preservation

Trust. It was vital for me that the Drayton family remain a part of Drayton Hall, because without them, Drayton Hall would not have become a historic site. In this interview in 2021 they share perspectives on Drayton Hall, especially its people. Drayton Hall is open exclusively to the family on Thanksgiving Day to gather, remember the past, look to the future, and enjoy.

Molly, could you describe your connection to Drayton Hall, and what it means to you?

Molly: I'm a direct descendant of John Drayton, the founder and builder of Drayton Hall. As a child, I didn't realize what a treasure it is. It was just part of our life. I didn't know most people didn't have such a wonderful place to go to on weekends. I didn't think about it being a great house. Today, I consider it a national treasure, an icon, that should be included in architectural and American history books.

Monty, could you describe your connection to Drayton Hall and what it means to you?

Monty: My major recollection of Drayton Hall is driving to it the night of our wedding reception. It was my first experience with the place. I'd never thought much about it until then. I was overwhelmed by the sight. That night it seemed as if there were as many firetrucks and firemen (to protect the house) as there were guests. Lit only by candles, Drayton Hall was magnificent.

Molly, could you describe some of your memories of growing up there?

Molly: This may seem crazy, but off the top of my head, a favorite memory is digging in the barn down by the river looking for the silver we thought was hidden during the War Between the States. We spent hours and hours and hours in that barn digging for silver we never found.

I also loved climbing trees at Drayton Hall. I was very good at it. Like all the Draytons, I have short legs, inherited from my father, and I was more like an animal going up these trees. Although the trees on either side of the house had good branches to climb on, there was nothing like the live oak in front of the house as you make that turn in the entrance drive because its branches came all the way down. Climbing trees means being footloose and fancy free to me. Nobody worried about us falling and breaking our necks. We had no restrictions. We had no boundaries. We could just go! That was the first real freedom I can remember, and the last freedom that I recall.

Monty, what are your favorite memories of Drayton Hall?

Monty: Family get-togethers on Thanksgiving Day! Drayton Hall is a wonderful venue. We enjoy being with the family and doing crazy stuff like trying to hit golf balls into the well. Charlie was the patriarch and presided, and his wife "Jerv" (Mary Jervey Drayton) was always much a part of it. Everyone congregated around them, and Charlie would tell stories.

Molly, when you were young, what were your favorite places at Drayton Hall? What was your Aunt Charley Drayton like?

Molly: One of our favorite places was the hidden stairs in the round stairwell. We loved going from one floor to the other one and not getting caught. They probably would have stopped us since a lot of steps were missing. I like challenges and was enticed by the inner staircase. I was also excited by digging for silver. We loved the basement too and looking for the silver down there. I don't think there was any silver because we never found it.

You know, I can't think of a single thing I didn't love about being out there! Except for when I went to spend the nights out there with Aunt Charley. I had to behave. She was a wonderful person, but wanted us to be seen and not heard. She wanted to be seen and not heard too. She didn't reveal much about her life. We loved hearing stories from Daddy about his childhood in Flat Rock, NC, Drayton Hall and 9 Church Street in Charleston, where he grew up. Aunt Charley was a great lady, but she was a recluse. That's the best way to put it.

Molly, could you describe Richmond Bowens?

Molly: I absolutely adored him — one of the finest men I've ever known. He was such a gentleman. I have his picture in a frame in my home with all of my family. I considered him part of it. I used to play with his children or grandchildren, I don't remember which, but we had a grand time. Richmond Bowens is at the top of my list of people I admire most, other than my father. He's among the top three people in this world that I truly admire.

I can't think of one thing in particular that illustrates why I feel this way about him other than he was always delighted to see us. He wanted to know how we were doing. He cared about us as if he were our grandfather or father. It didn't bother me at the time, but it bothered me later that he called me, "Miss Molly." I wanted him to call me, "Molly," but I think somebody told me I shouldn't say anything about it. Richmond Bowens treated us with more respect than we deserved.

What difference did race make?

Molly: None to me at that time. Zero. Perhaps race wasn't an issue for us because we were in segregated schools. We had Black servants, and we treated them with respect. They were part of our family too. I guess I knew the difference, but I didn't know the difference. Of course, I knew the difference between Black and White, but it didn't seem to make any difference. Psychologically, I probably knew there was a difference between servants in the kitchen and the owners of the house, but I didn't think about it much.

Molly, would you tell the story about the Drayton Family Memorial and your father?

Molly: When Richmond Bowens died, I knew he was going to be buried at Drayton Hall's historic cemetery for African Americans, and suddenly something hit me in the heart. If there's a place for Richmond at Drayton Hall, why can't there be one for me? Living in Augusta, I'd been struggling with a question: "When I leave this world, where am I going in the ground?" Then it hit me: "I want to go back — back across the Savannah River." Although I'd grown up in St. Philip's Church in Charleston, I didn't particularly care about going to the cemetery there. I wanted to go to Drayton Hall.

So I went to you, George, and asked, "What can we do? When I leave this world, I want to come home to Drayton Hall forever and ever. What can you do to help me?" You said, "Well, we'll have to ask the National Trust." I said, "George, if I have to crawl to Washington, I want to make this happen!" You looked at me and said, "I hope we can do this without you having to crawl to DC." I greatly appreciated that.

It took a couple of years to complete the process, but I didn't mention it to anybody in my family because I didn't know if it would come through. When I finally told my father, I said, "Daddy, I'm coming home!" He asked, " Y'all moving to Charleston?" I said, "No, Daddy. When I leave this world and when you leave this world, guess where we can go now? We can go to Drayton Hall. George worked it out with the National Trust so that we can go to Drayton Hall and be there forever and ever." Daddy burst into tears with joy. "That's the greatest gift I can remember ever being given, other than marrying your mother," he said. I'm forever thankful to you for asking the Trust on our behalf.

Why did being buried at Drayton Hall mean so much to your father?

Molly: Prior to the National Trust's taking it over, Drayton Hall had been vandalized. He was relieved to have it taken care of and put back in shape. He said Drayton Hall was closer to his heart than any other place — not Flat Rock in North Carolina, not 25 East Bay, not 9 Church Street. Drayton Hall meant the most to him, so when told he could be there eternally, he declared, "That's the greatest gift I've ever had."

Since then, a peace has come over me. It changed me to know I'm going home. I'm going back across that river. Once you told me that the National Trust said we could go there, I thought, "You know what? This is where Monty and I started the day we were married and where we had our reception. This is where I want us to end up." I don't think I asked Monty if he wanted to go there. He's just going.

Could that be one of those situations as in the scene from Book of Ruth, when she says, "Whither thou goest, I will go. Your people shall be my people?"
Monty: That's very apropos.
Molly: It's one of the few things in my life that I just did. It is one of my greatest gifts. It lifted something in me I didn't know was there. I can't express how peaceful it is to know this.

When the cemetery vault was built, I asked the contractor to leave small voids in the mortar between the concrete blocks so as the water table rises with the incoming tide, it will infiltrate the vault and mix with the ashes. As it recedes, the water will carry the ashes out into the marsh into the Ashley River and the ocean.
Molly: That makes me very happy.

Monty, what are some of your favorite places at Drayton Hall?
Monty: The Drayton memorial is certainly one of them. Also, the stairs in the front hall. At one of my first board meetings, we discussed how dangerous they were. I was reminded of bounding up those stairs after our wedding reception to change clothes. I didn't realize how close I came to dying. There are a lot of places in the house that I like to walk through and marvel at the architecture as well as the way the house was built, but those stairs are among my favorites. I like to look at them and remind myself of that evening.

Molly, what feelings arise in you when you look at Drayton Hall as a historical plantation, based on slavery?

Molly: I am not ashamed of slavery because that was a sign of the times and an acceptable practice. Do I think it was good? Absolutely not! It was awful. But it was what it was. A lot of good things at Drayton Hall wouldn't have happened without the slaves. I hope they were treated well. We were told by Richmond Bowens, who adored the place, stories about his family and his growing up there, and he spoke of Drayton Hall with love. I guess that's why my brother and sister and I become defensive when we hear about how horrible some plantation owners were to their slaves. I don't know how the Drayton family treated them. But Richmond Bowens did not know about any mistreatment. I can't imagine why he would lie about it to us. When he talked to us, it was with fondness. You can't change history. Slavery happened. We pray that it never happens again.

Molly, how do you feel about your father and uncle selling Drayton Hall out of the family?

Molly: That was one of the wisest decisions my father and his brother ever made. They saved it because they didn't have the funds, the knowledge, or the expertise to preserve it. As for the decision not to restore it to a specific period of time, I think that was excellent. Daddy would never have consented to the National Trust taking it over otherwise.

Why do you think Aunt Charley didn't add electricity, heat, air conditioning, or running water to Drayton Hall?

Molly: She didn't want to change a thing. She lived in the past, and that's okay. She was perfectly happy out there. She had some kind of electrical lines from the caretaker's house coming into the main house so that she could get electrical power in the first room on the left when you walk in. That's basically where she lived. She had a little Bunsen burner-type thing in there too. Aunt Charley was a recluse. As much time as I spent with her, I didn't really know her because I don't think she wanted to be known. I couldn't get inside her head.

Monty, now that Drayton Hall is an historic site, what are your hopes for the future?

Monty: First, we must make sure that we're successful in preserving the place. That's an expensive proposition. My hope for the future is to properly fund it and make sure its preservation continues. Second is to enhance the visitor experience and to put the house in context and tell the many stories about the people.

Charlie Drayton, Rebecca Campbell:
"Drayton Hall Could Help Bridge the Racial Divide"

2015 – Drayton Hall

Participants:
  George McDaniel: Executive Director of Drayton Hall.
  Toni Carrier: Wood Family Fellow, Drayton Hall; director of the Center for Family History, International African American Museum, Charleston, SC.
  Robin Foster: Family history research assistant, Drayton Hall; genealogist, owner and co-founder of Genealogy Just Ask.
  Jay Millard: Videographer.

George: *How are each of you connected to Drayton Hall?*

  Charlie: I'm just lucky enough to have been born into this family and still a part of it.

  Rebecca: I'm a descendant of Drayton Hall through the Bowens family — Catherine Bowens and Caesar Bowens. My connections go way back.

George: *The name "Charles" has a long lineage at Drayton Hall. Could you explain that, Charlie?*

  Charlie: I am the sixth Charles. The first Charles, born in 1744, was the son of John Drayton, who founded Drayton Hall. Now there are three more: my son, grandson, and great grandson, who is Charles the 9th.

George: *What does Drayton Hall mean to you?*

Charlie: It means just about everything. When I was growing up, I didn't realize it was so wonderful. It wasn't until later that I fully appreciated it. Transferring ownership of Drayton Hall in 1974 was traumatic because it'd been in the family for so long. But we couldn't pay the taxes, manage repairs, and keep the grounds. There was no way my brother and I could have handled it. But Drayton Hall still means an awful lot to me and to my children, and my nephew is now on the site council.

Rebecca: Drayton Hall means family. My ancestors are buried here. To me, Drayton Hall means Richmond Bowens, Willis Johnson, Catherine Bowens, and Caesar Bowens. I feel their spirits as I walk the grounds.

Charlie: Of those who Rebecca mentioned, I don't recall Caesar Bowens (*who died before Charlie was born*), but I remember Richmond well and considered him a dear friend. We grew up together.

George: *Tell us a story about Richmond Bowens.*

Charlie: He worked for my father prior to World War II. After my father died, Richmond went to work in Chicago. In the 1970s he came by my house and said he wanted to be buried at Drayton Hall and asked if I could help. So we got permission from the National Trust, which owned Drayton Hall, for him to be buried in the cemetery there as well as a job. He worked as Drayton Hall's gatekeeper (*serving as front-line ambassador, providing security, and selling tickets*) and later in the gift shop (*as a historian for visitors about family and community life*). After he died, his widow asked me to speak at his funeral, as she did you, George. It was a very touching time.

George: *What did Richmond mean to you, Rebecca?*

Rebecca: Richmond meant family. We did many things together. His daughter Gloria and I played together. He brought Gloria and little Richmond to our home for my grandmother to babysit. After he moved to Chicago, he'd visit in the summer and was more like my uncle than a third cousin.

Toni Carrier: *What were your fondest experiences at Drayton Hall?*

Charlie: Things that stand out are my two daughters having their parties and wedding receptions here. All occurred in the winter, and we were blessed with good weather. My Aunt Charley was not in favor of it, but she let us use the house. Fireplaces were open, and we had firemen here for protection, and no smoking, of course. With so many memories, it's hard to pull out one in particular.

Rebecca: My fondest experience is visiting the cemetery. Whenever there's an event there, that's when family members — north, south, east, and west — come to Drayton Hall. The dedication of the arch, for example, was great, and we could socialize.

Jay Millard: *What was your favorite place on the plantation?*

Charlie: Probably the woods, where I spent most of my time. My father would let me bring a friend, and we'd take off. Three or four mules roamed around and were fed in the barn. We also had sheep, which were mowing machines *(for the lawn)*. We played games and did lots of fishing in the pond and the dredge cuts. We'd hunt, and though I hated to shoot anything, I did anyway. We just had fun.

Rebecca: The cemetery. I visit Cleveland Johnson and my other relatives. They have no tombstones, but we know they rest there. You can now visit Richmond Bowens and his wife Velma there too.

Jay Millard: *What was your scariest moment here?*

Charlie: I don't remember a scary moment, but we did have hurricanes. After a big one in the 1950s, the house survived beautifully, but the grounds did not. It took me an hour to get from the house to the river climbing over and under fallen trees. I don't know how this house has survived years of war, hurricanes, earthquakes, *and* family!

Robin Foster: *How has knowing each other enriched your lives?*

Rebecca: Charlie has enriched my life. In the 1970s Richmond got interested family members together and said, "Look, let's come to Drayton Hall. We need to get involved because the legacy is there. Our ancestors were from Drayton Hall. We need to move on. I'll teach you. Come on." My sister Catherine and I followed him. Richmond introduced us to Charlie. He said, "I'm older, but Charlie and I played together." So we met you, Charlie, and then Anne, your children, and grandchildren. It's like we have become a part of the Drayton family because every time we see each other, we just hug and love. There was no hatred. No going back hundreds of years to what happened!

Charlie: No question about it, and I hope it remains that way forever.

Rebecca: No question! Thank you.

Charlie: I remember being with your family and Richmond and others, and how wonderful it has become. No acrimony at all. We got along well together.

Rebecca: We sure did!

George: *What are your thoughts about an interpretive center at Drayton Hall?*

Rebecca: I'm plugging for an interpretive center. It would be meaningful for the Drayton family and for descendants of the enslaved people to tell the stories of the many things that took place here.

Charlie: I think that's a great idea to tell the stories of the families, Black and White. They're human-interest stories.

George: *What messages would you like the new center to convey?*

Charlie: That the house is different from anything else today, locally or elsewhere. It's been in the same family for these many years. Even though it now belongs to the National Trust, I consider it still part of the family and always will. My children definitely do.

As for the whole site, I wish the other houses were still here. I remember them well. A woman named Binah lived across the highway when I was very young. My father used to pick her up, or walk over to her place and get her. She took care of me until I was three years old or so. *(An interview with Binah's great-grandson, the Rev. Roosevelt Geddis, is on page 80).*

Seven or eight houses were along a road off the entrance drive. They were wooden and relatively small, the predominant feature being a chimney. I remember this because after the houses had gone the chimneys were still standing. I remember vegetable gardens and chickens, but not pig pens or smokehouses. Most families had automobiles. The houses were cared for, and as far as I knew as a child, the people who lived in them seemed happy. I used to go down and chat with them. It was wonderful. I miss those families being here. The last house I remember was there before World War II. When I came back from the Navy, all were gone. The museum shop was typical of them — one big room around a fireplace, and small bedrooms.

Rebecca: When you walk the grounds now, it's as if no one lived here. But there were houses, as Charlie said. We need to interpret those places and identify life. I'd like for the interpretive center to answer questions: How did the Draytons treat their slaves? How were they fed? What were their occupations? Were they rice growers? Did they do a lot of fishing? What vegetables did they grow? Were they able to go to church and worship, and if not, did they have a praise house on the premises because African Americans coming from Africa have always been religious people? They believed in singing and shouting and, you know, praising the Lord. When did they socialize? What did they do on the Fourth of July and Christmas because enslaved people from Africa brought socializing with them? For those holidays, did they barbecue a pig and have a gathering?

Robin Foster: *How might museums connect descendants of former slaves and slave owners?*

Rebecca: The main answer is to find a key person. Here it was Richmond Bowens. Thanks to him, we got to know a lot of the Drayton people. Richmond was wonderful in every respect. I distinctly remember when he was working at the gate. Our people would ask him, "What are you doing here at a plantation? Why are you doing this?" He'd say, "I'm a Bowens, and this is my home. I love it here." Some of us were surprised. Later when he gave talks at the gift shop, people were amazed at what he said about what did and did not go on here.

Charlie: My father said that, when he was a boy, Christmas was a big event here. People who lived here had a good time together. They were given presents and so forth. We sang spirituals. Spirituals were a big item then and have always been with me too. I remember the Society for the Preservation of Spirituals. One sung here is "Honor the Lamb," and another is "Hand me down, hand me down, hand me down my silver trumpet, Gabriel." They're beautiful.

Rebecca: We sang spirituals, too, and also learned how to clap. You got to have the timing for that. We practiced as children — grew up with it. We heard the songs, and began clapping. Our feet moved, and our whole body moved with it … We know we are Africans because we have the same rhythms — our feet move, and then our hands and bodies the same way. We are African descendants!

Toni Carrier: *What is necessary for sites to make connections and bring different people together?*

Charlie: I'd say to families: "Come here with us and find out something, and learn. Come not only to Drayton Hall or Magnolia or Middleton but also to plantations where your families may have been. It would be wonderful. It's part of their histories. Rebecca, that's *our* history.

Rebecca: It goes beyond the Drayton and Bowens families. George McDaniel has played a great role at Drayton Hall. We met him through Richmond, who said,

"You need to meet George McDaniel." "Who's George?" I asked. So Catherine and I met George and his wife Mary Sue, and we talked about Africa, where he'd been in the Peace Corps. George said, "Look, we're going to start working with Bowens and Drayton families and other descendants, and together have events." So we did event after event — had a birthday party here for Richmond — and brought hundreds of descendants to Drayton Hall. This joint interview is a result of what George and the Bowens, Drayton, and other families have done. I recommend it to any other plantation or historic site.

The harder you work, the closer you get, the better you know each other. You feel the tension ease. You feel the love. You feel the hatred ease. One thing we've learned at Drayton Hall is that we always love.

George: *What are your thoughts about the African American cemetery?*

Charlie: That's one of the positive things — the recognition of the graveyard. The entrance *(a wrought-iron open arch designed by Charleston blacksmith Philip Simmons)* that's been erected and the love that's gone into getting together and meeting, all have been a tremendously positive step.

Rebecca: That was one of the events which brought the descendants back to Drayton Hall. When families began to open up to the cemetery programs and descendants of the enslaved people came back, that's when love drifted in. With the open arch, the spirit goes in and goes out. That's the way we want to do — flow in and flow out as the living people.

Toni Carrier: *Have you learned anything about your family from one another that you did not know before you met?*

Charlie: I've learned that my own family, particularly my daughters and my son, love to come to Drayton Hall, and to meet with you, Rebecca, and your sister Catherine, and other descendants. We are all family.

Rebecca: We learned that he could sing Negro spirituals. It was a shock when Charlie got up on the platform in the cemetery and sang. We asked ourselves, "How did he learn them?"

Charlie: In 1926 my father compiled a book of the spirituals sung here — 29 of them ... I sang a few. Two of the songs originated at Drayton Hall. Anne and I sang one — "Honor the Lamb" — at the cemetery dedication in 2008. (Charlie sings it again):

Honor the Lamb for the good He's done.
Honor the Lamb. Honor the Lamb.
Honor your mother for the good He's done.
Honor the Lamb. Honor the Lamb.
Way over yonder in the harvest field.
Honor the Lamb. Honor the Lamb.
Angel working on the chariot's wheel.
Honor the Lamb. Honor the Lamb.
Never seen such a thing since I been born.
Honor the Lamb. Honor the Lamb.
People keep a-coming but the train's done gone.
Honor the Lamb. Honor the Lamb.

Charlie: And it goes on for 49 verses.
Rebecca: Really!
Charlie: And your ancestors would have sung that too!

George: *As descendants of slaveholders and of the enslaved, what would you like to say as take-away messages to visitors?*

Charlie: Know that we are good friends. We're here together, and this is *our* home — both of us; all of us!

Rebecca: I would say that my ancestors did live here. They were born here, and I am a descendant. I'm also a part of Drayton Hall.

Charlie: Definitely you are!

Rebecca: Definitely! Because my ancestors were born and lived here and now because of my relationship with the Drayton family, I feel a part of Drayton Hall.

Charlie: I would like to say to you Rebecca, that you are my good friend and that you are just as much a part of Drayton Hall as I am, and my family is. I'd like people to know that we are all from Drayton Hall. Not just me, not just you, but all the people who were born here, who had any connection to Drayton Hall. We all belong to Drayton Hall.

George: *How can sites like Drayton Hall help bridge racial divides?*

Charlie: Richmond Bowens became the link between the two of us — and to the cemetery and to the meetings with people whose ancestors were born here. I hope more groups like us get together and enjoy each other's company. Drayton Hall can help bridge the racial divide by having more meetings together, by having the cemetery become a genuine part of the visitor experience.

Rebecca: Drayton Hall can help bridge the gap and build racial harmony in America by using the cemetery. It's where our history is. You go and look at a tombstone and see the birthdate and death date and the family name. It tells the history of where you are. Most people look for relatives, and that gets people together, and then they can sit down around a table and talk about the racial problems we are facing. I would like for Drayton Hall to extend itself, to have a retreat with plantations like Middleton and Magnolia and others, so we can explain our feelings to each other. This releases tension and could move us into other areas as well.

Charlie: I couldn't agree with you more. It's a wonderful idea.

Annie Brown Meyers:
"Values My Mother and Father Taught Me"
2012 – Drayton Hall

Annie Brown Meyers was a descendant of the Bowens family and niece of Richmond Bowens. Her mother, Lucille Bowens, grew up at Drayton Hall and probably named her daughter after her mother, Anna Bowens. She instilled in Annie the values she had learned from Drayton Hall's African American community, values which, in the 1960s, inspired her to become involved in the civil rights movement. She passed away in 2018.

Annie Meyers recollected her visits with her grandmother Anna Bowens Mayes, a widow who had re-married and who lived on the Drayton Hall property. She perceived her grandmother's small, frame dwelling, currently exhibited as the Caretaker's House, as the "big house" and the brick mansion next to it as an outbuilding. She paid it little attention. Her account suggests that it was not the size that made a dwelling the "big house," but rather the perception of the dwelling's residents.

George: *What is your connection to Drayton Hall?*

Annie: It's through my mother, Lucille Bowens Brown, who with her siblings was born here, as was her father, Richmond Bowens. Her mother, Anna, was born and raised down Ashley River Road near where Tobias Gadson Boulevard is now. I came to know about Drayton Hall through my mother's family. My grandfather, Richmond Bowens, was a farmer at Drayton Hall. He had a son, also named Richmond Bowens — my mother's brother, who's given you a lot of history.

Mother told us about her childhood, how they played in the yard and other things. When she was growing up, her job was like that of a chambermaid. She went to the main house and took care of the bathroom area. She said her father died when she was young and that her mother married Bud Mayes, who took care of the livestock at Drayton Hall. (*Livestock included horses and mules, which were housed in a barn destroyed in 1989 by Hurricane Hugo. Sheep grazed on the lawn while cattle were across the Ashley River Road.*)

What was your mother like?

She was a quiet person who said, "I do what I can do. I get it over and done with. I don't make a lot of fuss about it. I don't ask a lot of questions. If someone tells me to do something, I do it to the best of my ability." She taught us to never say "yes" if we didn't mean it, that we must be faithful to our word because it's our bond. Of all her siblings, she was the shortest, but she carried a lot of weight. When she spoke, everybody listened. They looked to her for guidance.

Tell us about your grandfather.

Richmond Bowens died when my mother was young. I never met him. Mother and her siblings said he was tall, dressed nicely, and was a deacon of Springfield Baptist Church, down the road from Drayton Hall. Some would call him a leader. He dedicated his life to the church and his family. He was a caring person. I have Mother's picture of him wearing a top hat and a nice suit jacket.

Did your mother share instances in her life when her parents' values helped or shaped her?

Mother's values came from her parents, who were family-oriented and did a lot for their children. If asked her name, she'd say, "Lucille Bowens Brown," and emphasized the Bowens part because she was proud of it. Her mother, Anna Bowens, was strict and taught her children to be devoted to what they did and to look out for each other. My mother got that from her parents.

Elaborate on values your mother learned from her parents at Drayton Hall.

She learned to cook and sew, although she didn't sew as much as her sister Emily. But Mother made our dresses for school and little scarves and things for the choirs. I grew up down Ashley River Road from Drayton Hall near what is now Tobias Gadson Boulevard, which was the country back then. Mother's main thing was cooking. If company arrived unannounced, she'd go into the kitchen and whip up a meal in no time. Everybody liked her fried chicken. They could always smell Lucille's fried chicken cooking. She'd make fruitcake during the holidays and lemon meringue pie and cook turnip greens or collard greens. Red rice and shrimp was my favorite.

I didn't learn to cook in Mother's house. She did all of the cooking, washing, and ironing. But all of us children had responsibilities. I cleaned the kitchen and mopped the floors. But cooking was a no-no. It was her responsibility as a wife to cook the food. She also ironed because Daddy was a foreman at the Navy Yard. He had seven or eight shirts, and she washed and starched them, using a little spray bottle. As the shirts dried on the line, they'd stiffen. She folded them carefully and put them in his dresser.

I went to Immaculate Conception School, operated by the Catholic Church in Charleston. We never ate meat on Friday. We had seafood. I couldn't wait to get home and eat, but we had to wait for Daddy because nobody got in the pot before he got home. Mother learned from her mother that everybody had to wait until their fathers got home. We took baths, and put on clean clothes, and when Daddy arrived, we were ready to go to the table.

When her brother, also named Richmond (see his interview on page 7), planned a visit from Chicago, he'd call and say, "I'm going to be there next week, and want herring and rice." She would fix herring and rice for him, and he'd take some home. It was one of his favorites. I didn't care for it, even after she soaked the herring for a couple of days. Still too salty.

Mother made potato pie, peach pie, nut cake, and pound cake during the holidays, but fruitcake was her specialty. People in the neighborhood stopped in and watched so they could learn. Sometimes she'd go to their houses after they bought all of the ingredients. She'd say, "Now add this much of this or that, and always stir in one direction."

She baked cake late at night because she said if someone walked on the floor or slammed the door, the cake might fall. She'd get up at 4 in the morning, take one cake out of the oven, then put another one in.

There were teenagers who lived nearby whose father had left their mother and 12 children. They hunted coons, squirrels, and things like that, and sold them in our neighborhood. Daddy would say, "If those Edwards boys come by, get whatever they got because they need the money." Mother would buy a coon and fix it for dinner.

What were your parents' family connections to Drayton Hall and Middleton Place?

My father was in the Navy, and after his discharge, he worked at the Charleston Naval Shipyard. Born in downtown Charleston near Fielding's Funeral Home on Logan Street, he moved to Middleton with his mother and lived there until he married my mother, who was at Drayton Hall. They were about 20 at the time. My father's mother was Mary Sheppard, who lived at Middleton Place. She was a famous cook in the restaurant there for years.

After my mother's father died and her mother remarried, my granduncle Samuel Bowens, and his wife, my aunt Lillian, kept my mother under their wings. They pampered her, considering it their responsibility to look after my grandfather's children. Samuel and Lillian Bowens didn't have children. He didn't say a whole lot, but when he did talk, you'd better listen. I don't recollect Uncle Sammy mentioning any bad times at Drayton Hall. He said everybody worked together, respected each other, and there were no ill feelings about being there. He never said anything negative that his father or mother said about slavery.

Did you speak or hear Gullah growing up?

No. Only in the last 15 or 20 years did people start talking about it. Even though my great-grandmother was born and reared on James Island, where a lot of people talk Gullah, she always spoke English.

When I was young, a girlfriend and I visited Beaufort and went into a restroom. Teenage girls were there talking Gullah, and we couldn't understand a word they said. Sounded something like "*yippedeyippetherero*." I said, "We need to get out of here because I don't understand them. I might say the wrong thing, and they might take it the wrong way." Coming up, I never heard anybody speak Gullah.

When you were growing up, did you visit Drayton Hall?

My first recollection of visiting Drayton Hall was when my uncle who was married to Sadie Mayes Burns lived here with his son Thomas. He sold religious pictures, and his little house is what is now the museum shop *(the Caretaker's House, now the Richard and Jill Almeida Gallery)*, which was closer to the brick house than now. A set of gates was not far from the reflecting pond. I remember Daddy getting out of the car, opening the main gate by the highway then stopping to open the second gate. The headlights shined on my uncle's house, and I used to get so excited by looking at that house. That gave me a warm feeling, like a peace. I think that's the peace that my uncles and my mother felt when they were here. My visits had to have been in the 1950s.

If you could ask these ancient live oaks questions, what would you ask?

I'd ask, "Did anybody climb you? Did they make a swing on one of your limbs? Were you manicured by the people that lived here and did that make you strong? Was it you that made the people strong? Did they imitate their lives on you?"

What questions would you ask of the main house?

"How was it to live in the main house? Did those who did appreciate the service they got from people who worked there? How did they relate to them? Were they satisfied with the work?"

Describe growing up during segregation. What led you to get involved in Charleston's sit-in movement and the hospital strike?

We were taught, "Know your place, and stay in your place." You knew when you got on the bus where your seating was, and did not question it. We must sit where we were supposed to sit and do what we were supposed to do. Mother always said that, when we were inside a store, "to make sure you get a receipt, and that the merchandise you buy is put in a bag" because if anybody said we stole something, we'd have proof we had paid for what we got.

My mother, who died in 1998, would also say, "There's a change that's gonna come," although she never made a big issue of it. "You gonna get involved with the movement or you're not gonna get involved with the movement." When I demonstrated, she never said not to. It was my choice. I got involved with the sit-ins at Woolworth in 1960 and 1961 and at Kress in 1961. We'd go around lunchtime, sit at the fountain, and order something. We used to have to go to a little back area to order food and they would bring it round by the back door and serve you, but we couldn't sit at the counter. Mother never did say, "You can't do this, or you can't do that." She always said, "You got to live up to what you believe in."

I was involved with the movement downtown even though I lived west of the Ashley River. After listening to my friends from downtown, I wanted to get more insight into myself. I've never liked secondhand information or hearsay. I was curious and wanted to take part in what they were doing. It was something positive. The values my mother and father taught me and the values I learned from the nuns at school affected me. They taught us to be positive and always encouraged me to do my best. If you can make a difference, participate in whatever you needed to do in order to make a difference. I figured I was going to be a part of making a difference.

Getting involved with the movement made me more mature. I got the pleasure of being a part of it. I worked at the hospital, and in 1969 Union 1199 came and said, "We're going to go on strike. Are you willing to go on strike?" I said, "Yeah, I'm ready." At that time, I was more hardcore. Whatever it took, I was there. I marched. I went to jail. When I called my momma and them to say I was in jail, they asked, "You are where?" I said, "They locked me up." My momma replied, "Oh, my goodness. You know what I told you: 'If you go out there, you know the consequence of it.' You want us to come and take you out?" I said, "No, I'm going to stay right here."

Ralph Abernathy, Mrs. King, and Jesse Jackson came. It was interesting to listen to them. They always gave positive encouragement to believe in yourself.

How do you feel coming to Drayton Hall, a plantation where your ancestors for generations had been in bondage?

The peace that I feel is the peace that my ancestors left here. My grandparents and my parents and my parents' siblings had a peace. They were comfortable here. They loved Drayton Hall and there were no ill feelings, so it wasn't like a place that they never wanted to visit again or wanted to associate with. It was always positive things that they said about Drayton. That's why I don't feel any hatred towards it. It was just a peaceful feeling, and every time I come up here, I still get that feeling.

Someone listening to this might think, "She's just putting the interviewer on. He's asking questions about Drayton Hall, and she's just saying that to please them." How would you respond to that?

If anybody thought that I was putting on with everything I've said, they would be highly mistaken because if they ever met any of my ancestors that were here — my uncle, my granduncle, my aunts — they would tell you that they enjoyed being a part of Drayton Hall. I go by what they have told me, and the peace that I have, knowing how they felt about it.

There was never any harsh feeling about anybody at Drayton Hall or the connection with them. It was always positive. I don't have to make it up. I don't have to rehearse it because I only speak what I've been told. I've been witnessing, especially with my uncle Richmond Bowens, because this is where his heart was, even though he had left for Chicago. His heart was always here. Anybody who spoke with him, he would always tell them about Drayton Hall. That's all I can say.

What final thoughts do you have about Drayton Hall?

My final thoughts about Drayton Hall are that [begins to cry] I like to keep the memories I have that were given to me by my family. I'd say, "Keep hope alive. Don't look at anything that was negative. Look at what was positive." Carry on their positiveness from living at Drayton Hall. I'd say I appreciate what they went through. When I come out here, I have that peace.

I don't know if it's because Uncle Richmond was buried out here because I know that's what he wanted — his last wish. It makes me happy. I'm proud to have been a part of them being a part of Drayton. I get full [laughs] when I think about them, and I know they're resting. If they could come back today and relive it, I'm more than sure that they would do it without a second thought. So that's it. Signed, sealed, and delivered.

Lucille Blunt:
"Just a Regular Life"

2012 – Drayton Hall

Lucille Blunt lived at Drayton Hall for four years with her great-uncle and great-aunt, whom she considered her grandparents. She gives important details about their tenant home place, inside and out, and the landscape and "kids' community" around it as well as the connection to Magnolia Plantation, where her grandmother tended the gardens. As important, if not more so, are descriptions of her grandparents' lifestyle and values, especially those of her grandmother.

Participants:
Mrs. Lucille Blunt, George McDaniel, Carter C. Hudgins

George: *What is your connection to Drayton Hall?*

I lived at Drayton Hall from about 9 years old till I was about 13. My grandmother, Rebecca Washington, worked next door at Magnolia Gardens. I was born at Runnymede, located just past Magnolia, and lived there till I was about 9. I came to Drayton Hall because my mother got a job downtown and married. I stayed with Isaac and Rebecca Washington until I went to high school downtown. Rebecca was my mother's aunt, so they were my grandaunt and granduncle. I loved them as my grandparents, and they accepted me as their granddaughter.

My family's roots are in this area. My grandfather, Isaac Washington, was from Green Pond, South Carolina. My grandmother Rebecca talked about being born right round this neighborhood. My mother's name was Viola Stokes, and my grandmother's parents' last name was Miller. That's all I know. You did ask me about Miss Binah, and I heard my grandmother talk about her living across the highway from Drayton Hall.

Could you describe your grandparents' house?

It was a frame cottage, two rooms and a kitchen with a big yard. After I left, my grandfather added another room, which they used as a bedroom, making it four rooms. The house was not painted and had a tar paper roof, I think.

Grandmother swept the yard every Friday night, though sometimes she didn't have to. There was no grass. In the front yard was a big oak tree with a wire swing, where kids swung all the time. Out front my grandmother had some flowers, like lilies, but I'm not sure. Also, out front was the well. She raised chickens, guinea, and ducks. If you were facing the house, the hog pen was on the left side, and the cow pen on the right. The chicken house and outhouse were in the back, the outhouse on the left side. I can still picture my grandmother walking to the well, and in the afternoon, going to feed the hogs, and taking the cow and putting it in the pen and milking it.

Could you describe the interior of the house?

They had a living room, bedroom, and kitchen. I slept with my grandmother and my grandfather. When I first went there, my grandmother had newspapers on the wall, and after I left, she added wallpaper. She didn't have a stove, only a fireplace with a mantle in the living room. Oak chairs were in the living room. In the kitchen she had three or four white chairs and a kitchen table. In the bedroom she had an iron bed and a very nice dresser — an antique — with four large drawers. When they added the room, they got another bed and chest of drawers for it and a wood stove for the kitchen.

How do you think your grandparents acquired the antique dresser?

I don't know, but when they died, a lady took it and had it re-stained. I called her and said I'd like to get it. She said I could pay a thousand dollars for it, but I didn't give her permission to have it. She just went and took it. My aunt didn't know what to do. I don't know where my grandmother got it. She also had beautiful antique lamps because she gave me one and her son, one. When they moved from Drayton and up Highway 61, they had to hide the antique stuff in their house from people trying to get things.

Where did your grandmother cook?

My grandmother cooked in the fireplace. She had a large, cast-iron frying pan with a lid, and when she made biscuits, which everybody loved, she put hot coals on top of the lid. When she cooked rice or grits or whatever, she had something or other to set the pot on in the fireplace. That's how she cooked all her meals in that fireplace. When she got a stove, it had four burners and a warmer on top, so when she'd cook a pie or cake or whatever, she put it up in the warmer.

Whether in the fireplace or on a wood stove, my grandmother could cook! My favorites were her biscuits, potato pie, and potato pudding. The doctor wouldn't let her eat grits so she had cream of wheat for breakfast and also ham, because the doctor said that ham was the only meat she could eat. For dinner, we'd have greens, okra, and whatever. For Sunday dinner, she'd kill a chicken, and we'd have fried chicken, or sometimes she would stew it down, and we'd have vegetables like okra soup, greens, or string beans.

Did you hear Gullah spoken?

When I got older, I heard about Gullah, but my grandparents didn't speak it. They spoke regular English. I didn't hear anyone around here speaking Gullah.

Where did you go to church?

Olive Branch Baptist Church on Highway 61 before you get to Middleton was my grandmother's church, so we went there. She sang in the choir, and my grandfather was on the usher roll. They were faithful to that. On Tuesday nights, my grandmother would go to one of those little houses in a row at Magnolia for a prayer meeting, and on Thursday, my grandfather would go. Ladies on one night, men on the other. They weren't special buildings, just one of those houses.

I wouldn't be left at home, so I'd go with my grandmother. They'd sing and pray. No instruments or preacher. Just the ladies singing and praying and enjoying being with each other. I think I remember them singing "Precious Lord," "I Want Jesus to Walk with Me," and other spirituals and hymns. Afterwards, they would shake hands and head back home.

Was your grandparents' house the only one in that area of Drayton Hall?

There were two houses, my grandmother's house and her sister's small house, which were close together. Her sister was Martha Dennis. We couldn't see the other houses. Fields were on the left side and in the front. I couldn't see the cemetery and don't remember any funerals there except Richmond Bowens' because my mother's family is buried at Ramsey Cemetery up Highway 61 between Magnolia and Middleton. A path led from our house to the highway. Our school was at Runnymede, just past Magnolia.

What was your "kids' community?"

Kids'd come by after school and played in the yard since it was big. We'd play ball, Sally Go Round, and different things. My grandparents stayed inside most of the time. They didn't fish in the river, but boys did, and in the creeks. I wouldn't because I was afraid of worms. I'd just sit and watch. Since I was an only child, older kids would walk with me to school at Runnymede. They lived around in different neighborhoods all the way to Bees Ferry. The teacher picked them up at Bees Ferry in her car and dropped them off on her way home. When school was over, kids would often come by and play. It was fun living at Drayton Hall.

What do you remember about the Ashley River?

The only thing I can remember was that my mother's brother lived in Lambs on the opposite side of the river. Mr. Bennett from Magnolia, or somebody else would take us across in a boat, and we walked from the river to my uncle's home. I'd get so nervous because the boat wouldn't go straight. It'd go upstream or downstream. I'd cry out to my mother, "Why doesn't the boat go straight across?" She'd say, "It has to go with the tide." I remember that.

When you look back on those times, what general thoughts come to mind?

Nothing special. It was just a regular life. I didn't know anything better. I enjoyed it, going to school and the kids. We had fun.

Carter C. Hudgins: *Do you remember any kind of equipment or roads left over from the phosphate mining times?*

No, I don't.

George: *What was your grandmother, Rebecca Washington, like?*

My grandmother was medium height and worked next door at Magnolia tending plants — weeding and watering. She was a very kind-hearted person. She would do a favor for anybody and was always willing to share food. When you came by her house, the first thing she wanted to know, "You want something to eat?" I'd ask her, "Why do you give all the biscuits away?" She'd say "Honey, all you gonna do is eat it. If they want it, I give it to them." She was that type of person, and her husband was the same.

We were close. If my hand hurt, her hand hurt. One night I did get a spanking. My granddaddy was sitting down, and I pulled the chair out from under him. She had a long pine needle straw and spanked my leg with that pine needle. She declared, "That was bad. Don't ever do that." [Laughs] I hugged and kissed him and told him I was so sorry. That was the first and the last time she made me cry. She was a kind person, so kind.

Why did you move downtown to live with your mother?

She had moved downtown for a better paying job and rented a house at 60 Spring Street. She got married, and I moved in with her to go to school downtown. When she grew old, she spent her last four years with me, dying in 2000. Her siblings have passed too.

When you were about to get married, what did your grandmother do for you?

I got married at my mother's house, and she did a lot for the wedding. When I got engaged, my fiancée and I went to her house and told her we planned to get married. She talked to us, or rather told us, "You don't have nothing to worry about. I'm going to see that you get whatever you need. Go pick out your dress and cake." I picked out my dress and she gave me the money to pay for it. We went to a baker on Spring Street (in Charleston), ordered a cake, and that was it. To pay for them, I think she sold two cows.

Joann Bowens Huger, Catherine Smith:
"Community"

2012 – Drayton Hall

Joann Huger and her older sister Catherine Smith grew up at Magnolia Plantation and Gardens and were kin in as a yet undetermined way to the Bowens family of adjacent Drayton Hall. Catherine sat listening by her sister during the interview but preferred to let Joann answer.

Participants:
George McDaniel, Joann Bowens Huger, Catherine Payne Smith, Toni Carrier

George: *Could you describe your background and how you are connected to Drayton Hall?*

Joann: I was born March 1, 1951, at Magnolia Gardens in one of its cabins, the last of five children. Growing up, we had a community and a lot of fun. We had hard times too because Momma was sole support of our family. She and Dad had separated. I used to work after school. Back in those days, you didn't make much money, but with five kids, she needed help. I stopped school in the 11th grade to help Mom pay the bills.

Magnolia was a beautiful place, and after all the tourists had left, they let us have fun. We could go fishing, crabbing, and shrimping. We could race and play baseball. We'd cut a long wisteria vine and "jump rope" with it, even do Double Dutch. We'd climb trees — they called us tomboys — but the girls did it better than the guys, who were afraid of heights. We grew up in a cabin at Magnolia, where my father, Joseph Bowens, worked on the grounds and married my mother, Eloise Bowens. My father grew up in the Red Top community. An old road diagonalled to Magnolia and Drayton Hall, making it closer than it seems now. Soon after I was born, my father left Mom. His parents were Robert and Elizabeth Bowens.

Could you describe your grandmother Bowens catching alligators?

My grandmother used to catch alligators, skin them, and sell the hides and meat. Back then, people loved alligator meat. Grandmother was short and of medium build. She was mean and strict. She had a big hook, dove under water to alligators' dens or holes, and snag them. She didn't use bait. She'd wrestle them underwater and hook them. I heard that one time she and my granddad were in the boat, and she told him that when the first head breaks the surface, hit it with his paddle. Instead of the alligator's, it was her head that came up, so he knocked her in the head.

Richmond Bowens used to tell folks how Elizabeth Bowens "wrestled" alligators in the ponds and phosphate mining cuts around Drayton Hall. She charged admission to watch from the pond's edge as she hunted gators by hand, as her granddaughter describes.

JoAnn: She did a lot of other things. She used to cut wood, tie it in a bundle, put it on her head, and tote it. They used it for heat and to cook meals on a wood stove. They had a big iron pot for boiling clothes to sterilize them. She made lye soap in the pot, and you bathed using lye soap. That iron pot, that's what they used to use back in those days.

I didn't hear much about her son, Joseph Bowens, my father. He was in the Army. Back then, people kept things isolated. They didn't tell you things.

Tell us about your mother Eloise Bowens and your home at Magnolia.

My mother provided for us, and she was a gardener. It runs in the family. She did that, and her father and mother did that, and me too. We all worked at Magnolia Gardens. She was a sweetheart. She'd take care of us the best she could. Back then, they didn't want grass in the yard so one of my chores was to rake the dirt clean. Girls washed clothes and guys cut wood. We had a wood heater and cooked with one too. We had chickens and a field with corn, okra, peas, and all that, which made things a little bit easier.

Could you tell us about the field at Magnolia that Johnny Leach planted for families in the community, including Drayton Hall?

Johnny Leach planted a sweet potato field, and people from the Magnolia and Drayton community shared it. Everybody could have a little of everything that was growing.

When you were growing up, did you speak Gullah? Did your parents or anyone else at Drayton Hall speak it?

My parents did not speak Gullah. We didn't either. I've heard Gullah — from people of Yonge's Island or when we went downtown to King Street. They short-cut words. Yeah, I heard it, but wasn't tempted to speak it. I'd say, "Oh, no, that doesn't sound good at all." Too much of a short-cut. [Laughs] Bring the word out.

Where did you and children in this area go to school, and did you go through desegregation?

I went to elementary school and to Wallace High School on SC 61, but I think they tore that school down. In the higher grades I went to St. Andrews High but quit in the 11th grade to work at Magnolia because Mom was struggling. When I was at St. Andrews, they were desegregating the schools. It was different. The work was harder. Back then, we hadn't gotten the up-to-date books; we had had the way-behind books instead. It was hard to get adjusted. We learned that people you thought were bad weren't. You made friends. I didn't face any violence. Everybody tried to get along and do the right thing. Teachers said, "You gotta treat each other equal. Don't treat them bad because of their skin color." There were nice teachers who'd step up to the plate to help you to get your work done.

Did you ever come over to Drayton Hall from Magnolia?

Yes, to see Miss Mamie, who lived on the west side of the highway across from Johnny Leach. I don't remember her last name. We'd go over and steal plums from her tree. Also, Miss Hattie Haynes lived there, raising her two grandchildren, Tom and Brulah Mae, whose mother had died. *(Author's note: Toni Carrier thinks this is "Nanny Notes" or Hattie Hopkins, grandmother of the Rev. Roosevelt Geddis, also interviewed.)* They lived in an old wooden house. But we were more interested in playing and not really paying attention to the house. When you went to older people's houses, they wanted you to stay outside. You had to go outside and play, so we'd jump rope, play marbles, tag, and hide-and-go-seek.

Could you see the cemetery at that time?
The cemetery was grown up. I don't remember it. The "high ground" was grown up in the trees.

If the Ashley River could speak, what questions would you ask?
I'd ask, "How did the Bowens come to Drayton Hall?" I want to know where my family originated and how they got here so I can pass it on to my children. Kids ask you questions, and I don't have the answers because I don't know myself.

If you could ask the live oak questions, what might you ask?
I would ask the live oak, "How many people got hung on it?" Those were hard times. If you did something wrong, you suffered.

If the main house could speak, what questions would you ask?
I'd ask, "How many staff did it take to keep the house going and looking good?"

When you think about Drayton Hall, what comes to mind?
I think about the beautiful house and how my ancestors helped establish what you have now.

When you think about your ancestors working here during slavery and after freedom, what emotions come to mind?
A good emotion. This brings it out. I appreciate my ancestors and feel good about what they did.

If you could speak to younger generations, what would you like to say?
I would tell them to check family trees and see what their families went through to get us where we are today. A lot of times they don't appreciate that. Everything's more computer-oriented now. There's drugs and violence. If they understood what their ancestors went through, I think they would appreciate life better. Back then, they were refused an education. Now, they can get education but are dropping out. I'm going back to get my GED (general education degree). You're never too old to learn!

What are some of your recollections of Richmond Bowens?

Richmond was a fun person. He was strict, and so was his wife, Velma. We were kin in some way, and I wish I knew how. He was a loving person.

How do you want to be remembered?

When I pass, I want people to think of me as having been a good-hearted person who tried to help everybody. I was a Christian person.

What does Christianity mean to you?

It means serving my God, doing what He asks, following His rules. Christianity is helping others, showing them love. He says you got to love the enemy, and that's a hard thing to do, but when you're working for Jesus, you have to do that. Do you want to make it into His kingdom? Then, do the right thing! Ain't no "ifs, ands or buts" about that.

Were you raised that way?

My mother was a strong Christian. She went to Springfield Baptist, and a lot of times she had to catch a ride, but she did it. She kept the Christian life in the house. You had to do the right thing. She was a single person raising us, so we had to abide by her rules.

Catherine Brown Braxton — Rebecca Brown Campbell
Descendants of Drayton Hall

Catherine Braxton, Rebecca Campbell:
"I feel the spirits of my ancestors ..."

2015 – Drayton Hall

Catherine Brown Braxton and Rebecca Brown Campbell are sisters who grew up in Charleston in the house their grandfather, Willis Johnson, purchased after he left Drayton Hall in the late 1800s to work in the city. His mother, Catherine Bowens Johnson, was born enslaved at Drayton Hall, and now her namesake, Catherine Braxton, serves on the governing board of the Drayton Hall Preservation Trust.

George: *How are you connected to Drayton Hall?*
   Catherine: We have a long line of ancestors from Drayton Hall. I am the granddaughter of Willis Johnson Sr., who was born here as a free man, the son of former slaves. My great-grandmother was Catherine Bowens Johnson, whose name I carry. Her two brothers, Caesar and John Bowens, were enslaved here. Though a plantation, Drayton Hall is important because we cannot leave our ancestors out of our lives. Slavery was not a good thing. No way! However, there were things that took place here that were passed on to us. So, we have an appreciation for Drayton Hall.
   Rebecca: My great-grandmother, Catherine Bowens, and her son Willis were born at Drayton Hall. As children, we didn't come out here. However, when we were adults in the 1970s, our cousin Richmond Bowens, Caesar Bowens' grandson,

returned from Chicago and initially worked at the entrance ticket office. He invited me to come. He said, "This is where your grandfather and your great-grandmother came from."

The place was overgrown. I was not impressed. But as I walked the grounds, I felt the spirits of my ancestors. I still do whenever I come. I'm a part of this place, and they are too. We may not have seen our ancestors, but we know them spiritually.

When freedom came to your family at Drayton Hall, what did you hear happened?

Catherine: Catherine Bowens and her husband, Friday Johnson, did not leave the plantation. They died here. Their son Willis left with the idea of owning property since land ownership was very important to him. My family kept all the records and photographs. They were organizers, like we are today. When we left for New York, my mother didn't pack them. She said, "My brother Frank is here, so we'll leave them and later come back." When we did, it was all gone. His wife cleared the house and didn't want the old stuff, so we lost all that.

Why do you think your great-grandparents stayed at Drayton Hall after emancipation?

Rebecca: It could have been that they loved the place. But when freedom came, they didn't have funds because slaves weren't paid. They were provided with food, clothing, and necessities but no money. They could stretch out on faith and leave without anything. But they didn't. They had children. They stayed because they were provided for. What was best? Wandering around with no place to stay? That's not easy.

Catherine: After freedom came, Catherine and Friday Johnson stayed because they had to have their needs met and had children, one being my grandfather. They were free to leave, but they stayed because of their children. That makes sense.

When your grandfather left Drayton Hall, what did he do? What were his values?

Catherine: When he became an adult, Willis Johnson Sr. left Drayton Hall because he was born a free person and probably thought: "I want to be on my own. I want to control myself and what I have." He was determined to purchase his own home. A document shows he paid $3,000 for property, which was a lot of money at that time. My grandfather taught us not to spend every dime we had. If we were to set it aside for a rainy day, we might be able to buy a house and then another. Not everybody did. But he did. I think this exemplifies values he got from his parents at Drayton Hall and that were instilled in my generation.

Rebecca: Willis Johnson walked from Drayton Hall to Charleston, worked, and eventually bought the house at 35 Calhoun Street, which is still standing. Although my grandfather bought the first house in 1937, the second house on the property, which is known as 35½ Calhoun Street, was built by his sons, Frank and Andrew Johnson, as a final test in their carpentry apprenticeship in the 1940s. We're trying to maintain those houses because they are representative of the historic Ansonborough section of Charleston. African Americans call it the "Borough."

If you saw a picture of Uncle Frank Johnson, a son of our Drayton Hall grandfather, you'd know why we called him "Dapper Dan." He was always well dressed, took pride in his work, and married a schoolteacher, but they never had children. Like his brothers, he was an excellent uncle and helped raise us since our father was sick when we were young. Particular about his foods, he did not eat many fats and sugar and drank milk only from Coburg Dairy. He was the last person to reside at 35 Calhoun Street — the front house — dying in 1998 at perhaps 83.

What role did the church play in your family when you were growing up?

Rebecca: Willis Johnson was a strong believer and regular church-goer at Mount Zion AME. He was taught that you had to train up a child. You must attend Sunday school to learn the Word of God and be a part of the youth program. You must pay at least 10 percent to God. He taught spiritual lessons. Since his parents had been enslaved at Drayton Hall and later were tenants, they had a lot to be bitter about, but he did not give in to anger. He knew the value of love. He was a steady man. He was organized. It had to be right. He sent his sons off to get training to be craftsmen. That's the way he looked after his family. His children must be educated and ready. He was also a community person. His home was called "the house of refuge." When my grandfather left Drayton Hall, he could read and write. Whether or not there was some type of school or training there, I don't know, but he taught his wife how to read and write since her family had worked in rice fields near Jacksonboro.

If you could go back in time and ask questions of your ancestors who were enslaved at Drayton Hall, what would you ask?

Rebecca: I can see them now in their spirit. I'll ask, "Were you happy on the plantation? How did you feel when you were shipped to America? How did you survive coming across the Atlantic? Were you afraid when you were on the block, waiting for someone to buy you like cattle?" I just can't continue because it's a hardship for me to go into depth.

If that large live oak at Drayton Hall could talk, what questions would you ask it?

Rebecca: It would tell me that some of my people were hanged there. They could have done something accidentally, or not listened to the master, or stolen food or money and were punished. Many things could have happened. (She stops talking momentarily.)

I froze just now. So many things happened with that tree and at many other places here. If that tree could talk, it would have stories to tell.

Catherine: Since those live oak trees were here with my ancestors, I'd ask them to tell stories of things they witnessed. One might be about someone having been hanged. Or, I might ask, "Did our ancestors have a meal under this tree? Were they able to gather there for a prayer meeting? Did they care for the tree and groom it? Did my great grandmother Catherine Bowens or her brother Caesar ever sit under this tree?"

If the Ashley River could talk, what questions would you ask?

Rebecca: I'd ask, "How many bodies of African slaves are lying at the bottom?" Also, "How many Africans did you feed?" — because there are shrimp and fish in it.

Catherine: "Did anyone attempt to swim across this river to escape?" And if so, "Did they make it? Were they caught and brought back? Were these people who attempted to escape directly related to me?" The waters sometimes get very rough. "Did anyone accidentally die attempting to get across?"

If the Ashley River Road could talk, what would you ask it?

Rebecca: "How many sang songs as they passed through here? Were they barefooted? What kind of clothing did they have? Were they cold? Did they hide in the woods, trying to escape the plantation? After freedom, did my ancestors travel this road to go to church? When my grandfather walked this road to get to Charleston, was he alone? Were there other ancestors who walked this road, leaving Drayton Hall?"

Catherine: When you're a slave on a plantation, it's like being in a prison. You couldn't leave unless you got permission, and if you left without permission, you were "running away." If you were caught, you could be sold, whipped, or have other punishments. I love traveling the Ashley River Road, and I wonder if they tried to escape by way of the roadway. The enslaved had no freedom to just walk the road as we do today. Were there law enforcement officers or such around to bring them back? If they did get back, there was almost certainly some type of punishment. Were any of those who attempted to escape successful?

If the main house could talk, what questions would you like to hear?

Catherine: It's my understanding that my ancestors were house slaves, which means they were living somewhere close to the big house. It's my understanding that my great-grandmother Catherine Bowens managed the kitchen, laundry room, etc. Where would her family's house be located in relationship to the big house? Where was the food prepared for the big house? Where did they do the laundry? Did they actually serve the family? Or did they just bring the food over, then the family served themselves? Were they required to work after "normal" work hours?

Rebecca: Did my ancestors help with the brick masonry? Did they help build those beautiful staircases? What did my great-grandmother do? Did she cook? Clean? Help raise the children? What did my great-grandfather Friday Johnson do? Did he bring wood for the fire to keep them warm or to start the breakfast in the morning? Who helped raise the vegetables for the table? Who made the bread? How did they operate the big house? Who did the work?

Here's a picture of Richmond Bowens Sr., Richmond Bowens' father, who died before you were born. What does this picture tell you about him? (See photo section.)

Catherine: I see a person deep in thought. He's well dressed, which means he has pride in himself and whatever he did. He seems capable of doing whatever he needed to do and to be a go-getter.

Rebecca: He looks like a preacher — ready to occupy a pulpit and start preaching. He has a comfortable, pleasing face, and like Uncle Frank Johnson, he seems like "Dapper Dan." He has clothing of quality and is wearing his Derby, so he apparently had sufficient funds. He has an intelligent look. Not that you could tell a book by its cover, but he looks like he's standing solid.

Could you tell us your recollections about Richmond Bowens?

Rebecca: Richmond meant so much to me. He regularly visited my grandfather, mother, and uncles on Calhoun Street. After he had gotten a job as a chauffeur in Chicago, we went up there, and he drove us all around Chicago. We were like celebrities and felt happy and so rich. We just sat back. We had a beautiful dinner at his house with his wife Velma, who was a superb cook. He was a loving person. Although he was actually my grandfather's first cousin, I took him as an uncle.

Could you describe the relationship between Charles Drayton, the last owner of Drayton Hall, and Richmond Bowens?

Catherine: Before I met Charlie, I'd heard a lot about him. He was the person I expected because Richmond had talked about him so much. They grew up and played together and had little favorite songs and favorite foods. They were of different colors but like brothers.

Rebecca: I think Richmond was older than Charlie. When he came for the memorial for Richmond, Charlie cried and cried and cried. His daughter had to take control because Charlie had lost a friend and brother. He was the type of person that Richmond always said he was.

Could you tell us about the blacksmith, Philip Simmons, who designed the memorial arch visitors see at the African American cemetery at Drayton Hall?

Catherine: I've known Philip Simmons since I was little because his blacksmithing shop was near our home at 35 Calhoun Street. Now his work is in the Smithsonian, and his gazebo is at the Charleston Airport. In spite of all his fame, you never heard him say, "I'm this. I'm that. I don't like this person." A kind and loving person, he and Uncle Frank used to work together, with my uncle doing the carpentry and he the blacksmithing. When Uncle Frank died, he gave the eulogy. We called him Uncle. That's the kind of relationship we had.

Rebecca: Catherine and I were on the committee to design a memorial for the African American cemetery, and we commissioned Philip Simmons and the Philip Simmons Foundation. Our committee had first wanted a gate, which is what Philip has made all over Charleston, but we decided on an arch because it was open all the time. Our ancestors had been through hell and back, and we didn't want them to be closed in by any gate! We wanted their spirits to flow in, flow out, fly all over Drayton Hall, and be a part of this site.

Philip designed the arch with birds in flight, but was unable to actually make the arch because of his infirmities due to aging, so he passed the blacksmithing to his nephew Ron Pringle. I believe he spiritually transferred something to Ron because it was carried out so well. We're proud of it. We are happy. Philip's hand is on that. His design is in that. The dedication of the arch was one of the best moments.

What would you say to African Americans about preserving their history?

Rebecca: I would say to consider coming back to their roots. They need to keep in touch with relatives who stayed behind, to do research, especially oral history, preserve family heirlooms, and pass them on. A family reunion is a good starting point.

When you think about racism, slavery, and then segregation, bitterness can easily rise to the surface. How did your family with connections to Drayton Hall respond to such situations?

Rebecca: When those occasions came up, we saw how our grandparents responded, and that guided us. In some families the hostility is still there, but in our family, we were told, "You need to put it down."

We were brought here against our wishes, and many slaves were killed, so what do we do? Dr. Martin Luther King says that's a tough thing. We have to come to the table and communicate and stop this foolishness. If we pass this burden on to the next generation, it might become even worse. We want to be better. Slavery and the harsh treatments, that's a burden. I personally don't want to carry a load. Consider forgiveness. That's what I have done. We have to continue to work on it. It's an ongoing struggle. We are all God's children. While our skin color is different, we all have red blood. Now, if you see any other color, do let me know! Alright! So, it's a struggle. I'm not going to show any meanness. That's ignorant! I want to show some intelligence. These are some of the ways that I've handled it.

What do you hope people will learn from this conversation?

Rebecca: There is no gain in being ignorant, which is what I say to people who act in a prejudiced manner. It's a matter of ignorance. We need to show love. Sometimes people make me upset, angry, but I am not going to stoop to those levels. I can't tell you the verse in the scriptures, but it says, "Come now, let us reason together." If we could just have some reasoning, we can turn the page on hate. I'm not talking only about the Whites, but many Blacks too. I say, "Let's come to the table and reason together." Let's talk about what has happened in the past. We don't need this to continue. It has got to end at some point! It's a slow process. I may not live to see it, but it will happen. God has given us space and time to think about it and to get our lives together. America is too beautiful to go on like this. We need to do better, and love and share and treat our neighbor as we would treat ourselves.

What are your final thoughts about coming to Drayton Hall, a plantation where your ancestors were enslaved?

Rebecca: I believe in education. For example, Catherine and I were there when Richmond was working as a guide on the gift shop's front porch. Visitors were all around him. He had a book of family photographs and other old photos about African American life, which he explained to them and educated them about our history. He told the group who Catherine and I were. That made me feel even better about Drayton Hall. He sought to educate. Whenever I come now, I get that same feeling as when I first came out and as Richmond had. The spirits of my ancestors were always with Richmond and me. I feel them with every footstep and in every place. I go in the house or on the grounds, and they are there. I feel good that they are here.

What is your perception of Drayton Hall, the place where your ancestors were enslaved?

Catherine: People ask me: "Why do you folks keep going back to Drayton Hall? Wasn't it a plantation? Weren't your ancestors enslaved there?" I agree and explain that you must know where you come from in order to know where you're going. How do you get that? You have to go back into your history to your ancestors. Slavery, no glory! But if you take that and one's ancestors out of one's life, where are you going to go? We can't say, "I don't want anything to do with it." No, we don't want it to happen again. But we can't leave our ancestors behind! I know that my ancestors — the Bowens, the Johnsons — left a legacy at Drayton Hall. And I intend to see that legacy go on and to pass it to the next generation.

Four Generations of Draytons:
"Memories and Hopes"

2015 – Drayton Hall

Participants:
   George McDaniel: Interviewer
   Charlie Drayton
   Chad, son of Charlie
   Charles, son of Chad
   Charlie, 4 years old, son of Charles

Charlie, when you came to Drayton Hall when you were about your great grandson's age, what did you think of the place?
   Charlie: I didn't think about it. I had no idea of the significance of it other than the fact the family owned it. I used to love to come out here, wander around, and climb trees. It was fun. So much so that as I grew older, I used to ride my bicycle from downtown out here. I do remember Aunt Charley's dog, Nipper. The Ashley River Road was a dirt road with maybe two or three houses. We were in a forest.

Chad, what did Drayton Hall mean to you when you came out here?
   I probably didn't come out here much until seven or eight years old because we were living in California, but after we moved here, I remember having my birthday parties here with my friends every year. Like my father, we climbed trees. We had a game where we would sit at the house, race to the live oak tree, and climb the limbs to the middle, and whoever got there first won a candy bar. I also learned to shoot ducks here. My parents had gatherings with their friends virtually every Sunday, and kids would come out. They'd drop us out of the car before we got to the house, and we'd run around the place and come back about five o'clock, and they'd have something to eat. The one thing I'd have to say is that nothing bad ever happened here. I never got into any trouble here. It's just a place where everything was good.

As my father said, it was a country place, not some historic place. It was just a place where we came almost once a week and had picnics. That's how I felt about it from eight till probably sixteen years old.

As the grandson, Charles, what are your recollections about Drayton Hall?

When I was five'ish, the thing I remember is the live oak tree almost in line with the road coming in. Before Hugo, those branches drooped down probably a hundred feet from the trunk, touched the ground, and came back up. I remember climbing them. I guess climbing trees runs in the family. I remember getting measured in the growth chart room, which was a big deal to me when I was little.

As the great grandson, Charlie, what do you like to do at Drayton Hall?

Charlie: Play games. Sometimes I roll down the mound. I don't know how to climb trees.

Chad: The tree limbs are gone now, so you can't climb those trees anymore. Growing up, I remember we'd have ball games out here — football, fizz ball. My friends would come, and we'd toss the ball around. The steps of the house to the sundial atop the mound was the field. Nobody got hurt. We ran through the woods. I remember helping to plant about 10,000 pine trees not far from the cemetery in about 1960.

I'll never forget that Drayton Hall is where I learned to drive. Aunt Charley had a 1937 Packard with a big stick shift and running boards, probably a foot-and-a-half wide. When I was about 10 or 11 years old, we could drive that thing around.

Charlie, as you grew older, do you remember certain moments when you realized that Drayton Hall had a deeper meaning to you?

Absolutely. After I got out of the service after World War II and came back to live in Charleston, it became a part of me. Its significance hit me hard. No question about that! I saw it anew.

One of the most distinctive attributes of Drayton Hall is its survival. It's old. It has survived hurricane after hurricane after hurricane. It has survived the war and the family and has never had electricity. I don't know why, but I loved it that way. Magnificent!

What about your memories, Chad?

The first time I realized how special this place was when I was seventeen years old at my sister's party. Having had a few drinks (when I wasn't supposed to) and standing out in front of the house and looking at it, lit by candlelight, was just unbelievable. That memory is still in my brain, "Wow, what a special place this really is!" It wasn't the historic value. It was just incredible that there we are in 1967 or '68 and this house is lit by candlelight and there are people in there partying, and I'm seventeen years old and having fun. What a spectacular place! The historic part didn't kick in until later. After its sale is when the significance of what Drayton Hall meant to us and to the state and nation hit me.

Chad, what were your thoughts about your father's selling Drayton Hall?

I was not in favor of it. I don't know how candid to be, but I didn't want to sign the documents to break the will. I may have been the only one who felt that way. That hurt took a while to get over. I'll say it: For my portion of the sale, I asked to be given 20 acres or whatever. My father went to the National Trust and asked for that. They said no. It had to be all or nothing. That upset me, because shortly after it was transferred to the National Trust, a large portion was sold to the State of South Carolina. If they couldn't sell it to me, how could they sell it to the State of South Carolina? That was where my mind was. That's how I felt, but I've gotten over it.

As the grandson, Charles, when did the historical significance of Drayton Hall hit you?

Its significance didn't really hit me in an ah-ha moment. However, in the last five years you have brought me in to speak to classes and conferences, and that's solidified my understanding of the site's historical significance. Growing up in a later generation, I knew Drayton Hall was historically significant. When I was in third grade, I came out for a school program and in the sixth grade, participated in Charleston Day's Junior Docent Program and gave tours. For training to be a Junior Docent, we came out five or six times over a month-long period. To my classmates, it was a field trip. To me, I was going to my kingdom and getting to show Drayton Hall off to everybody. I felt like the big man on campus. However, when you asked to participate in classes and conferences, I've had to stop and think about the site, and that has made Drayton Hall's significance more real.

Would you have preferred to see Drayton Hall restored to its 18th century glory?

Charlie: No, I think what they're doing is correct. I don't think it should be restored nor should furniture be displayed in the house.

Chad: I like what they're doing. Keeping it as it has been as opposed to restoration is where I'd head.

Charles: The decision to preserve it was the right one because when you restore, you pick a time period and a place, and you recreate that. But when you preserve, you have the opportunity to tell an entire story. The story of Drayton Hall is not just an 18th-century story. While it begins in the 18th century, it's a 19th-century, 20th-century, and now a 21st-century story. We discover new things all the time that add to that story, and we're able to do that because it's a preservation site as opposed to a restoration..

Chad, when your grandson is 70 or 80 years old, what would you like for Drayton Hall to mean to him?

Chad: When my grandson is roughly my age, my hopes are that he will be having Thanksgivings here with family and cousins and friends. That's a very special occasion for our family. We really appreciate your allowing us to do that. It's a great way to give thanks.

Charlie: I couldn't agree more.

Charles: I hope that Drayton Hall is a part of his life and that he feels like there's been great work done to maintain the building and grounds because the Trust has accomplished a lot. I also hope that Charleston is still here in 80 years and not underwater, as it may be. I hope my son has a connection to Drayton Hall, and that whatever form it takes will keep him coming back and that there are Thanksgiving celebrations with the family. I hope he wants to bring his children and grandchildren here so that the relationship with our family and other people involved will be sustained.

How has what we've done with your family and African American descendants touched you?

Charlie: I am delighted to say that racial relationships at Drayton Hall have improved considerably in the past years. Richmond Bowens, whose family came to Drayton Hall many, many years ago, always loved it here and wanted to come back here. He went away during World War II and in the 1970s was delighted to get back. It was home to him. Recently, we've had gatherings of members of the families whose slave families lived here, and I have kept in touch with some of them. As a matter of fact, I see a descendant almost every day at Bishop Gadsden, where I live. We've become close friends, and I hope that will continue. I've never heard of one incident where the people that worked at Drayton Hall were beaten or in any way taken advantage of. I won't say it didn't happen, but I never heard of it. Some descendants still love to come here, I can tell you that.

Chad: It's a deep issue to overcome, but I think Drayton Hall is doing what they can to help the situation. To me, there has never been any animosity with African Americans here. My personal relationship was with young Tom Burns, the African American whose father was the caretaker here. Many times, when we came out without my parent's friends, I'd play with young Tom. He was a friend. I hope the world will get to the point where there are good people and there are bad people, and it doesn't matter what color they are. Unfortunately, there is a lot of hate and extremists in the world, and that's something Drayton Hall can help to overcome.

Charles: As far as Drayton Hall's role in the evolution of race relations go, this site is where histories were brought together a long, long time ago, intermingled for several hundred years, and then were sent out and spread apart. The descendants I've spoken with feel a connection to this place. They feel their ancestors when they step out here. Drayton Hall has embraced that. As long as it's trying to build bridges between generations and races, that's all you can hope for. It's not a role defined for conventional historic sites, but it's a role Drayton Hall embraces well.

Chad: There are people holding grudges about what happened 150 or 200 years ago on both sides. However, as Catherine Braxton, a descendant, says, "We've got to move on, and come to the table." I agree.

Alison Rea:
"The Personal Is Always the Most Interesting."
2021 – Drayton Hall

Alison Rea is a direct descendant of original owner, John Drayton, and his oldest son, William Henry Drayton, 1742-1779. William Henry was passed over in John's will, and younger son, Charles, inherited the plantation. Renowned as a state and national leader in the American Revolution, William Henry's career was cut short by disease. He died in Philadelphia while serving in the Continental Congress. His son, John Drayton, was a founder of the College (now a university) of South Carolina and twice a governor of the state.

Alison's maternal grandfather, Charles de Vere Drayton, a Washington D.C. lawyer, was a great-grandson of Gov. John Drayton. Charles' daughter, Betty Drayton Taylor, was Alison's mother. She loved Drayton Hall and her family. She was most proud of her many years engaged in improving life for others by lobbying for better mental health care in Colorado and being active for political change as a Democratic district chairwoman, among other roles.

George: *When you were growing up, what did Drayton Hall and the Drayton family mean to you?*

Alison: I grew up in Denver, Colorado, so South Carolina and Drayton Hall were far away but still a living part of our family's landscape. My mother, Betty Drayton Taylor, and her father, Charles de Vere Drayton, were proud of their lineage as a descendant of William Henry Drayton, the oldest son of John Drayton, the original owner of Drayton Hall. In fact, Mother wished she'd kept her maiden name and filled our house in Colorado with portraits of ancestors.

As a child, what was that like?

We thought Mother was trying to create a museum. Since I've always loved history, I found family history interesting and was pleased to know what my forebears looked like.

What did Drayton Hall mean to your mother?

Mother shared her father's love of Drayton Hall, and both were proud to be part of a family that had made such significant accomplishments politically and built such an amazing house. Throughout her life, Mom visited Charleston. As my grandfather got older, he wanted a last trip to South Carolina where he'd grown up, so off he and Mom went to visit friends, cousins, and Drayton Hall. The night he returned to D.C., he died peacefully in his sleep.

What was Drayton Hall like when you first saw it?

It was in 1973, a year before it was acquired by the National Trust. I was traveling with a friend. The caretaker had been alerted. She lived in a mobile home to the left of the house as you drove up. The grass was tall, the place deserted. The caretaker came out with a gun on her waist. She said it was to kill snakes in the grass. What a contrast to Drayton Hall, which sat serenely in the middle of empty quietness, unblinking to time. It was amazing to see this giant, incredibly formal, sophisticated building enduring another era — quite haunting and lovely.

We had grown up with pictures of Drayton Hall, so it was familiar. However, in person, the house was more impressive than I expected. I remember the whole visit and the unlikely pair of us exploring an otherwise abandoned and empty house and grounds. The caretaker loved the place and knew a lot about it, which she shared. We imagined what life there had been like in its prime and in the many years following.

Why should people care about Drayton Hall in particular and sites like it?

The value of Drayton Hall and sites like it is to help people understand the past and ask deeper questions about it. It's not like a dream of Tara from *Gone with the Wind*. It can provide a real examination of the full range of life across the plantation — from having a guy who had the money and the interest in building such a sophisticated "white elephant" in the middle of this swampy place to the many enslaved people having to do the work of building and maintaining his dream and lifestyle. You can't help but consider how Blacks and Whites were treated so differently and had such different histories. Historic plantation sites can show how people actually lived with those realities.

I think sites like Drayton Hall have more resonance today as more Americans of all races show interest in learning their family histories. People want to know their heritage regardless of how great or awful it might have been for their forebears.

Drayton Hall, especially without the costumes and pretend antebellum frills, offers a particularly accessible experience. Seeing this in person makes it easier to understand how the past informs the present and the need to do something to repair the damage.

What led you to get involved with Drayton Hall?

I'd grown up with Mother and Papa's love of it, but it was your ability, George, to make the place relevant and interesting. It wasn't just about how the rich White people lived or about the furniture and stuff. Now there are stories about everybody. I like the idea of gathering stories. The personal is always the most interesting.

What's your favorite memory of Drayton Hall?

The Drayton family reunion in 1988 when Mom and I came down. I met Randolph Drayton, son of Frank Drayton, one of the two brothers who sold Drayton Hall. Randolph was delightful. He had a contagious love of the place. He said, "Let's sneak into the place tonight." So we did. First, we sat by the pond as you approach the house and watched the swamp light up with little phosphorescent creatures and listened to the frogs and other night creatures. It was beautiful. You could see Drayton Hall in the night glow with that perfect Palladian architecture. We walked down to the Ashley River and went swimming and could see the house lit up by the night sky. We too were lit up because of the phosphorous in the water.

Why did your mother choose to give a bench by the river in memory of her father?

Because they both loved Drayton Hall. They felt that our side of the family shouldn't be forgotten, despite William Henry's not inheriting Drayton Hall. The bench is in remembrance of our side of the family. I couldn't have picked a spot more meaningful.

What do you think about Drayton Hall's role in preserving the Ashley River?

I love that Drayton Hall has not only conserved the house and grounds but also the land across the Ashley River, so that one looks out at a lovely unmarred landscape empty of housing developments and other ugly things. That kind of conservation is also important for all the birds and other creatures that live in the marsh and nearby land. I'm proud of the vital role Drayton Hall plays in preservation of the Ashley River region. It makes the museum more relevant. People need more parks and wild spaces. One of the reasons people go to Drayton Hall is its beautiful grounds. It's restorative.

What do you like that Drayton Hall is doing? What should it do in the future?

I like that the house is empty. This helps to clearly see and appreciate the architecture and room designs. Even more so, one must use one's own imagination to visualize how the enslaved people lived, or what a dance would have been like in the great hall.

I like the programs Drayton Hall is offering virtually so that I can participate from New York, and others can participate from wherever they are in the world. For instance, there is a program, gleaned from family papers, about the role of the enslaved people from Drayton Hall in driving the plantation's commerce on the Ashley River and other waterways. Since historic sites like Drayton Hall are a natural locus for discussion of slavery and racism, I hope the momentum continues.

I like the way Drayton Hall and its new visitors' center found ways to make the objects, the building, and the land speak. Thanks to archaeology, scholarship, and story gathering, new things are being learned about how everyone lived there. Because I'm interested in porcelain, I find it interesting to see examples that have been dug up and show what was fashionable at the time of the house's heyday. I love the grounds because you can get lost — with your binoculars looking at the multitude of birds or simply in your own thoughts.

L-R: Johnnie Leach and Isaac Leach. Credit: The College of Charleston, Charleston, SC

Johnny Leach, Isaac Leach and Johnnie Mae Leach Gibson:
"Hand Come. Hand Go."

2012 – Drayton Hall

Johnny Leach grew up on Runnymede Plantation, a short distance up the Ashley River from Drayton Hall, and then worked at Magnolia Plantation and Gardens, the historic site adjoining Drayton Hall. Magnolia is owned by descendants of John Drayton. Johnny supervised crews working on the gardens and grounds. In the mid-20th century, the Drayton family hired him to take care of the Drayton Hall landscape, which was no longer a working plantation but instead a place in the country for the family.

Joining him for this interview are his son Isaac Leach, born in 1958, and daughter Johnnie Mae Leach Gibson, an Air Force veteran who returned to Charleston. By the time Isaac and Johnnie Mae were born, most of Drayton Hall's African American community had moved, but Johnny attended funerals there. The recollections of all three shed light on the places, practices, and especially the values of African Americans at Drayton Hall and Magnolia, values other scholars have documented across the South and the nation.

Participants:
   Johnny Leach: Long-time resident of Magnolia Plantation and Gardens
   Isaac Leach, Johnny's son
   Johnnie Mae Leach Gibson, Johnny's daughter
   George McDaniel, interviewer, executive director, Drayton Hall
   Toni Carrier, Wood Family Fellow, Drayton Hall
   Robin Foster, family research assistant, Drayton Hall

George: *How are you connected to Drayton Hall?*
   Johnny Leach: I was born in 1923 at White Hall in Colleton County. When I was seven, my granddaddy died, so I moved to Runnymede, the plantation upstream from Magnolia, where my grandmother raised me. My uncle had a small farm on both sides of Ashley River Road, so I hoed and plowed there behind a mule. After serving in World War II, I returned to work at Magnolia, supervising crews in the gardens. We planted camellias, azaleas, dogwoods, junipers, magnolias, and oaks and grafted all kinds of plants, my favorites being azaleas and camellias. I also worked at Drayton Hall. I took care of the lawn and trimmed the landscape.

That's a big lawn, how did you keep it up?
   Johnny: It wasn't much to keep up at all.

What are your connections, Isaac and Johnnie Mae?
   Johnnie Mae Leach Gibson: I was born and grew up at Magnolia. Since I didn't have any friends at Drayton Hall, I had no reason to visit. What Drayton Hall and Magnolia mean to me is freedom. Growing up here, I never heard of anything bad happening, so it's a good place in my mind. It's a part of my history. I'm proud of it. A lot of people don't have a place to reach back to and think about. Drayton Hall and Magnolia are always in my psyche as something to reach back to. Why is that important? To the generation today, everything is about technology. They don't have a place to go back to.
   Isaac Leach: I've lived at Magnolia all my life and have always been interested in the history of Drayton Hall, having heard my father talk about it. The woods between Magnolia and Drayton Hall were my favorite place, but when I ran into a snake on the path to Drayton Hall, it turned me away for a long while. Still, I thought Drayton Hall was beautiful.

What does it mean to you to have lived on a plantation?

Johnnie Mae: My father loves the history. It means a lot to him. He thinks the programs at Drayton Hall and Magnolia are good for the younger generation to know. History happened. We can't change it. My father is often asked what it's like to live on a plantation. He says it's safer than any place else he can think of to live. Kids are born innocent; it's what they are taught that matters. At the dinner table my parents never discussed things as "being bad." My father thinks that what Magnolia and Drayton Hall are doing now is going forward, not back. What happened is in the past. Magnolia and Drayton programs are for the future, and that's good.

What were the churches that people from Drayton Hall and Magnolia attended?

Isaac: Olive Branch Baptist, Springfield Baptist, St. Philip's AME, Castle Chapel, and Bull Chapel. Bull Chapel was close by. My father said it was a frame church, about the size of Olive Branch, painted on the outside and inside, with a homemade altar and pews with backs. Lizzie Bowens (an aunt of Richmond Bowens of Drayton Hall) was a leader. Most people from Drayton Hall and Magnolia went to Springfield, but some, like Lizzie, went to Bull Chapel. Almost every family went to church. About 25 or 30 people attended Bull. Almost everyone walked, though some had a horse and wagon. Other than my father, I know of no one still living who attended Bull Chapel.

Could you describe the African American cemetery at Drayton Hall when you were in your 20s and 30s?

Johnny: It was a little on the bushy side. The caskets were made of wood and were homemade and brought by horse and buggy. To mark the graves, people cut small tree trunks about the size of a camellia bush, and drove them into the ground at the head and foot of the grave to about two or three feet above ground. That way, you'd know where not to dig for new burials. If there was a cross or headstone, the family would put one there. I don't remember possessions or objects of the deceased being placed around the graves.

Could you tell us about the store at Drayton Hall down by the Ashley River?

Johnny: It was not a great big store. It was wooden, located near the canebrake and run by old man Tom Champagne. He was a tall, nice, Black man and weighed about 175 to 180 pounds. He lived right near the store. He was not from Drayton Hall. The store was near the river because a lot of people lived along the river, and folks went up and down it. Tom sold basic necessities. I don't know about buying things on credit. I never had occasion to ask for it. He treated people right.

What does it mean to treat someone right?

Johnny: If I can help you, I'll do my best to do so. You treat somebody how you want to be treated. Show your love.

Isaac: We had an expression, "Hand come. Hand go." I give you a hand because someday you might do something for me. My father taught us that.

Johnnie Mae: My father is a giving person. If he gives somebody something, he expects them to give to someone else. He brought us up in a good household. We never wanted for anything — always had plenty of good food and meat on the table.

Johnny: I take pride that I've never had any trouble with my children. I thank God that He has given me everything I've ever asked for.

Is there a specific instance in which this "giving" was illustrated?

Johnnie Mae: When they slaughtered a hog, they shared the meat with the community. For years, my father would pick up people who worked at Magnolia who didn't have a car and give them a ride to and from work. He was always giving back, and we saw those things. He had 12 or 13 boys, and none of us ever went to jail or even got a ticket.

Isaac: I think this was because of how we were raised and where we lived on the plantation, away from trouble. We never had people come bother us on the plantation.

What did you learn from your family and community, Johnnie Mae, that guided you in your career with the Air Force?

Johnnie Mae: I learned that everyone does not live the same or have the same, but it doesn't make one less of a person than the other. I didn't have a lot, but I knew where I came from and how to cherish that. In the military I used that and helped the next person. The person who had more than I seemed to be helped more by me than I was able to help them. For these reasons, I wanted to live on Magnolia when I came back to Charleston. Magnolia is a special place to me. Even though it was a plantation, it was home. There was always love in our household. I always wanted to come back. The entire place was our playground. We had a ball living there, and this place is peaceful to me.

Mr. Leach, in looking back on your life, what would you like for people to remember about you?

Johnny: I would like for everybody to remember that God is a good God. He said He wouldn't disappoint you. I'm holding Him to that and am doing the best that I can because I know one of these days I'm going to meet Him. We got a song we sing: "You gots to move. You gots to move. All God's children gots to move one of these days."

I want people to say, "I knew that old man. He was a good man in his day. He tried to help those who couldn't help themselves." One day we're gonna die, and I want to die happy. I know that if I treat my neighbors right, like I wish to be treated, when I come to the end of my journey, I'll be able to hear the Lord say, "Servant of God, well done. Your battle has been fought. Your victory has been won." Stay on your bended knee, and you'll be alright one of these days.

Isaac: That's what I'm talking about when I talk about Magnolia. It's happiness. People need to visit places like Magnolia and Drayton Hall and learn about more than just history. They need to know about compassion and caring.

If you could go back and ask your ancestors a question, what would it be?

Isaac: My father would ask, "Did John Grimke Drayton (the owner of Magnolia before and after the Civil War and an Episcopal priest at Old St. Andrew's Church on Ashley River Road) do everything I've heard about? How did their lives compare to slaves on other plantations?

Johnnie Mae: I would ask the children how old they were when they were pushed into slavery? Was it hard? Did they have enough to eat? Could they read? If so, who taught them? Were they happy? How did they have to behave as adults? How did they deal with hardship? Did they think about escaping? I can't imagine a child who would want to grow up in slavery.

Do you remember any stories of slavery days at Magnolia or Drayton Hall?

Johnnie Mae: We never heard of our enslaved ancestors. We heard about my father's grandfather, who was a constable and owned a store, and they lived pretty well until he died. That's when my father moved in with Uncle Jay and Aunt Eliza at Runnymede. We heard about the good things, not stories of slavery.

Mr. Leach, what does the Ashley River mean to you?

Johnny: Sitting by the river makes me think about the past. It's a happy place for me. One day I was by the river and saw God. I don't know how to explain it. Now when I look down the river, I pray and release all my concerns to God.

Frank B. Drayton Jr. and Thomas M. Drayton:
"Helping People To Link the 1700s to the Present Day"
2015 – Drayton Hall

Frank B. Drayton Jr. is the oldest son of Frank Drayton, who with his older brother Charlie were the last owners of Drayton Hall. Thomas is the son of Frank Drayton Jr. They were at Drayton Hall to record the height of Thomas' young son on the growth chart in the main house. In this interview, they reflect on Drayton Hall's people, including Frank's great-aunt Charlotta (Charley) Drayton and why she didn't modernize Drayton Hall, as well as the reasons for its sale out of the family, and the site's impact on them.

Interviewer: George McDaniel

George: *Frank, what do you think about this growth chart in the "library" room of Drayton Hall?*

Frank: I'm amazed it's still here with the earliest recorded history from 1891 to the present. There I am. There's my father, Frank B. Drayton, 4/16/41 or 4/06/41. That looks like the last time he put it on there. He was born in 1923, and my uncle Charlie in 1919. Now we're adding the 10th generation. I'm the eighth, Thomas is the ninth, and Thomas Middleton Drayton Jr., the 10th. My father, unfortunately, never got to see his grandchildren. I feel fortunate to watch two grandsons now being measured on the wall and do hope to see a great-grandson.

It's great that Drayton Hall allows us to do this. Our family history can keep going. You may see growth charts in other houses in America but never with 120 years of names of the same family.

Thomas, what do think about the growth chart?

It's wonderful we're allowed to do it and to see history from the late 1800s to the present day. Now we're adding my son, Thomas Middleton Drayton Jr. Measuring my son on the wall will make him a part of the house forever and a part of history.

Frank, what are some of your earliest memories of Drayton Hall?

My earliest memories are of coming here for picnics after church on Sundays. The children would be let loose and run wild. The big oak tree, which now, unfortunately, has lost a lot of its branches, was our climbing fort. We were like animals climbing up and down and scurrying about because the limbs reached all the way to the ground. Hurricane Hugo and time have taken those lower limbs.

One time I remember distinctly. There were a bunch of kids around. Our family was not much into alcohol. When we were told to get drinks, we went and got a couple of beers, and at seven years old, popped them, and took them to our parents, who said, "Oh, no, no, no. That's not the kind of drink we meant."

My biggest memory was on my sixth or seventh birthday party here. Right in the middle of it, a flyover of about 40 planes came low from the Air Force base across the river. Everybody was in awe, "Wow! Look at this." I thought they were doing that for my birthday!

A sad memory was coming out here one night with a friend from high school or early college. We'd heard people had been having parties out here. I brought a shotgun just in case. The house door was open, and when we walked in, we discovered that the Adamesque mantelpiece had been taken from the drawing room. As we were leaving, a pair of headlights came on out of somewhere and chased us down Highway 61. I didn't know who it was. I actually pointed my shotgun at him so we could "get out of Dodge."

Thomas, what are some of your earliest memories? Your favorite memories?

Thomas: My earliest memories are of coming out here and running around like a little kid should. Living in Charleston, you don't have these open areas, so just running on the lawn, rolling down the mound in front, playing on the steps outside, climbing the oak trees, and just being a kid outside was great. We also tried not to fall into the pond because Mother told us alligators were in it. I remember getting measured on the wall.

My favorite memories are of Thanksgiving. We'd all come out here as a family, everyone bringing a dish. A couple of years ago, we put all the children on the measuring wall. We'd throw the Frisbee, play baseball, go to the river, sit and relax, have drinks, and eat turkey for Thanksgiving dinner. Another favorite memory is of my wedding on the front lawn.

Frank: I had the privilege of seeing both my sons married here. Other favorite memories are of Molly and Anne Drayton's wedding receptions and a formal dinner we attended. Seeing the house lit at night, you felt like you were in another world, another century.

Frank, when did you realize the historical significance of this house?

When I was in my early to mid-teens, I knew it was a special place. However, when Aunt Charley, who was my great aunt, got older I knew something was going to happen. That's when I realized how significant it was. When my father and uncle inherited it, we understood it was a huge undertaking to preserve the house and that it wasn't something our family could do. We checked with various foundations to no avail. When the ball got rolling with the National Trust, I absolutely saw the significance of the house.

I wrote my senior thesis on Drayton Hall at the University of South Carolina under Dr. Walter Edgar. When I studied the history of the family and read diaries from the late 1700s to early 1800s, I saw the significance of this plantation and all the other plantations in the family, which spread throughout the state and into Georgia.

My wife, Marley Drayton, worked at a local school. One day a child, who was going on a field trip, said, "We're going out to visit your house today. I hope we won't disturb anything of yours."

Thomas, when did you realize the historical significance of Drayton Hall?

Thomas: When I was born, they had already sold Drayton Hall to the National Trust so my experience of coming out here was different from my father's. Growing up, I'd heard of Drayton Hall, Drayton Hall, Drayton Hall, and by coming out here, I slowly realized what it was all about. In first grade we came on a field trip, and I loved it. Learning about and appreciating Drayton Hall is non-stop.

Frank, tell us about the vandalism of the 1960s? Why did your father and uncle decide to sell Drayton Hall?

Lack of security was one of the main reasons why we sold Drayton Hall. We couldn't keep a close watch. In the late '60s, high school kids stole numerous pieces of furniture and stored them in a garage. One of their friends was a friend of mine and told his parents, who called my father and Uncle Charlie. Word got back to the thieves, so they drove out and dumped all the furniture on the Ashley River Road across from Magnolia. We went out with the police. I saw the furniture lying in the woods, the Chippendale tables broken. Nothing was ever done because our fathers were scared that somebody might come back and do even more damage.

An "urban legend" holds that the mantelpiece from the drawing room was stolen when a helicopter landed on the lawn and crooks came in and took it. Something spooked them, so that was all they got. Who knows whether it's true, but in fact, the mantelpiece was stolen.

Selling Drayton Hall was nerve-wracking, but the best my father and Uncle Charlie could do. We could not keep it up, and the National Trust has done a wonderful job. With the new Drayton Hall Preservation Trust, I think Drayton Hall will go even further.

Frank, why should Drayton Hall not be restored to its 18th-century splendor?

The preservation, not restoration, of Drayton Hall is a wonderful thing. The architecture speaks. The walls show what the house was. To some, not having furniture is a disadvantage. They say, "Oh, it's just a bare house," but you've got to understand its architectural significance. The furniture comes later. You can find furniture in almost any museum, and soon we will build an interpretive center for furniture and other artifacts.

Thomas, what do you think of your grandfather's decision to sell the house and about the site's preservation rather than restoration?

My grandfather and his brother made a great decision. We might not be sitting here today if they had not. That was a great decision to keep it like it is. The house grew with the times as shown by all the different rooms, each with ceilings, mantelpieces, or other features from different time periods. The house shows how a Southern plantation, and even our nation, evolved.

Frank, could you tell us about your great Aunt Charley?

I have memories of coming here when Aunt Charley was alive. It was stark. How could somebody live with no electricity or running water? She had an electric hot plate set up on the windowsill to heat food. She had different kinds of furniture — Chippendale tables in the main hall, modern beds, old beds, and an old linen press. It was unique to see 20th century, 19th century, 18th century all thrown together. The house was big and old and scary and dark. I didn't want to spend the night and never did, but my father and uncle did, and they loved it.

Right up until she died in 1969, Aunt Charley was unique. On Sunday afternoons in the spring and fall we'd come see her here or at her house on the Battery, which her father had built. She lived on the second floor. She had a dog, Lucky. People would walk down the Battery and see Lucky sitting in the window, looking out at them.

She collected many, many items. One of my fondest memories is of a huge Victorian dollhouse in the attic that's now at The Charleston Museum. She had a garage and carriage house full of stuff. She had a touring Packard — a 1936 or '37. I can remember her riding around in that. She was never mean to us and let us plunder through her stuff. She was a lovely old person who loved to collect things and held onto whatever she thought was a treasure, which as it's turned out, has indeed become a treasure.

I don't know why she didn't add running water or electricity to Drayton Hall. Maybe deep down she had a feeling of leave it like it is. Also, the cost would have been prohibitive. Walls would have to be torn out to put in plumbing and electricity. She may have felt it was a grand structure and didn't want to mess anything up by modernizing it. She was ahead of her time.

Frank, should a historic site like Drayton Hall devote staff time and funding to manage change in its environs?

The concerns about what happens up and down the river are critical in keeping Drayton Hall in its present state. The viewshed across the river is very important, and Ashley River Road has been here since the early 1700s. Growth is going to happen, but the road and the river and the land around them are too fragile. There are other places for growth. How we manage growth is a question that's going to take long, hard answers. There are opposing sides, but in the Ashley River Corridor, there is no room for unmanaged development.

Frank, what roles do you think historic sites like Drayton Hall can play in improving race relations?

That's a tough question, but Drayton Hall has taken a lead in bringing former descendants together. George, you've done a remarkable job. It's important to get everybody talking. You might read that this group of people won't talk to that group because one was the master and the other enslaved, and we want nothing to do with any of it. It's wonderful that people from Drayton Hall can talk, and we've had several discussions. I was part of one, and it was great getting everybody at the same table. An example is a program you organized in Charleston. I believe it was the first of its kind in the country, with descendants of slave owners and slaves talking about history and the future in a roundtable-style discussion. It could serve as a foundation for getting different races together and discussing. There are going to be hard feelings, but those programs help with race relations here and throughout the country. We set a good example in Charleston.

How has Drayton Hall affected your life?

Frank: Growing up, I'd go places when I was young and people would say, "Oh, you're a Drayton." At first, I didn't know what that meant, but gradually I realized the significance of this big house in the country. Being a descendant of people that helped form Charleston is a huge part of my life. I still go somewhere and someone says, "Oh, Drayton," and look at me a little funny, whether it's in a good way or a bad way. Some ask, "Oh, are you part of Drayton Hall? Do you still own Drayton Hall?"

Thomas: Being a descendant of the Draytons has affected me in many ways. As I grew older and came here more, I realized how Drayton Hall helped shape Charleston and what it means to others.

Frank, if we were to lose Drayton Hall, what difference would that make?

Frank: Whoa! I'd be devastated. It's one of America's greatest architectural showplaces. Number two, I want to be buried here. I don't know what I'd do if its destruction happened in my lifetime. I don't want to think about it!

Why do you say that you want Drayton Hall to be your final resting place? You'd be dead. Why care about the place?

Frank: My final resting place will be where my family has been since the 1730s. Very few people in this country can say they are a part of something like that. Although it's no longer in our family, we still come out here on Thanksgiving Day. Having my cremains here would be a continuation of my being part of Drayton Hall's history. It would be as if my life and death would have come full circle.

Thomas: Drayton Hall is a part of history. The house itself has gone 250 years with people living in it and is now a part of the National Trust. Whenever you come out, you can forget about your cell phone and get immersed in history. My being buried here brings everything full circle. It connects me with the place forever. Our names will be there by the river, and visitors might say, "Wow, the family is still connected to Drayton Hall!" They will see we have feelings for this place and remain involved. All of that will nurture among visitors a sense of connection to Drayton Hall and help them link the 1700s to the present day.

Greg Osteen Howard:
"A Special Place in My Heart"

2021 – Telephone Interview

Greg is the granddaughter of Charlie Drayton and daughter of Molly Drayton Osteen and Monty Osteen. She lives in Augusta, Georgia, is the mother of two daughters, and has become a successful painter. In this interview she reflects on the significance of Drayton Hall to different people and what it has meant to her. She chose Drayton Hall's bank on the Ashley River as the site for her wedding to Kevin Howard, with four generations of her family in attendance.

George: *What does Drayton Hall mean to you?*

Greg: Drayton Hall is one of a kind. Did I know this as a child? No, but I knew none of my friends spent time with their families at places like that. Drayton Hall was, and still is, a gathering place for my mother's side of the family. It's our family tradition. It wasn't until I was a young adult that I made a true connection to its historical significance — not just to my family's history but to our country's.

I think that's why it is so enjoyable for all my family members to take friends and guests to visit there. You can actually watch the connection unfold. When my husband Kevin came to Drayton Hall for the first time, I could tell what was going through his mind: If walls could talk! If trees could talk! I bet Indians stood right here! He certainly appreciates Drayton Hall because of the family connection, but now finds personal connection and interest through the stories it generates. If you allow it, Drayton Hall can ignite so much.

As an artist, what do you think about Drayton Hall?

Art creates an array of emotions. I wouldn't even attempt a realistic approach comparable to photography. I'm more inclined to try impressionism or maybe even abstract! But I wouldn't want to leave out the details of the gates or omit the trees and river, the ceiling of the first-floor great hall, the staircase, or the molding around the windows. Maybe a series!

One of the first pieces of original art my mother gave me was a watercolor of Drayton Hall. I enjoy it every day as it hangs over my bed. One day, I'll have fun painting Drayton Hall!

When you saw it as a girl, what do you remember as your first view?

My first memory of Drayton Hall was the day it was handed over to the National Trust, but that might be because of the photographs. I do remember my brother handing the key over to signify the change of ownership. Of course, the significance of that day didn't become a reality until I was older. Until many years later, I never knew how difficult that decision was for Pop (Greg's grandfather, Charlie Drayton) and how he struggled with it for years afterward. Positioning Drayton Hall to become a designated landmark that could never be destroyed (at least not legally) was an act of love of place. As hard as it was, Pop came to know deep down that he'd done the right thing. He got to a peaceful place.

Without the aid of photographs from that day of transfer to the National Trust, what are your earliest memories of Drayton Hall?

A lot of times when you're young, you see something that seems big, whether it is your house or a church, and when you revisit, it doesn't seem so big anymore. However, with Drayton Hall, that hasn't happened. It was grand then, and it's grand now. As I look back, Drayton Hall was so much fun. Unlimited game playing, fellowship, and food: sometimes we were muddy, sometimes we were cold, and sometimes we were sweaty. Our families have come full circle, and the next generation of children are having the same experience.

Drayton Hall is where my two girls, now 17 and 20, have spent every Thanksgiving Day of their lives. I'm grateful we've been able to continue this tradition. Now that Drayton Hall is a museum, they have more opportunities to connect beyond family. Drayton Hall is a part of their history books and elementary school field trips and is highlighted in presentations during Black History Month. When my daughter was a third-grader, she proudly spoke of Richmond Bowens as an important African American descendent of slaves at Drayton Hall and as a close friend of her great-grandfather Charlie Drayton. The oral reports that bracketed her presentation were about Michael Jackson and Venus Williams.

How did you see your mother feeling about Drayton Hall? How have your and her feelings evolved?

When Mom's telling a story about Drayton Hall, I've never seen her not smile. I'm sure she wishes she could go back in time and play in the gigantic azaleas that flanked the path to the river or search for imaginary treasures in the barn destroyed by Hurricane Hugo. Luckily, her memories have made great stories for the generations to follow. And because Drayton Hall now has an interpretive center, we can share our treasures and have a place for future discoveries.

Speaking of treasures, years ago Mom gave me a beautiful porcelain bowl that I had on my dining room table. I put a plant in it. I didn't think anything of it until the day she told me that when she was a child it was under her bed for use as a potty. I had used it to serve salad for a dinner party! Now the beautiful porcelain bowl (chamber pot) is at Drayton Hall and might be on exhibit in the new interpretive center as a decorative arts object.

What are your thoughts about Richmond Bowens and African American history at Drayton Hall?

My last memory of Richmond Bowens was when our family drove over to his house on Thanksgiving Day. He might have been sick. Three generations of Draytons were welcomed into his home where he was surrounded by several generations of Bowens family members. The connection between him and my grandfather was contagious. We all felt the love and admiration between the two old gentlemen. We didn't say much, just enjoyed their interaction.

Drayton Hall has done pioneering programs with African American descendants over the years that involved the Bowens family and others. I was asked to participate in a descendants' program that you organized at the South Carolina Preservation Conference. Continuation of these efforts is essential to keeping the history alive and understanding of the stories by future generations.

Since Confederate monuments are being pulled down, why should Drayton Hall be spared?

Drayton Hall is the oldest representation of Georgian Palladian architecture in our country. It is our responsibility as Americans to protect it. Removing monuments is saying we can't handle history. History comes from the Greek word "to know." Drayton Hall should be spared because there is so much more to know.

What are your thoughts about letting Drayton Hall be destroyed?

We would lose a connection to our past. All that lived and died at Drayton Hall are deserving of a place for their descendants to not only pay their respects and to mourn, but also to celebrate evolution of the human race.

Can't they read about that in a book or watch a movie? Why do we need the place?

One cannot duplicate a sense of place, which ignites emotions you can't get from reading or watching a movie. The place authenticates. I think that's the most important word. I'm for preserving plantation sites like Drayton Hall as teachable moments and for telling stories. There are many more to tell.

Greg's daughter Molly, a student at the University of South Carolina, adds her thoughts:

Drayton Hall holds a special place in my heart. This historic landmark has meant much to my family, and I'm proud to be a part of its legacy. It's where I've always gone to celebrate Thanksgiving. It's where my mother and step-father were married, and it's where my great-grandmother and great-grandfather are buried.

As I've gotten older, I've learned more about its history and how unique it is. Preservation of Drayton Hall shows how far we have come as a nation and human race, and it is essential to never forget that. Destroying Drayton Hall risks encroaching on future discoveries, but most of all it would deprive our country of a one-of-a-kind architectural gem. Being the oldest great-grandchild of Pop (Charlie

Drayton), I want nothing more than to help support the place that meant the most to him and to keep it as a special place to our family and future generations.

The Rev. Roosevelt Geddis & Lorraine S. White:
"No Matter What Happens in Life"

2015 – Drayton Hall

Lorraine White is the retired choir director at Alston Middle School in Summerville. For years she brought students to perform and to participate in Drayton Hall's school programs. Her father, the Rev. Roosevelt Geddis, is a Methodist minister whose maternal grandparents and probably his maternal great-grandparents lived and worked at Drayton Hall. In 2012 Drayton Hall dedicated the African American cemetery of the 1790s, and I invited Lorraine, whom I knew. I introduced her to Charlie Drayton, the last owner of the property. She asked if he knew her great-grandmother "Binah," who lived at Drayton Hall. Charlie's head tilted back and with a big smile, he said: "Binah? When I was little, my parents used to bring me out here, and it was Binah who took care of me. Her name I remember well." They embraced.

Rev. Geddis, could you describe how you're connected to Drayton Hall?

My great-grandmother, Binah, was here, and my grandparents, James and Hattie Hopkins, who was Binah's daughter, came here in the 1910s or early '20s. The youngest of their children, my mother, Luetta Hopkins, was not born here, but my uncle Francis Hopkins, who was raised by my grandparents, and my cousins, Willie Hopkins and Elizabeth Hopkins, were here, working on the grounds. When my older brother, George, was a baby, he lived with them. They all have passed on.

Lorraine, could you tell us your connections to Drayton Hall?

I first got involved around 1998 when fellow teacher Becky Dingle and I received a grant to teach students about Gullah culture. We came to Drayton Hall and had a wonderful performance of music, dance, and public speaking, using the mound in front of the main house as a stage. Afterward, when I spoke to my father about it, he asked if I knew that my great-grandparents and great-great grandmother worked on the plantation? "I did not know that," I said.

Now it was personal. I wanted to know more about what happened at Drayton Hall. What was it like? Where did they work? What were they doing in the kitchen? I wanted to know what my fore-parents did to pave the path that got me where I am today. What happened to them, be it good or bad? I needed to know.

Rev. Geddis, did you visit your grandparents here? What stories about life did you hear?

I hadn't been born when they lived here, but I heard a lot of stories. It means a lot to me to know that my grandparents worked here and were able to survive no matter what they went through. They raised my Uncle Francis right here. Even though he had a deformed leg and walked with a crutch, he became a carpenter who would leave his crutch on the ground, climb ladders to the tops of houses, and work.

This place means a lot to me. Every time I pass by, I think about Grandmama and those who were living in that little house on the other side (west) of Highway 61. Years ago, you could see it from the road, and I'd always tell the guys I worked with, "My grandparents used to live in that house over there." I was born in 1936. My grandfather James Hopkins died in 1948 and my grandmother Hattie Hopkins in 1955, so I'd gotten to know them.

Could you describe your grandparents?

James Hopkins was a tall gentleman. Everyone looked up to him. When he spoke, everyone listened. He was quiet, but would get your attention. He was a Baptist preacher and worshipped at Springfield Baptist Church, down Highway 61, then moved to Magnolia Baptist Church near Givhans. My grandmother Hattie was a Methodist and worshipped at St. Phillip's AME Church until they moved up Highway 61, where she went to Canaan United Methodist Church.

My grandmother was short, loved to work in the garden, and cook. We'd go to her house looking for that good meal that only grandmothers cooked. She was good-hearted and loved the Lord. In church, she sat in Amen Corner for the older ladies. In the opposite corner were the older men. In our culture, we say "Amen" in response to the preaching. Amen means: "I agree. Everything is alright." They loved to sing, usually a cappella, such songs as "I've Got to Go to Judgment to Stand My Trial."

While they were at Drayton Hall, Grandmother grew collards, string beans, mustard greens, white potatoes, cabbage, and all that. In her greens and cabbage, she would put in smoked butt's meat, the fat part of the hog, which would bring out the flavor. They had a lot of chickens, so she'd fry or stew some along with dumplings. She baked biscuits that were out of sight. My grandfather would declare, "Hattie, these biscuits got good sense!"

All his life, my grandfather James Hopkins was a farmer, and I presume he started at Drayton Hall. He grew mostly cotton and corn until he got too old. He didn't have much education, but he could read and write, and every time one of the children was born, he would write it down in the Bible. I have that Bible at my house. I'm sure he had that Bible when he was at Drayton Hall because my mother, Luetta Hopkins, being the youngest, was the last on the list.

I remember going to segregated schools and getting the used books from the White schools. I was always wondering when that would change, and thank God, it finally did. However, one thing my grandfather instilled in us was to look for the message in a book, not its ragged condition. Comprehend that, he said, and you'll go places in life. In the midst of segregation and all it meant, he let us know that we were somebody. He tried his best to share things we didn't understand.

Did you hear a story about your grandfather in a racially tense situation with a White person?

One day a White man tried to slap him, but had only one hand. My grandfather, who was a religious man, turned the other side of his face to this gentleman, who slapped that side. My grandfather didn't say anything. Not long afterward, the man was working at his cotton gin, stuck his only hand in something, and got it cut off, so he had no hands to slap somebody. He could use his nubs. One day he went up in his barn loft to throw hay out to the cows, fell out, and broke his neck. Now, we don't know whether his death was because of what he did to my grandfather, but it could have been God's judgment, His Hand.

How important was family in your life?

Lorraine: Although I didn't know my father's grandparents or great-grandparents, the importance of family they instilled in him was vital. Their shared values were passed to me. Like my father, his mother Luetta and her brother, my Uncle Frank (Francis Hopkins), who was raised and worked at Drayton Hall, loved to sing. I too was blessed with a good voice. I was a leader in the children's choir at church. One day in choir practice, a girl got jealous and said, "Oh, you think you're something 'cause you got a nice voice." I got upset and ran out of the church, and Aunt Thelma, my mother's aunt, came after me. She said, "God gave you a voice, and he didn't give you a voice to sit on. He gave you a voice to use. Don't you let anybody tell you that you're not good enough!" If she had not come out to talk to me, I probably would have stopped, but God had her there to say, "No, you keep on! Don't let anybody stop you from your dreams."

As you look around in this cemetery at Drayton Hall, what does it say to you?

Rev. Geddis: I'm thinking about all those who lived and suffered hard tasks in this place. Some lived a long life; some probably lived a short life. I see so many graves, which lets me know that they were cared for by friends and loved ones. As we sit here, it reminds me of my destiny. One day I, too, will be among the silent group in some cemetery. For many, there is no marker, nothing to let you know who's there, but one thing we can be assured of, God knows who's in these spaces where there are no markers. May God bless them. May God keep them forever in his care. And I know one day, sooner or later, if Binah is out here somewhere, we will meet again. Yes.

Lorraine: When I look at this cemetery, there are few gravestones to indicate who's there. For most, their only recognition is a sinkhole. This cemetery speaks volumes. It gives me a sense of hope to know they lived and worked here, and that despite the conditions they had to work under, when they thought they'd never make it, they did. The cemetery says no matter what you go through in life, there's a path for you to follow. That path leads to death. But when you do die, there's a savior waiting for you, who you've been longing to see.

Going down that path, I'm sure many have said, "I've opened my mouth to the Lord, and I won't turn back." I'm gonna see what the end is going to be. This is what this cemetery is speaking to me: "I've gone through many trials, but I didn't give up. I'm gonna go on. I'm gonna meet my Precious Savior who has guided me through everything I had to go through."

As I sit in this cemetery, it's like I can hear them say, "Go on. Remember the past." This is the present now, but also there is a future. In the future, there is great hope, a sense of pride. There's a sense of dignity that says, "You had a rich culture, and you still do." Because of this, I say, "God, I'm so grateful that my fore-parents had an opportunity to come this way." Hard though it may have been, now that I'm learning more about my history and my connections to Drayton Hall, I'm happy to learn all of the things I did not know. I thank God for the opportunity to be able to come and reminisce and look around the plantation and ask, "What were my people doing? How were they treated? What games were children playing? What songs might they have sung?" While I'll never know, I can get a sense of what it was like by being here.

Maybe they sang a song like "Take My Hand, Precious Lord." As I sit here, there are tears in my eyes because I'm grateful my father's here and I've learned things I didn't know about my family. There's so much history that is untold and that needs to be told, especially chapters in African American history.

There are many bodies in Drayton Hall's cemetery that don't have anyone to talk about them and tell their histories. It is very important for others to know so they can plot their course and say — even though they were in slavery, and slavery did happen, and it wasn't a good thing — I'm not gonna let it get me down. I know that it says in Philippians 4:13, "We can do all things through Christ, who strengthens us," so no matter what happens in life, we can learn from the failures. I believe America is learning from the failures, and it's for us, the living, to say we want to correct what was done in the past now and in the future.

Hear the Rev. Roosevelt Geddis and Lorraine White sing the following at www.mcdanielconsulting.net/drayton-hall-book/:
1. "Take My Hand, Precious Lord"
2. "You've Got to Stand Your Test at the Judgment"
    [Reverend Geddis heard his mother sing this at Canaan Church.]
3. "Touch the Hem of His Garment"
4. "Give Me Jesus"
5. "Trouble of This World"
6. "Drink This Water" [Reverend Geddis says this is a really old song]
7. "Do Lord Remember Me"

Catherine Braxton and Rebecca Campbell:
"Let Us Come to the Table"

2015 – Rutgers University, Newark, New Jersey

I was invited to participate in this symposium by Clem Price, a friend in the history department at Rutgers University-Newark. Invited to be the keynote speaker at the Historic Sites Luncheon of the National Trust for Historic Preservation in 2014, he dedicated his presentation to me. Shortly thereafter, a lethal heart attack struck him down. I dedicated this presentation to him. With me were descendants Catherine Braxton and Rebecca Campbell. Unfortunately, Drayton family descendants could not join us. I asked questions of 10 images of Drayton Hall and asked them to respond. The complete video is available at www.mcdanielconsulting.net.

My introduction: The etymology of the word 'history' is not memorization or lecture, as history is so often taught, but inquiry. A historian learns by inquiry. Often history is taught as something far away, but with museums and historic sites like Drayton Hall, the presence of history can be felt. That's why we preserve historic buildings, artifacts, and places. By asking questions and connecting places and things with stories, we enhance their evocative power.

George: *Here's a slide of an advertisement for the sale of "Negroes" from the "Rice Coast" of West Africa at Ashley Ferry, a short distance down the Ashley River from Drayton Hall. What are your thoughts?*

Rebecca: Charleston was one of the most powerful places for enslavement. Sullivan's Island is where ships arrived, where Africans were put in pest houses to quarantine them. Charleston people enslaved many, many people. We have forgiven them. The Word of God says you've got to forgive, and we'd like to move on. That's why I am here. I'm speaking for the betterment of our country and the betterment of the generation that is here and the generations to come. [Applause]

George: *An exhibit at Colonial Williamsburg entitled, "Rich and Varied Culture," featured the decorative arts in the American South, including 18th-century artifacts from Drayton Hall. Here is a branding iron, which was used to brand enslaved people. Before it was exhibited, we asked members of the Drayton family along with you, "What should we do?" The Draytons agreed. Could you describe your answers?*

Rebecca: It should be shown. We have hidden too many things in our families. We have hidden them in churches, and we've hidden them in America. It needs to be known. The truth must be spoken.

Catherine: I don't have any problem with showing this, but when I see it, I hurt, imagining that my ancestors were branded like cattle. I'm still in the healing process, and that's why I do what I do. I want others to understand what happened. It really happened. We have to get through it. But in getting through it, there needs to be some healing. It's a process, and we have to get it going.

George: *This is an image of a live oak tree in the curve in the entrance lane in front of Drayton Hall, maybe three to four hundred years old. If this live oak could talk, what questions would you ask?*

Catherine: "Were any of my ancestors hung on this tree? For what reason?" There may have been many "reasons." Maybe they did not comply in doing a task or whatever.

Rebecca: I believe that some were hung on the tree. They might not have done anything to deserve it. Maybe the owners just didn't like how they looked. "Hang him!" You know it's not always that you didn't do their job right, or you didn't follow directions. It's because, "I don't like you or your attitude. Hang him!"

George: *This is a shard of 18th-century colonoware, or low-fired pottery, derived from a West African tradition brought to colonial South Carolina and found by archaeologists at Drayton Hall. When you look at an object like this, what questions come to mind?*

Catherine: I want to know if my ancestors used anything similar to this. What did they prepare? Was it a water jug? Was it something to prepare food in?

Rebecca: I have a different version. If I were enslaved, I'd be tired at the end of the day. Get out a toddy! Get high. Sleep until it's time to go back to work the next morning. That's what I'd use it for. [Laughing]

George: *Here is the Ashley River Road — today a National Scenic Highway — that passes by Drayton Hall. What questions might you ask of it?*

Catherine: I'd like to know if my ancestors used this road to go to church. They were religious people. When freedom came, they and other freed slaves founded the Springfield Baptist Church, still located on Ashley River Road.

Rebecca: My grandfather, Willis Johnson Jr., used that road to leave Drayton Hall, where his parents had been enslaved, and walked to Charleston. There he bought land, and I was raised in his home in Charleston. Many of you may think this sounds silly, but start studying your genealogy and record everything you can from your oldest relatives. We regret we didn't record our great-grandmothers and grandmothers.

George: *What are the key messages you'd like for this audience to leave with?*

Catherine: Slavery happened. Let us come to the table. We have got to heal and move on.

Rebecca: I want to leave two words with you: "Love" and "Forgiveness."

[Applause]

INTERVIEWS
Friends

Peter and Patti McGee:
"There Is a Two-Word Answer"

2020 – Sullivan's Island, South Carolina

Peter McGee, a Charlestonian and prominent attorney, was instrumental in the initial preservation of Drayton Hall. A National Trust for Historic Preservation trustee, he served on Drayton Hall's advisory council for many years and became its chairman. Patti McGee, a native of Marion, SC, is an active preservationist in Charleston and was advisor from South Carolina to the National Trust. In this interview, among other things, they describe the key role of Frances Edmunds in the preservation of Drayton Hall.

Since you're a Charlestonian, Peter, what did Drayton Hall mean to you growing up?

Peter: I didn't know anything about it. As a boy, my father was a trust officer of South Carolina National Bank and had a close tie to the owners of Middleton Place, the Pringle Smiths. We'd go to Middleton for Sunday dinner maybe twice a year. This was a thrill because it was a beautiful place. Tourists would be there, for at that time, it and Magnolia were the two main spots on what we called the River Road, which we now refer to as Highway 61. To me, Drayton Hall was, in a word, almost meaningless.

The first time I laid eyes on it was decades ago when Patti and I went up the Ashley River with my friend David Maybank. We knew where Drayton Hall was and had carefully tied up our boat on its riverbank. Ascending the bank, I saw Drayton Hall. It's not an overstatement to say there was a "wow" impact. I was old enough to recognize architectural beauty, and this place had it! We felt like we were trespassing, so we walked around the building and left. That was my introduction to Drayton Hall.

Patti: While we may have known how important Drayton Hall was, the Drayton house downtown was the one we knew since it was on the corner of Atlantic and East Bay and owned by Miss Charlotta Drayton, who also owned Drayton Hall. She had a pair of Staffordshire dogs that sat in the window, and as you rode by her house, it was straight out of Charles Adams! We'd heard about the wonderful debutante parties at Drayton Hall and about Miss Charlotta being there every spring with her help in spite of the fact that there was no plumbing or electricity. These wonderful stories about the historic family home prompted us to sort of trespass and peek at it. It was quite a thrill! I don't know whether we told anybody right away. The house became more and more appreciated and just had to be saved because it was unique to Charleston and unique in this country.

The other thing I remember so well is that Sara Hastie Low, a Drayton descendant, had a candlelight supper downstairs in the main hall, not on the second floor. I was there. Candles filled the place, even tiny votives in the fireplace. It was probably one of the last family parties they had there. But oh, was it elegant! Magical! That evening is one of my favorite memories of Drayton Hall.

What led you, Peter, to become so involved in historic preservation?

Peter: There is a two-word answer: Frances Edmunds. For a number of years, the McGee family and the Smythe family had been staunchly involved with the Second Presbyterian Church. Because I lived nearby and they had a wonderful tennis court, I got to know all three Smythe children: Frances, the oldest, and then Austin and Henry. They were older than I, but eventually the law firm I created with my friend Ben Moore merged with the law firm of Austin and Henry Smythe, so we all practiced law together.

As a youth, I had gotten to know Frances. When she was with the Historic Charleston Foundation in the 1960s, she sought to update zoning laws, which dated to the 1930s, in order to extend the range of the historic district up the peninsula and to achieve other goals. When she asked her brother Henry for a young lawyer to help, he recommended me. That's the first time I worked with Frances.

Why do you think so many women have been involved in preservation?

Patti: That's an excellent question because women were, without question, the earliest leaders in Charleston. Perhaps it's an appreciation for the domestic. It wasn't just saving one house but saving the community and the whole environment, which quickly became important for Charleston, a unique community and a historically and architecturally important place. Women had the time to volunteer as docents. That's how I became involved. If you had a desire to learn about decorative arts and antiques and to take many courses and do it as a volunteer, women had the time to do that. Men handled the legal and financial ends. In the early days, they couldn't get away from work to go volunteer in a house, but housewives could. Charleston is so lucky to have had those earlier women.

Frances Edmunds had a lot to do with it. From the very beginning, she saw the value of Charleston's being a living, thriving, viable city. It wasn't Williamsburg because it had not been reconstructed. These were the real homes. People lived here, worked here, played here. She instilled in us that we wanted people to see Charleston as an active city, as a real community. We were not Disney World.

What led you, Peter, to the preservation of Drayton Hall?

Peter: Again, Frances Edmunds. We knew Charles Drayton and his brother Frank wanted to sell it, so she came up with a strategy, and I helped. We needed three organizations: the Historic Charleston Foundation, the state of South Carolina and the National Trust for Historic Preservation. Since the Trust was having its annual conference in Charleston in 1970, we organized a tour exclusively of Drayton Hall, not of Magnolia or Middleton Place. We didn't want Drayton Hall to be bought by a rich Yankee or anything like that. We'd spring it on them, "Isn't this a wonderful place?" The Trustees would be enthralled. Afterwards, when we said, "Now don't you think …?" the Trust's leadership would say, "Yes, we do." Once they saw it, National Trust leaders — James Biddle, Gordon Gray, and others— would recognize that saving Drayton Hall was vital. From the site, we returned them to their hotels, so for their whole time, we'd given them Drayton Hall by themselves. From that event, a series of steps took place, culminating in Drayton Hall becoming a Trust site.

What do you think Drayton Hall has offered the public?

Patti: When you involved both the Draytons and the Bowens and began to tell the parallel stories of the two families, you were ahead of your time, George, and that's what makes the site come alive. You've had great guides, ones who loved history enough to be knowledgeable and interpret the place in the light of how the plantation owners and the slave community lived, which is so integral to interpreting any of the antebellum places. The way Drayton Hall is opened up for people gives them a rare chance in person to appreciate Palladian architecture. As for the Draytons, they treasured Drayton Hall and lived in this house and used it into the 20th century for debutante parties and weddings, making it integral to the identity of their family. You've kept them engaged. I think all of that is wonderful, and not many places can say that.

Peter, you were on Drayton Hall's board for years and chairman of the board. Why bother?

Peter: I enjoyed it. It was fun to get something done that ought to be done.

If you were to summarize Frances Edmunds in a few words, what would you say, Peter?

Peter: Smart, lots of ideas and determination. I had a lot of fun working for Frances.

Why did Frances Edmunds care so much about Drayton Hall?

Peter: Because she cared about a lot of things.

Patti: She was passionate about Charleston. When they were saving and acquiring the Nathaniel Russell House, she fell into that first job, and that's what led to the formation of the Historic Charleston Foundation. Frances had a way of making it impossible to say "No." She had the ear of the bankers and the ear of the highway department and knew where people were that you had to be in touch with to get things accomplished. She stepped on a toe or two, but not many.

One story about Frances: When I went onto the board of the Garden Conservancy, I was seated next to a man who had been involved with the National Trust, knew Frances, and liked her. He asked her, "How do you get the leaders in your community to get behind these wonderful projects like Drayton Hall?" She quietly looked over at him and said, "Oh, just a little pillow talk."

You were saying earlier that she did not want someone "from Off" to buy Drayton Hall. Could you describe the likely effects of that on Drayton Hall?

Peter: From the outset I knew that we were not going to let this property get away. We needed help, hence the game plan I described.

Patti: We didn't want it to become a victim of that second Yankee invasion in which houses were owned not by people who lived and worked here but by those who come for a few months. Charleston wasn't their home. Somebody used the word "token wives." They have "token houses." When somebody has to have a house in Charleston, a house in St. Croix, and a house at every ritzy address, it's a loss.

At the same time, there are people who've come to appreciate what a unique city Charleston is. You've got them on the board of Drayton Hall. My friend Ben Lenhardt thinks Drayton Hall is wonderful. We need them.

I'll ask you an imaginary question. Imagine Frances Edmonds still living and as strong as you remember her. Now imagine she's on television's The Late Show with Stephen Colbert, Colbert being your son-in-law. Can you imagine the conversation they would have?

Peter: It would be pretty damn good.

Patti: I think it definitely would.

What kind of things do you think the two of them might talk about?

Peter: Lots.

Patti: He would have a lot to say about his hometown. He doesn't talk about Charleston too much, but I think he'd recognize that she was a person who helped make Charleston as special as it is. That would be fun to see. Oh, Lordy! She would give it to him as much as he would give it to her!

Charles H. P. Duell:
"I've Known Drayton Hall All My Life"

2015 – Drayton Hall

Charles H.P. Duell recently retired as president and CEO of the Middleton Place Foundation, a historic plantation on the Ashley River upstream from Drayton Hall. A leader in historic preservation and site management, Charles played a major role in the preservation of Drayton Hall and in shaping its early character as a site open to the public.

Could you tell us about your background and how you came to know Drayton Hall?

I have known Drayton Hall all my life. When I lived in New York, I came to Charleston as a young man to visit my grandparents. They lived downtown on East Battery next door to Charlotta Drayton, whom we called "Charley." On our way out to Middleton Place, we'd drop by Drayton Hall to see Charley and maybe have a picnic, so I've known Drayton Hall all of my life.

What is your connection to Middleton Place?

My grandparents owned Middleton Place, and I had no idea I'd ever be involved with it. But in 1970, I inherited it. I formed a nonprofit organization, the Middleton Place Foundation, and was selected to be its president and chief executive officer, a position I've held for nearly 50 years. As for typical commercial or residential development of Middleton Place, there wasn't any question that would happen. The greatest satisfaction is the feeling that our stewardship has made what we had a little better than if we hadn't been there. That's the pleasure of those of us who have worked to save Drayton Hall and Middleton Place. I believe a sense of history and a sense of place are essential to the human psyche.

Describe your role in the acquisition of Drayton Hall and the roles of others and organizations.

I joined the National Trust in 1968, and after getting to know a lot of its people, was invited to become an advisor representing the state of South Carolina. By the time Drayton Hall was acquired, I had become a trustee. My mentor, Carl Humelsine, who was chairman of the National Trust and president of Colonial Williamsburg, came down, helped guide the development of Middleton Place, and attended the ceremonies when Drayton Hall was bargain-sold to the National Trust.

Another mentor of mine was Frances Edmunds, a Charleston preservationist who loved Drayton Hall. She influenced Frank and Charles Drayton's decision to sell Drayton Hall, raised the first $300,000 including a gift from Sally Reahard, to buy it, and led to the tripartite purchase of it by the Historic Charleston Foundation (of which she was president), the State of South Carolina, and the National Trust.

There is no way she could be over-appreciated. Influential with the mayor, she was outspoken and felt strongly about preservation of the Ashley River region. For example, when Interstate 526 was built, she insisted it not have an interchange with the Ashley River Road because she could foresee the negative impact of commercial developments and parking lots. Thanks to her, the interchange was moved west to what has become the Glenn McConnell Parkway. If you look at that area today, you can see what might have happened to Ashley River Road and the drive to Drayton Hall if not for Frances.

What attracted you to Drayton Hall in those early days? What decisions were made that shaped what one sees today?

I became a student of architecture at Yale and was fortunate to have a great professor, Vincent Scully, who refined my thinking about Palladio and his influence on Georgian architecture, including Drayton Hall. In addition, I was influenced by Robert Marvin, South Carolina's great landscape architect, who was on Drayton Hall's advisory council with me. With Frances as chairman, we had a lot of discussion as to what the Trust should do with Drayton Hall. One example was the mound on the land front of Drayton Hall, which was added during the Victorian period. I had a tractor with a front-end bucket on it and volunteered to drive down there and remove the mound. It mars the image as you approach Drayton Hall. However, the National Trust believed Drayton Hall should show the evolution of the site and not pick a point in time.

Some of us felt differently. By no means were we insistent on everything being restored to a point in time. What I felt, and still do, is that you research, study, and then try to focus on the soul, or essence, of the property. Drayton Hall is a masterful piece of architecture, and the original two flankers created a kind of Queen Anne courtyard, which would have been a rectangular space that one drove into on arrival. Since the Victorian mound was probably put up temporarily, it would have been easy to restore that Queen Anne courtyard feeling in approaching Drayton Hall. You'll never see another Palladian building that has a mound blocking the front of it. Since my idea got shot down by Robert Marvin and the Trust, I put my tractor in reverse, and the mound stayed.

In the 1970s another critical issue came before the site council. After purchase from the Draytons, the land was divided into two parts, with the Trust owning 125 acres, including the main house, and the State of South Carolina owning 500 acres of forest on both sides of the road, managed by the park system of SC Department of Parks, Recreation, and Tourism. Thinking the state's parks needed more pizzazz, its staff drew up plans for a kid-friendly park with ocean-action pools and other intense activities. After considerable discussion, the site council got the state to agree to a passive park, which now serves as a buffer to development from Charleston.

The last debate was what to do about conserving Drayton Hall without embellishing it. After much discussion and a final report, it was decided that Drayton Hall would be a historic property that would not be repainted and not be wired and plumbed, but kept as it was.

What role do you think historic sites like Drayton Hall and Middleton Place have in helping race relations?

Historic sites have many opportunities to help race relationships. Both Middleton Place and Drayton Hall have made a real effort to talk about, interpret, and celebrate the contributions of African Americans. After all, they actually built Drayton Hall. They built Middleton Place. They built the gardens. They tended the livestock. They did the work that enabled the house to function, and they manned the schooners on the river. It's not rewriting history, but it's completing the valuable, historic story of what has happened on both properties. One of our friends, artist Jonathan Green, notes how important it is for students, especially African American students, to get involved in history and learn that it wasn't all doom and gloom; as horrific as slavery was, they had things to celebrate. He likes to focus on rice culture and on the skills, knowledge, and rice-related activities Africans brought to this country. At plantation sites like Drayton Hall, students can see where their ancestors lived, what they did, and where they had come from in Africa. They can learn about not only their building the structures and taking care of everything, but also bringing with them skills and knowledge. For example, to the culinary world they brought their knowledge and methods of cooking yams or okra. A lot of foodways in the South would not be enjoyed were it not for African contributions.

In addition, at Middleton Place and Drayton Hall the attention to the cemetery of African Americans is important as is our connecting to descendants and producing family reunions. Given the kinship of families at both sites, joint reunions of descendants of Middleton and Drayton families along with descendants of the enslaved Africans of both sites could demonstrate a shared history. Sites like ours can provide the setting for people simply to say how they feel about the experience and to talk informally and get to know one another through dialogue.

One thing we have not yet approached but will when the time is right, is cross-racial sexual relations. They seem to be somewhat off the record, but we probably will be talking about it more as time goes by. It may be that people will eventually get DNA testing to find out what the relationships are. While the topic hasn't broken into the mainstream of Southern plantation sites, that's the kind of conversation that will come up in the future. In fact, there is no Black history without White history, and no White History without Black history.

What do you think historic sites in general, and Middleton Place and Drayton Hall in particular, can offer which a classroom alone cannot?

According to books like John Naisbitt's series *Megatrends*, museums and historic sites have become, and will continue to become, more and more the teachers of history because, sadly, in the required curriculum in today's schools and colleges, history has diminished. The burden, or the opportunity, stands on our shoulders to properly teach history and more. We offer students hands-on, tactile experiences. If you're teaching colonial American history in the classroom, children may be daydreaming or doodling, but if you take them to a historic site and show them actual rice fields and explain the human endeavor, it becomes, "That was a lot of work, wasn't it? A lot of skills were involved." They can see it. Historic sites educate students in ways that a classroom alone cannot.

Why do you think historic preservation is important? What are challenges Middleton Place and Drayton Hall have faced and will continue to face into the future?

History is essential because it gives you context. Without a context in which to operate, you're flying around in outer space without a guide. History in turn is made more understandable by historic preservation because when you walk through

Drayton Hall and hear the stories about its people, you can see where they lived and worked, and use your imagination. It's like reading a book. You use your inner vision to imagine. Places like Monticello, Mount Vernon, Middleton Place, and Drayton Hall make the setting credible, tactile. The more you connect those places to people, the more history becomes a story. History is non-fictional, and non-fiction can be more powerful than fiction because it really happened.

Many challenges in preservation go far beyond preserving and interpreting the historic site. You and I and others have worked on things like preserving the context surrounding these historic sites and ensuring the region is not subjected to suburban sprawl. To do so, Drayton Hall actually has bought property across the river to ensure its viewshed would remain forested. Looking ahead, our successors will be battling to see that the Ashley River region is protected and that, for example, Ashley River Road is not four-laned because of impact on the historic properties. While many challenges may seem peripheral, they are essential to the preservation effort for all historic properties.

Why are historic sites like Drayton Hall and Middleton Place important to the region's economy and business development?

Several answers arise, and probably the non-economic ways are the most powerful. It's like asking, "Why is art important to the economy?" The answer is that people are interested in it, motivated by it, stimulated by it, and given pleasure by it. I like to think that Drayton Hall and Middleton Place are like fine paintings in a gallery. In addition, tourism is the largest economic engine in Charleston. We need to continue to recognize the importance of heritage tourism versus honky-tonk tourism. Heritage tourists appreciate honest history based on research and documentation, and they eat at our tables, stay in hotels, visit museums and sites, and produce a tremendous multiplying effect as quantified by research numbers.

Is there a place at Drayton Hall whose stories you'd like to hear if that place could talk?

I'd like to hear everything from pillow talk to dining room table discussions. I'd particularly be interested in hearing people talk about the garden. Of particular fascination is the foundation of the serpentine walls extending from the east façade of the house, for they bespeak a degree of landscape architecture that we don't know. Also interesting would be discussions among the enslaved African American servers in the basement of Drayton Hall as they're preparing things to go up to the dining room — an upstairs/downstairs thing.

How would you assess this quotation from John McCardell, former vice chancellor of Sewanee: "I answered a call and received a blessing?"

I'd respond by saying I feel fortunate to have been lured into historic preservation. I love my job. In many ways we're gilding the lily, aren't we, because what's here at Middleton Place and Drayton Hall is already pretty darn good. Just constantly asking ourselves how we could make this or that better is a lot of fun. I'm fortunate to have a staff of very capable people who work hard and who become very proprietary about Middleton Place. I encourage that. I want them to think of Middleton Place as theirs and to love it. They do. I'm a lucky guy.

For a brief video about Frances Edmunds, see:
https://bit.ly/AboutFrancesEdmunds

Gene Wilkins:
"Sally Cared"

2015 – Indianapolis, IN

A well-respected attorney in Indianapolis, Gene Wilkins was Sally Reahard's adviser for many years and executor of her estate. She loved Charleston and had visited Drayton Hall soon after college. Miss Sally, as she was affectionately known, made her first donation to the National Trust for Historic Preservation, when it was looking for a city to locate its Southern Regional Office. She bought the historic Aiken House in downtown Charleston and offered it free to the National Trust. Thus, its location in Charleston.

When I became Drayton Hall's director, I introduced myself to Miss Sally. Shortly afterward, she mentioned to me that she was selling tulips to raise money for her college. That struck a bell because my mother had done the same at Sweet Briar. So I asked Sally, "What was her college?" She said Sweet Briar, and remembered Mother, and

sent me copies from her annual with pictures of Mother. I later asked one of Mother's Sweet Briar classmates about Miss Sally, and she remembered her. However, no one knew how wealthy Sally was because wealth was not shown off back then.

Upon Sally's death in 2003, she left an estate of approximately $180 million dollars, which she gave to non-profits. Between $500,000 and $3 million were given to the Historic Charleston Foundation, The Charleston Museum, the Preservation Society of Charleston, and the Lowcountry Land Trust, plus about $73 million to the Nature Conservancy. The second largest bequest, $16 million, went to Drayton Hall as an endowment, $3 million of which could be devoted to its new visitors' center, now named after her.

A perceptive judge of character, Miss Sally did not like sycophants. From experience I learned how she, even though in Indianapolis, managed to keep a sharp eye on what was going on at Drayton Hall. She got information from people she knew who came to Charleston. Often in our telephone conversations, Miss Sally would ask about this or that, and I wondered, "How in the world did she know about that?"

I respected her, as did Gene Wilkins, who in this interview offers a very human portrayal of a lady some might have seen as an "eccentric" or a "moneybags." She was much more.

Participants:
   George McDaniel, interviewer
   Gene Wilkins, Sally Reahard's attorney, estate executor

When one looks at Drayton Hall, what does one see of Sally Reahard?

1. Drayton Hall itself as she made the lead private gift
2. A fire hydrant as she paid for city water from North Charleston to be piped under the Ashley River to Drayton Hall to provide water for drinking and fire safety
3. The terne roof on the main house that withstood Hurricane Hugo
4. The cottage for residents to provide on-site security
5. Preservation of the main house, inside and out
6. Archaeological research
7. The improved entrance lane
8. The administrative building
9. Rock revetments to halt riverbank erosion
10. Purchase of land across the river to secure Drayton Hall's viewshed
11. Approximately $50,000 a year in budget support during her lifetime

12. An endowment for general operations and hiring of professional staff
13. New visitors' center

Why do you love talking about Miss Sally?
Because she was the most unique individual I've ever met.

How did you meet?
I was the senior partner at Ice Miller, which had over 400 lawyers, and the head of our estate planning section said I should meet Miss Sally Reahard. I lived nearby and made an appointment to visit her at home. On came the largest snowstorm Indianapolis had ever had. That didn't stop me. Sally was not used to having people walk in the snow to visit her. We immediately hit it off. Our values were the same, and we knew a lot of the same people. We arranged a date for the following Wednesday at 1:30 pm. Since she rarely left her house, she began to rely on me as her eyes and ears in Indianapolis. For 15 years, I spent three hours every Wednesday afternoon with her.

What was Miss Sally's background? How was that expressed in her house and lifestyle?
She came from a fairly aristocratic background. Sally liked things to be rich but not gaudy. In Ohio, the Aul family was very prominent and had a lot of money. When Sally's mother was pregnant with her, she went to stay with the Aul family in Ohio so that Sally would be born a Buckeye. Sally's mother didn't want to have a Hoosier. After six months, they returned and Sally's father built a house on fashionable Meridian Street, not a mansion, but a pleasant house. In the early '60s, Sally built a house nearby and was her own architect. It's a one-story, brick Williamsburg Colonial — functional, with a lot of space. Because she loved plants and flowers, particularly daffodils, she had a beautiful garden and selected a leading landscape architect. She preferred single flowers. When she sat at her desk, next to her would be one flower, perhaps a tulip, rose, or daffodil. Sally received lots of flower arrangements, but every night she'd put them in a closet with no heat, and in the morning, she'd take out one flower. The bouquets lasted for weeks. Making the arrangements last for a long time is typical of her, but she'd rather have had one flower to begin with.

Although we lived nearby on Meridian for 43 years, Sally only visited my wife, Patty, and me twice. She came to see our flowering horse chestnut trees and hollyhocks. We had a beautiful English country garden. Patty had served as president of the Indianapolis Museum of Art's horticultural society and traveled the world to see gardens. Sally came for fifteen minutes but wouldn't come in for a cup of tea. She walked around our yard, saw the plants, and that was it.

Since she gave away so much money, why did she not wish for places to be named after her?

The biggest part of that answer is that Sally was very close to the brothers Eli and J.K. Lilly, with whom her father had worked since 1905. He rose to become the company's vice president. The Lilly brothers had a fairly strong rule about not making gifts with their name on them. For example, Mr. Eli made 16 huge gifts, none of which were "naming opportunities." To Sally, the Lilly brothers provided a model for carefully planning charitable donations and for not doing philanthropy for self-promotion.

When you see this picture of her standing in the water and with her smile, what comes to mind?

Sally was a perky woman. She had a lot of beaus. She liked men better than women, and that was true her entire life.

What were Sally Reahard's values?

I'd say absolute honesty was her biggest value. She did not tolerate fools and phonies. She was not glamorous, nor did she seek to be. For example, you would think that a lady with absolutely unlimited funds would have jewelry. I bought her two little pieces of costume jewelry in Venice for eight or 10 dollars apiece, which she loved. One was a pseudo diamond of about 25 carats. She got a lot of pleasure out of putting it on.

I remember taking Sally a quarterly dividend check from Lilly for $838,000. Her only comment was, "Damn, what shall we do with it?" I said, "Let's go to this fine jewelry store and buy a pin that you can wear," but she wouldn't do it. She liked her little pin from Venice.

What were her special interests? What was her philosophy of philanthropy, Drayton Hall being an example? Was religion a factor in her philanthropy?

Although Sally became a recluse, she was well informed. Friends who kept her up-to-date on what was going on in town and elsewhere. She wanted to be useful and for her philanthropy to make a difference. Towards that end, we came up with a list of 200 possible beneficiaries, which was cut to 65. She left an estate of about $180 million, all disposed of upon her death. The smallest beneficiaries were $371,000 for Meals on Wheels and for Visiting Nurses. All gifts were useful.

One problem was what to do about a charity that could use unlimited funds, and there aren't many of those around. An example of an organization needing unlimited funds is the Nature Conservancy, so Sally left it about $73 million, their largest gift in the U.S. Since Drayton Hall did not need unlimited funds, she gave you an endowment of about $16 million. During the year, special needs did arise. For example, one year when I was in Charleston and had lunch with Connie Wyrick, chairman of your board, I learned that Drayton Hall needed money to balance its budget. Having Miss Sally's power of attorney, I wrote a check for $160,000 to put you in the black since she trusted Drayton Hall's board and you.

Sally was uncertain as to her own feelings about religion and did not let it influence her philanthropy. Although she had been baptized an Episcopalian and was a member of St. Paul's Episcopal Church, I don't think Sally was deeply religious. Religion was one of the subjects we never talked profoundly about. That was her choice. She was not "laying up treasures" some place because she needed to be a "good" woman. Miss Sally did all of her good works purely for philanthropic reasons and to be useful. That was the real joy in working with her because that too is my theory. It's difficult to teach philanthropy.

Why did Sally become a recluse?

I don't know exactly. I have a feeling that Sally's mother did not approve of her leaving the nest. Sally and I never talked about that. I know that she was close to her father and not to her mother. After her mother died, she could have gone out, but she didn't. She was reticent about traveling. The world came to her. I think she saw everybody she wanted to see.

What is a story that illustrates Miss Sally's lifestyle during the time you knew her?

A favorite, which she told me, is, when she was elderly, she drove to the pharmacy and asked her houseman Ralph to ride in the passenger seat and tell her when the traffic lights turned green. She looked across the street to the Shell station and asked, "Ralph, do we need gas?" He got the book out of the glove compartment and said, "Miss Sally, no. We don't need gas." She said, "I got cross with Ralph" and said, "Ralph, I don't remember having gotten gas. When did we get gas?" Ralph says, "A year ago July." "How far have we been?" she asked. He said, "Thirty-seven miles."

Why do you think she loved Charleston?

Charleston was the epitome of the Old South. Sally had lived a couple of years in Virginia at Sweet Briar College, a private girl's college, where she met Charlotte Kent, who married into the Pinckney family of Charleston. Her daughter, Jane Pinckney Hanahan, was chairwoman of your board. Charlotte invited Sally and her mother to Charleston in about 1928, and they loved everything about it.

Throughout her life she continued to be interested in Charleston, taking its newspaper and having a Charleston phone directory. But she never went back. She had gone up the Ashley River and saw Drayton Hall. She liked the house, which was pretty decrepit at that time. She loved the Ashley River too, especially standing at what at one time was Drayton Hall's dock and looking across at the wetlands. When you became director, she saved a lot of those wetlands from development.

Since you were describing her love for Charleston, why was it that she didn't come back?

As a recluse, Sally did not go into downtown Indianapolis after 1957. She wanted to remember it as it was, but wanted to be of help there. Perhaps she had the same feeling about Charleston.

Why do you think she loved Drayton Hall?

Sally liked Palladian architecture, and Drayton Hall was, in her mind, the best example in the United States of Palladian architecture. Sally loved the fact that Drayton Hall had not been changed and had no heating, air conditioning, electricity, or water. Even Charlotta Drayton used an outhouse for years. That was exactly the sort of building Sally loved.

The house was built by slaves, who carved the banisters. Wonderful plasterers made its beautiful ceilings. Sally felt very much that one of the important things that she could do in her life was to preserve this kind of architecture and this particular house.

Could you tell us why she left such a wonderful bequest to Drayton Hall?

Sally felt that Drayton Hall wasn't merely important; it was vital because there is no other building like that. She was impressed that architects from all over the world came to see it. Leaving Drayton Hall an endowment of about $16 million plus the $2 million endowment she'd already established, she felt Drayton Hall was the most important monument she could leave a gift to. Drayton Hall made Sally happy.

What would you like to be your takeaway message about Miss Sally, one that illustrates what people ought to know about her?

Miss Sally's heart was in the right place. She was not selfish in any way. I gave Drayton Hall the rock I gave Sally on which is carved the word "Care." It stood outside her back door. That rock is meaningful because "care" is a word important to me and that I want my grandchildren to know. The difference between a great lawyer and a good lawyer is care. And the difference between a great philanthropist and a giver is care. Sally cared.

Ralph (Bo) Reahard and Stanley Reahard:
"Drayton Hall Was One of Her Projects"

2016 – Summerville, SC

Ralph (Bo) M. Reahard III is a nephew of Drayton Hall benefactress, Sally Reahard, and son of her brother Ralph. He grew up knowing "Miss Sally," as everyone called her, as a beloved aunt. His wife, Stanley Smith Reahard, was born and reared in Summerville, South Carolina, and described "Aunt Sally" perhaps more as an "outside observer" might. Together their recollections shed light on Sally Reahard's values, lifestyle, and the influences upon her philanthropy.

George: *What do you remember about Sally Reahard as a person?*

Ralph Reahard: My earliest memory of her is when my parents and us four children would visit my granddad and her — they lived together — almost every Sunday after church and at Thanksgiving and Christmas. We always had to knock and wait for her to answer the door. Aunt Sally was always excited and had cookies and milk for us. She never forgot our birthdays. For years and years, I got pajamas, a bathrobe, or a tie. When we went off to camp, she wrote us letters. She never forgot.

How did you come to know Miss Sally?

Stanley: Over 40 years ago, I married into the Reahard family. The first time I met Aunt Sally was when Bo and I were dating or engaged. We immediately bonded because of my being from Charleston. She loved Charleston, and we would chat about it. Any time I saw her, she had gathered the latest gossip or maybe newspaper articles about Charleston. If the children were with me, she had tea and cookies and little things she thought would interest them.

Her living room was formal, and she was too. She always wore a dress and little spectator pumps, had her hair done the same way, and was very polite but engaging and fun.

We have boxes of her slides, which are mostly of things, not of people, which may say something. She liked photography and painting. When she was younger, she was pretty, full of punch, and kind of jaunty.

What was Sally Reahard especially interested in?

Bo: Mostly environmental conservation and historic preservation. While she obviously had an interest in the Charleston area, she was active around Indiana and in Leland, Michigan, since our family had been going up there since the mid-1930s. She supported the environmental conservancy and other projects there. As for historic preservation, my grandfather was not engaged in it. It was something Aunt Sally picked up and thoroughly enjoyed.

Tell about your grandfather's association with the Eli Lilly Company and how he influenced your aunt?

Bo: My grandfather grew up in Ohio, went to pharmacy school in Dayton, became a certified pharmacist, and became connected to Eli Lilly. Eli and his brother J.K. started the company near the turn of the century. They hired my grandfather, who moved to Indianapolis and retired as vice president, responsible for marketing and production. He was very formal. Every Sunday when we went over for lunch, he wore a tie. Even on vacation in Michigan, pictures show him wearing a coat and tie.

Aunt Sally and Granddad grew up in the Mid-West, went through the Depression, and were frugal. My grandfather didn't travel. Early on, he was compensated with stock options and accumulated Lilly stock, which was the source of the wealth he transferred to my dad and Aunt Sally. They were more interested in leaving a legacy than spending that money themselves.

With all her wealth, what was Miss Sally like?

Bo: Widely read, Aunt Sally had a broad range of interests and the money to pursue them. She loved nature and had Audubon portfolios in her house. But for some reason, she tended to be a homebody. When her dad died, she could have been footloose and fancy free, but she did not choose to do that. She never married and lived with her parents. After her mom died, she stayed with her dad until he died in 1971. She didn't go to a lot of parties. If she got together with close friends, it was to have tea in the afternoons. I don't remember Sally ever having a drink of alcohol, but we were not there at five o'clock.

Sally Reahard came to Charleston a few times and loved it, had wonderful friends, but didn't return. Do you have any insights as to why?

Stanley: The story Aunt Sally told my mother, who was of the same generation, is that she came to Charleston when she was at Sweet Briar for Christmas parties, and things like that. She had a lot of Charleston friends. One who followed her around was Billy Carter. They spent a good bit of time together, and she was quite smitten. One day when she arrived on the train, Billy met her at the station and told her that he did not want her to hear it from anybody else first: he had asked for Grace Hanahan's hand in marriage. Aunt Sally was heartbroken, and within 24 hours she got on the train, went back to Indianapolis, and never set foot in Charleston again. From what I've heard and experienced with Aunt Sally, once she made up her mind about something, there was no changing it.

Billy Carter's son, Heyward, and his wife, Eleanor, were stationed outside of Indianapolis when they were young. Aunt Sally had kept up with people, including Billy Carter, who told his son, "Be sure and look up Sally Reahard when you're in Indiana." Heyward and Eleanor visited and begged her, "Please come back to Charleston. There are people who love you and who would love to see. You can stay with us. We would love to entertain you." She never did. I don't know if the hurt was that deep or whether by that time in her life, she wasn't traveling.

Could you explain her philosophy and methods of philanthropy?

Bo: Aunt Sally preferred privacy. She was low-key in her giving and everything else in the way that she lived, I don't think many people knew the fortune she had. After she died, a reporter with the Indianapolis Star wrote a story about the "unknown philanthropist" of Indianapolis, outlining all the money she had given away. When my niece saw the story, she called her dad, absolutely shocked: "What the heck! Aunt Sally had that much money to give away!"

Aunt Sally researched the organizations she gave money to. If a project interested her, she opened her checkbook and did something significant. If not, she didn't. For her whole life, Sally had a legal firm in Indianapolis that she worked with, the same one my dad used, and probably my grandfather too, because they tended to stick together. We understand that legal firm had an attorney who had one client, Sally Reahard. Every Wednesday afternoon at two or three o'clock, she would have tea ready, and they would sit in her dining room, go over their papers, and decide what they were going to research or support that week.

What made her mad? What didn't she like?

Bo: Aunt Sally was not happy with me when I had very long hair. And I think she was pretty disappointed when Frances Edmunds, the Charleston preservationist, dropped her. She declared, "Frances won't communicate with me anymore!" I know that hurt her feelings. At the same time, Sally could be pretty demanding of your time.

Did you ever hear from her why she liked Drayton Hall?

Bo: She never told us anything other than Drayton Hall was one of her projects. I have no idea how she got connected. I simply thought it was another one of her Charleston projects. Frankly, I didn't really know much about Drayton Hall until we moved down here and came to visit a number of times.

What stories might you tell that paint a picture of Sally Reahard as a real person?

Bo: Aunt Sally had a great appreciation for family. She was very fond of my father and was always very, very good to us. Very generous. I think her example of philanthropy is something that will be passed on. While we don't have the funds she had, giving is something we've always encouraged in our children as well.

Another story is that Aunt Sally had decided that making a left-hand turn was too dangerous; it was safer to stay on the right-hand side of the road and only make right-hand turns. You'd never have to cross oncoming traffic. When she went out driving or had someone drive her, she made sure to have right-hand turns to get there. She would figure out a route from home and a route to get back with all right-hand turns. She might go five miles out of her way, but who cares? It was safe.

After my grandmother died, my grandfather and Aunt Sally had a modest, one-story brick house built in the early 1960s a short distance from the larger house where Sally had grown up. She had antiques, and perhaps it was a Thomas Elf secretary from Charleston that she gave to her niece, my sister Joan, who lived in historic Philadelphia. After Sally's death in 2003, Joan helped to manage Sally's estate and worked with the appraiser, who assessed the value of everything in the house. In the garage was her old 1970s car. They came up with a total value of $13,000 for the household goods. She'd given much away, but that shows how frugally she and my grandfather lived. It's just what they did.

Stanley: Another story is she gave money to St. Vincent's Hospital in Indianapolis to build four suites for patients needing longer term care. She thought hospital rooms were dreary and patients needed a sitting room and things like that. Although she'd never have said so, maybe she thought she might be there someday. After she broke her hip when she was in her 90s, she was afraid to go back home and stayed in one. They couldn't get her out. She pretty well told them, "No, I'm not going!"

That's the last place we saw her. She had the cutest haircut because she didn't have anybody to do her hair the way she had always kept it. Somebody gave her a pixie, but if you complimented her on it, she would not respond because she didn't like it. She liked her hair the way it was for 50 years.

I had to laugh the other day because I had not signed up for the luncheon at Drayton Hall since I didn't know if I was going to be in town. I called that morning and asked, "Do you have a spot available?" A sweet young lady replied, "Yes, we do. We have a spot at somebody or other's table." I said, "Good. I'd love to take it." She said, "How do you spell your last name?" I said, "Kind of like Sally Reahard." She goes, "Yeah, I thought that was what you said. Okay. I got it." It's nice to float along on Aunt Sally's coattails. We miss her. She had lots of energy. Wonderful coattails!

Bill Weeks Describing Sally Reahard:
"An Extraordinary Person"

2015 – Indianapolis, IN

Bill Weeks is Professor Emeritus and the Scolnik Chair in Conservation Law at Indiana University's Maurer School of Law. In 1982 he became the second state director of the Nature Conservancy in Indiana, headquartered in Indianapolis, and for years worked with the Nature Conservancy in Washington. He and Sally Reahard were friends. Who was this lady who made such a difference in Drayton Hall's recent history? Bill Weeks gives insights.

George: *What was Sally Reahard like when you first met her in 1982 and as you came to know her over the years?*
Bill: When I first met her, she was as gracious as could be. Since I was a new director of the Indiana Nature Conservancy, an organization important to her, I knew she was assessing me. But she was careful to make me comfortable. Innately attuned to nature, she possessed a keen sense of responsibility. She was constantly aware that her resources could be traced to the success of Eli Lilly and Company, and she thought about that and the example the Lillys set. I'm not saying she tried to pattern herself after them exactly, but she was very conscious of them.

With its modest house, her property reflected her values. For example, she had a larger than usual lot — but not huge — with little areas where she kept wildflowers so birds could use them. Such places reflected her interest in nature and her idea of stewardship. She had no interest in ostentation with respect to her resources. Her property was nice, comfortable, and conveniently located, but wasn't designed to make a statement about her wealth.

As a major donor to local and national organizations, what influences shaped her values?
Certainly, her father was important, for she talked about him regularly. Her

education at Sweet Briar College made her worldlier than you might think and colored her view of who she was and her relationship to the world and to other people. The Lilly heritage meant a lot, for they, too, were interested in nature and historic preservation. Their early support for the Nature Conservancy influenced her.

She was aware that her fortune came from someplace else and believed she had a responsibility for its stewardship. To her, stewardship meant using her money wisely and prudently and not flaunting it. It meant being careful with her investments, and I'm not talking simply about financial investments, but also charitable investments. It meant finding out if something, whether it's a corporation or a non-profit, was going to be a good investment or not, and also seeing what the management structure was.

What attracted Sally Reahard to Drayton Hall?

As she looked back on her life, Charleston represented a time and experience that were important, and Drayton Hall was most important. While it was associated with her Charleston experiences, Drayton Hall reached back to a time she was very interested in. She was far too sophisticated to wax romantic about its past, but there was something about the way of life, the landscape, and the culture that extended beyond her personal experience. The fact that it had survived for so long was important to her and became one of the reasons she was committed to its continued survival and thriving.

Her own house reflected her values. You couldn't visit without seeing a model of Drayton Hall, at least a small one. We talked about Drayton Hall projects she was involved with, such as this renovation or that landscape issue, or the last hurricane and how Drayton Hall survived it. We'd talk about conservation along the Ashley River. What came through was her admiration for Drayton Hall and her hopes for it. I think the reason for those hopes is connected to the intangible things I mentioned before.

Every improvement contemplated at Drayton Hall interested her — whether it should happen, how it was going to happen, and when. Also important were plans for the public to experience the site, even traffic patterns or tour routes through the house. She thought about them. Her discussions illustrated her desire for good stewardship.

Why did she not return to Charleston and visit Drayton Hall?

Both Charleston and Drayton Hall were so important to her. Everybody changes over time. One might think that she'd like to revisit them when older and see if things that had impressed her still did. The best answer about why Sally didn't travel back to Charleston is that the earlier phase of her life was done. She was doing something else. Everyone who grows older sees things happen that are undesirable, or they get into situations they are not familiar with. It's not that she was scared to leave her house or Indianapolis. By the time I knew her, those decisions were settled. She had done the traveling she wanted to do. She was home. Her support structure was sound. She didn't have extraordinary needs, but everyone appreciates a support structure. It's as if she no longer asked herself that question.

Since we all have feet of clay, what were some of hers?

Sally's world experience was limited. She had a limited number of people she saw and had been influenced by many things decades before. For example, when the notion of women as managers or as non-profit leaders developed, Sally Reahard was dead set against it. This was well past the time when most people were happy to have women managers. Having said that, Sally Reahard was open enough to reassess even when she was in her 70s and 80s. As with anyone, certain things in our minds we think are settled, and we're glad not to have to agonize about them anymore. She had lots of those things, and they made her comfortable. Change makes people uncomfortable. It made her uncomfortable. But on balance, she was able to accommodate it.

What do these pictures of Sally Reahard tell you about her?

You've given me one picture of Sally Reahard as I saw her many, many times, one in her yard in her elderly age when I knew her, and another where she is standing with her feet in a lake as a young woman. I see the same person, not a different person. You can see the 50 years difference in age, but she is smiling in both. What I see behind the eyes is the same person. The person standing with her pants rolled up in the water is the same person in a dress, sitting in her front yard — smiling.

What are your takeaway messages about Sally Reahard?

Most important is that she was an extraordinary person and extraordinarily generous. Most people of wealth try to decide what kind of legacy to leave. Sally Reahard had decided a long, long time ago that half of her wealth would go to charity. That decision was not reached casually, but it was settled. Does it mean she wasn't concerned about her family? No. She was very concerned about that. She talked about her family all the time, but her decision reflected her sense of stewardship, which was a motivating force for the time she spent on the business side of her life. When I say the business side, I mean the management, or stewardship, of her fortune, both as investments and as philanthropies. It was more than generosity. It was her commitment to stewardship that was extraordinary.

What are your closing thoughts?
It's been a pleasure to talk about Sally Reahard and for you to preserve accounts of her. She was extraordinary. We often don't take the trouble to make sure such people are remembered. I appreciate your asking me about her so that she won't fall into that void of forgetfulness and will be remembered.

Donald and Katherine Willing– Reflections on Sally Reahard:
"A Gift"
2015 – Indianapolis, IN

Don and Katherine Willing, who lived in Indianapolis, were dear friends of Sally Reahard from their first meeting in the mid-1970s until her death in 2003. In their interview, they describe why Sally Reahard loved Drayton Hall, including a story about why she gave the lead donation to secure Drayton Hall as a National Trust site. All of their stories shed light on who Sally Reahard was as a person and why they saw her as a "gift."

How did you meet Sally Reahard, and what were your thoughts afterward?

Don: I first met Sally when her dad passed away in the middle '70s because I represented Indiana National Bank, the executor of her dad's estate. We connected immediately. We had common interests for we were both nature lovers and liked the forest, wildlife, and birds. While we talked about business, our common interests are what led to our friendship of 25 years or so. During the last several years of his life, she had been the caregiver and companion of her father, a widower, and had a close relationship with him. I got the picture that she was closer to her dad than to her mom

Kathy: Through Don, I got to know Sally and found her to be a lovely, gracious lady. She'd invite me to her home, and sometimes, I'd bring the children, whom she liked. Sally, or "Miss Sally" as everyone called her, was one of the brightest women. She was friendly and laughed and made jokes about herself. She asked questions. She wanted to know what you were thinking and was well-informed. Whenever I'd walk in the door, she'd give me a hug and a kiss and had the brightest smile and the brightest eyes.

How did Sally Reahard describe her first visit to Drayton Hall in the 1930s? Decades later, why did she donate to acquire Drayton Hall from the Drayton family?

Kathy: Miss Sally's first trip to Charleston was in 1934, when she was 26, and it was pivotal. Since her father had been sick with pneumonia, her mother decided in early March that they needed to go to Charleston, where it was warmer. Arriving by train on a warm night in her winter clothes, Sally recalled looking at the houses and the palm trees and then turned the corner and saw the harbor. She said, "I was hooked." Since her brother had measles and her father remained ill, Sally and her mother rented a car and drove to see Drayton Hall since someone they'd met at the hotel had recommended they do so. At that time, Drayton Hall was a private home, but the caretaker told them, "Please come in. You're welcome to look around." Sally said when she walked into the house, she felt like she had stepped into a dream from the past. That's exactly when she fell in love with Drayton Hall.

Afterward, Sally had little involvement until the early 1970s, when she read something that said Drayton Hall was for sale, so she stepped in. She'd never forgotten it. She said she responded with both excitement and fear, because she wanted to make sure that it could be kept. She wrote Peter Manigault, who was a trustee of the National Trust at that time and who lived in Charleston. She didn't know Peter but knew that was where she needed to start in order to make something happen. She also talked to James Biddle, president of the National Trust, and he encouraged her. In collaboration with other groups, she donated the money to buy the house for six hundred and something thousand dollars. That was the beginning of it. But only the beginning as we know.

Why did Sally Reahard remain interested in Drayton Hall?

Drayton Hall was a reflection of Sally Reahard whenever she took on a project. She was interested in every phase of it. Not just the building, but the people who were there, what was going on, and how she could help it become a high-caliber museum that people would want to visit and then have the same feelings she had when she visited it.

Sally had many interests, but at the forefront was history. She'd fallen in love with Charleston. It was almost a romance, and subsequently she fell in love with Drayton Hall. Sally went to Charleston seven times. From her college days at Sweet Briar, she had good friends there and enjoyed being with them, but she did not go after 1940. She preferred to have her friends here and in Charleston to be her eyes while she remembered Charleston as it was. However, she had this little red book, which was a walking tour of Charleston, and whenever Don and I went, we literally went through the whole book with her.

Did she tell you what her hopes were for Drayton Hall?

Kathy: Her hope was to make sure that Drayton Hall was of museum quality. She wanted to see it preserved as is and protected from encroachment, which is why she did many things donors do not do, like supporting archaeology or protecting the river and making sure the land across the river didn't get developed. She wanted Drayton Hall to be something that people could appreciate just as she had.

Could you describe Sally Reahard as a donor to Drayton Hall and other non-profits?

Kathy: Sally did not want her name on her donations' accomplishments. In the attic, which had stairs leading to it, her various projects lined each side of the aisle in the center. Always immersed in them, she had projects going everywhere.

We all have our idiosyncrasies. What were Sally Reahard's?

Kathy: Despite the pots of tea that she prepared and consumed, she ate no sugar. Even when she offered cookies for everyone who came to her house, she would encourage you to take them and then say, "I'll have some later."

Don: Looking at that picture of her standing in the water with her pants rolled up reminds me that Sally had told me she's had lots of beaus, even serious ones. She was so attractive. In that picture, she's young, beautiful. One day she told me why she had never married: her mother had never approved of any of her beaus enough for her to marry them. I thought that was a sad chapter in her life, and I think she thought she'd missed something.

Looking at this picture of Sally Reahard in her front yard, what words come to mind?

Kathy: Look at her wonderful smile.

Don: It's her terrific smile and her bright eyes, and the way she turned her head. You can almost see how smart she was. She's paying attention.

Do you have stories that illustrate how much Drayton Hall meant to Sally Reahard?

Don: During one of our visits to Drayton Hall in the early '90s, we were walking towards the Ashley, and Kathy picked up a pinecone and some nuts and leaves, maybe from a live oak. We gave them to Sally. You would have thought we'd brought a golden carriage. She set them on the hearth beside her fireplace. She said we could have not brought her anything better than those natural things, which fit in with her love of nature and her love of Drayton Hall. Everyone who visited Drayton Hall tried to think of something, as we did, to bring her, generally from the gift shop. But this absolutely was the best gift anybody could have brought her. It touched her. They sat there for as long as I can remember, kind of like a little nest.

What is the first word you think of when somebody says "Sally Reahard"?

Kathy: Treasured friend.

Don: I agree.

Kathy: We don't really think about her money. We think about a treasured friend. She shared herself with all the things that were important. She was a gift.

Paul Wenker:
"She Was Happy She Did It."
2015 – Cincinnati, Ohio

Paul Wenker, Trustee of the Robert A. and Marian K. Kennedy Foundation, was the attorney for Marian (Madge) Kennedy, advising her on financial affairs. Across the Ashley River from Drayton Hall was forested land, whose owner had no interest in easements but in September 1994 he offered me an option to buy the land by the end of the year. I accepted. Since Drayton Hall did not have the money and no funds were offered by the National Trust, Madge Kennedy stepped forward, as described in Paul's first-hand account. Thanks to her, visitors do not see condos across the river or hear the cacophony that apartments produce, but instead see marsh and forests. In thanks, we built the Robert A. Kennedy Memorial Library in memory of her husband, which may be seen today along with the scenic view across the Ashley.

Paul, could you describe what your relationship was to Madge and Bob Kennedy?

Marian, or rather Madge, and Bob lived in Cincinnati all their life. Since Madge was an interior decorator, my father worked for her often as a house painter, interior and exterior, and would say, "Oh, we have to go over to Mrs. Kennedy's house for this or that." I really got to know her when as a young attorney at Rendigs, Fry, Kiely and Dennis, where I still work as an attorney, I started doing her and Bob's tax returns and estate planning, beginning in 1976 or '77. For over thirty-five years, I handled their affairs.

When she "did" my office, she made it fun because she knew how to use colors. Some of my partners would say, "Why are all these colors in there?" but they all blended. For example, she had a paisley and a stripe. People said, "You can't do that." But she did, and it looked wonderful. Because of her, my office became a place where people enjoyed sitting down and getting comfortable.

Her maiden name was Marion Elizabeth Klick, born in August 1906. Her family was upper middle class. She attended the University of Cincinnati and studied decorative arts, where she met Bob, who graduated in 1930 from the University of Cincinnati School of Architecture. They married in 1931 and were a perfect match — she in decorative arts and he in architecture.

What was Madge like as a person?

I think an apt description of Madge Kennedy is that she was a Southern belle who was born and raised in Cincinnati, Ohio. When I met her in 1976, she was about five foot two, fairly slight, white hair, very prim and proper. Whenever she went out, she always wore a skirt and a jacket with gloves and a hat and carried a purse. You couldn't help but like her. She was opinionated. What she liked and what she didn't like, she'd let you know. She wanted things done a certain way, and she was going to get it done that way.

Why do you think she and Bob liked historic preservation so much?

Historic preservation to her and Bob was vital. They loved traveling, but rather than use the interstates, they drove the back roads for two to three weeks at a time, visiting historical towns and places. I can imagine they would walk up to the home, knock on the front door, and ask politely if they might come in. That's the way Madge was. And that's the way Bob was—such a gentleman. They loved to explore many areas of the United States, especially the South.

Bob was primarily a restoration architect. He restored the Museum Center in Maysville and added to it. While he built some houses, he did a lot of additions to beautiful mansions. Using his knowledge and skills, he blended in any addition so that it didn't interfere with the architecture and established lines of the home so you wouldn't know it had been added.

In reflecting on Madge Kennedy, what are some takeaway messages you'd like people to know?

A takeaway for Madge was that she loved the South. She loved the whole South and what it stood for and its history. I sometimes would say that I think she would have loved to have been born in the antebellum South of the 1820s or 1830s. The one thing I always thought about Madge was that she was born 100 years too late. She would have loved that period of time. She knew more about the South than anybody else I ever knew. The other thing was that she was passionate about her decorating. She loved colors. She loved fine things. She loved to read and bought books not for decoration but to read them. Her house was a museum. She was set in her ways. She knew what she wanted but was always kind.

I can tell stories about her. She was doing decorating jobs until she was almost ninety-five and still had clients coming to her. For a long time, she had a car called "Ready Eddie," a 1984 Plymouth station wagon that she drove to South Carolina every year when she went down to Georgetown and Drayton Hall. I handled her legal and financial work and visited her on a regular basis, but I did not travel with her. When she could no longer drive (about 1999/2000), I had a friend of mine drive her everywhere. He said it was like "Driving Miss Daisy." She would sit there and tell him, "Do this. Go here. Do that." But the places were always interesting, and later, fascinating to hear about. I regret I didn't get to do that. She was a good client and a good friend. It's important to say that I enjoyed working for her.

Why did Madge and Bob come to love Drayton Hall?

I think Bob admired its Palladian architecture and just its atmosphere. The site was the preservation of a building, nothing else. Since Bob was into restoration, it was important to him, and Madge took it upon herself to continue that. She would talk about the Palladian style of architecture and Drayton Hall as "a perfect example." The setting too was wonderful for her — right outside Charleston on the Ashley River. It was a pristine place. I'm sure that even before the Trust acquired the property, they visited Drayton Hall. They often went to National Trust conferences and loved being able to visit historical places. When the Trust had its conference in Charleston in 1970, I think they were there for the tours at Drayton Hall. They probably contributed to its purchase from the Drayton family.

Why did Madge want the library built at Drayton Hall in memory of her husband?

Madge wanted to have the Robert F. Kennedy Library built at Drayton Hall because first and foremost, Bob was an architect. Second, they loved the Palladian style of architecture and so she chose the interior of Drayton Hall as the model for the library's interior. And third, because of his untimely death, I think she wanted to do something in Bob's honor and memory. They never had children. As both were the only children of their parents, they didn't have anybody else other than each other.

She talked about Shadows-on-the-Teche in Louisiana, but more about Drayton Hall. Those were her two favorite places, and when you think about it, they're very different. Shadows is a museum that has decorative arts. Drayton is the building, the architecture. I could see that of the two, she would say, "Palladian architecture, Drayton Hall. Husband, architect! That's where I want to put the library."

I think the opportunity for the library came after your campaign, George, to buy the land across the Ashley River and your persuading Madge to assist in purchasing that first tract of 27 acres. After that vacant land across the river from Drayton Hall was acquired, Drayton Hall and the National Trust said, "We want to build this library for you, Madge." While she participated in the design, she mostly left it to the architect, Jim Thomas, but said, "I want to decorate the library." She purchased all the furniture and fabric, chose the colors, and had that wonderful eagle carved by a wood carver in Cincinnati. She was at his place at least once or twice a week, making sure it was exactly what she wanted.

Madge was devastated when Bob died suddenly. They were devoted to each other. They did everything together. Bob was such a gentleman. I never heard a harsh word from him. He was level-headed, knew what he was about, and was devoted to Madge. In 1979, when he was seventy-two, he died of the flu. He was okay one day, and then dead within two or three days. That's the one thing she felt sadness about in her life. Bob was not there to enjoy the things she did. After he died, she talked to me about that, "I really miss Bob. I don't know why I'm still alive." Twenty-three years is a long time to be without somebody you loved. They were a great couple. But she kept going and was determined to have that library for him.

What do you think prompted her to respond so quickly to our need to buy the land across the river from us?

In connection with purchasing the property across the river, she called me one day and said, "Paul, we've got to do something." I said, "What's wrong, Madge." She said, "Well, the property across the Ashley River from Drayton Hall, they're going to build condominiums there. When you look over the Ashley River, you're going to see buildings and the view will not look good. What can we do about it?" I said, "Well, what did they ask you?" She said, "They need donations because the developer said he would sell it to Drayton Hall at a certain price." I said, "How much?" She said "Three hundred and fifty thousand. What can we do?" I said, "Madge, you can do that. You have sufficient assets to purchase the property." "Do you think I can?" I said, "You have all the Proctor and Gamble stock that you've gotten from your parents and that you and Bob invested. We can give them about three thousand or so shares and that would be more than enough for them to purchase the land." "Well, can you contact them?" And I said, "Sure. Madge. It's the best thing in the world to do." And so she did it.

I called you, George, and we worked out a charitable gift annuity so Drayton Hall could buy the land. While still providing income for Madge, her gift saved your viewshed, preserved the area around the site, protected the Ashley, and provided green space for North Charleston and habitat for flora and fauna far into the future. It was a win/win for everybody. She was happy she did it.

Esther Beaumont:
"Drayton Hall Speaks to Me"

2020 – Telephone interview

A native of Charleston, Esther Beaumont graduated from Tufts University, worked for the Central Intelligence Agency and the U.S State Department, and was stationed in Africa, Asia, South America, and Europe. A widow, she retired to northern Virginia and began to visit Drayton Hall regularly. It is thanks to her generosity that the George W. McDaniel Education Center was built. She explains why she cares about Drayton Hall and its preservation and education programs, and reflects on how Drayton Hall offers "a way through the hustle and bustle of Charleston's tourism."

What is your connection to Charleston and to Drayton Hall?

I was born in Charleston, but according to old-time Charlestonians, that does not make you a Charlestonian. Your family has to go back many generations. One of my earliest memories is being taken to White Point Garden by our maid when I was about three years old, and older women looking at me and saying, "Who are your people?" I remember thinking, "Well, my mommy is my mommy, and my daddy is my daddy." But any proper Charleston girl would know to say, "My mother was a Lucas and my paternal grandparents were Buist." It was like dog breeding, "I was whelped out of so-and-so by so-and-so."

I came to be in Charleston because this location was an opportunity for my father. Born in Oklahoma in 1903, he grew up there and pursued a medical profession at Johns Hopkins, his family having been from Baltimore. When the Medical University of South Carolina in Charleston lost its orthopedics professor, my father accepted the appointment. While I might regard myself as a Charlestonian, old Charlestonians consider me as somebody "from Off."

While I was still an infant, my mother learned that the local public elementary school had an outdoor privy for students. She was horrified. She looked for a school that offered indoor toilets for her daughter and selected Ashley Hall, a girls' school founded in 1909. So I got to mix with the elite of Charleston society without knowing anything about elite society.

My father built a house at 90 Murray Boulevard. We were free-range children, and nobody was very concerned about what we were up to. While I was too young to pedal a bicycle, I did walk around by myself or sometimes with a maid and my younger brother. We went to White Point Garden to exercise for the day. Later, I got a bicycle and pedaled up back streets and via Smith Street to Ashley Hall. I got my driver's license at age 14 and proposed to my father that since my mother did not drive, he could get an extra car and I'd take her grocery shopping. He saw through that, but I managed to get a car to drive myself and friends to school. I was a lucky young lady.

What was your career, and what led you back to Charleston?

I went to Tufts University because it met specific criteria: it was co-educational, offered cultural opportunities, and had snow. I majored in history and later interviewed with a mysterious agency that promised work overseas. It was the Central Intelligence Agency, and my first station was with the Consulate General in Tangier, Morocco. American ex-patriates and people from foreign countries were there. I was fulfilling my dream.

Later, I switched to the U.S. Army Library Service. In Korea I met an Army officer, whom I married and who later died from complications of a stroke. I worked for the U.S. Information Agency in Brazil, Indonesia, Zimbabwe, and Tunisia. After being assigned to Washington, D.C. and retiring, I returned to Charleston, bought a "time share," and invited friends to join me. Although they'd seen the world, they hadn't seen Charleston. You haven't lived until you've seen Charleston.

What did you think of Drayton Hall?

When I was growing up in Charleston, Drayton Hall wasn't on my radar. Many years later, when entertaining guests in Charleston, I said, "Here's a place I've never been to. Let's go to Drayton Hall." I saw it and was hooked. Drayton Hall has a unique quality that distinguishes itself from reconstructed Williamsburg. It is the original building with much of its original design. Changes in fashion had not transformed it, and I appreciated that. I thought, 'This really needs to be supported," and that's why it became the place to take my friends.

Why did you become more interested in Drayton Hall?

I was intrigued by its preservation programs: how you do paint sampling, examine the basement, the staircases, the roofing — the real bones of the building and how it's put together. It's an architectural discovery tour. It's not the superficial aesthetics you see with your eyes alone. You have to explore it critically. Drayton Hall speaks to me because it has stood for so long, and I want to be sure it continues to stand.

Its preservation philosophy sets it apart as does the fact they want to keep it as it is, and not to suddenly say, "The height of its style was such and such a certain year, so we'll repaint it to that year." The glory of Drayton Hall is that what you see is what you get. It could serve as a setting for virtual reality tours, in which visitors could select any year and see how Drayton Hall appeared in that year, all without changing the house they are touring.

Why are the environs of Drayton Hall important?

Drayton Hall is an exquisite gem that requires a worthy setting. You can't just put a fence around it and say, "We have this little sparkling thing over here." If you don't have the context for its existence, you don't have anything. Many years ago, they sought to maintain the original view across the Ashley River because if apartment buildings were built over there, it would have diminished Drayton Hall. You have to set your sights on a larger canvas to keep this jewel.

How might a historic place like Drayton Hall help address contemporary issues?

It might address issues like climate change and how to improve the environment for the present and the future. Its incoming tide from the east and fresh water from the west could be used to monitor pollution, global warming, seawater rise, and coastal flooding. Drayton Hall could show what can be done to halt degradation and improve the environment.

What structure, place, or object speaks to you at Drayton Hall?

The house and the ruin of an orangery is intriguing, but if walls could talk, it's the outdoor privy. I'm a historian and know a lot about the Roman Empire and the bath facilities and social interchange of that period. When the ladies got together after a social event, and were letting their hair down and other things too, to listen in on their conversations would have been fun. A drawing of the privy at Drayton Hall shows how it looked, and I was struck by the fact that it was a communal gathering place with adult-height and child-height seats. You can imagine families gathering informally in the privy. It's the one place that would assure you of absolute privacy. I think the privy has much to commend it.

What led you to donate to Drayton Hall and to name the educational building the George W. McDaniel Education Center?

I believe in giving money when alive and seeing how it's used. So I told you, George, when you were about to retire that I wanted to do something. We chatted about the possibilities of building a simple structure where school groups and regular visitors could gather and participate in programs. That segued into discussions about having a visitors' complex, which had been a goal for years. I said, "Well, why not?" I liked the Kennedy Library, a charming Georgian recreation that fit.

I chose to make major gifts to Ashley Hall and to Drayton Hall because they are locally based and part of my childhood in Charleston. I liked the design for Drayton Hall's visitors' center with exhibits, educational spaces, gift shop, and restrooms, all incorporated around a large live oak and garden. The center offers visitors a background in history and inspires support. Drayton Hall is educational and needed an educational building. Since I knew you, George, not the Draytons or others, I wanted it named after you.

How do you think technology and the experience of place affect education?

As we move further into technology and virtual reality, the experience of a place like Drayton Hall can bring visitors back to reality. I do see the positive things about virtual reality because you can show how different things that visitors see at Drayton Hall have evolved. For example, John Drayton was a man of his time, highly educated with great interests, so why not tap into the things he knew as a base, such as architecture, and move forward? On the other hand, getting out of the classroom and using Drayton Hall as a venue for education is critical. Students learn about simple things like the joy of archaeology, what pot shards can tell you, and the construction techniques of furniture. Let's find out how to spark interest.

Drayton Hall could also use history to link people together. It could show that if you're an American, unless you're a Native American, you're an immigrant from someplace else. Wherever people came from, even if you were enslaved from Africa, we have all become a part of the same world. As individuals, we can learn from each other and benefit by working for common goals. That's what America is all about.

How has Drayton Hall touched your life? What is your hope for it?

Drayton Hall has enhanced my opportunity to share the Charleston experience with friends "from Off." It's a highlight of everybody's visit. When you're in downtown Charleston's hurly-whirly of tourists and shopping and looking at buildings from the outside, you don't get that sense of tranquility available at Drayton Hall. You can bond with nature and with history and go beyond the typical hustle and bustle of Charleston's tourism. It's like what happened with Mount Vernon. It's a protected slip of land on the Potomac River today. My hope is that Drayton Hall on the Ashley River near Charleston, South Carolina, will have a status similar to Mount Vernon's.

Steve Gates:
"A Focal Point for the Sweep of History"

2015 – Drayton Hall

When this interview was conducted, attorney Steve Gates was chairman of Drayton Hall's Site Advisory Council. He helped form and later served on the Board of Trustees of the new Drayton Hall Preservation Trust, its first chairman. He and his wife, Laura, moved to Charleston in 1999, where his skills, intellect, and wry sense of humor soon enabled him to become a leader in preservation, conservation, and libraries. A few years ago, he suddenly passed away, leaving a void felt by many.

What is your background that led you to Charleston?

Steve: I was born in Florida, but my great-great-grandfathers were from South Carolina near Camden and moved prior to the Civil War to Georgia. Bankrupted by the war, they moved to Florida around 1880. My father was born there. I went to Yale for college and Harvard for law school and have spent most of my professional life in Chicago. When living in London in 1999, my wife, Laura, and I came to

Charleston, thinking about buying a house here later. But within 90 days we bought one here. The combination of Charleston's history, architecture, ambiance, walkability, food, and weather made it the perfect spot, and we've been here ever since.

When you saw Drayton Hall for the first time, what was your reaction?

When we came to Charleston, Drayton Hall was high on the list. We were smitten and have maintained an association either through membership or, more recently, active engagement. Three aspects struck me. When you drive up, there's the house, an icon of architectural symmetry and pleasing proportions that registers immediately as something unique. Second, the site, including the river, establishes a sense of place. It strikes you as something appealing, comfortable, and attractive, a place you want to visit as often as you can. Third, once you get to know Drayton Hall, you see it manifests the sweep of history. Here we are in 2015, and knowing John Drayton was born in 1715, we have the sweep of 300 years of American history played out on and all around this one spot. Drayton Hall gives you a sense of participation in that sweep.

What led you to become personally involved in Drayton Hall?

I became involved after becoming friends with people around town, several of whom had served on Drayton Hall's Site Council. Having an interest in it as a National Trust property, enjoying history, and knowing people who were on the council, I accepted the offer to join it.

What are your aspirations for Drayton Hall?

To greatly enhance the visitor's experience. The decision has been made, with which I concur, not to restore the site to a particular period of time. We can enhance the visitor's experience through more programming, upgraded facilities, and attention to things other than just the house that over the decades we've not been able to give top priority. We've had to limit the number of visitors who go inside the house, and without an interpretive center, we could not exhibit artifacts that help tell the story.

To achieve those aspirations, two things need to happen. First is the change in governance, which happened recently when Anthony C. Wood, George McDaniel, and I — after working for several years — got co-stewardship governance for Drayton Hall whereby Drayton Hall continues to be owned by the National Trust, but its management is leased to a separate non-profit, the Drayton Hall

Preservation Trust, whose board makes strategic and operating decisions. It's fine to have an advisory council, but advisors are different from fiduciaries, as I think the Trust realized.

The second step was designing, from a board perspective, the future of Drayton Hall and get it on a path of sustained financial stability. If we're going to undertake additional staffing, more programming, and new facilities, we needed a business plan that shows how our investments enhance the experience to the extent increased revenues reflect value. To have more people come more often for more and different purposes is a model we're going to soon develop.

To ensure the future success of Drayton Hall, it is my responsibility as chairman of the board to continue to attract the best possible members to serve on the board, people committed to and wanting to contribute to the success of Drayton Hall — the house, the collections, site interpretation, and marketing. We need board members who have fundraising skills to keep us on a financially sound basis and who can contribute to our strategic planning. It's also my job to make sure Drayton Hall moves forward at the same pace. Following George McDaniel's 26 years, we selected Carter Hudgins as executive director, whose staff is cohesive and feels the independence our new governance allows.

How has Drayton Hall affected you?

Drayton Hall affects me and has potential to affect others by providing an experience through which to view history. It's one thing to read about events that happened in a broad area over a number of years, but to see how they had impact on a specific location, family, or enslaved people. Personally, Drayton Hall is a focal point for my interest in history and architecture. While those may be general subjects, if you key your reading or your travel to a particular subject, it's easier to put things in context. For example, Drayton Hall sponsors trips. A trip to the Veneto region of Italy to see Palladian villas puts the imagination that created Drayton Hall into wider perspective, and you see the influences that caused it to happen.

Why not restore Drayton Hall to its 18th-century glory?

If Drayton Hall were restored to its 18th-century glory, it would lose a couple of things. One is authenticity, for there would be the temptation to furnish it and install air-conditioning, heating, and humidity control, which require electricity. None of that ever existed at Drayton Hall. It reflects a house built over 250 years ago that changed somewhat over the centuries due to its residents' choices, but was never modernized or even had plumbing. This is unique in America and in preservation efforts. To periodize it would result in a structure that only represents, say, pre-Revolutionary War America and ignore the fact that it was something different during the Civil War and something different from that when acquired by the National Trust in 1974. To pick one period to restore it to would alter the whole experience.

Also, since Drayton Hall can interpret the sweep of history, visitors of the future can pick from a variety of offerings, depending on the docents, their own interests, or the length of time they have. Different periods or topics could be a focus, describing how the site's appearance, uses, and activities changed from decade to decade.

Why should Drayton Hall care about what happens beyond its property lines along the Ashley River and the Ashley River Road?

Growth is coming at Drayton Hall from all directions. Driving out Ashley River Road today, you can still experience country appeal and charm before you turn into the driveway, and you feel as if you are entering a different place. In the future, it's important that this not be a site that is a surprise once you turn in the driveway but that visitors sense something historical as they proceed along the Ashley River Road. The same is true for the riverfront. It's important that visitors experience the site without the noise of jet skis or the sight across the river of housing developments or docks.

Over the last 25 or 30 years, Drayton Hall has successfully protected the site's environs, but it didn't happen by accident. Drayton Hall took on those challenges and argued for the protection of not just the view across the Ashley but of the environs beyond the viewshed, arguing it's all part of an experience that appeals to people. Those wanting to explore history shouldn't have that jarring effect of turning from over-developed sprawl directly into a smaller protected place.

How does Drayton Hall contribute to Charleston's economy, quality of life, and schools? What difference does Drayton Hall make in the larger Charleston community?

It has a great impact on the larger Charleston area. Tourism is a major business because people want not only to look, eat, or drink, but also to learn, and there is a great deal to be learned about history and preservation here. Attracting such tourists, Drayton Hall contributes to the economy. Offering educational experiences for schools, Drayton Hall and other museums offer experiences students carry with them more than just a day in the classroom would. By offering the opportunity to choose a program or a period to learn about, maybe even to pick two periods and learn more, Drayton Hall is a wonderful asset to education.

How do you think that Drayton Hall and other cultural organizations together contribute to the decision of significant leaders like yourself to choose Charleston as a place to live?

Over the last 15 years, we've seen Charleston attract newcomers of all ages who find it appealing due to the weather, quality of life of the entire Lowcountry, the walkability of Charleston, and the food. Compared to 15 years ago, the number of young people under 40 who have decided to make this their home is a testament to the appeal. To what is that quality of life attributable? It's access not just to open air, open land, beautiful scenery, but also the ability to take advantage of local institutions that are here year in and year out that deserve visits. People take pride in taking their visitors to see them, and I think Drayton Hall is at the top of that list. Being able to take friends and family to visit such places, to use what you've learned during multiple visits, and to support their organizations, all contribute to the charm of living in Charleston.

What are your favorite memories of Drayton Hall?

Some of my favorites are:

1. Having different docents take me through the house, because each story has a different emphasis, reflecting the variety of periods in the site's history. It may appear to be the same house tour, but no two tours are the same.

2. The grounds. When my wife and I come out by ourselves or with friends, we don't always visit the house. Sometimes it's for an oyster roast or a picnic. The setting is so appealing, so tranquil.

3. Drayton Hall's collections. Although they are housed here, they haven't been exhibited or promoted because facilities don't exist yet. Those collections can someday tell the story of life through the centuries.

Could you reflect on the importance of African American history and what you've learned about it while you've been associated with Drayton Hall?

An interesting aspect of visiting Drayton Hall is the opportunity to learn about the enslaved populations that lived here through the Civil War and the shift of formerly enslaved people into the post-Civil War era. It's important to interpret the site from the vantage point of all who lived and worked here. Our current programming interweaves African American history into the house tours, provides access to the African American cemetery, develops school programs, and has created tours that interpret the plantation system. It allows visitors to hear from African American descendants. All of this provides a total sense of place that George McDaniel and the administration for the last 25 years have emphasized. There are histories here, not just about the Revolutionary War or Civil War experience, but also about how people lived and worked.

Why it is important to build relationships with African American descendants in addition to Drayton descendants?

The site's total history includes the fact that today we have descendants of the Drayton family on the board of trustees of the Drayton Hall Preservation Trust as well as descendants of the enslaved population. It's important over time to keep participation and communication open so all can contribute for the benefit of the widest possible audience. That's a serious part of its mission, and to date, Drayton Hall is doing a good job.

If you could use a magic wand to fulfill your thoughts, what would Drayton Hall look like in 20 years?

The core would not look any different. While the house would have been visited by tens of thousands of visitors, we would have found effective but unobtrusive solutions for its preservation. For example, we just finished repairing the portico, which needed substantial improvements, but that project, now completed, didn't change its appearance.

What might be different? First, the experience of visiting the grounds will be different. A walk to the river and ponds, our paths through the woods, and the riverfront are under-utilized now, but will be made to come alive. Second, we will emphasize our collections. We will have a visitor's center, a place for our staff to work more efficiently, for our visitors to enjoy enhanced programming, exhibits, and video tours plus lunch and other benefits, such as an orientation movie. Visitors could make it a full day or a half day. They'd see our collections that interpret Drayton Hall's story through the furniture, ceramics, books, and personal objects that have been donated, purchased, or found through archaeological efforts. Twenty years from now, people will come often, stay longer, bring friends, and have even more enriching experiences.

Jenny Sanford McKay:
"Integrity. Respect"
2021 – Telephone Interview

 An Illinois native, Jenny Sanford McKay was an investment banker at Lazard Freres & Co. in New York before moving to South Carolina and managing campaigns for her first husband, Mark Sanford, a former U.S. Congressman and SC governor. Long active in non-profit initiatives, she focused her work as the state's First Lady on wellness in South Carolina, enhancing the Governor's Mansion complex, and serving on numerous boards, including Drayton Hall's Advisory Site Council. Published in 2010, her memoir, "Staying True," was a New York Times bestseller. She chairs JS Capital Management and lives in Mount Pleasant, South Carolina, with her husband, Andy McKay.

Could you briefly describe your background?
 I moved to South Carolina in 1991 and have been in the Lowcountry ever since, a little over 30 years. I got involved in the political world when my husband became a congressman and then a governor, and after our divorce, I continued to live in the Charleston area, raising my four sons. My new husband and I call South Carolina home and hope to spend the rest of our life here.

 I was introduced to you, George, through the Charleston Heritage Federation when you were its first chairman. When I moved to Charleston, Charlie Duell, president of the Middleton Place Foundation and whom I knew in New York, asked me to become its first volunteer director to help nonprofit cultural organizations communicate in the aftermath of Hurricane Hugo with a unified voice on city or state funding and other issues that needed to be communicated to the powers that be. Working with all of you was a great, great experience for me.

What was your first impression of Drayton Hall?
 The first time I saw Drayton Hall was shortly after I moved here. I was struck by its magnificence, not just by the building itself, but also the surroundings and

everything about it. I was in awe of the fact that the building was created with such intricate detail, especially at a time when it would have been difficult to navigate the waterways and to bring the materials, the craftsmen, and the talent to the site — all of those things necessary to build such a grand home.

I was struck by the respect for the preservation of the building itself, its heritage and what the site represented. Drayton Hall is much more than a building. It's an entire property with a history produced by the livelihoods of all those who called it home over many, many generations. It has seen lots of life. Many different things are rolled up into that one specific place.

In light of your busy life, what led you to serve on our board?

There was something magical about Drayton Hall. It had been preserved, not restored, and had no bells and whistles simply to attract tourists. It was all about authenticity. Its integrity spoke volumes. I thought the property was a gem for our state and wanted to continue its preservation.

What did you think about its education programs?

They were very hands-on. It was wonderful to see school children under the live oaks learning about the history of the site, sitting in the same place where its history took place. Drayton Hall is like stepping back in time. There's nothing like it. Your imagination is free yet informed as to what went on during those times.

What did you think about the archaeological excavations?

I appreciated the incredible attention to detail! You had brought in students, guides, and others to learn from the archaeologists how to excavate sites and identify artifacts and create a more complete picture of the site. You sought to learn how the landscape was designed, how it was used, and what life was like. It was fascinating to watch.

What do you think is the public's perception of historic sites like Drayton Hall?

The public perception of sites like Drayton Hall is positive. Anybody who has ever been there speaks positively about it. Having said that, the direction our growth has taken, especially in tourism, has not always been of the highest quality. I'm not so sure that we — and by that, I mean the South Carolina Department of Commerce, the Charleston Conventions and Visitors Bureau, and the golfing and beach tourism organizations — are trying to bring to the Charleston area the kind of tourists that appreciate a Drayton Hall, those able to distinguish between Drayton Hall and more commodified attractions.

Why do you think that golf, beach, hotels, and other large entities get more funding and marketing support while museums like Drayton Hall tend to be at the back of the line?

There are probably a number of reasons. Having been married to a politician for years, I know more attention may be given to the loudest voice in the room. Often nonprofit organizations like Drayton Hall are not among the most forceful. They don't have lobbyists at the statehouse or in city hall nor have commercial interests at stake. They don't have a lot of money and aren't willing to throw it at the political leadership of the day. That's a shame.

Sometimes the hidden gems in our midst, like Drayton Hall, get lost in the shuffle. We spend a lot of money and time trying to attract more tourists, but aren't paying enough to attract the more educated tourists or those with an appreciation for history. This is not unique to Charleston. It's nationwide. We have become a society intent on instant gratification. Everything, even our news, is entertainment. Lacking is respect and admiration for understanding the history that brought us to where we are.

As an outside observer of museums and historic sites, what might they do to broaden outreach and gain more support?

They're doing everything they can right now and need to keep doing so. They must understand that in this fast-moving world of social media, they need to connect more with people who are interested in history and in quality. Institutions like Drayton Hall have incredible stories to tell, and respect should be given to the cultural history that went into building them. We can learn from this and grow. I know that nonprofit organizations like Drayton Hall constantly struggle to find funds and benefactors, but they are out there.

If you have a quality asset, which Drayton Hall does, and if you have quality leadership like your board and staff, and if you get your message out to a broad cross-section of people who care about such properties, then you can maintain the organization and grow your base. In light of other trends out there now, it's not easy, but it's a fight worth continuing.

What do you think that historic sites like Drayton Hall can do to help bridge the polarization we see too often in our communities and nation?

What's being done at Drayton Hall — starting, frankly, with your leadership, George — is a perfect example for others to follow in terms of bridging gaps in our society. Respect is given to the oral histories and cultural history of both the African Americans and the Whites at Drayton Hall. You do not label something as good or bad, but present history as facts and whether good or bad, show how people lived on this property and what we can learn from their experiences. It's presented in a civil manner and inspires our respect and a drive for excellence in a way that is a good example for other organizations.

Respect is taught at home. If you are derogatory in your house toward somebody of a different ilk, your kids will pick up on that. They might grow up being derogatory towards other people. Respect is also grown at the institution. Celebrating heritage at Drayton Hall means the whole heritage.

You were looking into potential sites of slave quarters and talking to descendants of slaves and slave-owners on the plantation in a respectful way. What better example for others to learn from? Just because there is something negative in one's history doesn't mean it's impossible to peacefully coexist today and to learn how to move forward together. The educational experience you get when you visit Drayton Hall is an honest celebration of the whole of its history, good and bad. Isn't that what we strive for: integrity and wholeness?

Anthony C. Wood:
"Transformative"

2015 – Drayton Hall

A national leader in historic preservation, Anthony C. Wood is director of the Ittleson Foundation in New York City and was advisor from New York State to the National Trust for Historic Preservation. He joined Drayton Hall's advisory council in the early 2000s and became its chairman. When the Drayton Hall Preservation Trust was formed in 2015, he was chosen to serve on its board and has thoughtfully continued to guide the site into its future.

Could you tell us about your background, and how you got involved in historic preservation?

I was born in New York City but by first grade, my parents had moved to Illinois. My dad took his first and last teaching position at Eastern Illinois University in Charleston, a college town of about 16,000 residents in central Illinois. A family pastime was to get in a car and look at old houses. We weren't schooled in this or that style of architecture. Instead, the beauty of the old houses and neighborhoods attracted us.

My parents bought a wonderful two-story brick house, probably 1865-ish, out in the country, which has kind of Drayton Hall-ish dimensions but without the pedigree. I majored in history at Kenyon College in Ohio and spent a transformative summer at historic Deerfield. I got a wonderful offer from the University of Illinois' graduate program in Urban and Regional Planning, which is how I got into studying history in a more activist role. I was the guy in the transportation planning course who focused not on planning a highway, but on how citizens could stop it. Being merely a historian was too passive. My interest was in saving historic places.

Upon graduation in 1978, I went to New York City and worked for a local elected official, the Landmarks Preservation Commission, and then the Municipal Art Society. Mrs. Onassis (Jackie Kennedy) was involved and had just helped save Grand Central Station. It was an exciting time. Since I loved both philanthropy and preservation, I went to the J.M. Kaplan Fund, a foundation that funds preservation causes, and ultimately to the Ittleson Foundation. I taught at Columbia University, served on numerous preservation boards, and became advisor to the National Trust from the state of New York. I started the New York Preservation Archive Project and wrote *Preserving New York: Winning the Right to Protect a City's Landmarks*. Preservation is my passion and my avocation. It doesn't pay the rent, but it certainly makes life rich.

When did you first hear about Drayton Hall, and what were your thoughts of it before you visited?

I first encountered Drayton Hall because of my brother Stephen, who was a year older. After graduating from college, he wanted to work on historic buildings, so, following the craftsman path, he was accepted into the National Trust's Restoration Workshop, based out of Tarrytown at the Trust property Lyndhurst. While my focus was on the policy and advocacy side of preservation, he worked in a hands-on way on conserving sites in terms of repair, materials, and integrity.

In 1980 his team went to Drayton Hall when the Trust was still weighing options.

Should Drayton Hall be like other sites and be restored to its historical high point? Having no furniture, electricity, or running water, how should it be presented to the public? Stephen passionately told me about these questions. He strongly believed they should never restore Drayton Hall to a specific moment nor add furniture because it was unique and significant the way it was.

In August, the restoration crew was on the roof repairing the chimney when the scaffolding collapsed. I got a call reporting that my brother had been in an awful accident. I hopped on a plane, as did my parents from Illinois, but by the time we arrived in Charleston, Stephen had passed away. The next day we drove to Drayton Hall. Although my thoughts were elsewhere in terms of the house's architectural importance, I was struck by the magic of the place and realized how important Drayton Hall had been to Stephen. My family's approach has been to look at Drayton Hall as a monument to my brother. At age 27 he'd gotten into the best program, was working on one of the most important sites in America, and was doing what he wanted to devote his life to.

Drayton Hall became his legacy, but later my father felt that Stephen had been forgotten and felt detached from Drayton Hall, so I reached out to the National Trust's president, Richard Moe, who connected me with you, Drayton Hall's director. As a result, in 2000 Drayton Hall honored my brother on the 20th anniversary of the accident. This reconnected my family to the place. I was rolling off as a National Trust advisor, and you invited me to join the Drayton Hall Site Council, and ultimately I became its chair. You might say I lost a brother but gained Drayton Hall, which has led me to a richer understanding of preservation and a deeper knowledge of historic sites.

In thinking about historic sites, what do you think can be done to help remedy polarized race relations? What specifically might Drayton Hall do?

Historic houses and neighborhoods are not just about the past. They are important for the future because they enable us to explore today's issues where they happened. There is a power of place, of authenticity, of knowing you are on the very grounds — in Drayton Hall's case, a plantation — where both good things and atrocities took place.

Such sites are where contradictions in our history as a nation are to be seen. Being on the ground where history happened makes the contradictions real and allows us to empathize. I can't imagine a better place in America to have a conversation about race than at plantation sites like Drayton Hall. Such sites are beautiful, calm, and safe, and where contradictions like freedom versus slavery or equality and inequality are made obvious, as is racism. They provide settings where people can contemplate and discuss controversial issues, including school groups. With their upstairs/downstairs design, plantation houses as well as other historic houses in the nation offer opportunities to discuss contradictions integral to America's story. Discussing such issues takes leadership, and Drayton Hall exhibits that. It is committed to telling its story as accurately as possible through scholarly research and tactful education. When an honest depiction of what happened at such a site is offered and when it has courageous leadership, larger conversations can result and help bridge divides.

How can education be improved by using sites like Drayton Hall as a resource?

It seems like American education has been taken over by a mindset of teaching kids to score well on tests in order to get good jobs. Concurrent with that is a devaluation of teaching students how to think and be creative and thoughtful and engaged in society. With a better educated populace, people might not fall prey to shallow political leaders who offer simple answers to complex questions and then demand that we follow them. By teaching history, we encourage critical thinking.

Sites such as Drayton Hall are where students become excited about history. A historic site can be a gateway to history, whether the storyline be about the Revolutionary War, architecture, or the life and work of the enslaved and the slaveowners. They learn to appreciate history as a story about real people. With appetites whetted, students return to their classrooms and learn even more by going to a library, checking out a related book, or downloading a program. In such ways, historic sites become "intake valves" for learning about people and events and the intersections, challenges, and questions about life. That's why fewer school trips to historic sites and the loss of historic places reduce our stock of intellectual capital.

Historic preservation faces pressures manifested by cutbacks in funding and regulations, politicians railing against it, and too many people saying it's an obstacle to economic development and jobs. What is your response?

Historic preservation is an activist use of history and about making sure special places survive into the future. Despite its image, it is not antiquarian. It's about using history to enrich our lives and preserving the memory of what makes life worth living. Preservation enriches the human experience. Imagine your favorite city. Picture it now devoid of the places you love and that define it. Odds are that most have historic, cultural, or architectural significance. The roles those places played may have changed, along with the people, but thanks to preservation, the stage has remained intact, providing us with a sense of continuity and opportunities for the future.

Preservationists do have an image problem. Some people think we're against everything. We're not. We are about the future and for livability. Preservation has been one of the best revitalization tools and has helped save cities. Thank goodness we have places like Drayton Hall! That site can be a person's first physical encounter with history. Through that on-site experience, he or she might come to recognize that they have a Drayton Hall-ish place in their own community, and because it tells an important story, it's worthy of preservation.

Why not restore Drayton Hall to a particular period?

With support from a panel of experts, the National Trust made the decision to basically keep Drayton Hall the way it was when acquired. There's a genius to that decision. When I was a Fellow at Historic Deerfield, we gave tours of colonial houses, taking visitors into kitchens with huge hearths and numerous cooking items. They were looking at a 1920s or '30s understanding of what a colonial kitchen was, which we now know was not accurate. As tour guides, we said, "Isn't this an iconic colonial kitchen?" Visitors responded, "Yeah, this is just what we expected." Then we'd say, "Guess what? It's all wrong!"

The good news for Drayton Hall is we don't have to tell visitors a room looked like this 20 years ago and that we now know it didn't but can't undo it. By keeping Drayton Hall the way we received it, we don't run that risk. Thanks to virtual technology, visitors can see what Drayton Hall would look like if it had been restored to a time period, but as we learn more, we can make changes to the image on the screen, not to the actual room.

What stories might historic sites like Drayton Hall tell that resonate in today's time?

Historic house museums in America still suffer from a branding image because too many people still think about "blue-haired ladies," to whom, by the way, we owe a huge debt because they are the reason we have some of the great iconic sites. The world of historic sites has changed. For example, a group has banded together as sites of conscience where awful tragedies happened. Today's sites interpret modern architecture, industrial history, union history, the history of oppression, or LGBTQ history, such as The Stonewall Inn in New York City, which recently was designated a landmark. Many stories in America and around the world need to be told, and there is no better way to tell them than at places where history happened.

Even the unpleasant stories are important for society to understand. Historic sites can play a special role in helping people to understand what was going on and why. They can be places for conversations about controversial issues like racism, sexism, or homophobia and by doing so, become places for reconciliation. While that may be heavy thinking for historic sites, it is so real. That is the future.

As you look at the Ashley River, why should we care what happens to it beyond our property lines?

Historic sites aren't isolated spots detached from reality. They are part of a larger context. One of the great things at Drayton Hall, particularly under your leadership, is the realization that its historic preservation doesn't stop at the site's borders. To appreciate Drayton Hall, you have to be able to walk down to the Ashley River, look across it, and see the marshland to understand the historical context of the site. If Drayton Hall hadn't taken the huge effort to protect that view across the river, it would not be the same powerful experience.

These wonderful places weren't created in isolation and don't exist in isolation today. Imagine coming to Drayton Hall and there are Dunkin' Donuts and other shops lining the road until you get to our property line and turn in our driveway to find an historical oasis. Your experience of Drayton Hall would have been marginalized. Today, although there has been development in places, you drive along Ashley River Road and sense you're in the Lowcountry. You are not in Anywhere, USA; you are in a particular place. It's the whole place we have to seek to preserve.

Does simply being at a historic site and looking at the river touch your heart?

When I come to Drayton Hall, I arrive early, walk around the house, and go down to the river. Sitting at a bench and looking at the river grounds me in this place. It's magical. It almost has a spiritual dimension. I think about my family connection to Drayton Hall and my brother. I had a magical moment by the river. After my parents passed away, I came here and was sitting on the bench, looking at the river, and saw three dolphins. I thought of my mother, my father, and my brother, and it was magical for me. Being in this spot creates an opportunity for you to think that way and to have those feelings. I never come to Drayton Hall without having a moment down by the river. At historic sites, visitors need to have a place like that.

Why is scholarly research essential to a historic site, and how has the Wood Family Fellowship helped advance that at Drayton Hall?

Research is essential if the goal is to tell a story as truthfully as we know it. Accuracy and authenticity give a site historical authority. With this in mind and to honor my brother and my parents, I created — with help from many others — the Wood Family Fellowship. It's an opportunity for a graduate student or professional in the fields of history, preservation, archaeology, etc. to go deep into a particular topic at Drayton Hall, advance their knowledge and address particular questions selected by Drayton Hall. The Fellowship is much like a research and development component of a company or a government. That current staff members, including the executive director and two department heads, came to Drayton Hall as Wood Fellows is very satisfying to me and, more importantly, to the enrichment of Drayton Hall. I was a Bicentennial Historic Deerfield Fellow in 1976, which shaped my life. Establishing such a program at Drayton Hall became a great way to honor my family, empower future leaders in the field, and benefit Drayton Hall.

How has Drayton Hall transformed your life and career?

On the personal front, having lost my brother here changed our family dynamics. It brought us closer together. As young preservationists, my brother and I had talked about how someday it would be terrific to work on a project together, and, in a sense, Drayton Hall became that project. To Stephen, it was critical that Drayton Hall's philosophy not change, that it not be taken back to a moment in time, not be furnished or gussied up. I've been honoring his wishes in my continuing involvement with Drayton Hall and making sure the preservation philosophy remains secure.

Drayton Hall also gave me Charleston. It gave me an appreciation of the South I never would have had and has enriched my philosophy of preservation. Until then, I didn't understand the importance of spending your life or of raising money to sustain an iconic place. Drayton Hall opened a window into the importance of historic houses. My on-site experience at Drayton Hall corrected my misperceptions and led me to understanding the power of a place like this. Drayton Hall has made me a more well-rounded preservationist. The word "transformative" is an accurate one.

The earliest known image of Drayton Hall as built, this watercolor of 1765 by artist Pierre Eugène du Simitière (1736–1784) shows the influence of Renaissance architect Andrea Palladio and the Draytons' knowledge of classically inspired design. Palladio accented symmetry, a central block, and a tripartite plan. Drayton Hall's façade resembles Palladio's Villa Cornaro of the 1550s, about which the Draytons would have read in Palladio's *Four Books of Architecture*. The colonnades and palisades separate the more public landscape from the more private, where specimen trees were likely planted in keeping with the fashion of the time. After receiving a copy of the watercolor by mail anonymously, the author became a sleuth, located its owner in Winchester, Virginia, and verified its authenticity. Photo courtesy of James Lockard, owner

2015 - Drayton Hall across the pond. Photo - ©tonysweet.com

Compare this 1930s image with the one above to see the site's preservation, not restoration, philosophy. Photo courtesy of the Drayton Hall Preservation Trust (DHPT)

To see additional photographs, read more explanatory captions, and learn of connections to specific interviews and places, visit https://www.mcdanielconsulting.net/drayton-hall-book/

Carved stair bracket. - Colonial Williamsburg Foundation.

A Chinese red swatch illustrative of the trans-lucent, vermilion-based stain used on the mahogany wood-work in the stair hall, as seen in two places where brackets are missing. Photo credit: Benjamin Moore Vermilion 2002-10

The walls of the stair hall were originally painted a cream color and contrasted with the mahogany balustrade, wainscoting, brackets, and original newel posts, which were all stained a brilliant Chinese red. Conservator Susan Buck knows of no other colonial house in America with such a contrast in color. Its original plaster ceiling might have resembled the one in the drawing room. Photo - Willie Graham

Learn more in the interview "The Most Magical Place" with paint conservator Susan L. Buck, Ph.D.

2015 - Drayton Hall Drawing Room. Original, hand-crafted plaster ceiling - one of the few surviving from colonial America. Photo - ©tonysweet.com

1973 – Second floor Great Hall with original wall panels, firebox, and floorboards. Original plaster ceiling replaced by beaded boards after the Civil War, illustrating the fall of plantation society and the rise of a new order in both South Carolina and the nation. Photo - Willie Graham

Read more about the hand-crafted, dowelled, and most expensive 18th-century floorboards throughout Drayton Hall in Richard "Moby" Marks' "Time Machine" interview.

This centuries-old live oak in front of the main house evokes many different memories. If it could talk, what stories could it tell? Photo - ©tonysweet.com

L-r: Tenth-generation descendants Molly and Beatty Joseph create memories in the live oak that their grandmother Molly and great Aunt Anne loved to climb and to which their great uncle Chad used to race with friends. Photo - Greg Howard

Historic Ashley River Road, a National Scenic Byway, canopied by trees and used by generation after generation, beginning with Native Americans thousands of years ago when it was but a path. Photo - George H. McDaniel

The tree-lined entry as the main house comes into view, a sight seen by generations. Photo - Greg Howard

The Ashley River at dawn. Photo - author

Learn more about the river and spiritual beliefs in Johnny Leach's interview "Hand Come. Hand Go"

The land across the river from Drayton Hall. – Photo DHPT

Learn more in Paul Wenker's interview about Marian Kennedy, who led the purchase of this view.

A tranquil spot on the banks of the Ashley River. Photo - DHPT

The Drayton Family Memorial nearby. Photo - DHPT

Learn more in the "When I Was Young" interview with Charlie Drayton and Anne Drayton Nelson.

Charlie Drayton with daughter Molly and Aunt Charley Drayton, c. 1945.

L-r: Chad, Anne, Molly Drayton, c. 1949. Photos above courtesy Molly Drayton Osteen

Frank B. Drayton Sr., brother of Charlie Drayton. Photo – Frank B. Drayton Jr.

1966: The house lit by moonlight, candles, and headlights from cars for Monte and Molly Drayton Osteen's wedding reception. Photo courtesy Molly Drayton Osteen

Charlie Drayton with his wife of 64 years, Mary Gregorie Jervey Drayton, at the wedding reception of their daughter, Molly Drayton Osteen, at Drayton Hall, 1966. Photo courtesy Molly Drayton Osteen

L-r: Anne Drayton (now Nelson) and her brother, Chad Drayton, at the wedding reception for Monty and Molly Drayton Osteen. Drayton Hall, 1966. Photo courtesy Molly Drayton Osteen

Greg Howard, daughter of Monty and Molly Drayton Osteen, measures her daughter Beatty on the Drayton family growth chart in Drayton Hall. Photo courtesy Greg Howard

The 2015 Osteen-Howard wedding by the Ashley River at Drayton Hall. Seated, Charlie Drayton. L-r: Molly and Monty Osteen, Kevin and Greg Howard, Beatty Joseph, Drayton Osteen, Molly Joseph. Photo courtesy Greg Howard

Four generations of Drayton descendants at their annual Thanksgiving celebration in 2014. Charlie Drayton on the right with blue hat. Photo courtesy Drayton Family

Handwork of unidentified artisans. Photo – Willie Graham

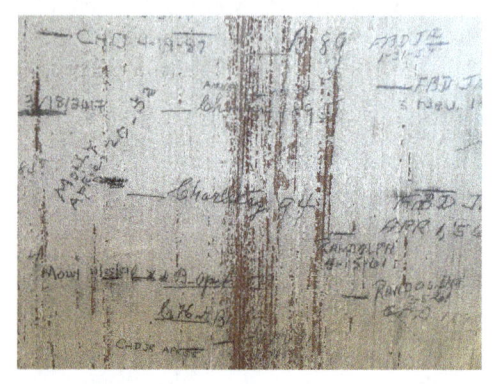

Five generations of Draytons on the family growth chart: Charlotta Drayton, or "Aunt Charley," 1894; her brother, Charles, 1890 and 95; his grandchildren Molly, Anne, Chad, Randolph, and Frank B.; great grandson, Charles H., 1987; and many more. See Drayton lines of descent and author's website for more. Photo – author

Charlie Drayton and Richmond Bowens, who knew each other since the 1920s. DHPT

Richmond Bowens leading a tour at Drayton Hall, c. 1991. DHPT

Toni Carrier, Drayton Hall's Wood Family Fellow and now Director of the International African American Museum's Family History Center, speaks about the importance of family history in a remembrance program at the African American cemetery at Drayton Hall.

Circa 1910, Richmond Bowens Sr., father of Richmond Bowens. DHPT

Circa 1915, young Richmond Bowens with (l-r) his mother Anna Bowens and aunt Harriet Mayes. DHPT

Circa 1993, Richmond Bowens (seated) at his 85th birthday party with relatives at Drayton Hall by a live oak their ancestors would have known. DHPT

"Leave 'em Rest"
The African American Cemetery at Drayton Hall

The Memorial Arch designed by blacksmith Philip Simmons for the African American cemetery, dedicated October 2010. Photo - Dan Stewart

Richmond Bowens directed us to keep the cemetery cleared but not to landscape it. Since his ancestors had done so much hard work on this earth, now was the time to "leave 'em rest." Those words are inscribed over the cemetery's memorial arch.

A procession of the descendants reading aloud the names of the hundreds at rest in the "Sacred Place," the African American cemetery at Drayton Hall, October 2010. DHPT

"I had negative thoughts about Drayton Hall because it was a plantation where my ancestors were slaves. The change wasn't until Richmond Bowens came back to Charleston, and I visited Drayton with him. Seeing the strength he had and the love that he had for Drayton Hall gradually changed my perceptions, knowing that my ancestors were there."
– Annie Brown Meyers

L-r Descendants Annie Brown Meyers and Shelby Nelson, son of Anne Drayton Nelson, at the 2015 Drayton Hall Descendants Program. Photo – Charleston Snapped Photography

Richmond and Velma Bowens headstone in the "Sacred Place," the African American Cemetery at Drayton Hall.
Photo - author

Brick in a c. 1750 Drayton Hall wall showing a longitudinal mark and three indentations, or fingerprints, before the brick was fired and probably made by an enslaved ancestor, who might be buried, unmarked, in the African American Cemetery.
Photo - author

L-r: Esther Chandler, Lonnie and Maria Bunch, Catherine Braxton, George McDaniel. Chandler and Braxton are cousins. 2010 - DHPT

To learn more, read the interview with Lonnie Bunch "The Sunshine of Remembering"

Drayton and Bowens families honor the 100th anniversary of Richmond Bowens' birth – September 2008.
Photos - DHPT

Recording Oral Histories at Drayton Hall - 2015

Interviewing l-r: Rev. Roosevelt Geddis and Charlie Drayton. DHPT

Front row, l-r: Annie Brown Meyers, Mrs. Blunt's granddaughter, and Lucille Blunt. Back row, l-r: Toni Carrier, George McDaniel, Joe Schmidt, Jay Millard, Carter C. Hudgins. Photo – DHPT

Interviewing Anthony C. Wood, Member, Board of Trustees, Drayton Hall Preservation Trust. Photo - DHPT

"Drayton Hall is kind of an anchor for me and my family. The why of that may be hard to grasp, but it matters somewhere deep in my core."
– Charles Heyward Drayton

L-r: Descendants Catherine Braxton, Charles Heyward Drayton, and Charles' father Chad Drayton at the 2015 Drayton Hall Descendants Program. Photo - Charleston Snapped Photography

Descendants at the 2015 Drayton Hall Descendants' Program. Front row, l-r: Annie Brown Meyers, Charles Drayton, Charlie Drayton, Shelby Nelson, Catherine Brown Braxton. Back row: Rebecca Brown Campbell, Frank B. Drayton Jr., George W. McDaniel Photo - Charleston Snapped Photography

Circa 1950s: Annie Meyers' grandmother and step-grandfather lived in the caretaker's house. When she visited as a child in the late '40s or early '50s, she told the author that she saw their house as the "main house" and the mansion as an "outbuilding." Her testimony shows how essential oral history is in illuminating significant points of view and in telling a more complete story. Photo courtesy of Molly Drayton Osteen

At the 2015 Descendants Program, l-r: Descendants Anne Drayton Nelson and Rebecca Campbell. Photo - Charleston Snapped Photography

Taking the Drayton Hall message to wider audiences, at Rutgers University, Newark, NJ, 2016.
Photo - Fred Stucker

Descendants, professionals, and friends gather at Rutgers University, 2016. L-r: Mary Sue McDaniel, Alison Rea, Catherine Braxton, Rebecca Campbell, Lonnie Bunch, Spencer Crew, Maria Bunch, George McDaniel. Photo - Fred Stucker

Charlie Drayton and daughter Anne at a 2008 Descendants Program at Drayton Hall. Photo – DHPT

With Elizabeth Drayton Taylor (seated), a direct descendant of William Henry Drayton and the mother of Alison Rea. Also pictured: Stephanie Meeks and her son John.
Photo - author

Don't miss the interview with Stephanie Meeks and the story of John's brick.

L-r: Anthony C. Wood, George W. McDaniel, Stephanie Meeks, Bob Barker. Photo - DHPT

With Billy Wingfield and Jenny Sanford McKay – good friends of the author and of Drayton Hall. DHPT

Fishing on the Cooper River. L-r: George McDaniel, Lonnie Bunch with spottailed bass he caught and released, and John Fleming.
Photo - author

The 2014 Portico Project

Ed Chappell. DHPT

Steel collars for support. Courtesy Craig Bennett Engineering

L-r: Richard Marks, Edward Chappell, and (back to camera) Craig Bennett conducting structural analysis. Courtesy Richard Marks Restorations

L-r: Craig Bennett, Richard "Moby" Marks, Trish Lowe Smith, and Gov. Henry McMaster at the 2017 ceremony for the SC Preservation Stewardship Award. Courtesy the Governor's Office

To learn more about this project, read the interviews with Susan Buck, Trish Lowe Smith, Craig Bennett, and Richard Marks.

Archaeology at the Drayton Hall Privy 2007

West wall of the 1790s brick privy. Along the back corner, or at its "north" end, one can discern just above the ground the row of arched bricks, indicating the large opening into which water was poured. Passing under the seats, the water "flushed" into the brick tunnel and to drainage ditches that led to the Ashley River. By conducting archaeology and examining the structure and by comparing it to Versailles, which in 1789 is said to have only nine flushing toilets, one can discern how this building's design represented advanced sanitation technology. Photo – DHPT

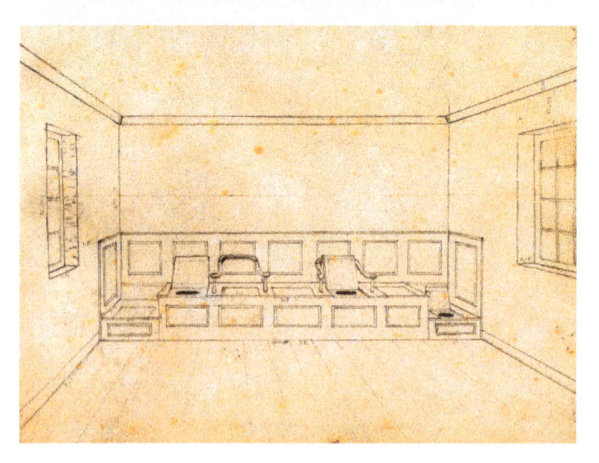

Lewis Gibbes' sketch of the interior of the seven-seat privy, 1846. DHPT

To learn more, read the interview "… Advanced for its Day" with Matt Webster.

"An Extraordinary Person" – Miss Sally Reahard

To learn more about Drayton Hall's wonderful benefactress, read interviews of Gene Wilkins, Bo and Stanley Reahard, Donald and Katherine Willing, and Bill Weeks.

The Sally Reahard Visitor Center

Opened in 2018 - Designed by architect Glenn F. Keyes. Photo – DHPT

"I hope people will appreciate our restraint with the visitor center because we were not trying to build a monument. The monument is Drayton Hall." – from the interview with Glenn F. Keyes

Gates Gallery in the Sally Reahard Visitor Center. Photo – Robert Oswald

"A Focal Point for the Sweep of History" – the interview with the late Steve Gates and his hopes for the future of Drayton Hall

The Lenhardt Garden at Drayton Hall

The Lenhardt Garden with a view to the George W. McDaniel Education Center.
Photo - Robert Oswald

Reception in the Lenhardt Garden. Thanks to Benjamin and Cindy Lenhardt, the garden was designed by landscape architect Shelia Wertimer and serves as the center of the Sally Reahard Visitor Center, connecting its disparate parts with an ancient live oak in the middle. The garden features plants cited in the journals of Drayton Hall's second owner, Charles Drayton, from the late 18th to the early 19th century, among them being the foxgloves seen in bloom. Perhaps he knew the live oak. In the background are the George W. McDaniel Education Center and the red Richard and Jill Almeida Gallery of the 1870s, which was originally the caretaker's house close by the main house and moved and now used to interpret African American family and community life at Drayton Hall.

To learn more about the landscape and gardens at Drayton Hall, read Shelia Wertimer's interview, "Walking the Landscape."

The George W. McDaniel Education Center

With Esther Beaumont who funded the construction of the George W. McDaniel Education Center at Drayton Hall. 2017 - DHPT

In front of the McDaniel Education Center with l-r: George McDaniel, Carter Morris, descendant Rebecca Campbell, Hampton Morris, Mary Sue Nunn McDaniel, and descendant Alison Rea, seated. Photo - DHPT

Read "Drayton Hall Speaks To Me" – the interview with Charleston native Esther Beaumont and why she cares about Drayton Hall's preservation and education programs

Friends & Visitors

Robert A. and Marian Kennedy. She had the Kennedy Library built in his memory, designed by architect Jim Thomas. Photo - DHPT

VIP Visitors circa 1970s, l-r: President Gerald Ford, First Lady Betty Ford, Frances Edmunds, and US Senator Fritz Hollings. Photo - DHPT

Left, c. 1991, in the cemetery where his ancestors are interred, Richmond Bowens uncovers a broken glass, which had been placed there as a traditional grave good. Photo – DHPT

Above: He holds a clay pipe fragment discovered while the Bowens house was being excavated – described in his interview. DHPT

Read Richmond Bowens' 1994 interview, "I'd like to see what's down there…"

Visitors join Shelia Harrell-Roye on a house tour. Photo by author

Read Shelia Harrell-Roye's interview, "Commit to Telling the Truth"

L-r: Descendants Lorraine White, Catherine Braxton, Charlie Drayton, and Rebecca Campbell attend a program at Drayton Hall, c. 2010. Photo - DHPT

Filming the PBS documentary "The African Americans: Many Rivers to Cross" L-r: Dr. Bernard Powers, Catherine Braxton, Skip Gates, Trish Smith, Kristine Morris, Rebecca Campbell, George McDaniel. 2012 - DHPT

Read the interview with Catherine Braxton & Rebecca Campbell, "I Feel the Spirits of my Ancestors"

To learn more, read the interview, "The Challenging Issues of Race," with Dr. Bernard Powers.

Center: Carter C. Hudgins, President and CEO of Drayton Hall Preservation Trust, with l-r: Trish Lowe Smith and Sarah Stroud Clarke. Photo - DHPT

"A National, Indeed an International, Treasure"
Read more in the interview with Carter C. Hudgins

Descendant Catherine Braxton engages the audience at the 2016 program at Rutgers University in Newark, NJ. Photo - Fred Stucker

Director of Museum Affairs Sarah Stroud Clarke explains "the Prospect" within the rare, English-made desk and bookcase, c. 1745. Photo - DHPT

To discover more, read "Drayton Hall Tells You about the Human Spirit Across All People" - the interview with Sarah Stroud Clarke

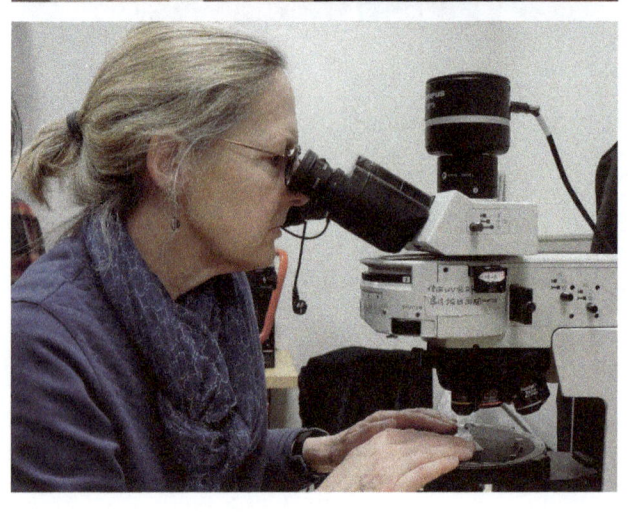

Paint Conservator Susan L. Buck seeks clues. Photo – Marissa Wang

Charlie and daughter Anne at the Drayton Family Memorial. 2005 - DHPT

L-r: Catherine Braxton, George McDaniel, Pam Brown, Tracy Hayes, Cathy Jenkins, and Rebecca Campbell pay their respects to Charlie Drayton at his memorial service in 2019. Photo - DHPT

INTERVIEWS
Professionals

Lonnie Bunch III:
"The Sunshine of Remembering"

2010 – African American Cemetery Dedication Presentation – Drayton Hall

Lonnie Bunch, 14th Secretary of the Smithsonian Institution, spoke at the dedication of Drayton Hall's African American cemetery (c. 1800), which consists of scores of graves and is considered a national treasure and possibly the oldest African American burial ground still in use in the country. Lonnie is the founding director of the Smithsonian's National Museum of African American History and Culture and a long-time friend of mine. At the time of this presentation, he served on Drayton Hall's advisory council, which was like our board. Throughout his career, he has sought to use history to enhance racial dignity, education, and understanding. He calls on each of us to expand the "ripple effect of remembering" and to continue to tell the story. If so, hard though it might be, his faith assures him that "our ancestors are smiling."

Lonnie Bunch: What a grand and glorious morning this is! We at the Smithsonian are proud of the work you're doing at Drayton Hall. I'm humbled, moved, and honored to be a part of today's dedication of the African American cemetery. This is a special moment, not just for Drayton Hall, but for a nation still struggling to come to grips with its tortured racial past.

When I was thinking about coming here, a man who shaped my career came to mind. He spent his whole life on a rice plantation, Friendfield, on the Waccamaw Neck above Georgetown, South Carolina. When I met him, Mr. Johnson was in his 90s, and we talked about the importance of plantations. He told me stories about slavery and about being a free man on the plantation after the Civil War. One thing he said that I've never forgotten is that my job as a historian is to help people to remember "not just what they want but what people need to remember." Those words — "people need to remember" — are crucial in helping us understand what we're trying to do. His words remind me of African American author James

Baldwin, who wrote, "History does not principally refer to the past. On the contrary, the great force of history comes from the fact that we carry it within us and that we are unconsciously controlled by it. History is literally present in all that we do."

So why did I come all the way from Washington, other than the fact George told me I had to? Why is today's dedication so important?

First, it encourages us to combat a great danger, the danger of forgetting. Not long ago I received a letter from a man who was very upset that the Smithsonian was interested in African American history. He said it stirs up unpleasant memories. He wrote, "After all, America's greatest strength is its ability to forget." He said historians like me should not be hired at the Smithsonian and added, "Best wishes for your continued success," which threw me off at first. But he's right in one way. You can tell a great deal about a people and a nation by what they deem important enough to remember, what countries build monuments to celebrate, and what graces the walls of their museums.

In many ways, we learn even more by what a country chooses to forget. This desire to omit difficult moments, disappointments, and moments of evil is instructive. In this country, the essence of African American culture is often forgotten. The story of enslaved people and their descendants is often lost in the mists of forgetfulness. But today, this dedication allows us to pierce the mist with the sunshine of remembering.

We know the names of some who were buried here, however most are known only to God. Today, we honor them all. We honor their sacrifices, their sufferings, and their impact. We also honor their joy, their resiliency, their lives. It's clear that we are made better thanks to the lives of the people who lived on this plantation. We stand on their foundation. Today is also important because it gives us a chance to re-position our thinking about our enslaved ancestors. I have been struck by Americans' limited knowledge of the institution of slavery, and by their conflicted sense of what slavery meant to the enslaved.

There are few opportunities to do what we're doing today, opportunities to discuss, learn, and wrestle openly with the impact, the legacy, and the continuing resonance of slavery. There is a need to help Americans understand that slavery matters because so much of our struggle to find racial justice has been shaped by that institution. So much of America's past — from politics to westward expansion, from economic growth to culture — was forged by the experience of slavery. Thanks to ceremonies like this, we help people honor in new ways those who were enslaved, to honor them because there are still people who are embarrassed by our slave ancestors.

I'm in awe of their ability to maintain their culture, their sense of family, their humor and their humanity. Despite the cruelties and the pain and loss that accompanied the institution of slavery, I am in awe of all the enslaved people who rest in this cemetery. I am amazed by their strength, by their faith that there would be better days — if not for them, then for their descendants. I wish we were as strong as those who went before us. I wish more people would realize that, even though our enslaved ancestors were bought, they were brave. Though they were sold, they were also strong. This ceremony is important because it allows us to draw inspiration and guidance from our African American past.

I would argue that there is nothing more inspirational than that story. I am so moved when I think of this culture, because who would not be moved by the oratory, the commitment to racial justice, and the ultimate sacrifice of a Martin Luther King Jr.? Who would not be moved by the artistic creativity of Betye Saar? Who would not be moved by the richness of the words of Langston Hughes and the quiet bravery of Rosa Parks or John Lewis? Who would not be moved by the family that left Mississippi for the South Side of Chicago, or the woman who demanded that her name be kept on a voter registration list in the 1960s? But I'll tell you, I am also moved by the people who rest in this sacred space, people who refused to let their tasks in the fields strip them of their humanity, people who kept families together, people who believed in an America that few could foresee.

Today, we should be moved by these people because although they are at rest now, their actions and their lives tell us not to rest, that our job is to struggle, based on their lives, for a fairer America, an America that remembers not only their loss but also their contributions to who we are. The Black past is a wonderful but unforgiving mirror that forces us to remember this nation's promises and its ideals. It's a mirror that holds all accountable. It's a mirror that makes those who are often invisible, visible. Today's program ensures that those African Americans who labored, who died, and who struggled here will be visible, and their voices heard. We may "leave them rest" today, but we will leave here, remembering.

Now let me thank George McDaniel, whose scholarship and career have shaped the lives of many, including me. Robert Kennedy once spoke about the power that comes from a ripple of hope. At Drayton Hall, you have created a ripple of remembering that is helping to change how and what America remembers. Your work here, as evidenced by this careful handling of this sacred space and honoring of memories, is noted nationally and greatly appreciated by those of us who work in places like the Smithsonian. This site continues to pioneer in helping plantations tell a fuller, more complex, and ultimately more satisfying history.

As a historic site, Drayton Hall demonstrates how illuminating the dark corners of the past makes us all better. There is nothing more powerful than a people, a community, and a nation steeped in history. There are few things as noble as honoring all of our ancestors, by remembering the known and the unknown, the Black and the White, the slave and the free. Thank you very much for allowing me to be a part of this ceremony that honors our ancestors, that helps us all remember because today, I know, as sure as I'm standing here, that our ancestors are smiling.

Bob Barker and Nancy Huggins:
"Those Early Days"

2015 – Drayton Hall

Bob Barker and Nancy Huggins were the earliest members of Drayton Hall's staff available for interviews. Bob Barker, a native New Yorker, was a gentlemanly raconteur, blessed with a sparkling sense of humor and an infectious laugh. Bob became one of Drayton Hall's most popular tour guides. Thanks to the record number of memberships he sold, his financial impact on Drayton Hall and the National Trust was immeasurable. Nancy Huggins, a native New Englander, started as a volunteer and later became Drayton Hall's popular and always welcoming gift shop manager. Their recollections shed light on the historic site's early days when funding, research, and staff were in short supply, but esprit de corps abundant.

George: *Could you describe your background and how you came to know Drayton Hall?*

Bob: My full name is Robert Edward Lee Barker. I come by it legitimately because my mother's family are Carters from Virginia, and General Lee's mother was a Carter. I studied at the Parsons School of Design in New York in 1948-49, where lectures about Palladian and Georgian architecture featured Drayton Hall.

When I was discharged from the Army in 1953, I came to Charleston for a simple reason: My great-grandmother had come down annually in the 1850s for the city's popular Race Week, and she wrote about it in her diaries. I went out to Drayton Hall and since the chains were down, I drove to the house. Miss Charlotta Drayton, who owned Drayton Hall at the time, was there and asked me to come in. I demurred because I'd arrived with a puppy, and puppies pee. She declared, "Dogs have been piddling on these floors for 200 years. Bring him in!"

She gave a wonderful tour. It was musty and dusty with the ground floor packed full of furniture, but it was one of the most fascinating house tours I've had. That was my introduction to Drayton Hall.

After I moved to Charleston and was looking for something to do, John Meffert, director of the Trust's Southern Regional Office in Charleston, told me about Drayton Hall's tours. "You've got a background in architecture. You can fake it if nothing else," he said. I volunteered, was later hired, and have been here until my recent retirement at age 82.

As many of our Friends, or members, know, we give new members a silver-plated "rice spoon." However, the "Drayton Hall spoon" began with the "Nelly Custis spoon," which I started carrying on tours. When we were stabilizing a ceiling, I described how much money was needed for preservation and used it as a pointer. Since we had a lot of them, at the end of the tour I told visitors they'd get a spoon if they joined. And they did! Our membership program had begun. When we ran out of Nelly Custis spoons, we started giving to each new Friend a silver-plated serving spoon, or "rice spoon," since rice was critical to the 18th-century Lowcountry and to Drayton Hall, and was often served in Charleston. I've been told that my sales of $400,000 in joint memberships to Drayton Hall and the National Trust total more than those of many Trust sites combined. I was given the Trust's President's Award and guess what came with it? A serving spoon similar to the one we give to new members, but while theirs is new and of silver plate, you gave me a sterling-silver spoon of the 18th century, made by Hester Bateman at that!

Could you tell us, Nancy, about your background?

I'm Nancy Naomi Grant Ryan Huggins. Since some of my family are related to Ulysses Grant, we have a Grant and a Lee on the same property, but we never fight! The first time I became interested in Drayton Hall was when I was a guide at Middleton Place. One day I parked out on Highway 61 and walked down Drayton Hall's entry lane. It was springtime. Dogwoods were flowering. In the tall trees, wisteria was blossoming. So fragrant! I thought I was walking into heaven, it was so gorgeous! After Mr. Gaskin, the caretaker, took me through the house, I decided then and there that I had to be a part of Drayton Hall.

I later signed on as a volunteer, and Bob had been here about a year. We worked as a team with him giving tours of the house half the day, while I welcomed guests at the entrance gate, and then we'd reverse roles. Visitors were few since they had to have an appointment for a tour or be a member of the Trust. Bob and I also did much of the "inside work," such as cleaning bathrooms and the house.

Who was the staff in those early days?

Nancy: After Drayton Hall was acquired by the Trust, it was closed to the public while research was underway, and the site prepared for visits. Archaeologist Lynne Lewis was brought from another Trust site to be director. Because important historical sites on the grounds had to be located and protected, we needed archaeologists, so they "camped out" in the main house.

Bob: Taking care of the grounds was the job of Bob Gaskin, a great guy who lived in a mobile home on site. Succeeding him was John Kidder, also a hard worker devoted to Drayton Hall. When Lynne was called to do archaeology elsewhere, I served as site director until Dennis Lawson was hired full time for the job. Our first office was the caretaker's cottage, which was moved in 1978 or so to become the museum shop. Originally, it stood between the brick privy and the main house. It had two rooms with back-to-back fireplaces and two little rooms at the rear, which served as our office.

Nancy: The cottage was moved because Drayton Hall needed a place for visitors to check in away from the main house. It became both our visitors' center and shop. We called it the "little red house." We cleaned it out and removed 16 layers of wallpaper, which included newspapers. Bob built shelves and cupboards for merchandise and made curtains and tasteful tablecloths. The shop was first in the front room, which was more open because the fireplaces were removed. Soon the shop expanded into one back room and then the other. We had little, hand-written receipts, and if we had $50 worth of sales in one day, we did very well. Bob also helped to choose merchandise because he has wonderful taste.

Around 1979 we added a little office to the side of the cottage, which became the kitchen for the whole staff. Since there was no water inside the shop, we ran a hose to the back window, and on an outside shelf, placed a pan. That was where we washed dishes. In the "office," a hot plate heated water for coffee, and later a sink was added. Space heaters and a ceiling fan provided heat and air conditioning. I'm happy to say that by the time I left as shop manager in the late 1990s, the shop's revenue had grown to about $200,000 a year! I loved it.

In the early days, what was the gatehouse and how did it function in selling tickets and welcoming guests?

Bob: The original gatehouse was on loan to us from the Salvation Army, which is why we called it the "kettle house." They used it downtown during the Christmas season until somebody smashed it with a car. So I built a gatehouse of plywood, two x fours, and windows I found lying around. It was an improvement but still had no heat, air conditioning, lights, or electricity.

Visitors would stop at the "kettle house" (later my gatehouse) and buy tickets. Then we would send them on down to the shop, or "little red house." Around 1980, our director, Letitia Galbraith, found a carpenter, Jim Crow, who built a new gatehouse complete with electricity, a telephone, and a propane heater. Our gatekeeper at that time was Richmond Bowens, a wonderful African American descendant who had grown up at Drayton Hall. He'd crank up the heater and get it so hot in there. It was fascinating!

Nancy: You wouldn't think sitting in a gatehouse would offer much, but it did. One time, a fox came up almost to the door, sat down, scratched fleas, looked at me, and walked on. While Bob wrote letters, bird-watching was my thing. We had a trial run using teen volunteers, but that ended when one of them got bored and used the telephone for international calls all over the world. His father got a bill for $90! That ended the trial run.

What were your main themes or stories that you conveyed in the tours?

Bob: We didn't have as much history about the Drayton family or African Americans as we have today because the Drayton papers were away in archives and, of course, not digitized or available to us. Basically, it was an architectural tour. It was easy to do because the architecture was right there in front of visitors. Once a guide learned a few terms, he or she could take people through. Visitors were fascinated.

Do you think that Drayton Hall ought to be restored to its 18th-century glory? Why or why not?

Bob: I do think Drayton Hall should be restored to its original glory. I'm not that taken by peeling Victorian paint. Since the detailing is so outstanding, it would be spectacular to see it restored. Though the Trust's decision-makers said it was a treasure and should not be altered, I think it should.

Nancy: I like it the way it is. I do love the colors you see now.

What are some of your favorite memories, Bob, or stories from your tours?

Bob: One of my memories is of two ladies from Georgia who arrived in a Cadillac limousine and took my tour. In my introduction, I explained how Drayton Hall's architectural style is "Georgian Palladian." Soon afterward, I heard one lady say to the other, "Why you know I grew up in Georgia, but I've never seen anything like this!"

Another favorite is about a young, attractive tour guide who loved to paint dead animals and skeletons. One day she picked up a dead bullfrog while returning from a tour while carrying her silver rice spoon, which interpreters use as a pointer. Some visitors asked her for directions to the Ashley River, so she complied. She noticed that their mouths dropped as they eyed one hand and then her other. Only later did she realize that she'd been giving directions, stylishly dressed, with a silver spoon in one hand and a dead frog in the other, directions at Drayton Hall, no doubt, they are still talking about.

My favorite was when Jackie Kennedy Onassis visited. She arrived with a city guide, and they stopped at the gatehouse. Former First Ladies are automatically National Trust members, so the city guide said to the gatekeeper, "I have a former First Lady, Jacqueline Kennedy Onassis, who would like to see Drayton Hall." Our young gatekeeper, perhaps one of those volunteer teenagers, walked out of the gatehouse, clipboard in hand, and declared, "I'll bet you have!" Taking off her dark glasses, Jackie looked squarely at him, and he dropped his clipboard!

Nancy: Yes, she did come out and was a gracious lady.

Bob: Since we had a lot of people on the site that day, I took her for a personal tour through the house. You don't often get visitors knowledgeable about architecture, and she was. At that time, we were repairing the plaster of the stair hall ceiling, so the upstairs was closed to the public and plaster dust was everywhere. I asked her if she still wanted to go upstairs, and without hesitation, she declared, "Let's go." We climbed over and through the scaffolding used for ceiling repair.

Ascending, she was wearing a black dress, but descending, plaster dust had turned it gray. It didn't bother her one bit, so intrigued was she by the house. She loved it!

What are your favorite memories, Nancy?

Nancy: I was not a history buff, but once here, I began to learn that history is more than dates and wars and became very interested in architecture, preservation, and conservation. I was able to give tours and know what I was talking about. It was fun to see people come into the house and on their face you could see, "Oh, this is an empty house!" By the end of the tour, they thought it was wonderful because of the way we presented it.

Bob: When a visitor learned the house was not furnished and said they didn't want to waste their time, I replied, "If you go on my tour, when it's over and if you're not satisfied, I'll refund your money." I never refunded anybody's money!

Bob, what do you think enabled you to sell so many memberships?

Bob: You've got to show your excitement in giving the tour and let your enthusiasm and interest rub off. You have to explain the benefits of membership. We also had a little competition among the guides.

What are your recollections about Richmond Bowens, the African American descendant who worked as gatekeeper?

Nancy: Richmond and I had a wonderful relationship. When he came down for his lunch or after he retired from working the gate and met with visitors on the porch of the shop, he would sit with me and the others and tell stories about his family and how much being at Drayton Hall touched his heart. He sincerely loved Drayton Hall. God rest his soul.

Bob: He was a wise man. If you had a medical problem, he was the one to talk to since he had a wonderful knowledge of herbal medicine, learned from his elders here. After he retired as gatekeeper and was working as an interpreter at the gift shop, people became so fascinated when talking to him that it was hard to get them to go on their scheduled tour. He was also a man of devout religious faith.

What are some of your favorite personal memories of Drayton Hall?

Nancy: As staff, we used to have cookouts and parties, and it was as if we had become a family.

Bob: My favorite memory is a recent one when my partner and I had our commitment service and got married here. I also remember receiving a call from our chairwoman, Frances Edmunds, about opening up the site for a photographer from England, a cousin of the Queen. We were asked to treat him very nicely. He came after hours when the property closed to shoot photos for a calendar. The models arrived and soon they were in costume — from the waist down. From the waist up, they weren't in anything! The photographer took pictures of them on limbs in the live oaks, in rocking chairs on the portico. I asked him if he would be kind enough to send a calendar to the president of the National Trust. I also asked Frances, "Do you know much about this calendar?" She said it was for some commercial calendar. So I told her what happened. She laughed. That was Frances.

Is there a place at Drayton Hall that you would like to ask questions about, or to hear it tell stories?

Bob: I'd like to hear stories from the ballroom upstairs. The parties that took place in this house in the 18th century would have been fascinating. Also, the dining room or wherever they enjoyed dining.

How has Drayton Hall touched your life?

Bob: Drayton Hall has touched my life because I've spent so much of it here. I love the house, but they wouldn't let me move in. I've met so many people. Some still send me cards every year because I took them through the house, and they loved it. They might not come back, but they loved the place.

Nancy: It's being able to drive down Highway 61 and then down the entry lane. No matter how many times you do it, Drayton Hall takes your breath away. I loved working here. I would be working here this very day if it wasn't such a long drive from my new home.

Who were some of the memorable interpreters at Drayton Hall?

Bob: There have been lots, but one in particular was George Boan, God rest his soul. He gave wonderful tours accompanied by his basset, Beau Drayton, which we'd given him, hence his name. If it was hot, Beau would lie in the brick fireplace of the room on tour because it was cool. If George got too long-winded and Beau grew tired of listening, he would pick up and sashay into the next room as only basset hounds do and in his own way say, "Time to move." He was very popular. People would come back to Drayton Hall year after year and ask, "Where is Beau Drayton?" We memorialized Beau by producing a tee shirt with his picture we sold in the shop.

Nancy: People loved George's tours, as they've loved Bob's. Bob puts his heart and soul into his tour, and that's why he's such a wonderful guide. He has fun on the tour and makes the people feel welcome, as well as providing information, so they want to become a part of Drayton Hall and see it preserved. That's why he sold so many memberships. Though we didn't know it at the time, those early days were special.

Letitia (Tish) Galbraith Machado:
"Philosophy, Interpretation, Education, Security"

2021 – Telephone Interview

A native of Spartanburg, SC, Letitia (Tish) Galbraith Machado graduated from the University of South Carolina, studied Fine and Decorative Arts at the Victoria and Albert Museum in London, and was curator of historic properties for the National Trust for Historic Preservation in Washington, DC. She became the director of Shadows-on-the-Teche, a Trust site in New Iberia, Louisiana, and served as director of Drayton Hall from 1978 to 1989. I succeeded her. During her tenure important decisions were made that provided a solid foundation and made Drayton Hall nationally known. Tish later was director of the Walter Anderson Museum of Art in Ocean Springs, Mississippi., where, now retired, she lives today.

Could you describe your first impressions of Drayton Hall?
I first saw Drayton Hall in 1963 when I was living in Charleston after graduation from college. Through a friend I met Molly Drayton, who suggested we drive out to the country to Drayton Hall. I'll never forget my first view of that great house standing solitary and beautiful on the landscape. Little did I know that my impressions that day would affect both the future of Drayton Hall and my own. I didn't see Drayton Hall again until I was curator of historic properties for the National Trust in Washington, DC.

Negotiations for its acquisition had begun. Others and I at the Trust recognized the rare resource Drayton Hall represented: the first use of a Palladian portico on a domestic building in the United States, and a building only owned by six generations of one family with no modernization and relatively fewer architectural modifications to its original details. The house warranted interpretation as an artifact in its own right. Of this approach, I was an outspoken proponent and was joined by National Trust President James Biddle and its architect, Richard Bierce. We championed preservation over restoration and leaving it unfurnished rather than furnished. We faced powerful opponents, but with the future of Drayton Hall at stake, stubbornness became a virtue. To their credit, the Draytons kept whatever reservations they might have had to themselves.

When you were director, what were the main sources of support for this historic site?

As Drayton Hall became more popular, admissions brought in more income. Dennis Lawson, the director before me, gets credit for starting the Friends, or membership, program plus the idea of using the rice spoon as a successful ploy. Bob Barker, a wonderful tour guide, was the master of inducing people on his tours to become a Friend. Our knowledgeable and enthusiastic guides stimulated great interest and appreciation among visitors, and membership sales increased.

Building our Friends program required a great deal of effort. We partnered with the National Trust, Historic Charleston Foundation, Preservation Society of Charleston, and South Carolina Historical Society to introduce the Friends program to potentially interested individuals. I personalized each letter whenever possible. Our newsletter, *Interiors,* let Friends know of our ongoing plans and accomplishments. To keep Friends and to make new ones, we offered a variety of programs for adults and children, which engaged the public and brought attention to Drayton Hall. Through such a massive effort, the Friends program grew into the largest of all the Trust sites and the most successful in fundraising.

Sally ("Miss Sally") Reahard was our angel. When I replaced Dennis Lawson, Miss Sally had reservations about a woman becoming the director of Drayton Hall, but she and I got past that hurdle and became devoted friends. Miss Sally was the go-to person for expensive but necessary projects. Among other things, Miss Sally funded our residential cottage, essential for on-site security. Drayton Hall will be forever indebted to her.

We carefully watched our budget and kept it down. The National Trust provided important technical support. I wrote proposals for grants. For example,

Drayton Hall was the first Trust site to earn a grant for general operating support from the Institute of Museum and Library Service, which we continued to get year after year. We partnered with others to get grants and used them to achieve multiple goals. For example, a South Carolina state grant and Historic Charleston Foundation grant funded our symposium on handicapped access, which we used to produce an illustrated guide for the hearing-impaired and to acquire hands-on objects that the sight-impaired could touch and feel. Support also came from our museum shop, which became one of the most interesting shops of any of the historic houses. People would come to Drayton Hall just to shop. In short, we sought diversified sources of support.

What were the major decisions made during your tenure? And why were they made?

We wanted to accent authenticity, documentation, and integrity and decided to use the building as an artifact to interpret preservation itself. We grounded our interpretation in fact and distinguished between documentation and speculation. We were always adding to or revising our interpretation without losing focus on the building. We organized tours around a simple statement, "This is how you look at this building." By pointing out details, we could talk about materials, craftsmanship, and design, and compare changes over time. Really gifted, our guides got people who previously knew nothing about buildings to ask questions. When asked how the Draytons got their money, for example, we talked about development of the cattle industry in South Carolina, citing from Rebecca Drayton's will, and about how the Draytons operated rice plantations down towards Beaufort, South Carolina, and along the Georgia coast. All of that surprised many visitors.

Why shouldn't Drayton Hall be restored to its 18th-century glory?

Visitors can go to numerous historic houses restored to their 18th-century glory, but with a few remarkable exceptions, they are restored and furnished in an attempt to recreate what might have been. Such an approach would be counterproductive at Drayton Hall because visitors would look at the furnishings, not the house itself, and a great opportunity lost.

Would you describe the development of Drayton Hall's education programs?

A grant allowed us to hire the former teacher Penny Reeves to develop our education programs. Under Penny, and later Meggett Lavin, our research and education programs became our major emphasis and they developed school programs, such as those for junior apprentices and the junior docents. When Penny left, Meggett took over, and our school programs and site interpretation earned local, state, and national acclaim.

What are your recollections about the interpretation of African American history and especially regarding Richmond Bowens?

Our interpretation of African American history was minimal, not because we didn't want to do it, but because we didn't have written information. We tried to bring in slavery and the "slavery" of phosphate mining. The only things we had were little excerpts from the Drayton papers, say, about Charles Drayton and his relationship with his carpenter and manservant, "my noble Toby, who died today." Since the Drayton papers hadn't been digitized as they are now, we had no access to them. We knew the names of some of the slaves, like "noble Toby," but the papers were still in possession of the Drayton family. Later, when they were available, we didn't have a secure place for them in the event of a fire, hurricane, or tornado, so they were stored in the City of Charleston's archives. One of the things I pride myself on was working with Charles Drayton and getting those papers for Drayton Hall. I'll never forget being in New Mexico when Charles called saying, "Tish, the papers now belong to Drayton Hall." Until then, the only thing we'd had access to was a little Drayton sketchbook and a card file with a few excerpts from Charles Drayton's diaries about African American history.

One of the best things we did was to hire Richmond Bowens. After he returned from Chicago, he was working as a school crossing guard in Charleston and would often drop by and tell me stories about Drayton Hall. Since we'd had trouble finding a good person for the gate, I asked Richmond, whom I knew to be personable and loyal, to be the gatekeeper. He was overjoyed.

He used to get upset, though, when people would ask him to tell them about bad things at Drayton Hall during slavery times. These questions made him uncomfortable because he had great affection and respect for the Drayton family, which he explained by this story about the recruiting of migrant workers: When he was young, recruiters made promises to Drayton Hall's African American men of high pay and opportunities to send money home if they came to Florida and worked in the turpentine camps. Once there, the men were imprisoned and beaten and afraid to run away. Word got back to Charles Drayton's father, who gathered some men, went down in their own trucks, and got the others out of there and back to their families. The Draytons were heroes to Richmond.

What are some of your favorite memories of Drayton Hall?

After the terrible accident in which Stephen Wood, Anthony C. Wood's brother, was killed while working on the roof, all the staff and Stephen's family made a big ring around the mound in front of the house and sang, Will the Circle Be Unbroken. That was special. Also special were the Halloween parties we had for Friends with pumpkins all over the place, and Richmond Bowens telling his "Will of the Wisp" story to the children, which they loved. The spirituals program was also special. After we asked Richmond if he could help us contact African Americans who could sing the old spirituals a cappella in the traditional way, he contacted a lady who was head of daycare for the elderly. With her elderly mother, they got together a group.

They were the real thing. At first, the audience at Drayton Hall didn't know how to react, but once they realized they needed to respond, it was wonderful. The Library of Congress came and recorded. Our staff picnicked with the singers, and we all had fun. Once I asked, "What was a change in technology during your life that made a difference?" An elderly lady responded, "The pump. We didn't have to carry the water from the spring." Such occasions meant so much to them and to us.

Is there a place at Drayton Hall that you'd like to ask questions of or to hear it tell stories?

I would like to be in the drawing room, having tea with Rebecca Drayton and Miss Charlotta Drayton because those two women were very important in the history of the property. I never knew Charlotta Drayton because when I went there in the 1960s, she was no longer going there, and had died by the time I became director. She did a lot to collect the words to the old spirituals and had such a deep love for Drayton Hall. I would like to ask why she'd go out there and live in such primitive conditions with no running water or electricity. I'd like to ask Rebecca Drayton about the cattle industry and the "cow catchers" and about where she lived before Drayton Hall. I've wondered how the flankers were used over time and where the linens and plates and other things were kept. Those two women would have informative answers.

Looking back on your years at Drayton Hall, how do you think you made a difference?

I was a very good director. I used my staff. We worked things out together. Which direction should we go in? What do we need to do? During those 11 years, there were many positive things that happened. If I had to enumerate, I'd say:

philosophy, interpretation, education, and security. The best thing I did was to keep those who wanted to gussy it up at bay. I consistently asked for documentation. I accented authenticity. We brought integrity to the site. We were not making up stories. We were getting rid of the glib things you heard at other historic houses. We were educating people.

How has Drayton Hall touched your life?

Eleven years of my life, I devoted to Drayton Hall: all the staff meetings, the directors' meetings, all the change-overs at the headquarters. I was there for three different heads of the Trust's historic sites department. One would ask, "Why pay guides; why not use volunteers?" I'd explain that, if you want quality, you have to pay for it. I was up against big obstacles, but we got it done. We developed a new and unique interpretation based on the house and on historic preservation. We were the first historic house in Charleston to allow children to come in, and even engaged young people to give tours. In our apprentice program, kids learned building crafts — for example, how hard it is to properly plane wood. They looked at the pilasters in the house, saw how identical they were yet planed by hand, and gained new appreciation for the skill and hard work of craftspeople. Our education programs became nationally known.

The staff and I addressed many issues: the Navy's Blue Angels' fly-overs shook the house and had to be stopped; the need for Slow, No-Wake signs along the Ashley River; encroaching development along the Ashley River Road; preservation of the view across the river; hunters poaching in Drayton Hall's forests; getting rid of feral hogs and the danger they posed; trespassing on the property; stabilizing the main house and ongoing maintenance; and construction of the residential cottage for security. Being director of Drayton Hall was for me a joy and a privilege. All that was accomplished over those 11 years was the result of the hard work and cooperation of the staff. Each and every one of my staff deserve a royal share of the credit.

Carter C. Hudgins:
"A National, Indeed an International, Treasure"

2016 – Drayton Hall

Carter C. Hudgins, the president and CEO of the Drayton Hall Preservation Trust, has known Drayton Hall longer than any of his predecessors. An archaeologist by training, he earned his PhD from the University of London. When I was Drayton Hall's executive director, he was selected to be a Wood Family Fellow, and soon his skills led him to be hired full time. Upon my retirement in 2015, he has taken Drayton Hall to new heights and has done so with devotion, intellect, and a good sense of humor.

Could you tell us about your background, how you came to Drayton Hall, and how you became interested in history, archaeology, and historic preservation?

I came to Drayton Hall as an infant. I was living with my parents in Savannah, and my grandparents had taken me for the weekend and brought me to Charleston. I don't remember anything about that experience, but can claim it. As far as my background in historic preservation, archaeology, and history, I came by it naturally because my father, being a historian, archaeologist, and preservationist, did drag us children to every historic site imaginable. For a while, I didn't want to have anything to do with history. However, during my sophomore year at Hampden-Sydney College in Virginia, I participated in an archaeology field school at Jamestown and caught the bug by working with tangible objects and the good people at that site. I graduated with a B.A. in history.

While there, I had a run-in with a professor who asked me to write a paper on Jamestown, so I used our archaeological findings from our field school. The professor gave me a D or an F, saying that, because none of the sources had been published, I couldn't use them. From that experience, I have questioned the written record alone. While that professor failed me, he actually inspired me to spend additional time at Jamestown, and following the conclusion of my Ph.D. in history and material culture, to move to South Carolina and to work at Drayton Hall.

There was an intermediate period when I was in high school and worked with Drayton Hall's maintenance and grounds staff during the summers of '96, '97, and '98. In a rebellious stage of my life, I was not a historian or preservationist and had little appreciation for a historic site. It was simply a job. At the end of the day, I was here by myself. Securing the main house and closing the site gave me a good bit of time to interact with the landscape and the house, one on one. In the twilight, it was magical. That experience planted a seed for my appreciation today for Drayton Hall and a reverence for the house.

What did you think about your work as a Wood Family Fellow? What did you do? Why stay here and not go somewhere else?

My experience was transformative. Although Drayton Hall is newer than Jamestown, starting in 1738 rather than 1607, it was apparent how many discoveries there were to be made. As a Fellow, my time was devoted to the research of the Lenhardt Collection of George Edwards Watercolors of the 1730s at Drayton Hall. That experience led me to researching Drayton Hall's museum and archaeological collections, which in turn opened the doors through which we're still moving today.

How has your thinking evolved over Drayton Hall? Are there markers that illustrate your evolution in thinking?

My initial scholarship at Jamestown was based on using material culture as text to understand the past, but upon arrival at Drayton Hall, I was confronted with a wider palette of resources. I'm neither an architectural historian nor a decorative arts expert, but a similar methodology of research can be used to analyze an object whether it comes out of the ground or has remained in somebody's dining room. That is: How was it made? How was it used? Why did somebody purchase or make the object? What did the object mean to the people who owned or used it? Those questions can be transferred from archaeology to decorative arts to architectural history. At Drayton Hall, we have all three, plus a manuscript collection, so there's a lot to work with.

When you began your Wood Family Fellowship, what did you focus on? What were the principal sources of evidence?

As you study history, one question leads to the next. In researching Drayton Hall's material culture, that's certainly the case as exemplified by the Lenhardt

Collection of George Edwards' watercolors. What was the story behind the watercolors themselves? Why had John Drayton acquired them in 1733? Answers shed light about him as an individual, his pursuits in natural history, and his intellectual prowess in literature, astronomy, and architecture. We're fortunate that many resources survive, and despite the fact that we know very little about John Drayton as written by his own hand, we can still piece together research of these other collections for a more complete understanding of him.

While it's ironic that John Drayton becomes a man of mystery due to a lack of written records, we need to think about another group of people, the enslaved Africans. They too didn't leave written records. Just as we have to piece together John Drayton's history using what survives in material form, we have to do the same thing with artifacts left by the enslaved community. Toward that end, we're cataloguing the archaeological collection.

What are your thoughts about Drayton Hall's preservation philosophy? What are its advantages and disadvantages?

Drayton Hall's preservation philosophy, which makes the site not period-specific, is both a blessing and a curse. There is great value to allowing the stories of the seven generations who lived and worked here to educate visitors. It's a curse, though, because it's incredibly confusing. In interpreting the site, we may want to think about the amount of attention we're applying to different generations. Although all of the stories are important, do they deserve equal time in our research and programming? That's a complicated question to answer.

The preservation philosophy is an evolving philosophy. As a colleague declared, the farther we get away from the 1970s and 1980s when the preservation philosophy was codified, our job becomes more and more difficult. Since aspects of the house have a shelf life, we are forced to evaluate repairs and conservation measures yet still uphold the preservation philosophy.

The preservation philosophy is valuable because it enables the site to become a timeline. Seven generations of Draytons and seven-plus generations of enslaved Africans and their descendants who lived and worked here have left imprints on the property. The challenge of the philosophy boils down to the significance of the site. One prime reason for the site's significance is that it's truly a survivor. Another is its design, for this is an extraordinary structure. Its initial design by John Drayton was the first of its kind in colonial America. However, some imprints on the house and on the property, whether intentional or not, cloud that. This is more apparent on the landscape, where preservation is a tricky thing because it's constantly evolving, and if you do not take proactive maintenance, you're left with an overcrowded mess. We're at a point now where we do need to take a more aggressive approach with the landscape, and we question whether we're preserving historical resources or preserving neglect. Since the house was occupied less in the 20th Century, a lot of once-cleared land has turned into wilderness. Do we honor those unintentional imprints on the landscape?

One value of Drayton Hall's preservation philosophy is that the imprints from previous generations remain both on the house and the landscape. If Drayton Hall and the National Trust had practiced restoration, things like graffiti in the house would have been covered over along with unintentional imprints like where candles burned some of the historic fabric of the house. Removing or covering them over would have taken away evidence of how the house was lived and worked in over time.

One way to think about the preservation philosophy is to conceptualize the house and property as being composed of different zones. For example, we are not doing pure preservation with the exterior because if we left it as it was when acquired, we'd have water intrusion and lose the historic house. As a result, we do a certain level of restoration on the exterior. However, on the interior of the house, I wouldn't dare do any restoration, such as a fresh coat of paint, because it would cover up things. Moving forward, we need to identify different treatment zones, both within the historic architecture and across the landscape, areas where we may have more stabilization, or even restoration in one place and more conservation in another.

How does work on the historical landscape, such as the large pond, fit into that zoned approach?

The two historical ponds, which one sees by the entrance drive, offer a perfect example of creating zones for the landscape and identifying different treatment levels for them. Their conservation is one of the more conspicuous projects Drayton Hall has taken on the landscape, the goals being to restore the quality and flow of water, to support aquatic life in and around the ponds, and to remove a lot of vegetation. The latter was necessary because the root systems of the trees and shrubs compromised the integrity of the banks by lifting them up and allowing water to seep through. If we had not intervened, removed the 20th-century vegetation, and then re-topped the banks, we'd have ended up losing this valuable historical resource, which is a survivor of some of the oldest inland rice fields in South Carolina. We're also intervening to educate present and future visitors and to enhance wildlife habitat. It's like the roof of Drayton Hall. If we had left the roof to its own devices, it would have eventually failed, taking with it the rest of the house.

What do you think about Drayton Hall not being period specific in its interpretation, or should there be zones for interpretation as well?

I think that the current interpretation is confusing for visitors. Trying to interpret seven generations of people, both free and enslaved, is complicated, and we could do more work focusing on the 18th-century and on what Drayton Hall is — that is, an architectural jewel with remarkable surviving material culture. Thanks to the preservation philosophy, we have a wider palette of resources than anywhere else in colonial America, so we should focus on that initial period, the long 18th century, when Drayton Hall was used as the primary home seat of the Drayton family. That's not to say those stories from the 20th century and the later 19th century are not important, but do they deserve equal time in our research and programming? That's a complicated question. For now, we need to expand the work we're doing on the long 18th century.

What projects have you been engaged in that you think have made the most difference, and how have they made a difference?

I've been involved in a wide variety of projects. One of the more significant is the Wood Family Fellowship. Thanks to that program, we've been able to build up Drayton Hall's preservation department in the last 10 years, bringing in specialists in archaeology, architectural history, and the decorative arts who have put Drayton Hall on the map. The research those individuals are putting forward has been well received on a national level, which has underscored the fact that Drayton Hall is a national, indeed an international, treasure.

What difference do you think our new visitors' center will make?

The construction of our new visitors' center will transform Drayton Hall. While the site's architecture and landscape are incredible, the new facilities will enable visitors to connect to the collection. We have an internationally significant collection of art and artifacts and being able to allow visitors to connect to those objects firsthand will enrich their experience.

Sarah Stroud Clarke:
"Drayton Hall Tells You about the Human Spirit across All People"

2016 – Drayton Hall

Archaeologist Sarah Stroud Clarke was a Wood Family Fellow at Drayton Hall and conducted numerous and important excavations. She is now the site's Director of Museum Affairs.

Could you describe your background, and what led you to archaeology?

I grew up in Virginia Beach. My father was career military and a history buff, so as a child, we were taken to Williamsburg and Jamestown, where I fell in love with archaeology. If you asked my mom, she would tell you that whenever I saw archaeologists working, I'd ask if I could do that when I grew up. She said, "Sure, you can do whatever you want."

I went to Randolph-Macon Woman's College in Virginia, where I told a professor I wanted to be an archaeologist. He encouraged me to participate in several important field schools. After graduating, I became a laboratory tech at Thomas Jefferson's Poplar Forest and later a staff archaeologist at Jamestown. After gaining my masters in Anthropology at San Diego State, I went to Syracuse University for my Ph.D. course work, where my advisor, Theresa Singleton, who's from Charleston, was a leader in colonial-era archaeology and African American sites.

What brought you to Drayton Hall?

Carter Hudgins and Matt Webster brought me here in 2007 because the archaeological collection needed to be assessed. While I knew Virginia sites, I'd had not heard of Drayton Hall. I took a wonderful house tour with Kathy Haney and saw the collections, which were overwhelming. For three decades, the National Trust had employed only one archaeologist, Lynne Lewis. Although she'd done a great job, she was responsible for the Trust's 20-plus sites, and Drayton Hall had suffered from the Trust's lack of investment in collections at its sites and in archaeological collections in particular.

After becoming a Wood Family Fellow in 2007, I assessed those collections and facilitated a proposal to the Institute of Museum and Library Services, awarded in 2009. Because I loved the work, I stayed. To be able to open each box and curate the artifacts within was an archaeologist's dream come true.

How have your thoughts about Drayton Hall evolved?

I went from not knowing anything about Drayton Hall to my world revolving around it. Archaeologically speaking, you never know what you're going to find. My work has evolved because as a team, we've taken Drayton Hall before broader national, even international, audiences.

As an archaeologist and the site's collections' manager, what are your thoughts about our preservation philosophy?

Drayton Hall's preservation philosophy enables us to better understand the past because it provides flexibility. We can research not only seven generations of Draytons but generations, even centuries, of Native Americans and African Americans. Limiting ourselves to one decade would ignore the vast majority of our collections and cut our ability to share knowledge. For example, in looking at the transition between John Drayton's period of ownership in the mid-18th century to his son Charles's in the late 18th and early 19th centuries, I can discern changes in material culture. They have different things, to be sure, but I can see how Charles is a product of his father in how he chooses to furnish the house. He has an aesthetic equal to his father's, but it represents the next generation.

Thanks to our preservation philosophy, we can delineate the evolution of African American material culture. We can show visitors how people used the site over time. For example, everyone uses a plate or a bowl so I can show them a bowl that someone 200 years ago was using and compare it to another from a different period. Archaeology becomes less esoteric when you start relating artifacts to people.

Do you think that these different time periods help visitors see the trajectory of history or do they leave with heads spinning?

Our interpreters have a challenging job because they're on the frontline and have to explain all this information within an hour. It's probably confusing, but we are able to talk about different people on the site. For example, Ms. Charlotta Drayton and the children's growth chart on a wall in the house is something visitors invariably react positively to. We continually try to figure out ways to distinguish time periods and to tell the stories more effectively.

In what projects have you been engaged that have made the most difference? Why?

I would say, first, was the research of the mysterious watercolor dated 1765. Arriving in the mail, it showed the house with large colonnades on either side, so we sought to validate its authenticity. Thanks to archaeology, we learned it was authentic and that the colonnades, which were no longer standing, had, in fact, existed. We also discovered a plantation complex on top of which Drayton Hall was built, which in turn has led to new findings.

The second project was the stabilization of the portico. Before that work happened, it was my job to investigate the area archaeologically. The knowledge we learned was used later, for example, by the structural engineer to figure out tricky mathematical equations. It was a team effort.

What did you learn about the construction of the portico by way of archaeology?

We learned how Drayton Hall was built. In most brick foundations, there's a stepped footer, even just of one step, or brick, to give the foundation a wider footprint for support. Some walls of Drayton Hall don't have a footer at all. I'm not sure I can describe the significance because I am not an architect, but it prompted me to think about those men in the trenches, laying the bricks, and what their knowledge may or may not have been, trying to construct a house of this magnitude. This was a new venture for many, who had not even seen a house of this scale or design and would not have known how things would work out.

We discovered that the staircase on the front of Drayton Hall is not tied to the rest of the building. This intrigued architectural historians because it suggests an earlier staircase. It seems that the house block was built completely, and the staircase was built in front of it at some time before 1765, when the watercolor of Drayton Hall was painted. I've love to get under the staircase to learn for sure, but they won't let me. [Laughs.] I've asked.

What do you think have been the most significant findings?

High on the list would be what we learned about John Drayton and how he used the house during its first decades. Looking at the house architecturally, we can see that he was trying to make a statement about who he was and how he fit in to the larger society. Archaeologically, we see that ambition mirrored in his material culture in, for example, the unusual amount of Chinese export porcelains he had. Most elites of that time would have been using white, salt-glazed stoneware on their tables. While our collections have a bit of that, their quantity pales in comparison to the quantity of porcelain John Drayton imported. So together, the architecture and the archaeology give us a more complete picture of the man.

The number of artifacts related to the enslaved population is fascinating. Unfortunately, documentary records neither tell us much about them nor do we even know how many enslaved people worked in the main house. While we've searched for and still can't find the locations of slave quarters, the sheer amount of material culture we have unearthed, like colonoware, tells us that a large population lived near the main house, so that adds to site interpretation. As we catalogue our archaeological collections, we will learn more.

As we move further through time, material culture becomes harder to use as evidence to distinguish one group from another. For example, in the 18th century, colonoware was being made and used by enslaved Africans and by Native Americans, but as technology advances in the 19th century, more access to lower quality manufactured goods makes it hard to say who was using what. No longer is there the "smoking gun" of artifacts to which you can point and say that one population is using it and another population is not.

If specific objects or places could speak, which ones would you select? What questions would you ask, and why?

We have an amazing collection of delft tiles that originally lined every fireplace on the top two floors, but we have no idea where each pattern went. As we work on our 3D modeling project, this is something we'll virtually re-install. I would love to ask those delft tiles where they belonged so we can properly furnish each room virtually without having to guess.

I'd love to talk to the colonoware to figure out who was actually making it. Were they enslaved people at Drayton Hall or was it made elsewhere and purchased? We have beautifully decorated colonoware in our collections. At what point did the maker decide to emulate English goods and use the same decorations on locally made objects? Answers would also tell us about the people making the colonoware.

Because I know the original kitchen was in the basement and have spent a lot of time excavating there, it's one of my favorite places. I'd love to go back in time and talk to the enslaved people working there and learn about their lives and how those rooms actually functioned. Answers would tell how Drayton Hall was operated on a day-to-day basis and what things were being used and how.

How can historic sites, and specifically the archaeology of historic sites, be used to build bridges?

As a historian and archaeologist, I'm learning about people in the past, yet I strongly believe that this work benefits our world today because it helps us to understand where we are. The shootings at Mother Emanuel came out of a place of ignorance and of not understanding different cultures and ethnicities. A goal of my work, specifically with archaeology, is to bring those topics to life. The ignorance some people carry around with them would be alleviated by understanding how diverse our nation's founding was. I feel that learning through archaeology might help people realize the contributions of each person and each group, and how we are more similar than we are different.

In looking back on our history, what are your thoughts about topics like slavery and historical diversity?

Thank goodness the institution of slavery ended. We should never sugar coat it because, even though there was a Black majority and it might seem like people were peacefully co-existing, there always was resistance. You can see this in the archaeological record. It's important to remember that slavery as an institution ended and why it was wrong. You simply must not enslave other human beings.

Maybe that's the point: People like Dylann Roof never learned about our diverse history and carry their prejudice around with them. The greatest lesson is that we're all in this together. There shouldn't be divisions based on the color of your skin, or who you love, or what country you came from initially.

Why do old places like Drayton Hall matter?

Drayton Hall matters on many levels. It matters that someone decided to build this building at the point in time he did. What was he trying to convey by this new building in this new place? I say new "place," not new "country" because Drayton Hall was standing decades before anyone thought about a new country or nation. To think about what all of that signified to him is fascinating.

Drayton Hall can also tell us about slavery and agriculture. Rice was a new thing to the English. How was rice cultivation established, and what was the synergy between the Africans who grew it and the landscape? Because we interpret all the generations, Drayton Hall offers many stories from the colonial era to the Revolution and through emancipation and phosphate mining to the present. Drayton Hall tells you a lot about the human spirit across all people.

Could you share some of your thoughts about Charlie Drayton, the last Drayton to have owned Drayton Hall?

To talk about Charlie Drayton is a treat. He and his brother Frank made the decision to sell the house out of the family to the Trust. It's been a wonderful experience to know Charlie and to work with him. He's volunteered with me for many years, washing artifacts. He hassles me about why we're doing this and what can we learn from these nails we're washing? He's been supportive of our work and talks about how hard it was for him and his brother to make that decision to sell. For Charlie, it's been gratifying to see the work of professionals, whether it's in my work as an archaeologist or Trish's as the preservationist, and to see the care given to his family home. He loves to see all the things we've been learning.

Charlie is the first to embrace all facets of history, whether we're talking about difficult objects related to slavery or things that his ancestors owned. He has embraced them all head on. It's been a wonderful experience to see someone now in their 90s open to those things that might be challenging. He has been exceptional in his praise of our work. It's been a great experience to know him. Charlie Drayton always has something new to tell us.

Damon Fordham:
"Tell the Truth"

2021 – Telephone Interview

A native of South Carolina, Damon Fordham is a respected teacher and devoted historian. True Stories of Black South Carolina *and* Voices of Black South Carolina *are among his publications, and he has taught at Charleston Southern University, the College of Charleston, and The Citadel. For several years he also worked as an interpreter, or tour guide, at Drayton Hall. He draws upon all these experiences to inform this interview.*

What led you to Drayton Hall, a plantation site, to work as a tour guide, or interpreter?

I started in either 2003 or 2004 and stopped in 2006. I'd been a docent at Boone Hall plantation, so when I heard of the opportunity at Drayton Hall, I applied. My position as adjunct professor at the College of Charleston was up, and its president was phasing out adjuncts. I love history. It's not work for me, yet jobs were hard to find. I grew up around older people who loved to tell stories about things they'd experienced. I grew to love getting up in front of people and telling stories. All of those things led me to Drayton Hall.

What is it that engages you about getting up in front of people and telling stories?

Number one, I'm a natural-born ham. Second, I love to teach and have been a heavy reader since childhood. Before teaching, I worked in radio in the 1990s and as a journalist and found that I could take things I'd learned and use them to make a productive difference in people's lives. I was able to get people to understand that little-known stories mattered. Transmitting that type of information is a joyful thing.

What was your first impression of Drayton Hall?

I wasn't sure how well I would fit in because it was a new environment for me. These were people who, by and large, were sort of old Charleston and somewhat on the aristocratic side at that point. Dealing with that element took a bit of getting used to — some individuals more than others. A lot of the tour was architecture-based, and I was not into architecture. But the historical aspect appealed to me. I grew up in the Bicentennial era, which gave me a superficial understanding about 18th-century history and the American Revolution. My Drayton Hall experience opened me up to the study of that century. The Civil War tends to overshadow the American Revolution, but if it weren't for the Revolution, we wouldn't have the United States.

When you drove down the entry lane to Drayton Hall and saw the mansion in front of you, what were your thoughts?

Not much at all. I had grown up here and was familiar with Boone Hall and places like that. I knew about the history of plantations and slavery and had read a lot of the ex-slave narratives and had heard narratives from my own family. It didn't really faze me. Being on plantations and speaking about the slavery experience can be emotional, but I look at that in the same way a doctor does who has to perform surgery. It's their job. I did then, and still have, an aversion to dressing up in costumes of that period. I did once and didn't enjoy that experience at all.

Did you say you had to dress up in costume at Drayton Hall?

It was for a Revolutionary War reenactment film, "All for Liberty." I played the role of a man, I think, named Samuel Drayton, who ran away from Drayton Hall in 1780 to join the British who promised freedom. I didn't enjoy it. I took off the costume and drove off as soon as I was done. That's the only time I ever had to deal with that.

Are there stories that illustrate your experiences as a tour guide, or interpreter, at Drayton Hall?

I was happy to get to know members of the Bowens family and learn about Richmond Bowens. He was an example of what I like to do. He used his experiences to educate another generation. I have a DVD about him, *I'd Like to See What's Down There*, which taught me a lot regarding the Black experience at Drayton Hall.

I also learned the story of Black Loyalists during the American Revolution. I had no idea about any of that. Their story opened a new world of study. Additionally, I became interested in going through Drayton's diaries and in seeing how honest and open they were about slave life. Drayton Hall guides made a decent effort in telling truthful stories about plantation life. So often with plantation tours, especially at that time, tour guides were more into dealing with the "Gone with the Wind" aspects of life since that's what people wanted to hear. Drayton Hall's guides were more honest, and with your Connections program on African American history, they were moving in the right direction.

What questions did visitors have that illustrated their thoughts or emotions about Drayton Hall?

I'd get the inevitable questions about slavery: "How do you feel about working at a place like this?" I'd say, "Well, this is my field. This is what I do. I study this period." I interpreted the site's history to the average lay person. Every now and then, like the incident with the costume, things would cut a bit too close, but for the most part, as a historian, this is what you do.

Were there any differences in the questions raised by either Black or White visitors?

Black people would ask more questions dealing with slavery while White visitors would ask more about the Drayton family and that sort of thing. That was understandable because people relate more to things they're familiar with, and at that time, fewer White people were familiar with Black history than they are now. What is interesting is that Whites wanted to learn more about the positive aspects of the Draytons while African Americans wanted some acknowledgement of the atrocities they'd heard about during that period. I just told the truth on both ends. I might explain how Charles Drayton did sell people and would have people beaten, which he cited in his diaries. We had excerpts right there. One thing I tried never to do is to sugarcoat things. I put it out there, and you could draw your own conclusions. I have no agenda, other than to tell the truth.

In light of Confederate monuments being taken down, why should slavery-based plantations like Drayton Hall be spared?

History is history. It's there for us to learn from. When it comes to monuments of the Confederacy, like the ones in parks in Charleston, I've used them as teachable moments to show how they took the ugly realities of the Confederacy, as stated in the Articles of Secession, and conveniently left things out and put this false narrative out there. I use these things to show the fallacy of all of that. As for the plantations, to get a full understanding of past experiences, people need to know what happened. When they see it brought into the open, they have an easier time imagining what went on. Plantations are important for the simple fact that the purpose of preserving history is to teach people.

Can historic plantation sites like Drayton Hall be used to bridge racial divides?

Bringing descendants of both the Drayton and African American families together is a capital idea. People can get both sides out in the open. That's important if we're going to move forward as a nation. In late April I posted on Facebook about Captain John Montgomery, who was the man who not only owned my ancestors in Spartanburg but who was my ancestor. I could have omitted his picture, but this man, like it or not, is a part of my history. Even though this man held my ancestors in bondage and fought to keep them in bondage, I have to acknowledge that he is the father of one of my ancestors and is a part of who I am. A lot of Americans don't like to acknowledge things like that, but it's the truth. You can't get anywhere if you don't tell the truth.

What advice would you give to African Americans who may be thinking about working at a historic plantation?

I would encourage them to study the era before they get into it. I was speaking to a conference of young people and was asked, "What websites should we use to learn about history?" I responded: "Library!" I said that because the vast majority of people nowadays, when they go look for things on the internet, they're not doing that to learn something new but to confirm their biases. That's not good research. People need to be more diligent and varied in their research. If you're going to learn about slavery or the Civil War, read the WPA ex-slave narratives, Mary Chesnut's diary, *Gone with the Wind*, or Thomas Dixon's *The Leopard's Spots*, which became the film, *Birth of a Nation*. Even things that are slanted or written in bigotry give you a point of view that existed at that time. That way, you are conversant on both sides of an issue and can present an educated point of view. I learned from reading Nelson Mandela that when he was imprisoned in South Africa, he made it a point to read both the materials of Black nationalists and of the White Afrikaners who promoted apartheid, so he could be conversant and deal with them better. I say the same thing for Americans today.

What questions should African Americans ask if requested to serve on the board of a plantation site?

I would ask, "What point of view are you trying to promote? What is your mission statement?" Looking at their programs, budget allocations, and investments in inclusion would be useful. Politically, I'm not with the left or the right. I'm a free thinker who wants to deal with, in the words of Jack Webb, "Just the facts." If a plantation site had an aversion to the less pleasant realities of history, there's not a lot I could do for them. Investing in programs of diversity and all that is a nice idea, but you must be cautious. A lot of organizations do things like that because it's trendy, so I wouldn't consider that as the main criterion for my joining a board. I would focus on how they do things on a day-to-day basis to see the realities of an organization.

How did you feel as an African American interpreter at a historic, slavery-based plantation?

Again, this is what I do. I was there to tell people the truth about what happened. As a historian, I'm trained to deal with unpleasant subjects. There were times I would not be pleased with a few things, like the issue with costumes, and every now and then, people asked questions or said things that rubbed me the wrong way, like whether the Draytons were good slave owners. People are looking for a way out from the unpleasant realities of the past. When they asked me questions like that, I realized why they were doing it: they were looking for a validation of what they had been led to believe was decent, but it wasn't. I told them the truth.

How would you respond when people asked you about whether the Draytons were good slave owners or not?

I told them what Charles Drayton himself said in his diaries — having to beat Billy or sending people to the workhouse on what's now Magazine Street. I'd give them the facts, based on solid research. I didn't then, and I don't now, have a history of going on propaganda rants based more on emotion than fact. I believe in dealing in the most honest level possible. I gave people answers derived from primary sources, so they could look anything up if they had any doubt of what I was talking about.

What do you see as the future of historic plantation sites?

That remains to be seen. Now is a time of confusion because you have people who are against historic plantation sites, but that movement is so lacking in solid direction and clear agendas that it's going to be relatively short lived. If you're going to have a movement, you can't base it on emotionalism alone and simply say that we're going to get rid of Aunt Jemima pancakes, the Cream of Wheat man, and all these other things. Okay. So what are you going to do that's going to make a genuine, positive difference in society, as opposed to a Facebook rant of the week? If you can't answer that question, I'm not interested.

A lot of what's going on now, while some of it is productive, will run its course. These things tend to come and go in cycles. In the past, movements have been specific about things that needed to be changed, whereas today I see things as going all over the place emotionally. I don't think that's a healthy thing. It would be good to have scholars, like Dr. Henry Louis Gates, who are very knowledgeable about these things, deal with genuine timetables and specific goals.

Right now, there's a lot of hostility toward these historic places because of the current social and political climate. I hope leadership will be developed to take plantations in a positive direction to improve the display of them.

I definitely want to say Drayton Hall has enriched me by enabling me to learn more about a period in history I knew little about. My college major was not African American history. It was U.S. history, post-Reconstruction. It was through Drayton Hall that I learned to be conversant in the pre-Civil War history of America, and that has helped me in innumerable ways.

Shelia Harrell-Roye:
"Commit to Telling the Truth"

2021 – Telephone Interview

Shelia Harrell-Roye is a native of Charleston. She graduated from the College of Charleston and earned a master's degree in history from there. After working at Drayton Hall for six years, Harrell-Roye now works in higher education focused on student retention and development. She lives in Winston-Salem, North Carolina, with her husband and loving fur-babies.

Brittany Butterworth

George: *When did you work for Drayton Hall, and what led you to work as an interpreter, or tour guide, there?*

I worked there from 2008 to 2012 after its being recommended by my College of Charleston history professor, Dr. Bernard Powers. Although he suggested the Drayton Hall job to diversify my resume, I was reluctant initially. I wanted to be a truth teller about slavery on the site, and would not deviate from that goal. I didn't know anyone there until I began working there. I then left to earn my master's degree and returned in 2015 to be Curator of Education. I resigned in 2017 because my husband was offered a career-advancement job in Winston-Salem, NC, where we now live.

When you first drove into Drayton Hall, what was your initial impression?

Sterile. Very sterile. I did not feel much. Honestly, it was not inviting.

When did your views change?

My supervisor, Craig Tuminaro, and my mentor, Peggy Reider, sparked the change. I told them upfront that I would not sugarcoat interactions of the planter elite and the enslaved people and that much more remained to be discovered. Many people of color wondered, "How will they present history?" I asked Craig and Peggy about that, and they responded, "Being open and not sugarcoating reality are what we want."

Are there stories that illustrate your experiences as an interpreter at Drayton Hall?

When I was Curator of Education, someone complained to me about what they thought was an inaccurate depiction of the history. Trying to calm the situation, I asked her in a polite but direct manner, "What can I do to help you walk away with a better feeling?" She replied, "I want you to tell the truth. I don't need to be refunded for my ticket. I don't need a special tour. I don't need anything additional. Just commit to telling the truth." I told her she had my word, and she thanked me. That was it. That's all she wanted. I think that's what most people want. She did not say our interpreter was lying. She said our interpreter was trying to not be direct about the truth. That happens at many sites. I have never forgotten what she said.

When I conducted tours, I tried to tell a story that included the status of various people at Drayton Hall and that illustrated what actually happened. My tour was all about people. I used words to paint a picture in a house which I thought was sterile and uninviting. But it was our canvas. An interpreter's job is to "paint" the story rooted in facts about what happened inside each room of the house. Information was available for each room, and it was more than enough to provide insightful glimpses into history. Some guides did this extremely well while others did not.

What are the advantages and disadvantages of an actual guided tour and a self-guided audio tour of a site?

A self-guided audio tour offers financial savings, less staff management, and time management by the visitor. The biggest disadvantage is the loss of human interaction. Your staff is often the main reason visitors enjoy the experience and why they continue to come or come back.

When you talk about truthful stories in each room, did that have to do with slavery and race and with African Americans being left out of the picture? Or was it women? Or something else?

You could tell stories about who occupied that space in terms of gender, race, or status and what was going on so the audience would understand. It should not be a lecture. It's a story. It's how you engage the guests. Metaphorically, you don't want to give visitors everything on the plate when they arrive. Instead, serve it in a way that they want to come back for more.

When my tour was assessed by Peggy Reider, we did not see eye to eye initially. "You have this information, so how can you make it engaging for your audience?" she asked. Indeed, for many visitors, history is dry and not intriguing. Interpreters need to make a connection, shape the facts into an interesting story. Thanks to the Drayton papers — digitized and accessible — we had more than enough material to get the audience intrigued.

Did you find a difference between the questions and responses of African American visitors and White visitors? Could you explain that difference?

In general, visitors were thirsting for knowledge and understanding. They did not understand the history of slavery or, for many, the founding of America and subsequent time periods. A clear difference was African American guests wanted to understand what happened and asked a lot of "why" questions. Most of our White guests wanted to know if slavery was really so bad, if it wasn't more like the extension of a family. Until I left in 2017, White people were still asking, "Was slavery that bad?"

As evidence, I could have focused on physical abuse but chose instead to focus on understanding interactions as told through the Drayton documents. For example, they tell the story of Affy, an elderly enslaved woman owned by John Drayton's fourth wife, Rebecca. I used those accounts to show how vulnerable the enslaved were and how the Draytons asserted their position in the social hierarchy. The truth is that Affy, under slavery, wasn't considered a person. She was considered property. Certain things were done for and to slaves based on status, not kindness.

Since you were active in education, what do think of on-site school programs?

This is an important topic now for museums across the nation. Students are stimulated when you paint them a picture of how things were and how they occurred. You must guide them, open a dialogue with them, and invite them to participate. Hands-on activities drive home certain historical points. Students need this stimulation, and the traditional classroom isn't the only place where they gain this knowledge. Outreach is extremely important. This pandemic placed a full stop on some public programs, but they were important then and they're important now, even more so.

Why can't school programs simply be given online?

Engagement happens when you're face to face versus online. Online can be sterile. It doesn't provide the stimulation most students desire.

How do you teach a painful issue like slavery to elementary school students?

That's difficult. What I found helpful — and it is something that was done at Drayton Hall when Peggy Reider oversaw training — is focusing on the main goals and messaging of the programs. You ensure that hands-on activities are based on age and how that age group can digest the information. Topics like slavery must be taught in steps. It's a difficult topic for young children and adults to understand, and with students, you go slower. They ask "Why?" and "Who decided this?" Since answers might be hard to understand, slow and steady should be the approach. However, it does no one any good to sugarcoat slavery or to act as though these things did not occur. It's important that they gain an understanding, and Drayton Hall's programs did so.

To show that enslaved people were property, we used the Draytons' inventory lists, so students could see the cost of slaves and that human beings were on the same list as animals, silver, or furniture. As students progressed into middle and high schools, we engaged them more deeply into those lists. I think seeing those lists created critical thinkers and taught a lot of history to students.

Why do you think many African Americans do not visit historic plantation sites?

Visiting is considered nonsensical. The stories told about what occurred do not convey what many African Americans consider to be honest, and most sites do not have a diverse staff. They believe they will not connect with the presentations, but that's true not only with Black guests. All visitors want to know about those who lived there, not just what they built or about the layers of paint. You must make it intriguing. It cannot be simply facts woven together that are of interest to only a few members of society. The information should be presented in such a way that reaches the wider community.

Changing the on-site story is good. But since decisions about time management and whether or not to visit a site are made in advance, how can sites like Drayton Hall remedy image problems and attract more African Americans?

Outreach is key. During my tenure, our outreach focused on working with schools, colleges, and other private organizations to spread the word about what we had to offer and how we wanted to provide resources. They could visit or we could work with them in person. I am not talking about numerous or pro bono programs but rather about marketing Drayton Hall as a resource to help in education and to improve the lack of knowledge prevalent in our society. It must be an assertive effort. The pandemic is a watershed moment for sites because they must decide how they want to be seen. If historic sites do not change their approach and become more inviting and direct about their histories, I fear many won't survive.

How can historic plantation sites like Drayton Hall be used to bridge racial divides?

I would not say they could be used to bridge racial divides, but they could assist in educating and providing a platform for dialogue. I recall conducting the Connections program, which focused on the African American experience. It was scheduled as a 45-minute program, but sometimes we'd be there for two hours because the questions didn't stop until I cut off the conversation. People remain thirsty for knowledge and to have conversations. You must train people to be facilitators. During my first years at Drayton Hall, training was extensive, and it was needed; many new interpreters were not prepared for questions they were asked. Training provided them with tools to answer questions, help them stick to facts, and to place their emotions aside. It was wonderful training that Peggy Reider, Craig Tuminaro, and others provided.

What advice would you give to African Americans thinking about working at a historic plantation site?

They need to assess their own feelings and what they can offer, and especially be open to the opportunity. Be open to the information coming to you, stand strong, and maintain integrity. Many things are going to be questioned, not just by guests but also by colleagues. That's because of lack of knowledge and exposure. You need to be sure the information is accurate and that you can tell visitors where it can be found. To most visitors, information is not important or relevant if it is not easily accessible.

What advice would you give to African Americans who may be considered for serving on a board of a plantation site?

Do it! Diverse voices are needed on every board and every committee. One reason many boards and committees make mistakes is because they are not diversified. Those voices are needed.

What are your favorite memories or stories about working at Drayton Hall?

When Todd and I got engaged, Drayton Hall had a "congratulations" party for us. Craig and the staff organized it. We gathered by the reflecting pond. Everyone brought food. It was not catered. It was not overly fancy. I recall other parties for us that were fancier, but my husband and I agreed that none were as warm as the one at Drayton Hall. That was because of the people, the camaraderie among the staff.

What did you like least about Drayton Hall?

Some guides unwilling to insert certain aspects of history into their tours. That's sad. The good news is they did not stay long, but it was difficult to work with that resistance. There were problems in using certain verbiage. Some interpreters were annoyed by having to use the term "enslaved." A lot of sites were not using that verbiage, but we were, and they did not like it.

What other questions would you want me to ask?

I want to add what is more of a statement than a question: Leadership matters. It is particularly important right now. Interpretations of what happened on historic sites must be direct — intentional. To tell the truth is not pushing an agenda or specific narrative. It's understanding that museum professionals have an obligation to be honest about what happened by presenting facts. We cannot sit on the sidelines. If we tell the truth, people will embrace the stories. They want to understand. But I question if the desire to put the truth out there is present. This has been and is an ongoing struggle and one on which we need to work harder as a community of lifelong learners and educators.

Why is leadership so important? Why can't it come from the ground up?

Leadership sets the tone. If supportive, it allows you as a professional to move forward productively with integrity and innovation. If support comes from the helm, collaboration is there, and success is achievable. It is leadership's job to guide and ensure that the team stays the course and moves in the right direction. You might hear people say, "It's actually from the "ground up," but the "ground up" can't do what's needed if there is no support and tools coming from the top — that is how it goes.

Tom Mayes:
"A Different Sense of Time"
2020 – Telephone Interview

Having served for more than three decades as an attorney for the National Trust for Historic Preservation, Thompson (Tom) Mayes is now its chief legal counsel. A devoted preservationist, he has taught, spoken, and written about historic preservation for years, the most recent example being his award-winning book, Why Old Places Matter, *which I recommend to all. Countless times I called him for advice when I was director of Drayton Hall, and unfailingly I was met with wisdom, honesty, and good humor.*

Growing up as a North Carolinian and a Southerner, what did history and historic preservation mean to you?
What made the difference was not that I grew up in the South, but that I grew up in an old community. My father was a farmer, my mother, a teacher, and we were a plain upcountry farm family in a stable farming community. We lived north of Charlotte near the towns of Cornelius, Huntersville, and Davidson. Early on, I became fascinated by old houses, and my father would take me to see the old places nearby.

Like lots of farmers, we stored hay and grain in old, abandoned houses. One of our family friends used a plantation house called Glenwood as a barn. Although shutters still hung by the windows, not a single pane of glass remained. It was this sort of rural experience that shaped my interest in old places.

My affinity for old places might be hardwired because ever since I was a kid, I was interested in historic preservation. In high school, my mother arranged for me to use the Davidson College Library, where I spent afternoons looking at architectural history books, including Plantations of the Carolina Lowcountry, with photographs by Frances Benjamin Johnston. Her photographs of Drayton Hall mesmerized me because while I'd seen photographs of old places in Charleston and North Carolina, none had the scale of Drayton Hall or were as architecturally distinguished and elaborate. I was fascinated by the way Drayton Hall seemed so empty, an emptiness that made the site evocative and powerful and enabled it to convey a different sense of time.

Roland Barthes used a term, "punctum," which when applied to fiction marks the moment — and I could be getting the definition completely wrong — when the reader realizes he has been touched in some way, or is in some larger reality, or has experienced a feeling or emotion that can't be easily articulated verbally. To me, Drayton Hall seems to have that mesmerizing quality of having pierced time. It broadened my sense of time because I could see that this place had survived. While it seemed nominally cared for and preserved, it had the quality of having been battered a bit and having come through a lot of changes and trauma. At that time, I didn't know it was missing two flankers and a panoply of outbuildings.

When I was in law school from 1982 to 85, I went to see Drayton Hall. Open to the public by the National Trust, it had become a pilgrimage site for me, as I'm sure it is for other people. I visited with a dear friend, and she and I both remember the visit to this day. It was thrilling to see it in person and in color, not in the black and white photographs from the 1930s.

What value do you think Drayton Hall and other historic sites have? Why should people care about them?

I wrote a book, *Why Old Places Matter*, which tries to capture the many, many reasons that old places matter to people. Drayton Hall represents many of its ideas. It is architecturally significant, one of the greatest Palladian houses in America, and represents the history of Palladianism — from the Roman Vitruvius to Renaissance Italy to 18th-century Great Britain and its colonies. It's also a place that's beautiful because of that evocative sense of time. Because it's preserved instead of restored, it feels like a ruin. That feeling I might have been sensing in the Davidson College Library relates to the idea of the sublime and to the emotional feeling people have when they experience ruins. Drayton Hall definitely has that quality, even though it's very carefully preserved. It has beauty, architecture, and history, but also ancestral ties for the descendants of all the people who lived there. For the Draytons and for the African American families and other families who have toiled there or been in bondage there, there's an ancestral tie to that place, and that connection to place gives the descendants a sense of belonging.

It's also a tourist's pilgrimage site and helps drive the tourism economy. People go to historic places to explore their ancestors, to experience the sense of beauty, to get that feeling of the sublime, to have that special sense that proportion, balance, and harmony of an architectural space offers. But most of all, Drayton Hall is one of those places that gives people a sense of continuity between the past and the present and the future. The fact that something like Drayton Hall has survived and continues to survive today expands people's sense of time and their connection to the past in a way that helps them be able to see the future. You and countless visitors have felt it. Old places like Drayton Hall have the capacity to broaden people's sense, not only of history, but of humanity, which can help them feel an openness to understanding other people and hopefully engender a broader empathy.

Old places can promote negative nostalgia. In the South, it might take the form of the "Lost Cause" concept of the Old South. Elsewhere, it might accent the idea that today we have to defend our heritage, represented by this beautiful site, because we've got barbarians at the gate. How can sites like Drayton Hall overcome the negative use of old places?

Drayton Hall cannot be a place that fails to fully acknowledge and educate people about the fact that it was built on the backs of people who were in bondage. It couldn't have been constructed otherwise. That's true not only for Drayton Hall, but of all plantation sites. They were effectively slave labor camps, where people were enslaved and their labor used to create immense wealth, not only in Charleston or the South, but in Great Britain and other parts of the world. That history not only has to be acknowledged but has to be front and center in any interpretation.

There are those who think places like Drayton Hall should be destroyed. I do not think that. They should remain for the many qualities they have, and also as a testament to the people who built them and labored there. While it's difficult to imagine that pre-Civil War world, we live with its legacy every day, and Drayton Hall has historically been at the forefront of talking about that history and acknowledging the connections to the living descendants of the people who were enslaved there or worked there. That work has to continue.

Preservation always has the danger of being manipulated to tell a narrative that supports an identity that is exclusive and used to keep people down. At the same time, these old places are the very places where the story can best be told of what actually happened and where the real history of slavery can be described. They are actually a testament to that reality. Plantation sites have not only the capacity, but an essential obligation, to tell that story. Otherwise, they are leaving out the reality of how they were created and why they even exist.

Why do people not care about preservation?

I'm going to push back on the question because most studies of the National Trust and in Great Britain show that the majority of people do care about preservation and old places, but preservation is always balanced against competing priorities, like property rights, free exercise of religion, or monetary issues around development and personal income. It's not true that people don't care about preservation. That said, we preservationists need to do a better job in asking people what they value. The more people engage in talking about and deciding the things they value in their own communities, the more they'll support the preservation of places like Drayton Hall. Sometimes, the places people value are surprising and may differ from what a trained preservationist would find in an architectural survey.

What were examples? What could we preservationists learn?

One example is Domino Park in Little Havana in Miami, a key gathering place for the community of people who came from Cuba from the 1950s forward. While from an architectural point of view it's not a place a trained preservationist would identify, it's a key part of the identity of that community. It's a part of people's memories, is used constantly, and is essential to their sense of belonging. It exemplifies the idea of continuity that I referred to earlier.

If you were a teacher, how would you teach about important places that are "non-architectural"? With architecture, one can point to something visible and explain why it's significant. How would you get people to appreciate something they may not see?

Getting people to understand historical significance requires learning how to approach and engage a community, so that it can identify the places that it cares about. That's a different way of thinking and a different skill set. There are a variety of ways this may be done, such as through mapping exercises, online devices by which people can submit things, meetings, or tours. Buildings other than the Drayton Halls may have high value, just not in the same way. For example, in Mount Pleasant, South Carolina, is the Phillips community, a historically African American community that does not have buildings that are architecturally significant, yet it's an historic place. It gives people that sense of belonging, memory, continuity, and history. Threatened now by a proposed new roadway, it is worthy of preservation because of those characteristics I've cited.

What issues in the future should become priorities for historic sites like Drayton Hall? How should historic sites change, and what should they be sure to keep?

People think of historic preservation as about freezing things, but it's actually about managing change and can even be an agent for change. When I think about the things that historic sites should keep, I think that they have to ensure they are telling the full story. If it's a plantation site, that means telling the story of slavery in an honest and meaningful way.

For Drayton Hall, one of the things to keep is that emotional experience people have when they visit the site, that sense of transcending time. Drayton Hall is one of the places in America where you can experience that sense of time most powerfully. It's not easy to give a crowd of visitors the space to have powerful experiences, but that's at the heart of why an old place like Drayton Hall matters.

More broadly, historic sites have to remain relevant and actively in use. The more a place is removed from the ongoing activities of the community, the less attachment the community feels to it. It's central for historic sites to be fully engaged with their communities and vice versa, so that people are forming memories connected to that site. For example, I have good memories of my visit to Drayton Hall when I was in law school and thus carry it with me. The more people get to experience a place, the more they care about it.

Drayton Hall should continue to build on the decision not to restore the historic core of the site. At that time, the inclination throughout the country was to restore an historic site to its period of greatest significance, yet the National Trust in consultation with the community chose not to do that, thereby allowing one of the most powerful aspects of Drayton Hall to be preserved and to continue to impact us today. One has to pay attention to a site's unique strengths and to what unique story it has to tell and build on that. In the past there's been a tendency for sites to want to mimic each other, so Drayton Hall offers the opportunity to show how preservation can be done in different ways.

What are some of your favorite memories or stories about Drayton Hall?

One of my favorites is the Watson Hill story (a mega-development of c. 4,500 homes and a commercial district proposed in 2005 a little more than five miles up the Ashley River Road from Drayton Hall). I had to propose to our Board of Trustees that the National Trust would agree to indemnify a property owner for the owner's actions in trying to stop the mega-development by blocking annexation by the city of North Charleston through their property to Watson Hill. The larger goal was to control the broader development around Drayton Hall. That's not something that a board of trustees would normally go for, yet thanks to our partners, the board approved it, and it made a difference in preserving the regional context of Drayton Hall.

My second favorite memory is going out on the river with you, George, and eating shrimp on an island in the Ashley. I remember that day and will continue to remember it. I saw the whole length of the Ashley River, which I'd never seen before, nor had I observed Drayton Hall from the water, a view that many people historically had beheld. And we did have Prosecco to go with Palladio.

Speaking of the Watson Hill mega-development and our appeal for legal help, you could have refused, but instead you jumped to join us. Why?

First, I loved the legal creativity of it, the crafting of a strategy. Second, I loved the idea of helping a couple who had set in motion the consequences for development that they did not anticipate. Third, I loved the idea of the partners that came together to make that happen. We were not standing alone. We were standing with a coalition of preservation and conservation organizations. At the root of it all is what a good lawyer does: he tries to achieve the goals of his client. Our goal was to prevent that mega-development. I was supportive of that goal. I remember our board asking a lot of questions, but at the end, they were very supportive. Congratulations to you and the team in Charleston that came up with that idea. It made sense.

Do you have other favorite memories about Drayton Hall?

I have memories of just being there. One of the things I've loved about Drayton Hall is that in the summer, spring, and fall, the house is open so that you feel the natural air as people would have years ago. I remember being in that upper hall and feeling the breeze come through in a way that keeps the connection between the building and the environment, with the smell of the river and the land meeting in that great old house. It's a simple memory, but real.

Helen Hill:
"Intertwine the Stories"

2020 – Telephone Interview

A native Charlestonian, Helen Hill is the CEO of Explore Charleston, the destination marketing organization for Charleston's Tri-County region. In addition to describing her thoughts about Drayton Hall, she assesses tourism and how museums and sites need to respond to visitors' interests and today's times.

Could you tell me what Drayton Hall and historic sites meant to you growing up in Charleston?

Helen: I'm blessed to have grown up in Charleston, and Drayton Hall has always been a part of my life. My earliest memory is seeing all that green grass. When I was young, it was a great place to run. I'll never forget running around back and thinking, "Wow, here's the river!" As an eighth-grader at Ashley Hall, I remember all of us laughing because we couldn't believe there was not a bathroom in the house! That's the same time we started to learn why Drayton Hall was so important, not just in Charleston or South Carolina but in the nation.

One of my favorite memories is of my Clemson internship when I had the opportunity to work with Fred Brinkman, director of the South Carolina Department of Parks, Recreation, and Tourism, who detailed to us his department's hard work in preserving the whole site of Drayton Hall. If we look at it today in 2020, where would we be, George, if you and Charles Duell had not preserved the things you did? Unfortunately, it would be very different.

As a tourism professional, what value do Drayton Hall and historic sites have? Why care?

Through my more than 35+ years of asking visitors why they chose to visit Charleston, the number one reason is always history. Numbers two, three, and four may change — food, outdoor recreation, and golf —-but history is always number one. That makes sense because history is Charleston's differentiating factor. There's not another Charleston, South Carolina.

Drayton Hall is knit into the very fabric of that. There's not another Drayton Hall. Many times, you and I have talked about the Charleston Heritage Federation and those places that make us different from any city in the world. We work hard to lift those up, because not only are we supporting historic preservation, but we're doing something good for the visitor by promoting something they're not going to see anywhere else. Charleston is definitely not Any Town, USA.

How do historic sites and museums contribute to the economy?

When people make a vacation-buying decision, Drayton Hall appeals to those interested deeply in National Trust projects or historic sites or to the couple who want to spend a lovely day outdoors and learn more about American history. From soup to nuts, Drayton Hall covers those. Other places may offer a nice beach, a fabulous meal, or great shopping, but there's not another place that has a Drayton Hall.

History is not static. When a man mailed you a picture of the Drayton Hall watercolor — the earliest painting of the house showing two flanker buildings — it was a view not seen before and shows we're always learning. That's magic.

I appreciate the decision made by the Drayton family when they turned their house over to the National Trust, knowing it was to be preserved, not restored. That too is magic because there's nothing like that elsewhere — where you can walk through and see change over time.

One of the greatest talks you gave, George, was when we were at Drayton Hall and trying to sell Charleston to JetBlue as a destination. In the drawing room, Lou Hammond, you, and the gentleman from JetBlue, were discussing the exposed brick masonry and how one can discern the evolution of a building by changes in the bricks. He's never forgotten that. He still brings that up to me. In fact, when he came back to Charleston, he took his wife to see Drayton Hall, so taken was he.

As a tourism professional looking at sites like Drayton Hall, what mistakes do we make?

You have to remember and re-educate folks about history. The magic of Drayton Hall is that its history goes from the beginning of our colonial past to the current day, but the story needs to connect to people. For that JetBlue executive, you brought the site to life by telling the story. Sometimes we get so busy sharing facts or details, we miss the magic of the story, but that's what people remember. You also need to tell them what you're trying to achieve.

You and I were blessed to know Charlie Drayton (with his brother, Frank, the last owners of Drayton Hall). What a great man, so unassuming! One of my best conversations with him was about the African American cemetery. He was proud of its preservation.

If you were teaching a course in tourism, how would you use Drayton Hall?

I'd use Drayton Hall as a centerpiece for how historic preservation can attract visitors by creating and intertwining the stories about architecture, landscapes, gardens, plants, and people. You've renovated the gift shop and sell things that are very Charleston, very South Carolina. The future is going to be about how people access things, as we do with the Charleston Heritage Federation, which you helped found. Your friend, Lonnie Bunch from the Smithsonian, was a big believer in joint tickets and in making it easy to visit. I also remember you teaching me about a viewshed. Thanks to your buying the land, visitors aren't now looking at condos across the Ashley River. As we look to the future, land conservation is going to be the story. If I were teaching a course, I'd say, "Follow this model."

How important is making your site easy to visit and in giving visitors the chance to manage their time?

People today have limited amounts of time and need to know what they can enjoy in a short while or in a whole day. "We're not going to go because we only have two hours" is a common barrier for visitation. However, if a visit is designed from a telling-the-story perspective, visitors can choose between the shorter option and the longer one and manage time accordingly. Offer visitors enough so they enjoy a wonderful taste in a short amount of time and let them know what the value is for a longer visit. Remember, there's magic in telling the story, but give visitors options.

How do historic preservation and tourism relate to one another?

Balance is the key. We've worked hard to market Charleston by appealing to folks interested in history because if we attract the wrong visitor, they're going to be disappointed. Charleston is not Orlando or Disney World. We know people want different kinds of visits at different times in their life. For example, we now market to grandparents and grandchildren. Is that a market for sites? You must show there's always something happening and give somebody a reason to come back. You want to create that repeat visitor.

Targeted marketing and having the right folks who understand and appreciate what they're coming to see is one key element. You need to make history approachable enough, so visitors don't feel as if they have to have a PhD to enjoy the visit. You've also got to use modern communication tools. For example, virtual reality could be used for tours and other offerings at Drayton Hall and other sites.

Why do you think visitors, especially African Americans, choose not to visit Charleston or plantation sites like Drayton Hall? What can be done to attract more African Americans?

Our historic sites, particularly Drayton Hall, have done a good job of telling not only the negative part of the story — like slavery, and there's no way to make it anything but negative — but also talking about the positive things that come from that. Some of the most amazing artisans were Black, as seen in Charleston, and you can't separate Charleston history from Black history because they're so interwoven.

Telling that story is key. For example, at the groundbreaking of the International African American Museum in Charleston, Congressman James Clyburn told how, despite the horrors people experienced during the slave times, African Americans were artisans, rice cultivators, cooks, and more. My friend and artist Jonathan Green agreed. That's the kind of story that will create the desire for African Americans to visit. The stories of a place and its people are intertwined. You can't tell the story of Drayton Hall without talking about both the Draytons and those people who were slaves and later, freed people.

How should a site like Drayton Hall convey research findings to visitors and not let time balloon out?

That's what I love about options for visitors. You first attract them with the main story and then offer options if visitors are interested. It's like reading a good book: get that first chapter right and the reader is hooked.

Technology may offer solutions. Look at your place and ask: What did Drayton Hall look like years ago? What was the same? Different? What was around the house? How did diverse people dress? You engage visitors by questions and by using visuals of what it used to look and feel like. You can go back to whatever period of time you pick. While many things are changing, the house provides permanence. That sells them on the fact that they can't believe the house is still here. There's magic to that.

Looking back on your career, what lessons have you learned as a leader? What do younger readers need to keep in mind if they aspire to be leaders?

The most important thing for any aspiring leader is to be curious. Curiosity is the most attractive trait. An example is the guy from JetBlue asking you about bricks. People want to talk about what they're excited about. As a young leader, if you are authentically curious about what you're doing, a lot of people will give you their time, talent, and treasure to train you. The second most valuable lesson is communication. Most often, when two people don't see things the same way, they probably haven't communicated enough to find out the other's opinion and to really understand it. Those two: being curious and communicating, especially curiosity. That's what makes you excited about getting up in the morning. It's fun. It makes life exciting.

If upon your retirement, a magic wand were waved and you woke up as director of Drayton Hall, what would you aim for?

That would be the best, best job right after mine. I would follow your footsteps, George, and do things necessary for historic preservation of not only Drayton Hall but also the larger community. I'd love interacting with people and telling the story of Drayton Hall. The story of not having a bathroom just flips people out, especially little people. It might help them to be more positive when they started feeling like "Oh, poor, pitiful me."

I'd work hard to tell more complete stories and make it clear that we're not changing the story but rather adding more depth to it. Our challenge going forward is how do we keep history interesting. How do we approach history in such a way that we capture people's imagination about the past as they plan our future?

How might historic preservation and historic sites benefit the future?

Historic destinations like Charleston and historic sites like Drayton Hall have an even more critical role in the future to play. That's what I was talking about with the marriage between preservationists and historians and tourism professionals. It's even more important that we intertwine the stories now, because we can't have a better future without understanding the past. While everybody wishes for a more perfect past, we need to talk about the triumph and tragedy more openly so that we know how to live in the future.

Matt Webster:
"This Privy Was Advanced for Its Day"

2005 – Drayton Hall

This interview was conducted by Alison Guss, producer from The History Channel for Drayton Hall's interactive DVD tour of the landscape. Matthew Webster was director of the preservation department of Drayton Hall and now serves as Executive Director, Grainger Department of Architectural Preservation and Research at Colonial Williamsburg Foundation. At Drayton Hall, he discovered architectural features in the main house and elsewhere, which he synthesized into new ways of interpreting the site, as exemplified by his perceptions of this late 18th-century privy.

Excerpts from "The Voices of Drayton Hall: An Interactive Landscape Tour on DVD," produced by The History Channel

What is the history of this privy?

Built in the 1790s by Charles Drayton, the second son of John Drayton and the second owner of Drayton Hall, this brick privy is the only remaining 18th-century outbuilding at Drayton Hall. The changes to it over its 200+ year history illuminate interesting chapters of Drayton Hall's story.

Originally, there was a window in the "east" side of the building, for today you can see the line from where the window was placed and where they built the chimney right into the window opening. Originally, the structure had no fireplace or chimney, only windows. It was a cold bathroom!

Its roofline has changed because the gable end is now oriented towards the river, or "east", but was originally facing the front, or "south," toward the front lawn. In the post-Civil war period, the building's function changed, and it became an office when they were mining calcium phosphate here. To heat the office, a chimney was added, so the roofline was re-configured to today's.

After serving as an office, the building was used in the 1920s as a residence by

Richmond Bowens, then in his early teens, and his brother Frank. Their father Richmond, the son of the enslaved Caesar Bowens, had died in 1920, and his mother had re-married. Richmond's mother, her new husband, and younger children (among them were interviewee Annie Brown Meyers' mother, Lucille Bowens) lived in a post-Civil War frame house located between the privy and the main house, which became the gift shop (now exhibited as a tenant house). This brick building's use as a residence ended when the chauffeur of Miss Charlotta Drayton stayed here whenever she visited her property. By that time, the caretaker's family, the Burns, resided in the postbellum frame dwelling by the main house. Both in use and appearance over time, this one brick building has changed considerably, so, like the main house, is a survivor.

How did this building function as a privy? What does it illustrate about 18th-century sanitation and hygiene?

As demonstrated by its drainage system, this privy was advanced for its day and illustrates how Charles Drayton, who earned his M.D. from the University of Edinburgh, thought seriously about health and hygiene. Along today's back wall at the northeast corner, archaeologists found a brick box with an opening on the side that fed into the brick-lined drain line along the back of the privy, about three feet deep. Above that line was the row of seven seats inside, as shown in a drawing of the 1840s. Two have arms, obviously for adults, while the two at each end are lower in height for children. Periodically the privies would be "flushed" by pouring buckets of water into the brick box feeding into the drain line along the back wall. Water would carry the waste down the drain line to the "west" wall of the building where an arch led to a long tunnel, also arched and completely constructed of brick that extended out from the west wall. Archaeologists have found that it then led to a drainage ditch at some distance and thence to other ditches and finally to the Ashley River.

Fortunately, drawings from the 1840s show the interior and exterior of this building and have enabled us to look for corroborating evidence in its architecture. While we knew the building had been a privy, it was not until these diverse sources of evidence — drawings, archaeology, and the building itself — had been examined together did we know of how it had originally functioned as a "flushing privy." Like the main house, it was complex and advanced for its time.

What types of artifacts did the archaeologists find in excavating the privy?

Archaeologists found broken glassware, clay smoking pipes, chamber pots, and other artifacts because privies often served as trash bins. For example, if somebody is smoking a clay pipe in the bathroom, then the pipe stems would end up out there. Broken glassware could be safely discarded into the hole. As for chamber pots, they might have been dropped, so all the pieces were picked up and thrown away, thereby enabling us later to re-assemble them. In fact, in Drayton Hall's collections is a creamware chamber pot from the 1790s to c. 1820, or from Charles Drayton's period of ownership. All its pieces were found while excavating this privy.

While serving a common use, what does the privy reveal about the uncommon status of Drayton Hall?

Like the detailing of the house and other outbuildings, the Drayton privy spoke to the status of the family. The Drayton Hall privy compares easily to the best structures of this form in the Americas. This includes the five-seat, heated privy at Westover in Virginia, the fortified privy at Stewart's Castle in Jamaica, and the finely constructed stone privy at Good Hope in Jamaica. Constructed of brick masonry with brick quoins at the corners, a molded water table, windows, stone steps, and even arms for two privy seats, its detailing was far beyond what would be expected for a building that served such a purpose.

These details, however, are not the only feature that sets the Drayton privy apart. It is the functional component – the large drainage tunnel that leads from the structure. Most privies have ports directly below for drainage and/or cleaning. The drainage tunnel carried the effluent away and could even be flushed. This allowed the seated to avoid the unpleasantness of effluent being held directly below. The Drayton Privy is yet another building that showed visitors the status of the family in 18th-century society.

Susan Buck with Recollections about Edward Chappell:
"The Most Magical Place"

2021 – Telephone Interview

A highly respected paint conservator, Susan Buck has worked on contracts at Drayton Hall for decades and knows its history well, including its original appearance thanks to her paint research. She was married to architectural historian Edward (Ed) Chappell, who both documented and made new discoveries at Drayton Hall for decades before he passed away unexpectedly in 2020. Both he and Susan lived in Williamsburg, Virginia, and worked on historic places around the world.

What is your background, and what led you into historic preservation and paint conservation?

Susan: I'm from Hanover, New Hampshire, and my family is from New England. After graduating from Williams College with a studio art degree, I earned an MS from the Winterthur and University of Delaware Graduate Program in Art Conservation in 1991 and a PhD in Art Conservation Research from the University of Delaware in 2003.

Because I started in art conservation, my entry into historic preservation was sideways. In grad school, I'd concentrated on furniture conservation and the analysis of varnishes and coatings on furniture. I began examining cross sections of paint samples from buildings and using them as evidence to figure out how a building had changed. Realizing I needed more training in historic architecture, I got my PhD in Art Conservation Research and used the Aiken-Rhett House in Charleston, SC, as my study site. That research gave me a solid background in architectural history and is how I came to work on historic buildings like Drayton Hall and to be on teams with architectural historians, conservators, and restoration specialists.

What led Ed into historic preservation and architectural history?

Ever since he was in high school, Ed was interested in buildings. When he got to William and Mary, there was no program for looking at buildings, so he majored in history but worked during summers with noted archaeologist Ivor Noel Hume at sites around Williamsburg. After graduation, he worked for the Virginia Historic Landmarks Commission and in 1977 earned his master's degree in architectural history at the University of Virginia.

When you first saw Drayton Hall, what did you think?

While I'd seen pictures, I'd never been there. When I first saw it, it was a beautiful, clear day with a blue sky. Driving down the entrance drive, we were right on the axis. The doors were open, front and back, so we could see through the building to the other side. I was coming from New England, where buildings are different. Essential to Drayton Hall's design was to permit ventilation to cool the building in the summer, which was not an issue in New England. I thought it was the most remarkable survivor! I'd never seen a building that had no plumbing and only minimal electricity or one where the woodwork was almost completely intact. It was the most magical place.

Did Ed ever tell you of his experience when he first saw it?

No. I wish he had.

What was your first project at Drayton Hall?

The project to stabilize paints on the woodwork about 20 years ago. Paint chips were flaking to the floor, a condition enhanced in some rooms by moisture condensing on the painted woodwork.

Why is paint a useful way of researching a historic house?

The classic questions have been, "What color was this room? Or, what was the color of the exterior when this building was built?" But that's only the beginning because the sequence of paint layers can tell us about alterations over time as well as changes in the pace of change and about changing styles and availability of materials. Because you can compare the time sequence on original woodwork or plaster with something that you think might be an alteration, the comparative layers may tell you when the alteration started or when something was removed or added. Paint is a powerful tool in deciphering the timetable of changes within or outside a building.

How do you date things, as at Drayton Hall, by researching paint layers?

When an expansion of a building takes place, the first layer of paint provides you with a solid, not-before-date. Also, certain pigments weren't available after certain dates, such as chrome yellow, which was not available here until 1812, or zinc white, which was not in use in architectural paints until the 1840s. You can also identify individual components in paint layers and get relative dates. While paint research is not usually as conclusive as archaeology, there are ways of comparative dating for paint layers. For example, we can look at the amount of dirt trapped between layers as well as the evidence of aging and sunlight exposure and get a sense of the length of time that a paint layer was exposed before it got painted over. Hand-ground paints from the eighteenth and nineteenth centuries are typically more coarsely ground with large, unevenly distributed pigments in comparison to commercial twentieth-century paints whose pigments are finely ground and evenly mixed. These give you a sense of relative dating. Researching the paint history in a building like Drayton Hall and putting all these layers and sequences together is like working on a giant jigsaw puzzle.

What are your favorite memories of Drayton Hall?

Since I've been working there for so long, it's hard to identify one memory. But I have to say, George, do you remember when you took Catherine Matsen, Nicole Grabow, and me on a boat ride on the Ashley River? That was the first time I'd seen Drayton Hall from the water. That was an important revelation, because I understood better how access to this site worked both from the water and from the land. It was beautiful being out on the water.

Some of my other favorites are working there when the Drayton family would come for a family gathering or after closing time and having the building entirely to ourselves. We were free to imagine how people lived.

What were some of Ed's favorite memories?

Ed always wanted to push the envelope and felt he never had enough time in the day to do what he needed to do, so he would often be left by himself at Drayton Hall with the key at night. He loved that!

What findings did you make at Drayton Hall that you think are the most significant and why?

The eye-opening find was the vermilion-based stain on the mahogany woodwork in the stair hall. Nobody had known of its presence, and once discovered, nobody fully understood how brilliant the color was when first applied or how expensive it had been. Finding it even in the most inaccessible places of the handrails and paneling was amazing. It made the stair hall a visually arresting area and far more important.

Another is that so much original paint survives in the interior and that every layer of paint applied from the time it was first painted in the mid-eighteenth century to the present. Charleston's climate, being moist and moldy, is hard on paints because they don't stick well to wet surfaces, but at Drayton Hall, everything's there.

Could you describe how brilliant that vermilion stain was?

It was a Chinese red, a red with an orange tone. And shockingly bright! Since it wasn't applied as an opaque paint, but as a stain, you would have seen both the design of the wood and the brilliance of the color. To get an idea, one may look at Chinese red lacquer objects, which are bright red with an orange tone. At Drayton Hall today, if you walk into the stair hall, the stain is now exposed because a couple of brackets have fallen off. In the sunlight, the color is vivid.

To see images of the vermilion stain, or Chinese red, see page 3 in the photo section or visit McDanielConsulting.net/Drayton Hall Book Project.

Could you tell us how Drayton Hall's rooms would have originally appeared?

All the rooms were painted cream color. Most rooms were monochromatic, but some had baseboards painted dark brown. If you walked from that huge entry hall into the stair hall, you would have seen a monochrome of cream-colored woodwork on the walls, but in the stair hall, all the mahogany elements of the twin staircases — the wainscot, handrails, and balusters — would have been stained brilliant orange-red, which would have stunningly contrasted against the lighter cream color.

Since the same cream color was on both the first and second floor woodwork, those two floors were not distinguished by color but by architectural elements. The paint was not matte. It did have a sheen and would have reflected sunlight and at night, candlelight.

Do you know of other houses in America that appeared like that?

This cream paint was not unusual because in the mid-18th century, it was a classic, elegant color for woodwork and was used as a background for textiles, rugs, upholstery, and artwork. Being durable, it didn't change color or fade because its pigments were stable. With white and yellow ochre and linseed oil readily available in the period, the only thing that would have been expensive was the vermilion-based stain of orange-red for the mahogany. In all the buildings I've studied in America or overseas, I've never seen such a contrast. It's unique to Drayton Hall.

What were Ed's most significant findings?

While the portico was a team effort, Ed was a key to its success. He helped find evidence of the original portico, discerned how it was constructed and how alterations took place, and figured out its evolution. Afterward, he was looking forward to immersing himself in questions about the exterior stairs on the river side. Were they made by a different builder? He also helped figure out the alterations to Drayton Hall's roof and cornices.

Since you've studied buildings in Great Britain, how would you rank Drayton Hall?

I think it's as equally important as the great buildings in the United Kingdom, because so much of it survives. My experience is that while you may get more generations of decorative paints in an aristocratic house or a "grade one" building, there's not the same respect for the evidence. You don't typically find them leaving everything in place and painting over it. Instead, the paints are removed. Once the evidence is gone, you can never go back, do more research, or apply different types of analytical methods. Drayton Hall represents a great respect for every phase of its history. The evidence is all there and decipherable. The Draytons lived in Drayton Hall and preserved it, but didn't make a great effort to alter it nor did the National Trust. What was there, the Draytons simply painted over, never stripping anything away. Simply leaving what was there and trying to stabilize it is an approach that is relatively rare in this country and in Britain.

How did Ed compare Drayton Hall to other buildings he'd studied in America and overseas?

Ed thought Drayton Hall was one of the best sites in the country in terms of what's there and its importance in architectural history. While there are buildings on the same grand scale in Jamaica, most have survived as fragments or been significantly altered. In contrast, Drayton Hall is intact.

What places at Drayton Hall would you like to research in the future?

There are always more questions to explore. For example, as the research on the stairs in the stair hall gets underway, I may be involved. Since they're going to open up parts of it, trapped areas of paint may enable comparative dating of alterations and provide intact surfaces not painted over.

The basement offers lime wash accumulations, which are fragile surfaces. Testing may enable us to figure out how to stabilize its flaking, vulnerable coatings, so that they, like the paint on the upper floors, are preserved.

The small, enclosed staircase could enable us to understand more about how it provided access from the basement up to the first and second floors and to the attic and how it might have been used by enslaved people. What limitations did it impose in terms of things carried up and down? If you were in a room that led off it, what did you see of that staircase? How did people, especially the enslaved, use it to move around the house from the basement to the upper floors in comparison to the Draytons and their friends?

While you were researching paint in the main house and overheard tours being given, how would you characterize the tour guides?

For the most part, the guides knew the building and the family history. It wasn't the kind of "singsong" tour you often hear at historic houses, but instead, you got the sense that the guides were deeply committed and that they were flexible enough to adjust their presentation to the particular interests of a given group. I was interested to see how each guide would approach both presenting the space and answering questions from visitors, and found the level of guiding to be very high. Also, educated visitors might have inspired the guides to become more engaged.

As they give tours of the house, how did the guides interact with you?

The guides wanted to know about new discoveries and asked good questions. If relevant, our findings would soon get incorporated into their tours. Sometimes when I'm working on a historic site, the guide pretends I'm not there, but at Drayton Hall, the guides were keenly interested in what Ed and I were doing.

What do you think is the future for Drayton Hall and other historic sites?

The first thing is to encourage people to return to historic sites and to experience in-person what they've simply seen on computer screens. You can't understand the smells or the size of the spaces or the feeling of being in a historic house just by looking at it on a screen. How are we going to coax people to historic sites? Many people want to go to see something new.

While I've not been to Drayton Hall since the audio tours started, I'll be interested to take that tour and compare it to in-person tours I've seen there. People do want guides so they can ask questions and interact with the site's knowledgeable people. I do think Drayton Hall is part of the leading edge of trying to interpret not just the Drayton family, but all the people who lived in the other buildings on site and participated in life and work there. With service buildings gone, interpreting their presence is a challenge.

Since those buildings are gone and Drayton Hall now has a more park-like environment, how do you help visitors see what is not there?

In recent years, Montpellier has done extensive archaeology behind the main house and found evidence of a dairy, smokehouse, and housing for enslaved people. Those are being reconstructed. Where there was once simply greenspace, now you can see buildings that people slept and worked in and where food was stored. I think this kind of physical recreation works well there and seems to be an engaging way of showing how the entire site worked. At Drayton Hall, I would love to see that approach at least explored.

How can historic sites like Drayton Hall and others help heal today's racial and cultural divides?

You've been reaching out to the families connected to Drayton Hall, an important first step. Sites like Drayton Hall should encourage visitation by people of all colors and backgrounds. Although I'm not an educator, I recommend reaching out to schools and attracting people when they're young and encouraging in them an appreciation for history and exploration. I know visitation is a struggle, Colonial Williamsburg being an example.

What would you like to say about Ed's relationship to Drayton Hall?

Ed never tired of learning more about buildings. It was thrilling to him to make discoveries, even small ones, and to share them. He was such a good teacher, generous with his knowledge. I think what Ed loved was that there was a real sense of community at Drayton Hall, as evidenced by people gathering for birthday parties or lunch in the conference room. He never tired of going to Drayton Hall and rejoining the family there. He felt comfortable and was impressed with your reaching out to the broader Drayton and African American community. I think he always tried to do that too and wanted the world to be a better place.

Craig Bennett:
"Every time I go, I understand something new."

2016 – Telephone Interview

Craig M. Bennett Jr., PE, is the president of Bennett Preservation Engineering, PC, in Charleston. A native Charlestonian, he is a structural engineer, specializing in historic preservation. In his interview he reflects on education and accents his work in stabilizing Drayton Hall's iconic portico, including the risks taken, the options considered, and the research that undergirded solutions.

Could you describe your background?

Born in 1953, I grew up in Charleston, but it did not look like it does today. No houses had paint, and that was fine, because if nobody else's house had paint, it didn't matter that yours didn't. Charleston changed dramatically in the '70s and '80s.

In an unusual move, I selected Georgia Tech, where I earned undergraduate degrees in Civil Engineering and in Architecture and a graduate degree in Structural Engineering. If I had not studied both architecture and engineering, I wouldn't be anywhere nearly as effective in historic preservation. After studying in France, working with Atlanta architect John Portman, and teaching at Georgia Tech, my wife Sandy, also from Charleston, said in the mid-'80s, "It's time to go home," and I said, "Yes, dear."

After working for excellent architecture and engineering firms, I founded Bennett Preservation Engineering to focus exclusively on structural engineering for historic preservation. While I've worked on structures in Washington, DC, including the Washington Monument and the Blair House, my main focus has been around the southeast, especially Charleston.

How did you come to know Drayton Hall?

Growing up in Charleston, I lived near Frank and Randolph Drayton, whose father, Frank Drayton, was an owner. I remember going to Drayton Hall with Randolph for birthday parties, and the most exciting thing was the prospect of digging around and finding the family silver!

All four of my children were in the Junior Docent Program, in which they learned about Drayton Hall and at the end of the year, gave tours to family and friends. That program had lasting effects, for all now support historic preservation. During their tours, I remember noticing structural problems, an example being the portico, and saying to myself, "That's unusual. There are some issues here," but at the time, I didn't think much about it. Little did I know!

In 2009, my company was successful in becoming part of a preservation team working on Drayton Hall. What a joy it has been ever since. Every time I go, I understand something new.

What is an example of a new understanding?

Our work on the portico had finished by March 2016, but when we were hired, we knew we had to understand its construction before devising remedies. One mystery was how the front masonry stairs were tied into the main block of the house since our stabilization of the portico would involve the stairs if they were joined to the main block. We had contractor Richard (Moby) Marks' staff remove a face brick, then drill three-inch diameter cores, or openings, into the masonry behind the brick, through the basement wall and into the void under the stair landing, and then inserted a camera on a stick. I'd devised it years ago and now call it the "original selfie stick." I should have patented it a long time ago, and I would have made millions! [Laughs] We slid a light in there and with the camera recording a video, slowly spun the camera around and pulled it out. We also took photographs.

All of that gave us a thorough understanding of the stairs' construction and timeline. We solved the mystery by seeing that the stairs were not tied into the masonry of the main house, but were simply built next to it. Since we now knew the construction of the portico's support system, we could safely design the shoring system for the columns, which rested on the portico alone. Had I proceeded without that complete knowledge of the support system, I could have dropped the portico. Not only would I have to leave town, I'd probably have to leave the planet!

As a structural engineer, how would you characterize the masonry construction of Drayton Hall?

Drayton Hall's masonry is beautiful. In this area, masonry was generally pretty good up until about 1840, and Drayton Hall is a perfect example of that. In 1840, things thinned out because people started using a different bond, making the buildings built after 1840 nowhere near as well built as those built before. Drayton Hall's Flemish bond brickwork is well worked out. In a horizontal course of Flemish bond, the bricks alternate in orientation one by one — that is, there is the length of the brick, or stretcher, and then the end of the brick, or header, which is turned perpendicular into the wall. That system locks the bricks in place. Over time, the wythes, or vertical sections of a brick, delaminate or separate from one another. In addition, they may crack or crumble due to weather, rising damp, or simply age. All of this weakens the wall. However, alternating bricks in orientation, as in the Flemish bond, locks the brick together.

What has your work as a structural engineer taught you about the people who designed and built Drayton Hall?

It's clear that Drayton Hall was designed by someone who had studied books on both architecture and construction and that it was built by craftsmen skilled in their trades. I strongly suspect that the architect didn't design every aspect of the structure but relied on craftsmen who understood how to build.

As a structural engineer, what do you think of Drayton Hall's preservation philosophy?

Drayton Hall's preservation philosophy has influenced both my work as a structural engineer and my assessments when I served on and chaired the city's Board of Architectural Review for a number of years. I wish more people adopted Drayton Hall's philosophy because we could understand historic structures much better. As architectural historian Bob Stockton declared, "Nobody is making any more historic buildings," so we have to be very careful how we treat them.

An example of the preservation philosophy is the portico. Since construction of the house in about 1750, the portico has seen several sets of repairs, the last being in about 1920 with the addition of concrete girders in the basement to support the portico's first and second floors. We had choices. We could have replaced concrete with concrete, but we now know that concrete was inappropriate for the long term. Or, we could have used wood that looked historical, but that would have created a faux historicism. Instead, we used wooden joists that clearly appear to be of our time period in order to make it obvious that this was a 21st century reconstruction of something that had been built, failed, been rebuilt, failed, and was being built now for the fourth time. Drayton Hall's philosophy calls for us not to restore things exactly to the way they were originally in order to enable people in the future to understand how things were first built and then changed over time.

Archaeological excavations in the basement found that the footings of the arches are but eighteen inches in depth and only spread a half brick, or two inches, on each side. Why would a house of this scale and weight not have had footers that gradually stepped out wider to create a bigger "footprint" to support the load?

That's a good question. These piers are unusual. At St. Philip's Church downtown, built in 1835, the footings descend about five feet into the ground and gradually spread from 30+ inches to 50+ inches underground. I suspect that the rest of the walls around Drayton Hall have exactly the same footing as those we found. What we know now is that the dead plus live load totals approximately nine thousand pounds per square foot, an extremely high stress on the soil for this area. I can't help but think that someone just didn't think that one through.

How has your work at Drayton Hall shaped your life as a structural engineer and as a person?

My work at Drayton Hall has reminded me again and again of the importance of going gently. We have to keep as much of the historic structure as we can, make as little change as possible, and not throw out our history. Several years ago, we were called to Bodie Island Lighthouse on the Outer Banks, a National Park Service site, to strengthen the stairs, so borrowing in part from Drayton Hall, we made modifications that were fairly unobtrusive and fit in gently with the architecture. At Drayton Hall, two key lessons I've learned: 1) to make modifications that are minimalist but effective in what they do; 2) to make changes that cannot be confused with the original.

I think so highly of this philosophy that in structures where I've to strengthen an original element, I'll refuse to take out the damaged part but instead build around it. This enables those who want to understand the structure to look at the original parts still in place, see the damage, and then the repairs we've made. That way, we aid future study.

How do you think Drayton Hall could be used to educate people about historical building methods and ideas?

Drayton Hall can offer wonderful ways to educate the public about historic structures and historic structural engineering. The new visitors' center could offer opportunities to understand how buildings were historically put together, especially in ways that visitors can't see. They could learn how a building behaves under stress and how the pieces are made, one at a time, and then joined together. The center could educate structural engineers about how structures were built three hundred years ago onward. Being able then to see Drayton Hall in person, they will be able to understand historical construction far better.

How could Drayton Hall address shortcomings in education?

Drayton Hall does a good job with education, and the new visitors' center could have displays, computer graphics, and that kind of thing. I admire how your architectural historian Trish Smith is showing people virtually how furniture appeared in the rooms

By capitalizing on opportunities presented by computers and the web, Drayton Hall could become a center for education, particularly construction education for this time period. It could show the sequence in which the house was built and how it changed over time. Software programs like SketchUp, which we use in our office, is easy to use in creating 3D models. In fact, we used SketchUp to produce a 3D model of Drayton Hall's portico, so we could understand whether its columns needed to be shored up. We asked, "If we take this piece away, will the portico remain stable?" It collapsed, making it obvious we had to shore the columns.

3D graphics could show how the masonry was built, how the floors were built in and added as the masonry went up, how a roof was put over the top, and then how the interior of the building would have been filled out. You could explain the construction technology from the 18th century and how it changed through different time periods. You could also show how craftsmen and laborers made the bricks and mortar and how they dug trenches, laid the foundations, laid the bricks in Flemish bond, and worked their way up. You could show how they selected and felled trees, cut and hewed timbers from them, and then shaped them into framing materials. On site or online, people could see how the masonry was done floor by floor, each floor serving as a platform for further construction, and how carpenters fashioned the roof frame and how roofers covered it. They could learn how the house needed to be "dried in," so that craftsmen could then finish it out, doing the millwork, plaster work, and stucco work. In sum, you show how the whole building came together, thanks to a number of different craftsmen from different backgrounds. People could then visit the main house and observe the actual bricks or framing timbers these craftsmen made and put into place.

You could explain that we don't know anything about these people: whether Drayton Hall was built by tradesmen who were in Charleston or came from overseas or whether it was all done by local labor, by freed men, or by slaves. However, their workmanship does tell us about the types of tools they used so those could be shown, and their skills and attention to detail pointed out in the house tours.

What do you think of interactive computer graphics or animated games using Drayton Hall as a subject? Might they allow people to design Drayton Hall? Might the computer determine whether the loads are properly aligned and whether the building would stand or fall?

Opportunities for gaming abound and could help reach wider audiences. Visitors might design the house. Would it stand up to different stresses? Or they might try to stabilize the portico. Which remedies might work or not?

As a structural engineer, why is a historic site important?

We might ask: "Can't we learn all of this through computer animation or by looking at photographs in a book?" And the answer is "No." We can't grasp the scale, touch the masonry walls, or put our eyes right up to the pieces of millwork that were cut with a plane and see the plane marks in the millwork. We can't see the marks of the adze in the timber framing. We can't carefully examine the mortar and see the little bits of brick in the mortar. We can't see the sand and examine the mortar's finish. None of that can be done from a distance. We have to physically get onsite and use the building as a laboratory for learning. As a laboratory, Drayton Hall should be accessible to students regardless of discipline, and especially to those studying architecture, engineering, and construction.

Over the years, who have been preservation experts from different backgrounds who have worked on Drayton Hall and influenced Drayton Hall's preservation?

A number of experts have influenced the site, and their fields illustrate the diversity of skills needed to preserve a site like Drayton Hall. They included Ken Johnson, the founder of Soil Consultants, architect Bob Shoolbred, and structural engineers Dave Fischetti and Bob Silman. It was Bob who declared, "Whatever you do, don't try and make that building earthquake proof! You'll ruin it if you do." I agree with him a hundred percent. Architectural conservator Lyles McBratney, my former colleague, wrote a good bit of the report we've just turned in to Drayton Hall. I've certainly enjoyed working with you, your successor Carter Hudgins, and staff members Trish Lowe Smith, Cameron Moon, and Sarah Stroud Clarke.

What are your favorite memories about Drayton Hall?

I enjoyed working with the people on staff and on the consulting teams, which to me is highly important. A favorite memory is our lifting the columns of the portico to relieve the load so we could remove the concrete girders below them in the basement. We were gathered together, and Richard (Moby) Marks, the contractor, asked, "We've got the collars around the columns so we can lift them. We've got the frame designed to lift the collars, and we've got four jacks, one under each of the frames. What pressure are we going to have to put on the hydraulic fluid in these jacks to lift the columns?"

My response was that we had to lift perhaps 30,000 pounds. We'd put plaster of Paris across all the places where the stone column might break free from its base, and placed linear differential transformers on the plaster of Paris so we could see and measure the cracks. I said, "I think it's going to take 600 psi for each jack." We took each jack up not all at once, but very slowly staggered the lift, jack by jack, maybe 50 or 100 pounds per square inch at a time, and kept watching the transformer. Finally, the plaster of Paris cracked, indicating that the columns had broken free of their base one at a time. One of the columns had broken free at 590 psi and another at 625. So close that we laughed about it, "We've never been so close in our lives, and we'll never be this close again!"

We had raised one column 500 micrometers, which is a half of a millimeter, and another, 200 micrometers, which is a fifth of a millimeter or the thickness of two sheets of paper. Since the load was off the concrete base, it didn't matter whether the distance was two micrometers or two feet. We could safely remove the support system of concrete girders without risk of collapsing the iconic portico.

We then proceeded to stabilize the portico for decades to come. As one person explained, "If you do a really good job in preservation, no one will see you've done it." I hope that that's the case. In the basement, people will see we've been there because they'll see 21st-century timber joists. They have the same geometry but not exactly the same look as 18th-century timbers, for they're a little deeper and broader than 18th-century timbers. Their connections to the walls are 21st century. Not only is this in keeping with Drayton Hall's philosophy but comparing the old and new will educate people about how this house was built almost three hundred years ago and how people have changed it through the centuries. I think my contribution has got to be that we've done our very best to treat the building gently and with respect and have sought to educate. To me, that's important.

Richard Marks:
"A Time Machine"

2016 - Telephone Interview

For decades, Richard (Moby) Marks, a preservation contractor in Charleston, has worked on the preservation and repair of Drayton Hall. Imagining the house as a "time machine," he explains why Drayton Hall was, and is still, unique and enables us to see, as only a contractor can, the processes involved in constructing Drayton Hall and the handwork of its builders, including the enslaved. Because of all that Drayton Hall offers, he envisions Drayton Hall as a center for preservation learning.

Could you tell us about your background?
I grew up in Scottsville, Virginia, not far from Charlottesville. My admiration for Jefferson, particularly his architectural side, spurred me to get involved with historic buildings. In 1973, when I was about 10, we moved here. Since I loved to work with my hands, I helped my dad restore three or four historic buildings. At Clemson, I studied architecture and construction management and upon graduation in 1985, started a historic restoration company.

What was the very first time you saw Drayton Hall, and what did you think?

When I was a student at Charleston Day School, our history teacher, Miss Leland, took us here. I was struck by how big Drayton Hall was and how impressive its features were. The second time was with the Center for Palladian Studies and two University of Virginia professors, Freddie Nichols and Mario di Valmarana. Their academic argument over American Palladianism, English Palladianism, and Georgian architecture was a telling example of how Drayton Hall serves as a resource for understanding — even debating about — our history.

How did Drayton Hall affect your early career?

After being in the restoration business for about eight years, I understood that the well-respected conservationist, Frank Matero from the University of Pennsylvania, was working at Drayton Hall, and that visit spurred me to study under him at Penn and to earn my Master of Science in Historic Preservation. Upon return, I set up a conservation lab and with others, persuaded Clemson to establish a graduate program in historic preservation in Charleston because its historical buildings could serve as a collection of learning labs unrivalled in America. I'd seen experts coming to Charleston, bringing students with them, but when they left, so too did their knowledge. Believing too in education, Drayton Hall has unfailingly encouraged our students to get involved and given them the chance to learn here from among the nation's best.

How has Drayton Hall affected your approach to preservation and that of others?

Drayton Hall has affected all aspects of our company because it has hired us for dozens of conservation campaigns, ranging from the brick masonry, windows, and stone steps and columns to the paint, paneling, plaster, and flooring to the roof itself. We've researched documents, artifacts, and the main house itself as well as other structures. As the National Trust and Drayton Hall required, we've developed an academic, systematic approach because if our goal is to maintain historical integrity, we've got to understand the materials themselves and forecast accurately the consequences of what we do.

Drayton Hall's preservation philosophy has made it the hallmark of historic preservation in Charleston. Every major technique has been done there, so students and professionals alike can evaluate performance over time. Our objectives have been to make interventions as light as possible and to extend the life of the building.

You don't rush into interventions because many of Drayton Hall's historical features are early, have not been radically altered, and need to be treated with reverence. In that sense, Drayton Hall is sacred.

What have you learned that visitors may not see? What might they learn that demonstrates 18th-century construction and design?

In keeping with Drayton Hall's mission, we incorporate education into our projects. Visitors learn: 1) how handwork was integral to its construction; and 2) historical buildings neither build nor preserve themselves. An example is our project to assess and repair Drayton Hall's historical windows, so they'd fit tighter in their frames and allow less draft. Setting up our shop under a tent near the main house, we encouraged visitors to see us working on the window sashes and to learn what we were doing and why. We've discussed the pros and cons of possible solutions. We could not do this in the private sector.

Most visitors miss how the finer points of the brick masonry show how Drayton Hall is a high style, Georgian edifice. The regularity of the brick work, the fine butter joints at each end of a brick, the tight lines of mortar between bricks, and the shaped and rubbed bricks in the jack arches of the windows and around the doors, all represent the highest form of construction in that era. The fine alignment of the Flemish bond brickwork is unparalleled. A mason today would have a hard time replicating all the techniques seen here.

If visitors could glimpse the original framing, they would see great craftsmanship and close attention to detail and joinery. Since everything was sawn by hand, visitors could see the saw patterns made in the wood by that particular kind of saw. They could learn that blacksmiths wrought every nail, that molding planes shaped every piece of molding, and that joiners mortised and tenoned the doors and windows. Thousands and thousands of wood joinery make up this building. Could visitors imagine how much effort went into felling the trees, hauling and sawing it, and molding it? What about getting the clay, winnowing it, putting it in molds to shape it into bricks, and then firing it? An advantage for visitors is that much of this work was done in an area about a half a mile radius around this building, so perhaps they could imagine the work sites. Could they imagine what a feat it was to take all of those raw materials and transform them by hand into what we see today as this grand building?

How might the chair rails and wall panels be used to educate?

To illustrate craftsmanship and the thought that went into Drayton Hall's construction, guides might explain the construction and installation of the chair rails and wall panels seen in every room on the first and second floor. To make the panels, the wood had to be laid out in some type of covered building, then fabricated into panels, possibly disassembled, brought into the room, and re-assembled. Walls are 20 feet long with many longer, and the panels required complex joinery, which had to neatly meet in the corners and then be connected. Fitting these large planes of paneling perfectly into their allotted spaces represented a tremendous amount of mortise, tenon, and pegging. Linear elements and perpendicular joints had to be made flush, indicating that craftspeople spent a lot of time with a block plane to get everything even. Chair rails had to be cut, molded by planes, and joined into place. Everything was then sanded by hand. It all had to fit together. Just one wall was a feat, not to mention two entire floors.

What might visitors not see about the floorboards?

Visitors may not appreciate the flooring because all the boards on the first and second floors were doweled together horizontally. When you look at pattern and price books of the day, dowelled floors were the most expensive. Why? Materials and hand labor. They would literally lay the floorboards down, drill holes horizontally by hand, insert a dowel, and drill another hole in the next board, and using the dowels, fit each board together like a puzzle. By keeping the floors level and secure, the dowels prevented the boards from moving up and down or twisting. While not visible to visitors, the doweling still keeps the floorboards even and straight just as we see them today.

What has your work on Drayton Hall taught you?

Materials speak to their time of use. For instance, good examples of the type of 18th-century ornamental plasterwork in Drayton Hall's drawing room have not survived elsewhere. They look more like clay and straw than lime and are certainly not gypsum plaster. St. James Goose Creek Church is the closest thing in this area that has the hand modeled, sculpted plasterwork that plasterers were doing in England in the late 1600s and early 1700s. That tradition transports you back in time and is the closest thing to a time machine. You have to get in the mindset of the people that did the work, understand their technology and their pattern books, and only then fix the problems.

I'm struck by how few examples we have to compare Drayton Hall to, and I strive to be sure that we're looking at the right thing. Two things have been essential: reversibility because we should not do something that can't be undone; and evaluating performance over time. Looking at one part of the building, we learn about other parts. For example, when we searched the attic for evidence of the original shingle roof, we found part of an internal roofing drainage system that was part of the original W-designed roof. We've made such discoveries on every project.

How does Drayton Hall speak to you?

Due to its scale, architecture, detailing, and joinery, Drayton Hall is unique. Whether that's a result of its having been one of the few survivors or its having been truly a rare example in its time of sophisticated architecture and extraordinary woodwork, joinery, and brickwork remains a good question. Everything was done to an expert level that shows an architect or a master builder superior to most any we've seen in Charleston. This is a very English house that exudes English detailing, proportion, and scale.

What's your favorite place?

My interests are in all parts of the building — from the brick masonry to the woodwork, framing, stonework, and plasterwork to the fine cabinetry finishes and moldings. I'm struck by the grand nature of its elements, especially the staircase and the ceiling in the drawing room. All of these parts are remarkable survivors.

As a contractor, what do you think are its strongest qualities?

Without exception, the strongest parts of the building are the masonry walls and the layout of the external walls as they relate to internal masonry walls. The perimeter walls are fortified and substantial. Tying the walls together are substantial floor systems. However, their long span underneath the second-floor great hall is the weak link. Buildings of this stature from 30 to 50 years earlier probably would have had summer beams, which were thicker. Exposed on the bottom side, they would have been seen from the first-floor great hall below. If beams of that larger size had been the case, the summer beams would probably still be there, and the structure would probably still look like it was originally framed. Instead, under the second-floor great hall, they made the summer beams thinner so they could hide them between the floorboards on top and the plaster of the ceiling below because it was stylish to not see structural elements. This illustrates how the house was a product of its era. However, the depth of the beams underneath the floor was not sufficient to support that long span, so it failed. The support underneath the second floor is the only part of the house that was insufficiently engineered.

If you were a tour guide, what would be your key messages in characterizing the construction and design of the house?

Drayton Hall is the closest thing we have in this country to an English manor house in the 18th century. In comparison to the average grand house in Charleston, it stood in advance. Whether the master builder was directly brought over from England or whether Mr. Drayton had plans he wanted followed, we don't yet know, but clearly it was sophisticated for its time. I would tell people that Drayton Hall is unique in America and is very akin to what you might see in England during the same time period.

I'd ask them to imagine seeing this house under construction. Unless you'd been to Villa Cornaro in Italy or seen Andrea Palladio's designs, you would have wondered how one could come up with this design. It was the first in this country. Since there were few published copies of Palladio's designs and since most weren't out until probably the 1730s, Drayton Hall was on the cutting edge of the discovery and the reinterpretation of Italian Renaissance architecture. It has a unique place in the history of this country.

I would also ask them to care about Drayton Hall's future because it is a rare survivor and a unique example of what the wealthy elite were doing in colonial America. It exemplifies the success of that class in South Carolina. The amount of money generated in the Lowcountry was far superior to that of other colonial settlements, creating incredibly wealthy individuals who could show off and build structures on par with those of the landed gentry in England. I would explain that the average building of the mid-18th century was simple compared to this house. Drayton Hall was a "skyscraper" for its day.

From your contractor's perspective, what do you think of the decision to preserve and not restore Drayton Hall?

That decision offers a unique challenge. How do you preserve a building and at the same time, let it become a museum open to visitation and not allow spaces to be altered? Because things inherently age and weather, how do you stop change? The challenge is how to keep the outer envelope in good shape, and on the inside, leave it as it was when sold to the National Trust. Over time, things were done for fashion and to "modernize" the house. They're all part of the story. The house is honest. It doesn't gloss over imperfections and blemishes. It reflects what happened in the South after the Revolution and the Civil War and into the 20th century. We are fortunate in that Drayton Hall was not destroyed by fire, hurricane, or man. If we listen, it has a story to tell.

What has your work as a contractor taught you about the people who designed and built Drayton Hall?

The people that built Drayton Hall were experts in every respect. They had the ability to take the raw material available in the Lowcountry — such as the clay for the brick, the shell to make the lime, the timber to make the framing — and transform them into building materials, which included both the structural materials as well as the finer elements like the joinery, finish work, and casework. They not only had the ability to construct it, but they came up with designs and the proportions on par with what their counterparts were doing in England. However, they were doing it in a remote site with harsh conditions in a part of the world they weren't that familiar with. Drayton Hall was the culmination of a keenly honed organization.

Since we don't have records of Drayton Hall's construction and cannot identify its builders, does the house itself allow us to get closer to nameless African Americans who probably did a lot of that work?

This type of building could not have been done without the enslaved artisans and laborers, who worked side-by-side with master builders. The sheer amount of energy it took to generate the raw goods would in today's world take heavy machinery and tremendous amounts of horsepower. Just think of the work necessary to dig and process the clay to make the bricks; to build, stock, and manage the kilns to fire them; to gather the sand and produce the lime, produced by burning oyster shells; to mix them with water to make the mortar; then to skillfully take all of that and erect the walls for this grand edifice. That's just the brickwork.

In the colonial era, you do not see this grand of a building in Pennsylvania or other areas. Why? Because Drayton Hall was the product of vast amounts of money coupled with the expertise available probably through master builders or carpenters who came over from England, and the presence of very trained, enslaved African American builders and laborers. While it's unfortunate that so many of the hands that worked on this building will never be known, we can look at Drayton Hall and see and touch their handiwork and know it couldn't have been built without them.

How has this work at Drayton Hall affected you?

Drayton Hall has allowed me to reflect on what I do on a daily basis and enabled me to understand other buildings we work on. It's given me an education. The more I learn, the more I see that I don't understand. Drayton Hall inspires me to keep learning. With graduate students here, we can utilize their talent, continue learning, and promote preservation.

How do you see Drayton Hall in the future?

My vision for Drayton Hall is that it become a center for learning. It would build on previous efforts, highlight the site's uniqueness, and broaden the knowledge of the historical people who did the work. Hopefully, we could identify them by name and map where materials came from. We have stone columns that are sophisticatedly carved and turned, yet we cannot connect them to names and faces. I've always wanted to put myself in the place of the people that did the work and go back in a time machine. If we could learn more about those people and what they did and how, wouldn't that be fascinating?

I'd like to see Drayton Hall become a center for preservation learning, where people could learn the processes involved in creating this space and then utilize that knowledge at other historic sites. Today's builders, architects, and workers doing renovation work are not always careful to document and preserve what's there, so we could teach them to document and retain historical materials without major alterations to them. They could learn first-hand about finishes, mortars, moldings, mantels, or staircases. Drayton Hall could promote historic preservation in the best sense of the word, for changes here are similar to changes made to all buildings over time. As at Drayton Hall, threats to a building's integrity and lifespan are common. Nothing stays stagnant.

Fortunately, Drayton Hall has come to us as a rare survivor and offers us a kind of time machine. As it takes us across time, our job is to understand what we are seeing, so we can educate the public about history and about what we are doing to preserve it. Publications, tours, public programs, school programs, workshops, and online media, all offer us ways to communicate what we've learned. My hopes are that what I have done here will: 1) extend the life of Drayton Hall; and 2) educate people about how and why we need to do historic preservation.

Glenn F. Keyes:
"As an Architect"

2016 – Charleston, SC

Glenn F. Keyes is a preservation architect who has been practicing in Charleston since 1986. Although he has worked on numerous plantations, most of his work has focused on historic homes on the Charleston peninsula. He was the architect charged with stabilization of Drayton Hall's portico and later with design of the new Sally Reahard Visitor Center.

Could you describe your background?

A Nashville native, I became interested in historic preservation when I was in undergraduate school at the University of Tennessee. When Palladian architecture came up, so too did images of Drayton Hall. I went on to study under the renowned Blair Reeves, earning a Master's in architecture at the University of Florida with a specialty in historic preservation, and in the mid-'80s, worked for South Carolina's Historic Preservation Office as its staff architect. That led to my first visit to Drayton Hall, and it's been a love affair ever since.

What did you think of Drayton Hall when you had only seen pictures of it and when you first saw it in person?

When studying American architectural history, Drayton Hall was the go-to image for Palladian architecture. The purity of architecture is something you rarely see in America. In 1984, I drove down that wonderful allée of oaks, and that moment arrives when you see the façade, just sitting on the knoll. While many plantations in the Charleston area have great settings, Drayton Hall is almost magical the way you approach it. Of course, I got out, walked around, and went inside, but that ah-ha moment is when I drove down that allée and saw it for the first time. You never forget!

As an architect, what attracted you to Drayton Hall?

Since Drayton Hall is unrestored, my experience changes every time I go. As an architect, I appreciate all the intricacies and how the pieces fit together. By its not looking pristine, you appreciate the architecture and the detail better than if it were brightly painted and restored. Since Drayton Hall has no furnishings, you see architecture and are not distracted by something else. Because there is so much to tell, the house engenders a sense of discovery.

What I like to discover are the details like window casings, cornices, crown moldings, or ornamental plaster ceilings, because they're so intricate that you can never really take them all in on one visit. It's nice to experience the house over time, to study it, and then, as an architect, to think about that on my future projects. It's one of the best to learn from.

What is it about Drayton Hall that makes it appeal to everyday people?

When working on a new project, we find that people are drawn to balance. Sometimes buildings don't necessarily work as symmetry, but people seem to feel that balance is required, even if it's not totally symmetrical. Balance is at the root of Palladian architecture and is one reason why it's been studied and built for so many years. It looks right and feels right. While it may feel expansive, it still offers a human scale.

What were your thoughts when you started working with the team of conservators on stabilizing the portico? What were its problems, and what did you learn?

That was my first experience in actually working on the house itself and enabled me to see behind the scenes. While I'd been on tours, I'd never looked up from the basement to the underside of the portico. When I saw problems with the 20th-century concrete beams supporting the portico, the thought of removing them was intimidating, because this is Drayton Hall!

I had to figure out how to overcome problems that had convinced previous owners to use concrete. I didn't take that question lightly because while we were taking concrete out, we needed to replace it with something. For historic buildings, we try to design fixes that stand up to the hundred-year test, which is contrary to most construction today. Because we respect the buildings and the technology of the past, we take that test seriously. It's rigorous because our solution needs both to fit within the preservation ethic of today and respect the architecture of the past.

As a result, the portico of Drayton Hall offered a fascinating journey into understanding its original construction, why it failed, and how we could stabilize it for the long term. At the same time, we wanted to make few visible changes so that the casual observer would hardly see what we'd done.

What options did you consider? What led you to make your final choices?

The portico's natural exposure to rainwater caused the problems. The first-floor deck is covered with a checkerboard pattern of square stone tiles, joined by mortar between them. Through cracks in the mortar, rainwater penetrated and was carried by gravity down to the portico's support system of concrete beams. Originally, the support structure had consisted of wooden beams, but due to water penetration, the beams had become wet, had weakened, and eventually had been replaced in the 20th century with concrete beams. However, water continued to penetrate and was absorbed by the concrete beams, causing the reinforcing bars within them to rust and thus expand, which cracked and weakened the beams, whose failure could cause the entire portico to collapse.

Over the centuries, the portico had gone through several generations of efforts to stabilize it. We knew that when rainwater passed through the mortared joints of the first floor's stone tiles, it went down into the concrete girders below, causing them to weaken and possibly fail. To maximize effectiveness of our remedies, we designed a system to keep the new support structure dry and devised three levels of redundancy. First, the stone tiles were carefully removed. Those in good condition were re-installed while deteriorated ones replaced. Next, the concrete beams were carefully removed and replaced by new floor joists of Douglas fir, which matched the size of the original joist pockets in the basement wall. Upon the joists, we placed a wooden floor deck and covered it with a bitumen roofing membrane to protect it and the joists below.

Since we knew the rainwater will inevitably find its way through cracks, however tiny, in the new mortar of the reinstalled stone tiles and in the roofing membrane, we designed a drainage mat below them so the rainwater could be channeled outward and away from the portico and not penetrate downward to our support system. Finally, we incorporated a tell-tale, which is a small opening through which water could drip onto the basement floor. Thanks to the tell-tale, staff could easily see the water dripping and alert us so that remedies could be taken before the problem became serious. Those steps enable us to constantly monitor performance, a key step in any preservation project.

Fortunately, Ed Chappell, architectural historian, discovered original pockets for the ends of wooden joists in the basement walls. Since the concrete applied in the 20th century had simply skimmed the pockets' surfaces, the pockets were open inside and intact. We were able to rebuild and reuse them and to size the new wooden joists to fit into them. Ed's research is an example of the sense of discovery you find every day at Drayton Hall. In fact, Ed's great knowledge of Georgian architecture and his ability to dissect and interpret a house were phenomenal to watch.

As with other preservation projects at Drayton Hall, this solution resulted from a collaborative effort, involving research, trial and error, mock-ups of designs, and much discussion of different options. Sometimes collaboration can be problematic, but this team worked together well. It consisted of Richard Marks, restoration contractor; Craig Bennett, structural engineer; Ed Chappell, architectural historian; Ashley Wilson, National Trust architect; and Carter Hudgins, Patricia Smith, Sarah Stroud Clarke, and other Drayton Hall staff; and me, the preservation architect.

Affecting our plans were physical constraints such as working within a prescribed depth because we were trying to put the floor back where it was previously. Longevity of materials was a concern. For example, modern products like the drainage mat are fairly new to the market so its aging process is uncertain. However, we felt that monitoring of the system by staff would tell us of problems. In its favor is that the mat is totally concealed, will not be degraded by UV light, and has been effectively used for outdoor decks in areas of high-water exposure like beach houses. Though more time-consuming, our team sought to use the best of technologies to create what we thought to be a superior solution.

We had to make choices, the support system being an example. As a preservationist, I'm prone to retain changes that have been introduced over time. Since concrete joists had caused damage to the historic building, it was not prudent to retain them. We considered aluminum joists because they would not rust but felt that the visual intrusion of aluminum was not what we wanted for visitors to see. Stainless steel had appeal, but it will rust. We decided to use real wood as joists, not chemically treated wood, and to find native wood that was structurally suitable and straight. Had we found quality heart pine or cypress, we might have chosen it, but we knew Douglas fir to be a superior framing lumber. It was milled in a Virginia mill specializing in timber framing. Thanks to its straight grain, it is strong and less apt to twist, check, and warp. It could fit easily into the joist pockets, and if problems were detected in specific spots, the joist could be strengthened by "sistering" in reinforcement.

We never arrived at a solution lightly. Ultimately, we chose to go back to the first period design, using wooden beams for support, and to develop a three-tiered system for water management, which included modern materials. I think that was the right way to go.

When this repair is explained to visitors, what would be the key points to make?

It's essential to interpret repairs because all buildings evolve, and the preservation of this era is different from that in the 1930s or '50s. You need both to learn from the past and to try to improve on it. Clearly, the Draytons had sought to do so and, instead of wood, put in a concrete floor, which was successful for many years. Learning from their choices, we decided to go back to the original design, albeit with contemporary interventions to make the flooring more watertight and to protect the support system. By blending old and new technologies, this solution respects the historic building, protects it for the long term, and can teach visitors about preservation.

How have these experiences at Drayton Hall affected your work as an architect?

I learned attention to detail. Drayton Hall didn't just happen. All pieces were designed with intentionality to make them functional and beautiful. Whoever designed it thought about how joints should come together and how a cornice should interact with the ceiling. Attention to detail is something I try to incorporate into my practice because thinking through the details is what makes the difference between a good project and a great project.

I hope my work will enhance the visitor's understanding of this great historic site. It's not just the house but the entire site that's important. It's been a great honor to work on the house itself and to design a new visitors' center to help people appreciate Drayton Hall all the more. It's also daunting. I hope people will appreciate our restraint with the visitor center because we were not trying to build a monument. The monument is Drayton Hall.

Jim Thomas:
"Significant for the Modernist Architect and the Traditionalist"

2021 – Telephone Interview

Jim Thomas is now Architect Emeritus of the firm he founded, Thomas and Denzinger, Architects, in Beaufort, SC. At Drayton Hall, he partnered with his friend, landscape architect Robert Marvin, in the re-design and improvement of Drayton Hall's entry lane in the 1990s and later designed the Robert F. Kennedy Memorial Library and the Drayton Family Memorial by the Ashley River.

Could you briefly describe your background?

A native of the Lowcountry, I was born in Charleston in 1942 and grew up in Beaufort. After studying architecture at Rensselaer Polytechnic Institute in New York State, I earned my Master of Architecture at the University of Pennsylvania in Louis I. Kahn's Studio. I apprenticed in various architectural firms in New York, Seattle, London, and Philadelphia, the latter in Kahn's professional office. After extensive travels in Europe, the Lowcountry called me back in 1973, and with my friend Hermann Denzinger, we established Thomas & Denzinger Architects in Beaufort.

For 48 years, I served as Lead Designer, and our designs won widespread recognition for their creativity and for their sensitivity to landscape and history. In 2008 we received the South Carolina American Institute of Architects' Firm Award (SC AIA) and, over the years, other architectural awards in South Carolina and the Southeast. From 2001 to 2020, I served as Lecturer in History and Theory of Architecture and of Architectural Design at Clemson University Architecture Center in Charleston.

What did you think when you first saw Drayton Hall?

Before visiting Drayton Hall in the late sixties, I hadn't seen photographs of it because those were the days before the internet with easy access to images of everything, so I didn't know what to expect as I drove down the sandy, bumpy oak allée. I remember, poignantly, the moment I first caught sight of the house. I was overcome with the sensation that I was in a dream. The venerable core of the old edifice was found standing naked in an enchanted clearing. All evidence of living pastoral support had disappeared. The mystique was intoxicating.

As an architect, what is it that impresses you about Drayton Hall?

On the most subliminal level, Drayton Hall impresses this architect because of its singular evocation of a sense of place which transcends the building itself. In a manner difficult to articulate in words, there exists a kind of silent balance between the house and its surroundings — the clearing, the forest, the river, and the sky. The architecture of the structure itself is certainly strong and reflects impressive tectonic excellence. But its magic lies less, I believe, in its superior craft, and more in its calm restraint. It is this synthesis of "strength of being" with its calm restraint that succeeds in gathering up both the open space around it and the natural elements of its environment into a unified whole.

A dream-like sense of poetry exists in this "place," in part, because in its present state, it is incomplete — there are missing elements of its narrative. There remains, for example, only an outline of its riverside garden; the flanker buildings are only suggested by a trace of bricks in the grass; the landing on the river is completely gone; any number of outbuildings have disappeared; the roof of the main house has been significantly altered. This "presence of absence" lends a compelling mystique. These "voids" allow the observer — be he an architect or a lay person — to dream and to imagine. Much like reading a poem, the beholder is given space to "read between the lines."

The mysteries of the surrounding voids intensify one's encounter with the stunning refinement and elegance one discovers in the architectural details which have survived. It is this contrast between the empty spaces and the ultra-refinement of the remaining fabric that brings a haunted quality to the sense of place at Drayton Hall. In the realm of the unknown, one discovers fragments of a lost civilization. It is an experience which has an edge.

Where can one see your work at Drayton Hall? What do they mean?

My work at Drayton Hall was intended to be unobtrusive. They are there, but they place only a light hand on the landscape. For example, my friend and landscape architect Robert Marvin and I were asked to improve the sandy entry lane because it suffered from ruts and washboarding due to heavy traffic, especially from tour buses. One solution was to asphalt the lane, but while that might seem practical, it would drastically change the character of Drayton Hall. We therefore decided to improve the road's foundation and drainage in various ways and to cover the lane with a "plantation mix" of sand and small granite, so it would seem as if "nothing was done."

When Marian Kennedy, who had given the donation to buy the land across the Ashley River from Drayton Hall and protect the viewshed, wanted a library built in memory of her architect husband, Robert A. Kennedy, I was selected. The interior space of the little building was considered to serve, discreetly, as a "quotation" taken from the historic mansion. The proportions of the room and the profiles of its paneling and trim are informed by one of the smaller corner rooms of the second floor of the main house. That quotation is shrouded, hidden, and protected by an exterior of cypress weatherboards, brick, and tin rendered as I imagined the vernacular of the many humble outbuildings which had existed on the plantation. It won a Carolopolis Award from the Preservation Society of Charleston and an Honor Award from the SC AIA, which described it as "a jewel."

I was also asked to design the Drayton Family Memorial for Drayton family cremains. It too was to be unobtrusive, so we selected a corner of the landscape by the marsh and river. You and I worked with a committee of landscape architect Sheila Wertimer, fellow architect Sandy Logan, a Drayton descendant, plus Charlie Drayton and his son Chad. Each contributed suggestions. The idea of the circle of stones emerged from my memory of the ruins of Stonehenge in southern England. The suggestion of eternity is implicit. Stonehenge has always intrigued me as remaining evidence of one of western man's earliest attempts to find meaning in his existence within the cosmos.

What can architectural students and practicing architects and even lay people learn from Drayton Hall?

The History & Theory Seminar, which I conducted for Clemson University's School of Architecture focused on what I consider to be the vital relationship between architecture and landscape. That relationship is believed by me to be an allegory of the larger issue of man's view of himself in relation to the natural world, indeed, to the cosmos. The objective was to encourage the students to consider the work of architecture to be a part of something, something greater than just the building itself as unconnected object or as something whose only meaning is to perform some functional task. To that end, I found at Drayton Hall a vision of wholeness wherein the architecture orchestrates a hierarchy and unity among the activities of man in time and the realities of nature. This carefully crafted Georgian/Palladian edifice is the condensation of an order which encompasses the gardens, the fields, the roads and pathways, the forests, the river, even the sky. This notion of wholeness, though it can be manifest in many different modes — reflecting differences in time and place, different architectures, different materials, changing values in society — is, at its deepest level, a universal ideal which can be striven for by architects everywhere and in every epoch.

The physicality of the building itself exudes a robust "strength of being," and it was certainly built to impress. However, what is admirable to the modern eye — and a model for students — is its honesty of construction, its simplicity of form, its directness, even, as I have said above, its sense of restraint. I refer to its integrity in the use of materials and detailing, particularly in the exterior brickwork which is both elegant and true to its own nature. I believe this apparent simplicity and contained, formal restraint is what enables the edifice to interact so successfully with the natural features of the site. Classical references, inside and out, are subordinated to a tectonic integrity of the structure and to a sense of the whole. To the extent that a building can, I feel Drayton Hall projects a message of "truth" which speaks to the spirit of man. So, I have directed my students' attention to these qualities, which are as significant for the modernist architect as they are for the traditionalist.

Trish Lowe Smith:
"Being the Best Steward I Can Possibly Be"

2016 – Drayton Hall

Trish Lowe Smith, Curator of Historic Architectural Resources at Drayton Hall, describes the challenges that the preservation of Drayton Hall presents and how she has sought to chart the best course forward.

Would you describe your background and what led you to historic preservation?

I grew up in Columbia, South Carolina, and from a young age, loved the sense of being surrounded by history. One of my earliest memories is sitting between my parents on a pew at the Washington Street United Methodist Church, and feeling so small as I looked up into the rafters. John Ruskin wrote of walls "long washed by the passing waves of humanity," and long before I could articulate that concept, I was drawn to it.

I was attracted to science, but to satisfy a liberal arts requirement, I had to take an art history class and realized quickly I'd chosen the wrong course of study. A special professor, John Brian, encouraged me to pursue historic preservation, and I ultimately came to Clemson's program in Charleston and earned my Master of Science in Historic Preservation. Through historic preservation, I found a way to merge my interests in science and architectural history.

Could you describe your first encounters with Drayton Hall?

I clearly remember the day I first came to Drayton Hall in 2008. It was my first week of grad school, and Peggy Reider, a long-time interpreter, gave the tour. I remember being intimidated because she was so knowledgeable about the building, and all of us thought, "Gosh, it's going to take forever before we know as much about a building as she knows." My first "work" here was a 10-hour volunteer project. I scrubbed artifacts for Sarah Stroud Clarke, our archaeologist, and then did a stone conservation project, wrote my Master's thesis about Drayton Hall, and was awarded a Wood Family Fellowship. I joined the staff full time in 2010.

Could you describe your work as a Wood Family Fellow?

I was tasked with creating a preservation archive. At that time, there was 40+ years of correspondence, reports, and so forth, related to the modern preservation of the site. My job was to sort through the collection and find ways to make it accessible and useable. The result is an archive that's accessible digitally and in hard copy, and that grows as our preservation work continues. It's been immensely helpful in my current job, because I've got a fairly clear picture of all the work that's been done, and a greater appreciation for all the people and their extraordinary efforts. When I get overwhelmed by projects and am tempted to press on without leaving a paper trail behind, I think about what a valuable resource the preservation archive is to me, and try to take the time to help my successors figure out what I was up to all this time!

What are your thoughts about Drayton Hall's preservation philosophy?

The preservation philosophy of Drayton Hall is unique among historic sites. While at first glance it seems like our approach would be the easiest one to adopt, I'd argue it's the hardest. Essentially, our task is to 'hold the line,' but with so many different materials and with the pressures of age, visitation, and environmental stresses, holding the line is a complicated and expensive undertaking. I wouldn't change it, though. Our light hand on the historic fabric of Drayton Hall has fostered so much discovery. I can't bear to think what we'd lose if we took a more aggressive restoration approach. Drayton Hall is a rare artifact, and it's appropriate that we treat it as such.

What led you to the careful research of architectural design books and their influence on Drayton Hall? What did you find?

My earliest research was about the influence of 18th-century architectural books on the design of Drayton Hall. Among some 700 volumes in Charles Drayton's library, he listed eight popular 18th-century architectural books. We already knew the over-mantel in the great hall came directly from a design book of 1728 by William Kent, *The Designs of Inigo Jones*, and the discovery of these additional titles offered greater insight into the influence of such books. To make real-world connections, I completed measured drawings and interior elevations of the entire interior of this house to 1/16 of an inch and compared them side by side with plates in these pattern books. Thus, my second year of grad school was spent at Drayton Hall with a measuring tape and sketch pad. If there's a better way to get to know a house, I don't know it!

What is the difference between measuring by hand as opposed to using a digital scanner?

Digital scanners are great for quickly and accurately documenting historic buildings, but for really understanding a building, I don't think there's any substitute for pulling tapes and producing hand drawings. Taking the time to look closely and methodically at a building reveals telling inconsistencies and directs your eye to important details that may be easy to overlook. It gives one respect for the place and has made me a more careful historian and conservator. You can't help but reflect on the craftspeople who built a building when you're looking so long and so closely at their work. I find it inspiring to think of myself as a protector and interpreter of their hard work.

I will add that although I'm an evangelist for hand measuring, I believe it's important to get those drawings into a digital format. After completing hand drawings, I used them to create CAD (computer-aided design) drawings, which are easy to reference, modify, save, and disseminate.

Could you describe your work in 3D modeling, and how it might educate the public about Drayton Hall?

Not long after I came to Drayton Hall, I started wishing for a way to see how the house appeared in the 18th century. We know about the original paint colors, furnishings, and how the building has changed over the years, and I was convinced that technology could offer a way to show these things without restoring the house. One day I happened to be talking to Ron Hurst, Chief Curator at Colonial Williamsburg, in the stair hall and told him my ideas about digital restoration. He said, "Funny you should mention that — we have people doing this very thing at Colonial Williamsburg. There's a fellowship, so please apply, and let's see how it goes." I applied and was awarded a 3D visualization fellowship at Colonial Williamsburg and learned how to use technology to digitally restore the house. That's something I've been working on for several years, and in addition to creating photo-realistic images of Drayton Hall's 18th-century interiors, the technology aids our research since it enables us to build models, which inevitably generate research questions.

Could you tell us about the work you did for the portico stabilization and what difference you made?

We've just finished a five-year project for rehabilitation of the portico at Drayton Hall. In 2011, we hired structural engineer, Craig Bennett, to study it and tell us what sort of interventions might be necessary. We learned that the concrete and rebar were damaging to both the portico and its historic masonry and that we had to make structural interventions or risk collapse. We researched the problem extensively, spending an entire year documenting and studying materials to glean every bit of information that might inform the repairs. We learned about two previous generations of wooden joists and about decay that had been damaging the structure since the 18th century. I spent hours underneath the portico, carefully chipping away at the concrete with a chisel and hammer. We had a hunch we'd find original joist pockets behind the concrete skim coat, and we did. We made measured drawings and collected material samples, including historic mortars. All of that clued us in to the several generations of repair on the portico.

As a result, we were able to document first-period wooden joists as well as later ones. We sketched everything. We worked out how the height of the first-floor deck had changed and did a lot of math, based on those drawings, to figure out how much room we would have for whatever new system we installed. We asked ourselves whether to use wood, metal, or precast concrete. Later, during the actual rehabilitation of the portico, every decision we'd made had been informed by our research.

How can your research and use of technology teach different audiences? Who might those audiences be?

Different people take away different things. Everyone learns something while here. I've seen that people visiting the site respond favorably to seeing us working on the house. For instance, I was doing a mortar re-pointing project and found that people were happy to see someone doing something the hard and slow way. They said our work inspired them to go back to their communities and do something to preserve places special to them. That's one thing visitors take with them.

Since we interact with a lot of students, my constant refrain is "Be a good intern or a good volunteer." I started here as an intern and now have had the opportunity to work with interns, one of whom works for us now. An important lesson that people can take from Drayton Hall is how to be a young professional, how to get started in preservation, and how to leave a mark to the good. While it may not be obvious what your path is going to be, the decision seems to sort itself out if you're willing to throw yourself into what you're working on.

If you could imagine being on a "Star Trek" mission and travelling decades into the future, what do you think people will be documenting and interpreting at historic sites like Drayton Hall?

3D technology will continue to be used to document and interpret historic sites for people in a way that's relevant and exciting for them. However, I really hope we will encourage people to put their devices away and just be in the place and soak it in without having this technological barrier. You don't need devices to have an engaging experience.

Since today's tablets and iPhones will be old fashioned decades from now, what ways of engaging people, such as holograms, might you envision?

We certainly don't shy away from embracing technology, but I wonder if, in the future, coming to Drayton Hall will be revolutionary because of what we don't do in the tech realm. Maybe the really advanced thing is to take a step back from all of that.

If specific places, structures, or objects at Drayton Hall could speak, which ones would you select? What questions would you ask it?

I'd like to spread the curiosity around and invite our visitors to be puzzled, curious, and frustrated right along with me. People love a mystery. They love the prospect that you're on the cusp of solving it. If we had the time and the resources to devote to some of our burning questions, we could absolutely answer them in the near future. That's an exciting prospect!

How do you think your documentation of Drayton Hall has contributed to the wider fields of research, historic preservation, and interpretation?

Perhaps my most basic contribution to the field has been my producing contemporary floor plans and elevations of the house and making them available to anyone needing them. The 3D digital models I've made of the house have helped us answer questions about how Drayton Hall was constructed, modified, and furnished over the years. My research with the Draytons' architectural books also made a significant contribution to the body of knowledge about the influence of such books.

From this and more recent research I've conducted, a significant picture is emerging of Drayton Hall's designer—presumably John Drayton—as a well-educated and worldly person who made very deliberate design choices to communicate his wealth and dominance and to reinforce the rigid social hierarchies which he believed in. Furthermore, these design choices have ripples through history that we feel very much today, and my work helps illustrate why the study of history, including architectural history, is so relevant to our lives today.

How has this work at Drayton Hall touched you personally?

This place has important stories to tell, and in stewarding the historic buildings here, I help ensure that there will always be an authentic and evocative setting in which to hear them. Countless people across several centuries worked to build and maintain these buildings, many under appalling conditions, and I believe that I honor their existence and their efforts by being the best steward I possibly can. It is an extraordinary privilege.

Why care about historic sites like Drayton Hall?

Drayton Hall has the ability to challenge people in a constructive way, particularly as we seem to grow increasingly polarized. Often, our visitors ask questions that are framed in binary terms. They want a story that presents people as either good or bad or with pure intentions or not, but that's generally not something we can give them. What we can offer, instead, is a thoroughly-researched history of the place, our enthusiasm for discovery, and a site that fosters important discussions about the way history impacts our modern lives.

Sheila Wertimer:
"As You Walk the Landscape"

2021 – Telephone Interview

Noted Charleston landscape architect, Sheila Wertimer, has worked on Drayton Hall's landscape for decades and articulates its significance in clear and heartfelt words. After taking her degree in landscape architecture from Cornell, she and her husband lived in Great Britain, where she photographed gardens and eventually moved to Charleston in 1979, because it reminded them of England. They envisioned staying here for a year or two. That was forty years ago. During that time, she has worked on important landscapes and gardens such as Mulberry and Milford plantations, the Spoleto headquarters, and the Swordgate house in Charleston, winning national recognition in the process.

What was your first impression of Drayton Hall?

After my having worked in England, the approach to Drayton Hall definitely reminded me of an old English or Scottish family estate — rugged, unadorned, and hauntingly dramatic. Because its landscape is unadorned, one can still appreciate the native beauty of this site along the Ashley River.

As you walk the landscape, I saw it to be clear and timeless and also unexpected and refreshing. The tranquility allows one's imagination to immediately question how it came into being and how it functioned over time. It encourages further investigation. I also saw how the house sits beautifully and unapologetically on the land and rises rather majestically as one approaches the site. It's a remarkable composition.

Were you familiar with the South Carolina landscape architect, Robert Marvin, who argued successfully for a preservation philosophy for the landscape, a unique approach in the 1970s?

I hadn't heard of him before I came, but Robert actually offered me a job. Sadly, I'd taken a position with the city and couldn't go back on that obligation. I admired his incredible work. While I'm not familiar with his thinking about Drayton Hall's landscape, I know he was interested in preserving the landscape in general and in preserving and highlighting the natural landscape. That became a signature of his. He sought not to obscure a landscape but to design delicately in order to highlight the timelessness and the beauty of the natural setting that surrounded his work.

That way of thinking about a landscape influenced me. That's what a really good landscape architect does. You never work on a blank slate. You're always working on a site with a unique ecosystem — some more so than others. Drayton Hall certainly has one. Whenever I come to Drayton Hall, one of the things I consciously want to do in terms of design is to check my ego at the door because its architecture and physical setting are so beautiful, so complementary. Being able to read the landscape and to let the landscape be read is most important to me.

As a landscape architect, what might you appreciate at Drayton Hall that lay persons may not?

As time goes by and more and more development happens, particularly along the coast, the unique situation at Drayton Hall becomes clearer and clearer. It's not been restored but preserved. That's obvious both in the architecture and the landscape. Because there are places with restored formal gardens or contrived landscapes around Drayton Hall and elsewhere in the nation, Drayton Hall affords one the opportunity to envision life not only when the house was built but as it evolved over time, even life predating the house.

When you look out over the Ashley River, luckily you see an unspoiled view. You can imagine being on this site at so many different points in history. It's not static. It's not cluttered. As you walk Drayton Hall's landscape, you get a clear appreciation for all its various ecosystems and the questions they raise.

Drayton Hall is allowed to breathe. It's just so clear, so unmanipulated, that you can't help but ask fundamental questions: What happened? Who lived here? What happened over time? Such questions may not occur to people if they're just handed a landscape that portrays a specific time period, no matter how beautifully it's done. In contrast, Drayton Hall's landscape is wonderfully mysterious.

The live oak at the turn of the entrance lane past the pond has evoked different memories and questions from other interviewees. How do you see it?

As a landscape architect, I see it first and foremost as a horticultural specimen, quercus virginiana, our native live oak. Secondly, I see it as a survivor. It's a tired old soul that must have seen incredible things and has incredible stories to tell. It speaks so quietly but so powerfully about the history of this site.

What might Drayton Hall's landscape teach landscape architects, historians, museum professionals, or visitors?

Simplicity, quiet reflection, and compassion. And patience — for lots of reasons. One is because you and I took a couple of rounds at this property and had patience. With that came understanding. It's important not to rush to a solution but to work on something quietly but consistently over time, which eventually yields results. We worked very hard to make sure that the new work we did was subservient to the house and the main approach.

One of the things I liked was working with Glenn Keyes to site the new buildings of the Sally Reahard Visitor Center so that within the woodlands, they wouldn't be visible from the main house. We clustered them. I worked to make sure that when people got out of their cars, they had a sight line straight through the visitor center to the live oak in the center of the courtyard and thence to the main house and the historic landscape. It was a strong axis but simple.

The other thing I'm pleased about was re-aligning the entrance drive in very much the English way. The house reveals itself and sort of rises from the landscape, but then you take the left turn between the two ponds, pass through the woods, park, and get out of the vehicle, and walk through the visitor center. There you see the historic house again but this time, on foot. You're immersed in the landscape. You're part of it. You're walking it. You're feeling the way people may have felt during various times throughout the site's history.

The other benefit is that from the house itself, one can no longer see cars coming around near the house and parking close by. We deleted from view all that 21st-century nonsense that we have to do.

Speaking of landscapes, could you describe the Lenhardt Garden you designed for the Sally Reahard Visitor Center?

The Lenhardts were terrifically enthusiastic and quite knowledgeable about certain types of gardens. We made sure that the courtyard garden stayed within the courtyard, that it had a specific garden design, and that it had a clear geometry and related to the new buildings in a more contemporary way. The garden became a beautiful sight, restful, welcoming, and enlivening, but not one that could be confused as part of the historic landscape.

One goal of the Lenhardt Garden was to educate visitors and enable them to see plants that Charles Drayton cited in his diaries of the late 18th to the early 19th century. We learned a lot and hope visitors have. We weren't able to use as many plants as we'd hoped because as Charles Drayton would have known, some years are good and some bad, and maintenance is maintenance. Some plants couldn't be found anymore. The climate has evolved, so some plants no longer thrive. However, Charles' diaries were wonderful because they forced us to expand our palette and reach for plants that weren't the kinds one would typically put in a garden where maintenance is a primary concern. We had some successes, some failures, but by and large, the garden was a wonderful challenge, and the successes pretty terrific.

The board of Drayton Hall was also wonderful. I cannot give Steve Gates enough credit for his patience, leadership, strength, and ability to quietly steer things.

Thinking of Drayton Hall, what words of encouragement and caution would you like to give to those responsible for a historic landscape, whether they be owners, museum staff, donors, board members, or landscape architects?

Be patient and let the landscape speak to you. There's very little that a beautiful landscape needs other than a little bit of love. A lot of times, in an effort to improve something, we end up creating clutter. A historic landscape, especially Drayton Hall's, needs to continue to live and breathe as it does now in natural, native simplicity.

Toni Carrier:
"A Sustaining Force"

2021 – Telephone Interview

Toni Carrier is now the Director of the Center for Family History at the International African American Museum in Charleston. An anthropologist by training, her dedication to African American genealogy led her to found the Lowcountry Africana project and to become a Wood Family Fellow, a program established at Drayton Hall by Anthony C. Wood. An accomplished researcher, she wrote histories of post-Civil War African American families at Drayton Hall. For a brief list of Toni's recommendations for family history and oral history, please see my website, www.mcdanielconsulting.net/drayton-hall-book/, or visit the Center for Family History online or in person.

Toni, what led you into family history research and genealogy?

I recognized a void. I was in the last year of my graduate studies at University of South Florida in the Africana Studies Department and was helping a lady trace her Black Seminole ancestry. I noticed how many records are out there documenting African American family history, but they weren't organized or in a place where people could find them. I was keenly aware, because of my work with this lady, that there's a strong yearning to know the lived stories of enslaved ancestors, yet in about 2003, there wasn't much out there except for the website, Afrigeneas, (www.afrigeneas.com). When I started doing the work, I came to Charleston and saw rich, archival resources — plantation papers, family papers, and correspondence — which documented the names of enslaved people and revealed a lot about their lives, but I was shocked that there was no organized effort to make that information available to people researching their ancestors.

I've been of the mind that if you don't like what you see around you, you should change it if it's within your power to do so. All I had to do was to start gathering materials and build a website, but that was easier said than done. Back then, we had to start from scratch, but within a year we managed to develop a website and make records available.

What led you to Drayton Hall?

What led me to Drayton Hall was my work with Magnolia Plantation in 2006 or 2007, when they commissioned me to conduct a genealogical study of enslaved communities on Drayton family plantations in South Carolina, Florida, Georgia, and Barbados. Quickly, we realized that many papers were at Drayton Hall, so I made my phone call to you.

What were your first impressions of Drayton Hall?

My first glimpse of Drayton Hall was when I was flying into Charleston from Tampa. Looking down, I asked myself, "What on earth is that huge house down there? Can you go there?" When I got to Magnolia, I realized I had been looking next door at Drayton Hall. What struck me was the grandeur of the house and how formidable a presence it must have seemed to the enslaved community. It represented the power to keep them on the plantation. If I were enslaved looking at that big house, I would realize that, surely, the owner of that house — and at that time, the owner of me — would have had the power to fetch me from wherever I tried to run. When I first saw that house, I pictured what an enslaved person would see when they looked at it. Surely, it would have said, "You are here forever or until we decide you're going somewhere else."

Could you briefly describe your research at Drayton Hall?

The first part was that work I did for Magnolia in about 2007, and it continues to this day since I still collect every Drayton family document I can find. When I first started researching the Drayton family papers, I was looking specifically for names and biographical details about the people enslaved at Drayton Hall and who lived there from Reconstruction into the 20th century. At your invitation, I gave brown bag, lunch-time talks at Drayton Hall, and that's how I got to know African American descendants of Drayton Hall. When I became a Wood Family Fellow, that's when we got into recording oral histories and connecting them to documentary records.

What did you learn as a result of your family history research at Drayton Hall?

I learned that the history of Drayton Hall is incomplete without the stories we recorded. We learned how people lived and their memories of the 20th century. We learned about how families interacted and saw themselves in relationship to other community members. Small phosphate mining communities of African Americans had sprung up on Ashley River Road, and we learned their names and locations, which would have been lost if we hadn't stepped forward. We learned about the values of families who lived at Drayton Hall, Magnolia, and other communities and how they mourned their dead and buried them. For example, Johnny Leach, who also appears in this book, described how wooden posts were set to mark the head and the foot of grave sites. That's something we'd have never known had we not asked him. We learned how the community pulled together for the greater good. For instance, Johnny Leach planted a field of sweet potatoes every year, which the community was welcome to harvest. We learned about children raised by adults other than their parents, like Lucille Blunt who was raised by her great uncle and aunt who served as her grandparents. Another child was raised by her grandmother. Those are important stories if we care to ask for them. They allow Drayton Hall to tell a nuanced, very human, and multi-layered story.

What sources did you use for your research?

I used Drayton Hall's records plus a variety of public records, such as census records, birth and death certificates, military and funeral records, and marriage records held downtown in the courthouse that not a lot of people know to access. We used probate records from people who lived at Drayton Hall that described their worldly estate when they passed and who they left it to. All of this we used to research the details learned in oral histories and to write my paper.

How important is oral history?

It's absolutely essential. Number one, the stories in oral histories are not in public records and exist in few places. Specific details from those interviews were not recorded anywhere until we transcribed the interviews. Oral history provided us a look at the lived human experience not typically recorded in normal sources or public records. You have to go looking for those stories. They're out there. Oral history enables us to learn history in ways that documentary sources alone cannot. Together with other sources, they tell a human story — the big, complicated, messy human story — but you have to care to ask.

If you were giving tours at Drayton Hall, what key messages would you convey to visitors?

I would say that there was a vibrant African American community at Drayton Hall after the Civil War. When calcium phosphate was discovered along the Ashley River at the plantations, a phosphate mining enterprise was created and took root there, for which African American labor was crucial. The wage labor offered by the phosphate industry allowed freedmen to have more flexible control over their time and their lives because they weren't pinned to the land as were sharecroppers. For some families, phosphate mining paid well enough to enable some of the women not to have to work outside the home, so they could concentrate on minding the home place, raising the children, and keeping community life together. At Drayton Hall, I'd talk about the houses people lived in, where they were located, how people lived in those houses, and their foodways. I would talk about the things people planted in their gardens and the animals they raised to sustain their families. I would talk about family and community values. I would talk about how the several communities that sprang up at Drayton Hall, Magnolia, and Middleton Place were related to one another and how community members helped one another.

How does this history fit into larger patterns of African American family history that you've researched? Is it a one-off? Is it representative? Both?

Maybe both. The community at Drayton Hall identified themselves as a community and saw themselves as a bit apart from others. I think that had to do with the fact that most of its people had generational roots there. The other communities that sprang up were people who had come from elsewhere to participate in the phosphate mining industry. So Drayton Hall was a little unique in that regard. However, Drayton Hall's African American community did have important similarities with other African American communities across the South up until the 1930's or '40s. They shared community values and pulled together for the greater good and for the greater good of individual members. There was a sense of shared community resources.

The good news is that our work is informing studies going on today. For example, there's a project going on right now about early African American communities in and around Charleston. Someone participating in it said they'd obtained my Wood Family research report from Drayton Hall and found it very helpful, so in a useful way, Drayton Hall's community was representative.

How were these family and community values used in the face of racial prejudice and segregation?

Family values and knowledge of the family history were a sustaining force. During the challenging times of Jim Crow and the struggle for civil rights, the people who were active in those movements grounded themselves in their family history. That was a sustaining thing for them. There was a sense that individuals knew who they were, had a solid grounding, and therefore had nothing to prove to anyone. They took that grounding and used it as a sustaining force and even a springboard to stand up for what was right.

Bernard Powers, PhD:
"The Challenging Issues of Race"

2016 – College of Charleston

Bernard Powers, professor emeritus of history at the College of Charleston, is the first Director of its Center for the Study of Slavery. The author of Black Charlestonians: A Social History 1822-1885 *and a co-author of* We Are Charleston: Tragedy and Triumph at Mother Emanuel, *he served as interim CEO of the International African American Museum and devoted years of work at Drayton Hall as a consultant and committee member, improving our site interpretation. To view a video of his presentation at the dedication of Drayton Hall's African American cemetery, please see: https://bit.ly/DrPowersDraytonHall*

Could you describe your background and how you came to Charleston?

Originally from Chicago, I graduated from Gustavus Adolphus College in Minnesota, a Swedish Lutheran liberal arts college, and majored in history. Interested in the American South and African American history, I earned my PhD in history from Northwestern University and wrote my dissertation on Charleston's black community, focusing on the Civil War through Reconstruction. As a graduate student in 1975, I came to Charleston for the first time. This was my first time in the deep South. In 1976, I returned to research for about five months and loved the vegetation, the historic buildings, the people who were so nice and friendly, and all of that. While still a grad student, I said, "When I retire, I'm going to Charleston."

In 1992 my wife and I moved to Charleston, where I taught in the history department of the College of Charleston, directed its graduate program, and served as chair of the department. I've spent my career trying to unearth and promote African American elements in South Carolina's history. I've learned a lot too. For example, you really don't have a full appreciation of the Civil War until you come to the South. It doesn't mean that much in the North. Here, you can see the past and the present intersecting with one another, bleeding into one another, enriching one another, and sometimes poisoning one another.

History is palpable in South Carolina, particularly in Charleston, as illustrated by a personal story. When a graduate student, I was researching and making notes in the county treasurer's office in downtown Charleston. This fellow came in to dispute his taxes, voiced sharp, loud words to an attendant, and left in a huff. Afterward, the attendants began to talk to one another about his gruff, rude behavior. One attendant said, "Yeah, well, you have to expect that from a Yankee." And I heard another say, pointing to me, "Shhh, there's one sitting over there in the corner."

When Northerners think of the South, they may think Whites and Blacks are at one another's throats. While we may disagree, to me issues of race are certainly as contentious in places like Chicago, Detroit, and Boston as here.

When you first came to Drayton Hall, what were your impressions?

What I expected were more buildings, some slave quarters, fields, and more evidence of a past African American presence. I took a tour of the main house, and the docents told about the White inhabitants and the grounds with just a bit about the African American experience. I left, thinking most of the people who lived here were black, but there's hardly anything said about them. My preconceived notions were affirmed. I didn't leave with hostility, but thought work needs to be done and that perhaps I'll play an important role in getting it done.

Many African Americans could never see themselves visiting plantations because of the hurtful things they symbolize. For them to visit, it would require a lot of convincing. However, I have a natural curiosity and saw plantations as important because this is where the experiences of so many people of my heritage took place.

As Drayton Hall changed, my feelings evolved. I've met Black and White descendants, which has been positive and has enhanced my appreciation for it. Now when I walk the grounds, I have a sense of reverence that I did not feel the first time I went. I remember thinking when the African American-focused tour was instituted, how great it was that Drayton Hall was doing that. I went out, took the tour, and learned things from it.

You've invited me to give talks. I've gotten to know the staff. I've participated in studies like the one trying to devise additional ways that the African American experience could be incorporated into the entire visitor experience. I've met descendants like Catherine Braxton and Rebecca Campbell and seen how they feel a spiritual connection. Drayton Hall's ground speaks to them. That level of connection is infectious and gives you a new sensitivity to the ground you walk on.

Projects like the African American Cemetery Memorial Project offered a rare opportunity for the descendants, scholars, activists, members of the surrounding community, and just everyone, because the committee you organized brought together all these different components in collaboration, each bringing their own experiences. A wooded area that had been overlooked now plays a central role in the interpretation of the property.

I remember the public opening of the cemetery perhaps in 2010 with perhaps a couple of hundred people there, Black and White, in attendance. Lonnie Bunch, now Secretary of the Smithsonian, spoke, and I had the honor of speaking, as did descendants. Two descendants, a man and Lorraine White, whose ancestors seem to be here, led us two by two into the cemetery, singing a spiritual onto that hallowed ground. It was the most spiritually moving experience.

When you see descendants of the enslaved being appreciated in that way and having their profile raised, and when you know that attention is being given to them in the interpretation of the site, you can't help but want to invest more and to do more and to send people there. I routinely direct people, "Go out to Drayton Hall. Go out to Drayton Hall." Now, based on what I have been able to do, Drayton Hall has become a part of me.

How do you see Drayton Hall in comparison to other historic sites?

Other sites could use Drayton Hall as a model worthy of emulation. One example is that its staff continues to learn, innovate, and think of ways in which they can do a better job. That's professionalism. Interweaving African American history so the visit becomes one experience and is positive despite the negatives like those earlier described. As at Drayton Hall, we need to remember that the goal ought to be a tour in which it's not possible to avoid the African American experience. A presentation that only separates creates an artificial presentation of what life was like in these places.

Having taught for decades, what do you see as the value of historical plantation sites like Drayton Hall?

Drayton Hall is important because it places students into the space where history occurred and can thereby enhance their perspective and appreciation. Drayton Hall is the site for a range of events from the eighteenth century into the twentieth, and African Americans played critical roles in all of them. Visiting this site gives any person an opportunity to imagine black actors and their respective roles in history.

In an essay you wrote about Drayton Hall, you recommended that in our interpretation, we juxtapose the architectural symmetry of the house and the asymmetry of racial relations to symbolize relationships between Blacks and Whites here and on other plantations. Could you elaborate and cite specific places to which that juxtaposition might be attached?

At Drayton Hall visitors see this asymmetry manifested by the inner service stairwell, which though out of sight, ran from the basement to the upper floors. When you see the hidden stairwell, it's like the spine of the human body, which is the centerpiece that everything revolves around. It's the hidden interior nerve way by which the people with less power move up and down throughout the house. As much as possible, they were supposed to be out of sight. Indeed, where the stairwell is placed tells you that the house was designed to ensure that they were. Their roles, however, were so important because this place could not have functioned without them in the same way that the body cannot properly function without a spine. Since I found that stairwell so striking, I used it as a metaphor in my essay. I hope the docents use it.

Because this property is on the Ashley River, the water offers opportunities to interweave into the African American presence. There is a long tradition of African American mariners and boatmen, who were a crucial part of Drayton Hall. Using the river, African Americans ferried people across it and conveyed products from Drayton Hall down to the markets of Charleston and brought products up from Charleston to Drayton Hall. The Ashley River linked this place to other riverine plantations up and down the coast and to the Atlantic. It was the strength and skill of Black mariners who provided the human linkage between Drayton Hall and other places via the water.

Black mariners sailed schooners and manned barges, which enabled them to learn about the larger world around them and to pick up some literacy, which they were not supposed to do but probably did. They acquired ideas by interacting with people on other plantations, White as well as Black. While we don't want to minimize the exploitative features and the brutality of life on plantations, they were not concentration camps because there was going and coming. The boundaries were not sealed. As enslaved people moved about, they had an opportunity to become more fully human and to educate themselves about different ways of living. The Ashley River therefore opened our eyes as to what this plantation experience was like, and helps us to develop a fuller appreciation of what enslaved people were like as human beings.

How might museums and sites better relate to African American museums like the International African American Museum or the National Museum of African American History and Culture in Washington?

As sites like Drayton Hall periodically review their exhibits, they should do so in a way that complements history museums. That's how we intend to develop exhibits at the International African American Museum because we realize we can only introduce visitors to our subject. We will send them to sites like Drayton Hall to learn more in the spaces where the experiences occurred. As we look to the future, we should also think about hosting such programs at each other's sites.

What roles might historic sites like Drayton Hall play in race relations?

The question of what role Drayton Hall might play in the difficult terrain of race relations is a critical one. In terms of interacting with public schools, Drayton Hall is doing good work because thousands of school kids come for on-site programs. They see the connections between the African American and Anglo American experiences, learn how the people in general are connected, and thereby develop a more complete appreciation of our common humanity.

Drayton Hall and Middleton Place have been leaders in organizing family reunions of descendants, which can go a long way toward breaking down barriers between people. By continuing these reunions into the future, you can sustain the good will built up in one gathering. The other thing you've done is to have Black and White descendants present the work of Drayton Hall at professional conferences and at meetings open to the general public. Black and White descendants can talk about their connection to Drayton Hall, their experience at reunions and other programs, and they're all hopeful.

One of the takeaway points is that if we today can see how hopeful these people are who are descended from where people had contentious relations, such relationships engender hope. I don't care how good of a master or mistress was on the plantation, fundamentally the institution of slavery was based on an iron fist. As

Richard Allen, the founder of African Methodist Episcopal Church, concluded, "My brother and I had a good master who treated us more like a father would treat a son, but even so, slavery was a bitter pill." So it was.

While there is ample reason for descendants of slaveowners and the enslaved to be hostile toward one another, that's not what you see. The lesson is that if we can see people from such disparate backgrounds come together in common accord, then that's a cooperative spirit worthy of emulation. If we could inject that into our challenging discussions of history and race, we'd be doing good.

W. Marvin Dulaney:
"Tell the Full Story"

2007 – Drayton Hall

This interview was conducted by Alison Guss, producer from The History Channel for Drayton Hall's interactive DVD tour of the landscape. Dr. W. Marvin Dulaney, historian, was former chairman of the history department and Director of the Avery Research Center for African American History and Culture at the College of Charleston. He went on to become the Chair of the History Department at the University of Texas at Arlington, TX, and is now Deputy Director of the African American Museum of Dallas.

What was the principal crop grown at Drayton Hall, and what were the activities of the enslaved work force?

This was a working plantation, not a park like one sees today. Coming down the entrance lane, one would have seen the big house but dotting the landscape were small buildings and workplaces, like a stable, slave quarters, and workplaces for enslaved African Americans to do laundry, carpentry, blacksmithing, and a variety of work. One might have heard the rhythmic sounds of the mortar and pestle and seen enslaved people working in the rice fields or heard them communicating among themselves in African languages or in Gullah about various things, perhaps even laughing. Today this may seem like a quiet setting, but the main thing a visitor would have seen and heard was people working and communicating.

Rice was the chief staple because it was a moneymaker. Enslaved Africans were imported to the Lowcountry from what was called the Rice Coast of West Africa because they knew how to cultivate rice. Many people don't know that Africans were imported specifically because of this skilled labor. They think of slaves as having been an unskilled labor force, but they had a highly skilled knowledge many people in this country didn't have. Coming from West Africa, they were also more resistant to malaria because of the sickle cell trait of their blood cells — not immune, but more resistant to malaria than settlers from northern Europe.

In the 18th century, how did African and European cultures intermingle?

African and European cultures intermingled on the plantation in a variety of ways. One was the language. The Africans combined their native languages, like Mende, Mandinka, or Wolof, with English, and even with Native American words, to create what is called the Gullah Geechee language. Another was colonoware, which has been found at Drayton Hall thanks to archaeology. Africans brought their own traditions of making low-fired vessels for cooking and eating and combined them with European and Native American techniques for making dishes, bowls, jugs, and other things.

Could you describe what it was like growing up as an enslaved person here?

I don't have knowledge of this particular plantation, but in general the enslaved child would have been born on the plantation and raised during the day probably by women while their parents worked. At an early age, he or she would have been taught some skill and practiced it later by working in the rice fields or doing carpentry, blacksmithing, cooking, housework, or tending livestock. They would have worked during the day, but would have had some kind of family life with their mothers and fathers. In fact, most historians have concluded that many enslaved Africans had family lives, and it was those ties that kept them on the plantations, rather than choosing to run away. Family life served to get them through the situation of having to work and not be free.

Looking at plantation life in the South, was it better for an enslaved person to be at Drayton Hall than at other plantations?

There may not be enough historical record to answer it, and by no means do I want to paint Drayton Hall as some sort of idyllic situation! Based on the historical record, I don't know whether it would have been better to be here or on Middleton, Boone Hall, or McLeod. What we do know, for example, is that during the American Revolution, some African Americans who were enslaved at Drayton Hall ran away, as did others on other plantations. The bottom line is that it was never good to be a slave on any plantation, because you don't have rights. You can't go and come as you please or control your life. To ask if it's better to be enslaved on Drayton Hall than on any other plantation is not a good question.

Looking at the Ashley River, what thoughts come to mind?

People of African descent used the river primarily as a means of transport, that is, transporting rice and other goods down river to Charleston, and then of course, bringing goods, supplies, and materials back up. While the enslaved didn't prosper from the river economically, it was an important contributor to commerce in this area. I'm reminded of the poem by Langston Hughes, *I've Known Rivers*: "I've known rivers. Ancient, dusky rivers. My soul has grown deep like the rivers." Langston Hughes talks about Africans building the pyramids and about the Nile and the Congo. This is similar, although here they were enslaved. They were moving goods and services up and down this river and helping to make this plantation and the Lowcountry prosper economically.

The Ashley River was important for African Americans who were enslaved at Drayton Hall as well as other plantations along the river because it served as a "commons." They fished, shrimped, and crabbed here. Some African Americans were called "fishing Negroes," because they fished and did a variety of things to get food and resources from the water. African Americans also commanded and piloted boats up and down the river for Drayton Hall. One enslaved mariner got in trouble, or got the Draytons in trouble, because he was piloting their boat and the law permitted only White pilots. He was by himself and had an accident. I think the Draytons got fined for allowing him to pilot the boat by himself.

Did African Americans stay on plantations like Drayton Hall after the Civil War and emancipation?

Many may be surprised that they stayed. For example, the Bowens family, who date back to when Drayton Hall was founded and the house built, stayed here and worked on the plantation as paid laborers. Many died here. On plantations like Drayton Hall many African Americans stayed after slavery because this was all they knew. They'd formed relationships with the family that owned the plantation and who provided important services or work. Further, it is not farfetched to think that African Americans stayed because the place was familiar to them. This is what they knew. This was their home. Many of their family had been buried here. Why go away from what you're familiar with? Some left and came back. A later example is Richmond Bowens, who was born here in 1908, went away, came back, and was employed here until his death in 1998. He'd become a plantation historian.

How do African Americans respond when they think about or visit plantations like Drayton Hall?

Over time, change has occurred. Five to ten years ago, when African Americans came to plantations, they didn't see themselves represented. They saw the fine houses, heard discussions about architecture and furniture, and experienced things that didn't relate to the presence of enslaved Africans and African Americans. In recent years and in some places at least, there have been attempts to include the African American experience, but the problem of getting African Americans to visit still exists. Who wants to come to a slave plantation that represents sadness, brutality, and things you can't feel good about? On the other hand, when African Americans do visit, the plantation may be so clean and beautiful that you don't get the sense of what it was like. It was like a lie was being told, and that made you feel bitter, discouraged, and sad. Would you want to come to a place that's going to make you feel bitter and sad because of the misinterpretation or lack of interpretation of your ancestors' presence?

How may historic plantation sites like Drayton Hall remedy such situations?

What we're doing today is very important, because we're telling the story about Africans and African Americans and their work on the plantation. We need to talk about the work, not just about good architecture and furniture, or ladies in long dresses, and parties. It was the work of the rice fields. It was the hauling of stuff up and down the Ashley River. It was the Africans who made a clear contribution to not only making Drayton Hall work, but to making the Lowcountry plantation and economic system work, which of course translated eventually into making the United States work, because so much of it was based on the plantation economy. If you tell the full story on these plantations, we can change attitudes that African Americans have about coming to plantations like Drayton Hall.

Ken Seeger and Jennifer Howard:
"The reasons why"

2016 – Summerville, SC

When this interview was conducted, Ken Seeger was president of WestRock Land and Development Company and Jennifer Howard, its Director of Marketing and Communications. Their views are important not only in looking backwards over the "Watson Hill campaign," but in explaining from a developer's point of view why managing development and conservation in their environs is imperative for historic sites.

Background: For decades, MeadWestvaco, a timber and paper company that has become WestRock, owned 72,000 acres from the Ashley River Road westward to the Edisto River. In about 2004, they began discussing the sale of Watson Hill, approximately 6,600 forested acres past Middleton Place, with Charles Duell, President of the Middleton Place Foundation. When those discussions fell through after several months, they sold Watson Hill to a company, which in turn flipped it to another. Using a template from a development in Florida, that company planned to develop those 6,600 acres into hotels, shops, golf courses, and about 4,500 homes.

Conservationists were surprised, as was I, by the news. I was on vacation when I received the telephone call and had never heard of Watson Hill. Since we'd finished the most pressing preservation issue of the main house, my priority was to plan and construct a much-anticipated visitor center. However, if the mega-development of Watson Hill succeeded, it would spawn suburban sprawl and traffic throughout the Ashley River region, transforming its historic and scenic character in irreversible ways. The visitor center would have to wait.

For several years, Drayton Hall allied with residents, political leaders, and local, state, and national conservation and preservation organizations and campaigned to determine Watson Hill's fate. We won support from local and national press. However, even though it was on the west side of the Ashley River and there was no bridge, the city of North Charleston managed to annex Watson Hill. Suburban sprawl was to become the norm. We lost.

Due to the recession, Watson Hill's owners went bankrupt in 2009, and WestRock re-purchased the tract. Led by the newly arrived Ken Seeger, WestRock placed conservation easements on Watson Hill and restricted development to what Dorchester County ordinances permitted, ordinances developed by the county council's "Watson Hill committee" on which I served. As a result, only about 1100 houses could be built, too many to be sure, but with an accent on clustering and open space and far better than the developer's plan. Although Watson Hill's development plus others in the future will alter the region, the worst threat to the Ashley River region and to Drayton Hall had been averted.

Could you tell us about your background and what led you to Charleston?

Ken: I'm from Buffalo, New York, and went to the University of Pennsylvania and then to the Wharton School of Business. For more than 40 years, I've been in the real estate development business and was hired nine years ago by WestRock's predecessor, MeadWestvaco, to take over responsibility for approximately 1.1 million acres of their land holdings, about 40% of which were located in South Carolina. Moving to the Charleston region in 2007, I became responsible for the Forestry Division, which was operating those land assets.

Jennifer: I grew up in a rural area in northern Illinois, where I spent a lot of time in the fields and forests. I spent a summer in Yellowstone, doing trail work, and that experience set me on my path to pursue a Forestry degree, which I now have. In 1998, I was hired by Westvaco's Forestry Division and have since worked in several different capacities.

Could you tell us what you thought of the Ashley River region and of Drayton Hall when you came here?

Jennifer: Moving here from the area of Florence, South Carolina, I was struck by the depth and integrity of the area's history, the number of historical places, and its natural beauty. The Lowcountry captured my heart.

Ken: Being an architecture and a wood-working buff, I was struck by Drayton Hall's architecture and was curious about how it had been constructed and the number of man-hours that went into building it. I wanted to know about who had lived there and what they had done and about what the other facilities of the historical plantation had been.

Jennifer: The first time was to visit you, George. What struck me was how understated Drayton Hall is. It's not a site that leaps out to tourists, but when we got there, your passion for the place and your personal tour left me awestruck. However, before I connect with the built environment, I connect to the land, so it was memorable to stand quietly on the grounds in the shadow of Drayton Hall and to imagine all the history that had come before.

Why should we care about what happens beyond the property lines of historic sites?

Ken: No place exists in a vacuum. Both it and people's perception of it are influenced by what's happening around it, especially if its context becomes degraded. The context for Drayton Hall is the Ashley River region, so it needs to be protected.

Jennifer: When I think about Drayton Hall and its place in the Ashley River corridor, I think about the ancient Greek phrase, "Follow the red thread," which led Theseus from the labyrinth. The red thread goes from Drayton Hall, Magnolia, and Middleton and to the natural areas around them. As with a red thread, Drayton Hall is connected to other places.

In the mid-2000s, the battle erupted over Watson Hill, which MeadWestvaco had sold. What led MeadWestvaco to sell that property?

Ken: Just before I arrived, the company had been selling property no longer needed to supply fiber to its Charleston paper mills, so we sold Watson Hill to a company that assured MeadWestvaco that it would be sensitive from a conservation standpoint. Unfortunately, after the sale closed, that party flipped the property for a substantial profit to a third party that proposed intense development. That was Watson Hill's status when I arrived and learned about the controversy.

MeadWestvaco had always been a community-involved company, so our management was upset with the community's consternation over Watson Hill. We looked for ways to resolve the situation because MeadWestvaco felt that it had been betrayed after it had sold the property but was powerless to do anything about it since it had been a legal transaction. We decided to wait to see if an opportunity arose to resolve the situation. With the bankruptcy of Lehman Brothers who had financed the acquisition of the property, Watson Hill went into foreclosure, and MeadWestvaco was successful in re-acquiring the property in 2009.

We told the community that if we re-sold the property, we would put density restrictions on it that would reflect the requirements of Dorchester County's Ashley River Historic Overlay District, which you helped craft, George, as opposed to the density allowed under the zoning laws of the City of North Charleston. We did so.

During the contentious battle over Watson Hall's future, MeadWestVaco did not publicly support the conservation of Watson Hill. Where was MeadWestvaco's leadership because its employee on the county's Watson Hill committee was adamant in support of its mega-development if that's what the landowner wished?

Ken: The whole transaction occurred within the Forestry Division, whose representative may not have reflected the feelings of John Luke, CEO of the company, and of our corporate people in Richmond. While they were aware of the controversy, they didn't appreciate what was going on. Upon my hiring, they said, "You should check into Watson Hill. People are quite upset." When I got here, I made a point of learning about Watson Hill as we began planning East Edisto, our master plan for MeadWestvaco's 72,000 acres west of the Ashley to the Edisto River.

Why didn't MeadWestvaco aid our campaign and explain the company's thoughts at public hearings or in a newspaper interview?

Ken: At the time, the leadership felt that since it was a legal transaction, they quite frankly weren't sure what they could do to change the situation. While they regretted it, the Forestry Division wasn't politically attuned and felt they could do nothing.

We were looking for allies, especially from businesses, because we were being accused of being anti-growth, of not respecting private property rights, and of supporting "big government" takeovers. Any offers would have helped.

Ken: The difference between the organization at that point in time, which was strictly a forestry operation, and the operation after 2007 is that we now have more people who are politically sophisticated and have beefed up our communications organization. That's why we re-purchased Watson Hill in 2009 and have now put density restrictions on it. We felt that the restrictions were important to the legacy of our company because earlier, we hadn't sold the property for high-density development. We'd been hoodwinked. In the end, we prevailed by buying Watson Hill out of bankruptcy and putting density restrictions on it.

To develop the right conservation measures for Watson Hill, I worked with conservation groups in the region, developed permanent covenants on the land, and put those lands under the control of the East Edisto Conservancy, the majority of whose board members come from the conservation community. We did that in a way that would not disadvantage our two masters: 1) our shareholders whom we had to look out for; 2) our community. One goal was to make sure that the long-term benefit to our community was a major component of whatever we did.

When told that companies must be responsible to shareholders and maximize returns by building typical subdivisions, how should historic sites like Drayton Hall respond?

Ken: You need to respond by developing an overall strategy, a key component of which explains why a holistic approach is needed — that is, one that includes supporting the community, its organizations, its regional economic development, jobs, and housing. It should explain why we need to let the land tell us what's appropriate and why you don't invest unless the location of property is appropriate for development. Looking at the development boom before 2007, we see lots of development done badly.

For sites like Drayton Hall and concerned stakeholders, could you describe what "developed badly" means?

Ken: By "developed badly," I mean property that's been poorly planned or designed with primarily subdivisions that have no character, services, or jobs in proximity to housing and are not walkable neighborhoods with a mix of uses. To develop plans for our East Edisto area, we sought public input and found that this region is not against growth as a concept, but is against growth not well planned or reflective of Charleston's character. These findings led us to create places that would accommodate the growth for decades, while other tracts like the Ashley River region remained for timber production, recreation, or rural homes, not subdivisions.

What is important for historic sites like Drayton Hall to do in determining the future of their environs?

Ken: Historic sites and conservation organizations need to understand the planning process shaping the future of their environs and get involved in that process rather than simply complaining after the fact. As areas grow and become more dense, there needs to be more coordinated planning and zoning at the town and county level, so when people buy property, they have a good idea of what they can do. Especially important is for sites like Drayton Hall to serve as venues to educate the public and to enable developers to talk to neighbors, the community, and government leaders so all can give input and understand what can be done with traffic, schools, infrastructure, and conservation being examples. Communication is critical, giving everyone a good sense of what you can do and not do and thereby helping business as well as the community.

Could you explain further about the communication and educational roles of historic sites like Drayton Hall in regard to regional conservation?

Ken: The predominant reason for suburban sprawl is that the further out you go, the cheaper the land is, which enhances opportunities for affordable housing. What gets forgotten is that homebuyers on the suburban fringe have to drive more miles to work, so they have higher transportation costs. Driving to jobs and services creates more trips on highways, which call for new or improved roads at taxpayer expense. People waste time on the road. In contrast, mixed-use developments have businesses and services in close proximity plus places where residents can walk, congregate, and get to know each other. They also make more land available for conservation.

As an alternative to the Glenn McConnell Parkway's extension, what do you think of the proposal to four-lane SC Highway 61, which passes by Drayton Hall, and for it to have a vegetative median?

Ken: A divided, four-lane highway would change the character of that scenic road entirely. Trees would have to be removed, including the wonderful live oaks and other trees that form a canopy. When you get closer to Charleston, to have a four-lane going through a lot of those developed areas might be very difficult to accomplish. Even if you thought you could preserve the look and feel of the Ashley River Road, four-laning with a median would be very difficult because of SC Department of Transportation standards.

How have Drayton Hall and the Ashley River region touched your life?

Jennifer: It tears at my heart when I see families become increasingly fragmented because their kids must leave for better opportunities. Places like Drayton Hall and the Ashley River region make Charleston a place that my kids want to come home to. Economic growth gives them the opportunity to come home, and the quality of life makes them want to come home. To me, that's what really matters. In the Ashley River region, there is such integrity of history under our feet.

Ken: I've moved here from the San Francisco area and was recently talking to someone who wanted me to talk to her son about moving here. She observed, "You've fallen in love with Charleston, haven't you?" I thought for a minute and replied, "As a matter of fact, I have. I haven't really thought of it in those terms, but I guess I have." Sites like Drayton Hall and places like the Ashley River region are the reasons why.

Eric Emerson:
"There Have to be Tangible Examples of the Past"

2020– Telephone Interview

W. Eric Emerson is Director of South Carolina Department of Archives and History. As former Director of the SC Historical Society, Eric lived in Charleston and came to know Drayton Hall. Later, when serving as Director of the SC Department of Archives and History, he served on Drayton Hall's Advisory Site Council and continues to be involved in Drayton Hall initiatives.

What's your background? What led you to work with historical organizations?

Ever since I was young, I've been interested in history. I grew up in Asheville, North Carolina, and majored in history at the University of North Carolina-Charlotte. Upon graduation, I became an Army officer, went into business, and then decided to get a master's degree and Ph.D. in history at the University of Alabama because I hoped to teach. When a job as editor of the SC Historical Society's historical magazine opened in 1998, I came to Charleston and eventually became the Society's director. In 2009, I became Director of the SC Department of Archives and History, which entails my serving also as the State Historic Preservation Officer and the State Archivist.

What was your impression of Drayton Hall before you visited the site?

I first came to Charleston in 1971 and returned in 1998 to work for the SC

Historical Society. In that 27-year period, Charleston had become a dramatically different and more polished place. As for Drayton Hall, while I'd heard of it, I didn't know it at all, so I had a vision in my mind that all plantation houses are similar. Nothing could be further from the truth, but that's the way I viewed it at the time.

What were your impressions when you first visited Drayton Hall?

I'd never seen that model of preservation. In a house museum you assume you're going to see a house frozen in time with period furniture, wall coverings, and other antiques. Drayton Hall, however, had left the spaces open, and guides talked about the spaces and the ways those spaces had been used. I thought, "Wow, this is a creative way of interpreting the structure and its spaces!" Of course, I could hear people on my tour complaining, "Is this it? This is a house museum. It should be completely furnished." As for me, I was intrigued.

Looking back over your career, what do you think are key lessons you've learned about historic sites?

The first is the question of sustainability because it takes a continuous stream of funds to maintain historic sites like Drayton Hall, and that's just to keep them from falling down. That does not include enhancing collections or doing further research.

The second lesson is that in order for any site or museum to not grow stale, they have to constantly evaluate and re-interpret. Because visitors are looking for something new, it takes creativity and money to offer something different, whether it's an exhibit, interpretation, or program. Otherwise, people will say, "I've been there, done that." Funders, too, are looking for something new and different, so you've got to maintain their enthusiasm. Adaptability from staff is crucial. Altogether, managing a historic site takes skill and hard work.

Why are historic sites like Drayton Hall important now and in the future?

I believe there always have to be tangible examples of the past, whether they are historic sites, artifacts, or documents — things from the past that people can see and touch, which enhance their understanding of history. As we become more attuned to virtual representations of life, whether they be videos or computer-generated imagery, it becomes more incumbent to maintain physical structures, artifacts, or artwork, and to do what digital representations cannot: connect people to the past in a tangible way.

A good example is when we show historical manuscripts to young people touring the Archives. Their eyes light up when they see the writing and the wax seals. Even though the documents are encapsulated in Mylar, they can touch them, turn it over, and try to read them. They capture the imagination not just of children, but the public at large. That's why it's important to preserve historical places. You can tell stories about a building, but if there's only a vacant lot or a new building there, something that helps you understand the past has been lost. There's no substitute for a tangible reminder to educate young people, and such reminders will be even more critical going forward.

Integral to our human nature is to want to be visually stimulated by historic objects and to touch them. That experience could include holding a mid-19th century document or object, or walking up the stairs of a 250-year-old house, or standing in the same room where people have stood for centuries and looking at the same walls. As you look around, you see the same landscape, at least in part, which previous generations would have seen, whether you are walking a battlefield or visiting a plantation. The experience sparks the imagination.

Why are historic sites like Drayton Hall important to the state of South Carolina and to their community?

Historic sites represent the history of a time and place. For example, Drayton Hall is emblematic of the period of South Carolina's history when the state was at its apex of wealth and prosperity. As George Rogers showed in *Charleston in the Age of the Pinckneys*, South Carolina during its golden age was at its best, and at the same time, at its worst. It was a period of great wealth and opulence for a small elite with all the attendant things like culture and education, yet all of that was created upon the backs of enslaved people working in horrible conditions in the rice fields of the Lowcountry. During that period, the wealthiest South Carolinians have never been as well educated or have supported arts or culture as much, when at the same time, it saw the worst of human traits being imposed upon hundreds of thousands of people. Sites like Drayton Hall represent that period. While it sowed the seeds of wealth and opulence, it also sowed the seeds of national disunion, which resulted in secession and the racial issues we are wrestling with today. That's why sites like Drayton Hall are necessary to our community, state, and nation.

What roles do you see historic sites like Drayton Hall playing in the future of history education?

History education is declining. Most frequently, people point to the rise of STEM (science, technology, engineering and mathematics) curriculum, which is being financially incentivized, not just by our state, but all over the nation and by our federal government. The focus on STEM education has placed history education, indeed all of the humanities, at a disadvantage. In addition, people have reduced history to a one-dimensional representation of the past instead of seeing history as a complex interplay of all human emotions and actions. It's the complexity and the humanity of all of us that enlightens us about who we are, what we are, and how events shaped us. The teaching of history with a focus on presentism has diminished that complexity. I've talked to a number of people who say, "I'll never let my kids study history, because it's just meant as a tool for political purposes." Such views place even greater strain on history education.

Places like Drayton Hall and other museums are vital because they enable people to come into physical contact with the past and become educated about the complexity of the human experience, rather than to see it as one dimensional. History should not be used solely to denigrate those who came before us, but instead to explain what made the world what it is today.

What do you see as the two or three biggest challenges or opportunities in historic preservation?

I don't mean to sound like an economic determinist, but I think money is a great opportunity and challenge. We see this in our work every day. If you pitch preservation as economic opportunity, you can get decision-makers interested in alternatives to tearing down old buildings. Through the State Historic Preservation Office, we offer tax credit programs, historic preservation grants, and other similar grants, so if historic preservation, as Drayton Hall does, benefits economic development, people support it. Thanks to such efforts, we've been able to promote historic preservation as an economic tool to counter the pressure from conventional development.

The other challenge is to keep historic sites, buildings, and communities from solely being associated with oppression in the past. If the public only see historic places as sites of injustice or only as evidence of human evil where bad things happened, it will be difficult to attract visitors and donors to help preserve those sites and pay for upkeep. If there's nothing triumphant about the human experience associated with an historic site and if it is only perceived as a site of oppression, then the people on whom you rely to fund the site's preservation will choose to spend their money elsewhere.

Keeping in mind that Drayton Hall was a plantation and carries with it all the impressions one may have of a plantation, what should plantation sites do?

Drayton Hall carries with it all the negative impressions associated with a plantation, so you have to interpret the site by focusing on the experiences of everyone who lived there. Much may be said for human resiliency, so when you're talking about the people who were enslaved and kept there against their will, you have to talk about their entire experience and include the agency that they brought into their daily existence. Even in the worst of circumstances, people tried to offset bondage by using faith and sheer willpower, to make it through terrible experiences and difficult times. You have to tell those stories. The days of interpreting any house museum as just an "upstairs" experience or only from the viewpoint of the plantation or estate owner are over. Sites can't survive like that.

This is not only an American issue. It extends to Great Britain and beyond. Public historians have found that people are just as interested in the stories of the people who served as well as in stories of the owners. We see that in British period dramas, such as *Downton Abbey* or earlier, *Upstairs, Downstairs*. You have to focus on stories about all the people. For example, Drayton Hall takes its story beyond slavery and describes postbellum people who continued to work on site and what might have kept them here and why they left. You have to tell as broad a story as possible yet be specific. You have to be honest and transparent. You can't hide history. You can't downplay terrible things. As to how you do that, it takes creativity, money, and a commitment to tell the stories of both the mainstream and the marginalized. People want to hear compelling stories at the very spot where the events took place.

What are your closing thoughts about Drayton Hall?

I wish I could be more optimistic about the future of sites like Drayton Hall, but it's becoming more and more difficult to find private funders willing to give large sums of money to historic sites and historic preservation. In recent years, the National Trust for Historic Preservation has decided to focus less on its historic sites in order to focus more on preservation in urban areas and on getting young people involved. Most young people, however, don't have extra money to donate to preservation, which is the nature of being young. Although they might like a historic neighborhood or prefer a local pub in a historic building because it's a cool place, are they preservationists? Or are they just someone that likes cool places and old neighborhoods? This extends to historic sites. As interests change, how do you continue to raise money for places like Drayton Hall?

What I see from my experience at the SC Department of Archives and History is that more and more organizations are turning to the government for money to support sites, whether through grants, legislative earmarks, or some other vehicle. They are relying far less on the donations of people whose families were involved in the longtime preservation of sites and communities to which they felt connected. In the future, how do you replace that feeling of obligation and connection?

Another problem is that, traditionally, preservation organizations and museums like Drayton Hall have gone to corporations for money for their operations and programming. Today, corporations are more likely to fund organizations associated with social justice initiatives, a focus that many preservation organizations and sites may find hard to meet. I see it becoming difficult for them to survive without government assistance. Does that mean that organizations like Drayton Hall will have to rely more on government and less on private donors in the future? That's a distinct possibility.

Looking into the future, I believe that competition for finite financial resources for historic sites will become more intense and that more and more museums and sites will be unable to sustain themselves. Do they turn to the government? Will the government be willing to become the main funder for these cultural organizations? If so, will the government make determinations about interpretation or programing or put restrictions on what a site can and can't do? While I don't have the answers, those are questions to ask now as funding becomes more difficult to secure.

Max A. van Balgooy:
"This Challenging Profession"
2020 – Telephone Interview

Max A. van Balgooy, Assistant Professor in the Museum Studies Program at George Washington University, teaches museum management, historical interpretation, and community engagement. A frequent author, he is president of Engaging Places, a strategy firm for museums and communities, and directs the History Leadership Institute of the American Association for State and Local History (AASLH). The former

Director of Interpretation and Education at National Trust for Historic Preservation, he and I worked on projects at Drayton Hall and taught AASLH's workshops on historic house museum management for eighteen years.

What is your background? What led you to work with the historic sites and history museums?

For forty years, I've worked with historic sites and house museums. I grew up in a town about forty miles east of Los Angeles. As a University of California student, I took part in "Education at Home," in which thirty students studied in Williamsburg, VA, for a semester and got to meet museum leaders, like Cary Carson. For the first time, I could see history in three dimensions, not as a flat page or photograph in a book, which made history more interesting and exciting. I switched majors from pre-med to history, and upon graduation, I worked three different museum jobs and fell in love with interpreting history because I could see the impact of history on visitors, students, or children. Those experiences led me to graduate school as a Hagley Fellow at the University of Delaware. Upon receiving my master's degree, I returned to the Homestead Museum in California for a dozen years before Jim Vaughan hired me as the Director of Interpretation and Education for the historic sites department of the National Trust for Historic Preservation in Washington, DC. When I left the Trust in 2011, I'd gained a national perspective on historic sites, which led to my editing books about interpreting African American history and reimagining historic house museums, working as a consultant for historic sites, and teaching museum studies at George Washington University.

What had you heard about Drayton Hall before you saw it? What was your first impression when you did visit?

I knew about Drayton Hall because it had appeared in books and articles, and you, George, used it in your presentations in workshops and conferences. Most memorable is the sepia-toned photo of Drayton Hall on the cover of *Interpreting Historic House Museums*, edited by Jessica Foy Donnelly. Drayton Hall's classical design dominating its surrounding open landscape is unforgettable. Some twenty-five or more years ago, my first visit reinforced that image as I drove through the wooded entrance and saw the house grow larger and larger and larger as I was approaching. It was more impressive than I'd imagined.

Since then, I've visited Drayton Hall several times on business for the Trust and always found time to walk the landscape and study the building. You'd given me the freedom to go in the house unsupervised, so I could explore and ask: Why is it oriented this way? Why is this room finished in this manner and not this room? Do the column capitals change according to classical hierarchy? Since it was deliberately designed, it was fun to puzzle out meanings and symbolism.

What are your favorite memories or stories about Drayton Hall?

While I enjoyed meeting Drayton Hall's board members, staff, and descendants of the people who had lived or worked at the site, what struck me was the interpretation. It integrated architecture into the overall story. That's unusual, since tours of most historic house museums will proceed room-by-room, pointing out furniture and listing facts. Because Drayton Hall had no furniture, you had only two choices: incorporate the architecture or ignore it. If you ignored it, you might as well give the tour in a parking lot. Instead, Drayton Hall highlighted the architecture. The house itself became the evidence, not merely an illustration or background, for interpreting the site's history. Because it was so unusual, it gave me a fresh way to see historic places and has always stuck with me.

Soon thereafter, James Madison's Montpelier and President Lincoln's Cottage were trying to figure out if they should be restored to their periods of greatest significance and re-furnished. Jim Vaughan, the National Trust's vice president of historic sites, and I used Drayton Hall as a model to exemplify that they need not furnish the house in order to tell great stories. Unfortunately, Drayton Hall is one of the rare ones. That makes it distinctive. There are far too many historic sites that interpret stories similar to one another's, have similar furnishings, and offer similar programs. It leads visitors to assume that if they've seen one, they've seen them all.

What are two or three key lessons about historic sites like Drayton Hall that you think critical to the future?

First, every historic site needs to be distinctive and tell a different story and find different ways to tell it. Second, historic sites are always of a place and need to capitalize on that. They are not like museums that have taken objects out of a place or out of context. Instead, a site has a unique context, whether that be the land or the community surrounding it. Because it's place-based, a site adds value to the local community, and that may mean being a good neighbor, telling the community's story, or being a center where the community can gather and talk about issues or celebrate its history. That relationship operates best when engagement flows back and forth. Third, though historic house museums are the most common type of museum in the United States, they are always the most under-resourced.

I emphasize these three points to show the link between interpretation and financial sustainability. Sometimes, the urge to be competitive and attract more visitors and donors makes boards and CEOs worry too much about their rivals. Rather than simply copy, the site should take advantage of its distinctiveness. Every site needs to find its own path and do something different, so we all win. It doesn't have to be a zero-sum game where another site has to lose visitors or donors in order for your site to gain support.

Managing historic sites like Drayton Hall is a complex responsibility, because the most important object in the collection is the most vulnerable. The house gets rained on. The sun shines on it. People walk through it. No museum would ever let that happen to their collections. Plus, its landscape (and community) is continually changing, growing, and dying. The demands of managing a complex organization that's under-resourced can force the staff and board to focus only on what's happening today or this year, rather than thinking long term. It also encourages staff to focus only on their site and become isolated from other museums. Limited capacity pulls management and governance into a limited frame of time and geography.

How might historic house museums like Drayton Hall balance lofty goals like engaging their community or helping to resolve issues like racial or cultural divides with the real world needs of finances, board relationships, and professional stewardship of the collections, like the house?

Nonprofits, not just historic sites and museums like Drayton Hall, are in the business of doing good, so almost any idea seems to be a good idea. No one would say that community engagement, addressing social issues, building financial sustainability, or caring for the collections is a bad idea, but pursuing all of them at once can be a terrible idea. It can pull you in several directions, leaving you unbalanced and unsatisfied. While good ideas aren't in short supply, a good filter is. A filter allows the best ideas to come through and keeps you moving forward at a steady pace. For house museums like Drayton Hall, that filter is a practical mission, a compelling vision, and guiding values.

Imagine a country road heading off into the distance. Mission is the guardrail that keeps you on the road. The mission explains your purpose, i.e., what you do and just as important, what you don't do. At the end of the road is your vision, i.e., your destination. The writer Jim Collins would call a vision a "big hairy audacious goal." The compass is your values, providing you with direction when the road is hidden by fog. When you're caught in a dilemma, values clarify your choices.

Organizations like Drayton Hall need all three components of that filter so that the board, staff, volunteers, and supporters can share a common path, making intentional choices that will move the museum in one direction. The theory is easy, but the practice is one of the most challenging aspects of managing museums. To achieve impact, organizations like Drayton Hall must have a shared mission, vision, and values. Here's some good news: house museums are the most common form of museum in the United States, so no museum has to do it all. If we collaborate, others can fill the gaps.

If a historic site like Drayton Hall aims to attract and engage a more diverse audience, such as African Americans, Hispanics, or recent immigrants, what should it do?

Like Drayton Hall, every museum wants to attract a larger and more diverse audience, but that desire can be a distraction from a more important question: What is your impact on your visitors? Too often, historic sites don't know much about their visitors or how the museum has improved their lives, except in the most superficial ways. While they take attendance and have anecdotal information, they don't have reliable information on the needs, interests, and motivations of their audiences. They rarely conduct evaluations of their tours and events or engage with non-visitors. If house museums were armed with this knowledge, they could design programs and activities to attract a more diverse audience and to provide something meaningful and relevant to them. Why would African Americans visit a historic site where their history was ignored? Why would recent immigrants tour a house museum like Drayton Hall if its interpretation is restricted to a time and place so remote it might as well be a foreign country?

More importantly, house museums need to be more sensitive to how their interpretation focuses on the same stories and experiences: entertainment in the parlor, meals in the dining room, cooking in the kitchen, and lots of bedrooms where nothing seemed to happen. Some people enjoy the familiarity, but others find it boring, irrelevant, or cloying. Since house museums like Drayton Hall have a long history of owners and events, let's choose those that provide distinctive stories for diverse audiences. And be sure stories are connected to universal and more meaningful themes, such as freedom, gender, ethnicity, or justice.

We need to put away the notion that museums like Drayton Hall have to serve everyone all the time. Certainly everyone is welcome, but with limited time and money, museums have to prioritize and select where and how they can have the biggest impact. Pepsi and Coca-Cola would love everyone to drink their sodas, but not even those huge corporations can attract and engage every American.

Where do you see Drayton Hall in the situation you've described?

Unlike most house museums in the United States, Drayton Hall chose to remain unfurnished and unrestored when it opened to the public in the 1970s. It seemed crazy at the time, and for some it's still unsatisfying. But that distinction created a different visitor experience that emphasizes architecture and historic preservation. Drayton Hall is thereby different from nearby historic sites, so it complements rather than competes with Magnolia Plantation and Middleton Place.

By the time I joined the National Trust in the early 2000s, Drayton Hall and a few other Trust sites were at the forefront in interpreting African American history. At Drayton Hall, you integrated African American history into the daily tours and programs. Too often, historic sites make African American history a sidebar or a separate tour. It shouldn't be. Since the history of the site was integrated, its interpretation should be, too, as should its school programs, public programs, even shop merchandise. Moreover, Drayton Hall interpreted African Americans holistically and respectfully. Slavery, for example, is an important story at Drayton Hall and other plantation sites, but too often it is treated as only hard work with tedious jobs, heavy tools, hot weather, and long days. In addition to work, Drayton Hall also discussed the resiliency, tenacity, joy, faith, and care among individuals and within families. It explored how life changed when freedom came and made historical and cultural connections between Africa and the United States — all topics that most historic sites overlook. History became bigger, expansive, consequential, and significant.

African American history is usually confined to slavery, which is why most African Americans don't want to visit historic sites. It was a brutal, awful part of their ancestors' lives. Civil rights is a topic most historic sites avoid because of modern-day controversies. Drayton Hall recognizes those parts of our history, but it places them in the much larger context of American history, allowing for a more complete and fulfilling story.

Because house museums can be found in every county and nearly every city in America, they can make an essential and crucial contribution to our understanding of our history and our future. That's what is keeping me going in this challenging profession.

Peter H. Wood:
"To Think and Imagine Differently"

2020 - Answers Written by Interviewee

Peter H. Wood is among the most influential of American historians in recent times. A Rhodes Scholar and PhD from Harvard, his book, Black Majority: Negroes in Colonial South Carolina from 1670 Through the Stono Rebellion *published in 1974, shook the study of the American past and led historians like me to look anew at history in hopeful and vigorous ways. For decades, Peter taught American history at Duke University and has now retired and lives in Colorado. In this interview, his connections to the Lowcountry become clear as does his understanding of history and his vision for sites like Drayton Hall.*

From your perspective, where are we now in interpreting Southern history to the public?

Approaches to the tangled tale of the early South have certainly changed greatly in our lifetimes. You and I have joined lots of others in trying to help along the way. For me, cultures are like individuals; to move forward effectively, they need an inclusive, honest, and forgiving view of their own history. We can't change the actual past, but we can open the darkest closets and explore them, confront the skeletons that hurt us all the most, and discard simplistic myths that get in the way of growth. In Southern Public History right now, as in almost every other national sphere, we're at a huge fork in the road.

Frankly, I often find the phrase "too little, too late" ringing in my ears. I look back and feel that positive shifts have been molasses-slow, and even those gains now seem endangered. When the country's 250th birthday arrives, will White supremacy still be ascendant? Will many still endorse a blame-the-victim version of American history that downplays the legalized ownership of other human beings as chattel property? I wish I knew what the 2020s has in store for us, after such a wrenching start. But let's imagine that our culture takes a road that leads towards a less selfish and more egalitarian future—based on sound science, broad history, and just law. If so, the Drayton Halls of the world will need to play their part.

In what positive ways could historic sites like Drayton Hall contribute to the future?

How do we find ways to move beyond an era of overweening hubris, corrosive nationalism, and widespread hostility to fact-based science and history? In the South, a less cramped and more relevant version of the regional and national past becomes important for whatever lies ahead. But let's think about two issues: deep-seated racial injustice, and the overarching threat of human-created climate disruption. Any hopeful march forward will involve swift steps in addressing both these massive challenges. I'm convinced that Drayton Hall and similar locations around the region can develop meaningful positive roles in relation to these two pressing concerns. With imaginative responses, they can secure their own futures and aid the wider public good. It's a daunting task, so not all will adapt and survive. The hundreds of plantation sites, with their varied budgets, audiences, and perspectives, will need to do some drastic re-thinking. But a few are well along in the process already.

It does sound daunting. Say more about how "drastic" change could become an opportunity.

Why "drastic"? Well, to put it bluntly, these stately mansions are large and enduring monuments to the wealth of a racist oligarchy, a clever and domineering one percent that attained far too much material wealth and political power at the expense of the vast majority. Does this mean such estates should be defunded, neglected, or even physically removed, like the misbegotten statue of John C. Calhoun that loomed over central Charleston for so long? Not to me. My hope is that, with work, these long-lasting sites can become part of the solution, rather than remaining—as many still do—part of the problem. In any best-case scenario, our culture faces its most drastic re-envisioning since the Civil War era. It would be exciting if these relatively small interpretive institutions could be among the first to rethink their role, not among the last. It will not happen overnight. But from the outset, almost all these sites have built-in advantages for addressing the two vital challenges that I mentioned.

First of all, so-called plantation sites represent the earliest and most difficult chapters of African American history, where Black residents usually outnumbered the White family in the Big House by as much as ten or twenty to one. So, they are first and foremost Black history sites; at least that's what I've always believed. And more often than not, the records exist to shed light on this world, even though much has been lost. I'll never forget your story about interviewing a Black handyman at the Stagville site in North Carolina who had been ordered to burn a stack of slave record books before the estate's papers were turned over to the Southern Historical Collection in Chapel Hill! On the other hand, I also remember watching Christine King, an impressive Black interpreter at the Old Slave Mart Museum in Charleston, engage a group of visiting middle school students when she shared and discussed a detailed list of victims on a sheet that had survived from an antebellum sale of enslaved people.

So these places can hold a transforming key to African American history; as we saw when Dorothy Redford became the site director at Somerset Place in eastern North Carolina, where her ancestors had once been enslaved by the wealthy Collins family. But these sites also have a bigger role to play when it comes to the second, even bigger, challenge: climate disruption. Our country's environmental awareness has been changing as slowly as its race consciousness, but in both instances the positive shift is undeniable. Places like Drayton Hall, which were once country estates, are now surrounded by mile after mile of suburban sprawl, whether in the Carolinas or the Chesapeake or the Gulf South. They survive because they have been protected by preservationists and conservationists such as yourself, and now we all stand ready to reap the benefits.

A model for me has been what Shawn Halifax and others have created at the Caw Caw Interpretive Center south of Charleston, with its mix of natural and historical resources. It provides a first-hand encounter with slave-built rice fields through its restored canals, but it also doubles as an accessible wildlife preserve and education center. In June 2018, I accompanied a group of teachers and students visiting South Carolina from Colorado, eager to learn more about the early Black past. At Caw Caw, Shawn led us on a canoe trip through those irrigation canals, and for the young paddlers I could see two worlds coming together in their minds. Suddenly, the natural world, with its mosquitoes and alligators, seemed intertwined with the historical world where unpaid African Americans had been forced to clear huge cypress swamps and grow rice that would pay for the mansions of White plantation owners.

How can the changes you envision occur?

It will take ongoing resolve from below to achieve the world of fact-based history and science I'm imagining. Public pressure must underscore the idea that Black Lives Matter not just in the present, but in reframing our collective past as well. Also, citizen determination (especially from the youngest generation) is making clear that any sustainable future for our species depends on a much more intelligent and less rapacious relationship to the natural world. But there will need to be changes from the top down as well.

So why not think big? A government report from 2017 showed that arts and culture account for nearly five percent of the American GDP, over 875 billion dollars annually, exceeding both transportation and agriculture—two sectors that have venerable cabinet-level positions. For half a century, you and I have watched the ups and downs of the earnest but underfunded National Endowments for the Arts and Humanities. I think the time is overdue for a new cabinet position, Secretary of Arts and Culture.

Such high-level federal endorsement could lead to a national rediscovery of our shared history not seen since the 1930s. Vehement resistance would only confirm the importance of the undertaking. And in such a rebuilding process, there would be a role for public history sites across the South, should they choose to play it. Here's one shift that I've advocated for several decades and that is now taking hold in the scholarly literature—and it doesn't cost a dime! The word plantation has taken on unduly positive and nostalgic connotations over time. So docents and site managers might occasionally slip the more honest characterization of "slave labor camp" into their brochures and their walking tours, if only to broaden the conversation.

That idea may seem small and simple, but "drastic" too. Can you say more about your thinking?

Way back in 1997, at a conference on Inequality in Early America, I gave a talk entitled Slave Labor Camps in Early America: Overcoming Denial and Discovering the Gulag. My epigraph was a quotation from Elie Wiesel: "If you suppress any part of the story, it comes back later, with force and violence." I began by saying, "We live in a nation in denial," and I argued that "we Americans are still unable to grasp the full depth of the huge collective wound that predated the country's founding and that haunted its infant and adolescent years." I went on to compare and contrast the Soviet Gulag with the South's original labor camps. The differences go well beyond cold weather versus hot weather. The older regime, where private capital exploited racial captives, lasted much longer than Stalin's modern state-run system for punishing political prisoners. The tundra of Siberia is not the swamp land of South Carolina or Louisiana. Still, I argued we could learn from the first-person narratives that describe the way people experienced the so-called Gulag.

It struck me that Americans had never developed a descriptive term that was as vivid, realistic, and suitably negative. So I quoted Richard Wright's astute observation that English speakers have traditionally suffered from "a genius for calling things by the wrong names," and I suggested that we need to question our overuse of the benign term "plantation". My essay was reprinted in several anthologies, and slowly the phrase slave labor camp is gaining traction. To many, it may seem jarring at first, but it has taken hold because it offers a clearer picture of the dark realms we are seeking to describe. There's no denying that millions of African Americans were enslaved in order to exploit their labor, and long before the invention of barbed wire, they were confined in stark camps and denied freedom of movement.

This modest proposal was not some form of political correctness; I was not arguing to expunge a useful word, plantation, which has had many meanings over time. Instead, I was plugging for a suggestive synonym that could help people to think and imagine differently. Granted, in any public space such semantic realism attracts some new visitors and discourages some old ones. But a few brave institutions, such as the McLeod restoration on James Island, SC, and the Whitney site near Wallace, LA, are challenging scores of other locations to shift their emphasis and their language. Each locality likes to be distinctive, even competitive, but institutions watch each other closely. If no place wants to be the first to make striking changes, no place wants to be last in line either. We need to widen our notions of collaboration.

Please expand on that. Why should historic sites like Drayton Hall collaborate and network?

I would like to see more networks that weave together regional historic sites. Places that stress different periods and perspectives can learn from one another, share staff insights, and encourage family visitors to make coherent and extended trips that go beyond a one-day-one-place foray into the past. Done well, a federal National Heritage Area can highlight African American history while also tying it to a wider regional and national past. In the North, I think of the Hudson River Heritage Historic District that stretches through New York's Hudson Valley, where slaveholding was commonplace among wealthy Dutch settlers. And in the South, the Gullah-Geechee Cultural Heritage Corridor was authorized by an act of Congress in 2006. It ties together public sites in four coastal states, and it helps to guide newcomers through the Lowcountry's unique history. But also introduces longtime White residents to elements of deeply rooted local culture that were skipped over in school classrooms and ignored by Chambers of Commerce for too long.

That leads to one other idea of networking and tying historical sites and stories together. Increasingly, colleges and churches are organizing Black history tours to visit significant places and weave a coherent story. You might call it Civil Rights tourism. Local jurisdictions are realizing that visitors who come to see the Edmond Pettus Bridge in Selma or the Legacy Museum and National Lynching Memorial in Montgomery also spend money at nearby eateries and hotels. But these efforts need to push back in time and spread out more broadly across the region. I noticed years ago that docents at many sites had a rich and detailed sense of their locality, but not nearly as firm a grasp on what had transpired in other parts of the South. Imagine a ten-day bus tour that began at Sullivan's Island and Drayton Hall in Charleston but ended up at Alex Haley's boyhood home in Henning, Tennessee, or the Nicodemus National Historic Site in Kansas. If docents from various sites took such a trip, they could learn from one another and then offer much wider context to their next tour group when they arrived back home.

If you were giving a tour at Drayton Hall, what messages would you want them to leave with?

Leland Ferguson has written about the utterly different ways in which a planter's family and their enslaved workers experienced the same landscape. I saw this when you took me down the Ashley in your outboard; it gave me a very different water-level view of the huge rice operations that once lined the river. I'd want visitors to leave with a clearer sense of the contrasting worlds and perspectives of all the people who lived here, and of the strange glue of deference, intimidation, and paternalism that kept it from falling apart or exploding. I'd make sure we went beyond talking and looking, since touching and sharing objects can count for so much. That's why I encourage site managers to plant gourds. Growing a gourd vine costs no money, and handling a dipper gourd, passed around by an informed docent, can help to put any visitor closer to the hard-to-conjure experience of enslavement.

How would you attract more African Americans and recent immigrants to visit the site or to attend or participate in its public programs?

"If you build it, they will come." Once uncertain visitors see that a particular site does not make them feel irrelevant or unwelcome, word spreads quickly on the grapevine. Two keys are having enough African American docents and making sure that all docents feel well-trained in their positions and well-supported by their administration. When tour leaders are comfortable and confident, anxious newcomers of all sorts will feel free to speak up, and it can be exciting to hear what they can bring to the conversation. I recall watching an excellent docent at Drayton Hall explain winnowing rice with a fanner basket. The onlookers included a family of recent immigrants. Afterwards, the mother explained to her children and the rest of the group, with obvious pride, that she had done the same thing as a child back in Southeast Asia.

Imagine you became Drayton Hall's director. Suggest a change you would make, and why?

I can't presume to tackle that question. I will say that several of my most memorable visits to historical sites have centered around interactions with well-informed role players. At Appomattox Court House, I chatted with a young man dressed as a Union soldier. Even when people asked him, "Wait, what do you do in real life?" he refused to get out of character, continuing to draw us into his world of 1865. It was amazing, but it takes special talent. I remember when Colonial Williamsburg finally got up the nerve to allow an African American to dress as an enslaved person and talk to the public! They hired an excellent Black woman, well trained in acting. She jumped through all their predictable hoops and cleared the way for others to follow her. Maybe Drayton Hall has crossed this bridge, but if not, it is worth a try.

How have experiences of historic places affected your thinking and hopes as a historian?

I recall the first time we met at Duke in the late seventies. Professor Larry Goodwyn was holding a party for new graduate students who shared his interest in oral history and African American Studies. As soon as you learned about my overlapping interests, you pulled me away from the festivities. I can hear your enthusiastic voice: "Peta, come with me. I've found something I want to show you!" After dark, we drove into the country north of Durham, and at the end of a long dirt road, the headlights shone through tall grass to illuminate the deserted house that had once been at the center of Stagville, one of North Carolina's largest slave labor camps.

It may surprise you, but that nighttime scene, peering through the grass at the ghostly white outline of a deserted house, made a lasting impression on me. After the tobacco company that owned the property finally transferred it to the state as an historic site, you went on, with your usual persistence, to locate and interview numerous Black descendants. Your work reminded me to leave the library behind sometimes, to walk the landscape and talk to people who know it well. The historian Simon Schama has called it "the archive of the feet." I can envision a time when impressive operations like Drayton Hall are playing an active role in helping the next generation understand the intricacies of a brutal southern past and the interdependencies of a natural world that mankind has put into dangerous disarray.

Joseph McGill Jr.:
"To Right a Wrong"
2021 – Telephone Interview

A native South Carolinian, Joseph McGill Jr. is the History and Culture Coordinator at Magnolia Plantation and Gardens and is the founder of the Slave Dwelling Project. For years he served as program officer with the Southern Regional Office of the National Trust for Historic Preservation and visited Drayton Hall countless times. He believes that preservation and education can be used to correct misguided beliefs and to uplift people. Best of all, he has turned that belief into action with his Slave Dwelling Project.

What led you to your current work in history?

I saw a void: the absence of voices for enslaved people at historic sites. Being an employee of the National Trust for Historic Preservation, I worked on preserving places that matter, but realized that missing from those places was the story of the enslaved people who'd lived there. They weren't missing from the landscape and buildings but from the story. There was no linkage. A solution I saw was to insert the stories of enslaved people by performing a simple act: sleeping at these places. Simple though it was, that act could bring these places attention, which I could leverage to let people who were doing the right thing know that they were doing right by those places. Also, I could give education and inspiration to those who weren't recognizing the enslaved as they should.

I was trying to right a wrong. The wrong was that the "Lost Cause" version of history gave me nothing to be proud of as an African American. I was given no desire to care for my enslaved ancestors. The history taught to me had to be purged from my mind. That wrong had to be righted. In the Slave Dwelling Project, we bring attention to the fact that we come from a proud past. For example, it was because of our ancestors that rice could grow and enable the landowners to acquire their wealth. Into existing narratives we insert specific names and specific stories.

What were your first impressions of Drayton Hall?

Magnificent. Architecturally, it demanded its place. In approaching it, it seemed to demand its isolation. However, it was devoid of the stories of those whose labor had enabled it to exist. That experience had to have been one of my inspirations to start the Slave Dwelling Project.

How has your impression changed over time?

The needle has moved from the middle to the positive because Drayton Hall has sought to be more inclusive in its interpretation of history. You've put time into recognizing the African American burial site. For regular visitors, you've produced daily programs focusing on African American history. You've exhibited the Drayton branding iron used to mark the enslaved. That took courage. I'd like to research visitors' reactions to it. Investigations for actual locations of slave cabins have been and are still going on. You've had Toni Carrier doing African American family research there, and that presents educational opportunities with the International African American Museum since she's with them now.

Since Confederate monuments are being removed and streets renamed, why preserve historical plantation sites like Drayton Hall, which were based on slavery?

Confederate monuments and plantation sites function in parallel. You couldn't have one without the other, but we have to caution ourselves. I look at Mount Rushmore and see two slave-owning presidents, but I don't want Mount Rushmore to go away. That's why it's incumbent on plantation sites to separate themselves from *Gone with the Wind* history. Even though a lot are removing "plantation" from their name, that's just a surface change. They need to acknowledge the fact that they were a part of the economy of that period and tell a more complete history of their places. Even if they wanted to interpret their sites architecturally, they could interpret slavery by looking at spatial segregation. For example, at Drayton Hall or in other grand buildings, visitors want to go through the front door and see that grand staircase. However, there's almost always a second set of doors and stairs, as at Drayton Hall, which the enslaved used, and that's an opportunity to use architecture to interpret spatial segregation. Or, if you need to find those fingerprints in the bricks, find them. If you need to find saw marks on the wood, then claim that it's highly likely that an enslaved person made them. Make slavery a real story that happened to real people.

Why should or should not African Americans visit historical plantation sites?

I think visiting can help us get over the historical trauma attached to plantations because we know that historically a lot of sufferings went on at such sites. We want to stay in our comfort zones. When typical visitors came to plantations, say, 20 years ago, they weren't coming to hear about the stories of the enslaved and preferred to stay in their comfort zone. For African Americans to visit plantations is hard and tough. Since I give daily tours at Magnolia Plantation and Gardens, our audiences are mostly White, although they've lately gotten younger and more diverse. I hope that trend continues. For that trend to continue, we have to have African Americans in the audience who can also keep the site in check, so the interpretation of African American history doesn't change simply because African Americans are or are not in the audience. If African Americans are not in the audience and the interpretation changes, that's a problem. Sites should consistently include the voices of all who inhabited that space. The story of happy slaves and benevolent slave owners is changing, and there are those who get upset, because that's the story they want to hear. African Americans need to buy tickets, show themselves in the audience, and participate.

A lot of African Americans are visiting places where their ancestors were enslaved. Plantation sites like Drayton Hall, Middleton Place, Monticello, Montpelier, or Somerset in North Carolina are reaching out to descendants, and we need to convince others to do the same. Some are worried about reparations, but reparations need not only be about money. It can take many forms. In North Carolina, if you are a descendant of an enslaved person at a state historic site, you get free admission to that site, and descendants can have family reunions free of charge. I think all plantation sites should do that, or at least offer a manageable number of reunions during the year. That's an example of things we need to do to attract African American visitors.

Why should African Americans join the staff of a plantation site like Drayton Hall?

You don't go to many plantation sites and see a lot of staff who look like me. Plantation sites need to make more of an effort to change that, even if it means bringing in someone occasionally to help, such as our organization. Our crew could come in two or three times a year, put on demonstrations of our enslaved ancestors, and help.

Why should African Americans join the governing board of a historic plantation site like Drayton Hall?

That's the governing body. I've talked to enthusiastic staff members of plantation sites who want to bring in the Slave Dwelling Project. We have that moment. However, that person has to convince their board that that's a good idea, but some board members are descendants of slave owners, even of owners who enslaved people at that site. There are a lot of "old dogs" on boards who want to stay in their comfort zone and not talk about chattel slavery. That's why African Americans should be on the boards.

Why should African Americans donate to historic plantation sites like Drayton Hall?

African Americans should donate because these places have to sustain themselves, and that takes money. Of course, that's a harder sell for African Americans. You get people coming up to the ticket booth, saying, "Why are you charging me? You've stolen my ancestors' labor for so long." But these places have to be sustained. Even if they're doing the best job of telling the story and being inclusive, they have to be sustained and should be rewarded. Sometimes it's the carrot and stick process. If you see a site not doing the right thing, maybe some of their cash flow can be disrupted if that can be done in the right way. On the other hand, those sites doing the right thing should bubble up to the top and reap the rewards, and African Americans should support them. Also, development officers need to be sure African American donors are sought out, but beforehand, you've got to make sure you're telling the whole story.

There's the argument that while it may be fine to do African American history, we need to feature architecture, gardens, and decorative arts, because that's where the money is. With your answers in mind, why is it important for African Americans to donate?

If African Americans want to ensure our history is told, we have to contribute. If we expect sites to be places to help with our history and education, they should be designed to appeal to all people. Reparations is not just about money. As I explain to my audiences at Magnolia, it's also my opportunity to stand before an audience and tell the truth. A donor can contribute to a fund to hire a black person, not to clean the place up, but to be a point person and decision-maker, so let's incorporate that into fundraising efforts.

We have to understand plantations as places of historical trauma since torture, rape, and whippings took place there. Black folks aren't visiting plantations or donating to commemorate those things. Instead, folks like me believe that donating is good idea because maybe we can change the narrative if decision-makers see we're putting our money where our mouth is. The money can go to the general funds or be restricted, however the donor and the site decide, but donating empowers us as African Americans. It encourages others to do the same and encourages sites to do the right thing. There are also the foundations, some run by African Americans or that plantation sites appeal to, and they have gone in the direction of inclusiveness and want to fund sites that tell the stories of all segments of the population.

If an African American were asked to join a board or to donate to a plantation site like Drayton Hall, what should they be mindful of?

They should be mindful of the communication or lack thereof to descendants of the enslaved at that site. Is there an effort to communicate with them? If so, at what stage is the site in that process? Descendants are going to be some of the first to come to you. If you find yourself on the board or donating and if the organization is not communicating with descendants, you need to find out why. They should be communicating with descendants. If you find they are not communicating, you should make communication a stipulation for you to become a donor or board member.

What do you see as the future of historic sites like Drayton Hall?

I see historic sites being more actively involved in public history and education. When we have a January Sixth with people storming the Capitol, I think that's a lack of education or rather misguided education. As public places, sites like Drayton Hall can right wrongs. The Dylann Roofs should not go to plantation sites and become inspired to do what he did. His manifesto is littered with photographs of plantation sites he visited, such as Magnolia or MacLeod on James Island. He visited plantations to get inspiration to do that. I think these sites are responsible for righting that wrong.

We can't continue to see the acts of people who have learned the wrong version of history at sites. We who work at sites should be the ones to educate these folks about the real history of this nation. Yes, these plantations existed, but they would not have existed without the stolen labor of those who were enslaved. Therefore, their story should be told through the graveyards, the fingerprints in the bricks, those marks in the hand-hewn logs. We need to pull out our archival materials and look at them differently. For so long, we've been looking at those papers from the eyes of the enslaver, but if you look at that paper from the viewpoint of the enslaved, we'll find out about that slave, those slaves, or that family they sold or that they took the whip to or that produced so much rice, thanks to their forced and unpaid labor.

Let's ask what the value of those barrels of rice equated to in terms of what the enslaved people could have made had their labor not been stolen. Let's use that information and turn it so that the public can think more humanely. Sites have to give the enslaved people names and make sure they are prominently spoken or displayed somewhere, so that visitors can know that there were people involved in this thing called "chattel slavery." Instead of "yield," we need to think of stolen labor. We now use the term "enslaved" rather than "slave" because no one's born a slave. It's the system that enslaved them. We've got to put the burden where it belongs. Sites have got to change this narrative and get people to think in the manner that they should about these sites.

Why should people care about historic preservation?

Historic preservation is important because that's the thing that keeps me going. That's my incentive. Eleven years ago, when I started the Slave Dwelling Project, I thought it was going to be "one and done" or just within South Carolina, but because of historic preservation, I'm still employed by the Slave Dwelling Project and am now employed at Magnolia because of the restored slave cabins. While historic preservation provides a revenue stream, it's also a passion for me. What we have to understand as a people is that what matters to you may be offensive to some. Slave cabins are offensive to some. That's why I made sure to have "slave" in the name of the "Slave Dwelling Project."

Preservation reveals our prejudices. That Native Americans didn't matter and that blacks were second class citizens may be seen in the places we choose to preserve. That's why the built landscape of the Native Americans is pretty much non-existent and why the historical built landscape of African Americans is there but is deteriorating quickly. Preservation is important because we tend to tell our stories through the buildings we preserve.

If American history is rife with racism and oppression, why get engaged in preserving such a history?

We got to figure out how to proceed because our history is full of racism, which was interwoven into the founding of this nation and has existed long before then. We should know that it has existed. When I was with the National Trust, there was this case in Missouri where we were talking to this lady who owned property with a slave cabin. We were talking to her about what she should do with the building. Using the Secretary of Interior's standards, we pressured her too hard. She tore it down. That's too bad. We don't want to go too far and must find the right approaches. We are changing a lot, and quickly. Since George Floyd's death, Confederate monuments have come down with less resistance. Many words have changed. Images are gone. Lady Antebellum is now Lady A. The Dixie Chicks are now the Chicks. Drayton Hall is in position to change our national narrative. Some will get upset, because they will hear a history that dispels the history taught to them. Some will see the branding iron and look away. But most will be satisfied with hearing a narrative that includes the stories of all who inhabited the space of Drayton Hall.

Michelle McCollum:
"A Compelling Story Is Not Enough"

2020 – Telephone Interview

Michelle McCollum, president of the South Carolina National Heritage Corridor, shares her thoughts about Drayton Hall and reflects on history and historic sites and how they can be used to build community. An experienced professional in tourism, she critiques historic sites and gives positive suggestions for the future.

What were your first impressions of Drayton Hall?
Growing up in the Upstate of South Carolina, my brother and I were lucky because our parents took us to historic sites and instilled in us an appreciation of the past, which seeded my educational journey as a history major. When I first visited Drayton Hall in my later teens, my love of history made me look at it perhaps with a more open mind than someone being introduced to it for the first time. I asked, "What did the site look like, and how has it changed? What did it mean to various people over time? How would I have felt growing up here?" Many people

are drawn to history and may reflect on such questions when they visit historic sites. However, sites need to be more creative and thoughtful and help visitors to enhance their imagination and understanding.

Why are historic sites important today?

Historic sites and history museums give us a sense of who we are as a people by helping us understand where we've been. They enable us to go back and experience, to some degree, what things were like in the past, thus providing context for the present.

What is your favorite memory about Drayton Hall?

I was by myself along the Ashley River. The SC Heritage Corridor had recently helped fund the interpretive project where you carried around an iPad that played a DVD, which presented the stories as you walked from one place to another on the landscape. You handed me an iPad and told me to go and enjoy. The weather was perfect. It was early morning, quiet. I watched that DVD program as I walked around, seeing historical photographs, maps and interviews with living Drayton Hall people and hearing their stories. I could understand how it all connected. I remember being near the river and becoming emotional. As I walked back to the house, I felt as if I was surrounded by people from Drayton Hall's past. That's my favorite memory of Drayton Hall.

Among today's competing priorities when time is in high demand, why should people care about historic sites?

Today's tourists care about more than "sun and sand" experiences. Historic sites provide an in-depth immersion into the past and provide a sense of place that people want when they travel. They introduce people to the places they are visiting and impart a greater understanding of where they are and why that place is important. For locals, historic sites ground them and provide a sense of belonging.

If people are interested in history and if a site is a good resource for them, why is visitation to historic sites and history museums flat to declining?

In my 25-year career in heritage tourism, I have seen visitation numbers rise and fall. While I'm a supporter of the STEM curriculum (science, technology, engineering, and math), the fact that we are no longer focusing on history and civics is affecting young people's desire to visit and experience historic sites. We are losing our love of history and respect of place. That's very troubling and is going to negatively impact sites like Drayton Hall.

What is the remedy for flat to declining visitation?

I believe the remedy starts at home with parents instilling a sense of responsibility to know the history of our people. In schools, we must tell the history of this nation in a way we are not ashamed of nor egotistical about, but as a human story and provide context to our progression as a country. No doubt, the interpretation of sites needs to be transformed but in the positive direction of being more holistic, telling both the good and ugly aspects of life.

The unfortunate thing is that many sites are competing for the same target audience and the same small piece of tourism's marketing pie. To remedy that, historic sites should market collectively. That's a hard thing to do because everybody is afraid that if they invest money into a marketing partnership, someone else is going to benefit from the dollars that they invest. Associations like the Charleston Heritage Federation are examples of what could be useful partnerships.

Communicating time management is vital because visitors weigh time in their decision-making. Historic sites like Drayton Hall should communicate options for use of time and let visitors know a visit can be of one or two hours or a half or full day. In advance, visitors need to know what they get by spending their time at the site and most importantly, know they will receive a quality experience regardless of the time invested.

If you were teaching a course in tourism, how might you use Drayton Hall? What contemporary issues might historic sites or plantation sites like Drayton Hall address?

I don't want it to ever become politically incorrect to visit a historic plantation. Historic sites and especially plantation sites could do a magnificent job of bringing the African American story to light and telling it in a sensitive way. I'd market plantations with the message, "We're here to tell the history. Please come and talk. Let's have a dialogue. We invite you to become an interactive part of what we're doing." Today, a top priority should be refining the marketing message and becoming more invitational. We don't want to talk to you. We want to talk with you.

What are the criteria that visitors consider when deciding to visit a historic site?

When considering a visit to a historic site, visitors weigh cost versus value. It's that simple. What is the cost? Does the value equal the price? The price is not only money, but time as I explained earlier. As for value, visitors are looking for amenities as well as great interpretation and programming. Once on site, places to sit and rest and to appreciate the place are important. People enjoy the opportunity to be contemplative. Sites also need to supply things that engage all ages, which even a house tour can do if evaluated creatively. If a child becomes distracted during a tour, so too are his or her parents and others on the tour.

If you want to keep people for a longer period of time, they need opportunities to buy food and beverage. If you don't have those two things, you're not going to keep them for long. At the very least, let visitors know to bring a picnic and enjoy the grounds. Because people want to be able to buy something to take with them from that site, good shopping is important.

As a tourism professional, what lessons have you learned?

One lesson: a compelling story is not enough. You've got to network with people. You've got to build a coalition of supporters around you and to talk to political leaders. You have to engage all your resources. You can't simply protect your site and think people are going to come. You've got to get away from your site, interact with your community, and pull people to you.

On my office wall is this quotation: "In the end, we will conserve only what we love. We will love only what we understand. And we will understand only what we're taught." While that quote focused on conservation, it's just as fitting for historic preservation and sites. Engage your community.

Why are heritage corridors or regional trails important to historic sites like Drayton Hall?

While the mandate of a heritage corridor or trail is conservation, preservation and education, economic development is critical. Why? Because people aren't going to worry about saving a historic building or spending money to visit a site if their water quality is bad or roads are crumbling. Only when a community is vibrant and sustainable do they start investing in preservation. The holistic approach of heritage trails helps sites because it leads to ensuring that preservation and sites are part of the conversation about the overall economic development of the community. By creating partnerships, historic sites get a place at the table.

What assets or debits do Drayton Hall or other museums overlook?

Please understand I'm painting with wide brushstrokes. While the staff may be passionate about their particular museum, many may assume that everybody else is just as passionate. If not, it's because they don't care. We've got to get better in both engaging people on site and beyond. Branding and marketing are crucial and must constantly change in response to the times. The way Drayton Hall branded itself four years ago is not the way it can successfully brand itself today. The marketing of historic sites is too slow to change. Programming cannot be boring. I repeat, it cannot be boring.

If somebody waved a magic wand and you became the director of a site like Drayton Hall, what would you aim for?

I'd say: "Let's move forward. Let's have meaningful conversations about race and history, get different state agencies and community and nonprofit organizations together, develop strategies, even beginning with small steps, but let's get started and move past the blame game or silencing people." If everyone retreats to their separate corners, conversation will stop. We cannot let this happen. We must engage people.

I'm worried about historic sites, especially here in the South. We've got to be proactive and craft a better narrative. Historic plantations are where honest conversations could be happening, thanks to the work you've done at Drayton Hall or Joseph McGill at Magnolia, Tracey Todd at Middleton Place, or Shawn Halifax at McLeod. Today offers a great opportunity for plantation sites to encourage people to come and visit and have conversations in a safe and respectful manner. We must engage. Respect is the key.

Elizabeth (Liz) Alston:
"Plantations teach us"

2021 – Telephone Interview

Elizabeth (Liz) Alston has served as chair of the Charleston County School District's Board of Trustees and been an active – and vocal – leader in a number of local, state, and national organizations. Growing up near Summerville, South Carolina, in a family with strong values but in a segregated world, she protested against those strictures with her friend and now-Congressman Jim Clyburn. In this interview she describes the arc of her thinking about plantations as well as why she came to serve on Drayton Hall's site council and how she sees historic sites as educational resources and historic preservation as a difference-maker to the good.

Could you describe your youth near Summerville? What values were instilled in you growing up?

I'm a Charlestonian, having been born in Charleston. but was reared about six miles from Summerville, South Carolina. Since my father worked at the Navy Yard and was the bread-winner, he wanted us to grow up in a well-protected community and in an environment as he had. My mother worked in the home. She respected family and was a genteel person. We were raised with Christian values. Instant gratification was not something we took for granted. We were taught not to speak when adults were speaking. We had to go to church. We were taught the work ethic. Mother made sure we had duties that prepared us for life.

In 1941, Daddy was sent to Key West with the Navy and stayed there until the war was over. Mother was young. I can remember her tears as she opened his letters with money inside. Later I mentioned that to my sociology professor, who asked if I'd told my father about that. I said, "No." So later, sitting on our back porch, I said, "Daddy, I remember when you went off and sent us letters and the money we needed, and I want you to know how much I appreciate that." You know what he did? He cried. He was a nice man. I remember that now with tears in my eyes.

As a child, I was smart, so I did the taxes for people in the neighborhood. We made friends with White people. For example, the mailmen were not African-American, but they treated us like they treated their own children. When I went to college, family members were proud of me, and then I became a teacher, a principal of St. John's High School on John's Island, and chair of the Charleston County School District's Board of Trustees.

How did those values influence your family's and your response to segregation?

I came up in the '40s and '50s, and our parents protected us from segregation. Though I grew up in rural South Carolina, my thought processes were more worldly than that environment thanks to my mother and father. My father worked at the Navy Yard as a shipfitter, constructing or repairing ships, and traveled with ships all over the world, so he knew more than South Carolina. When we traveled, we'd put our fried chicken in shoe boxes and only stop by those places that treated us fairly. Mother taught us that we were just as good as anyone else. Of course, I remember going to a segregated church and a segregated school, which is now Alston Middle School where your wife taught. I think I became a teacher because my mother had wanted to become one. Our parents had the ability to make sure we were protected and not subjugated to racism. It may seem strange, but it seems I see more racism today.

What led you to get involved in the civil rights movement?

I got involved when I went to South Carolina State University from 1957 to 1961. That was the first time that I had a course in Black history. My good friend, colleague, classmate, and partner in crime was Jim Clyburn, now a congressman. We participated in the marches at South Carolina State and later in what has become known as The Orangeburg Massacre. We were taught not to react to someone who spat upon you. We were trained to act like a lady or a gentleman and to act with dignity and move on. Recently, when I heard a professor lecture on the civil rights movement, I was surprised to hear my voice. My mother gave me a backbone, for she and my minister'd say, " If you don't stand up for something, you'll fall for anything." During the movement, when I was called racial epithets, it was like water off a duck's back.

One summer in the '60s, Jim and I went to New York, where I worked as a model. We had a platonic relationship and were very cautious not to join organizations that would cause you to fear for your life if you went against them. That's what happened to Malcolm X. Jim and I have remained involved in issues, still serve on committees and boards together, and have similar philosophies. When I've complained too much to political leaders, he's said, "Leave her alone!"

What were your first impressions of Drayton Hall when you drove down the entrance lane and saw the main house?

I resented the beautiful site our ancestors had built. I was bitter. I blamed the founders of those places. Later, after working as a docent at Middleton Place and seeing the work of Earl Middleton with joint family reunions there and then getting to know you, George, and serving on Drayton Hall's site council, I began to change. I listened to Richmond Bowens and his cousins, Rebecca Campbell and Catherine Braxton. All of that altered my thinking. There are still younger generations who want no part of plantations and question why I care, but like me, they could change.

If the ancient live oak near the curve in Drayton Hall's entrance lane could speak, what questions would you ask? What stories would you like to hear?

Recently, I've been reading books about the slavery period, and they've conditioned my thinking, yet the interesting thing is that they have thoughts similar to mine. I imagine that if the live oak could talk, it'd say it was horrified by what it saw of slavery. It would have preferred to have its limb cut off rather than have a person hung or lynched from it.

You force me to examine my subconscious feelings. Had I been a slave, I would not have survived. I would have killed the owner and then committed suicide rather than endure the injustices of slavery. I would not be here. But I try not to internalize it. That's all I can say.

If the Ashley River could talk, what do you think it might say?

If the Ashley River could talk, I figure it would say, "I'd rather run dry than accept bodies of enslaved people in chains thrown into my water."

Why did you join the site council of Drayton Hall?

Well, George McDaniel had something to do with it. You'd gone to Vietnam. You've benefitted from plantations, but am I going to hold that against you? I'm not going to not participate, because of my strong feelings about slavery. Staff members whom I'd gotten to know, like Tracy Hayes, helped as did other board members whom I knew. You were doing programs with descendants like Rebecca Campbell and Catherine Braxton, who spoke of their ancestral home as if they'd grown up there. They see its pros and cons. My friend Herb Frazier works next door at Magnolia Plantation. A lot of people said, "You're serving on the board of a plantation!", but I've served as a docent at Middleton Place and McLeod Plantation and had invited you to speak to senior citizens at Emanuel and brought senior citizens to Drayton.

"Stereotype" is not too strong a word because many African Americans have been taught that plantations are only a negative. However, that's where the records of our ancestors are, so my personal feelings are of little significance. As Mayor Tecklenburg, who has apologized for slavery, said, "We came on different ships, but we're all in the same boat." I feel that even though plantations were a bitter part of American history, we can't bury our heads in the sand. They help us understand how we got here. Much of the bitterness comes from the fact that we were not taught our history. Today, many of the plantations are opening up thanks to the George McDaniels of the world, so we can look at them from different perspectives. That's what I'm doing. Those are reasons I became a member of Drayton Hall's site council.

What lessons might we learn from sites like Drayton Hall that could guide us through these polarized times?

We could learn a lot from historic sites. For example, Middleton Place, thanks to Charles Duell and Earl Middleton, now has family reunions of White and Black descendants together. Some people may say, "If you open the door, it will be like opening Pandora's box with all of the evils." My best friend happens to be a white female, and I am not embittered by her past, which may have been privileged. I've read about the Tulsa Race Riot a century ago, and I could be bitter indeed, but I do a lot of public speaking and read the Bible and am religious and believe that is not the way. After all, it was African kings who sold some of us into slavery, wasn't it? We must study history, and though we may not understand it, we must try not to repeat the evils of the past. Plantations teach us that.

How might historic sites and museums like Drayton Hall enhance education?

Historic sites like Drayton Hall make history tangible. You go to a plantation and look at the houses that have been preserved but need not glory in them. There you can see the contributions of African Americans. When I give a tour of Charleston, I go around the Battery and point out fine homes whose owners had plantations, and it was their slaves who built the gardens or helped make the fine furniture. It will be an easier job with the young because many of them are more receptive to African Americans and other minorities than their ancestors were. I try to look at the good and see that we're educating the ones who will become the leaders of tomorrow, so that they may learn about the contributions of those people in the past. Even in teaching about slavery, we can develop self-esteem among minorities.

How might museums like Drayton Hall respond to public tragedies like the one you experienced at Mother Emanuel?

Just 24 hours ago, I was thinking about that massacre of June 17, 2015. I'm a trustee there. As you and other organizations did with us at Emanuel, what I'd like to see is collaboration among museums and communities. We had hundreds of artifacts that people had left in front of the church or mailed to us, which you helped us curate, organize, and store as best you could. Across the nation, there could be collaborations, so people wouldn't have to come to Mother Emanuel or to a school to see an artifact that someone sent. Collaborations among museums and communities or even schools and libraries could result in local or traveling exhibits and programs. A digital committee could produce links.

Why is historic preservation important?

A lot of the people don't know their history, and that's what causes so much misunderstanding in the world. I'm a preservationist and belong to such organizations as the South Carolina African American Heritage Council. Too often, self-esteem is low among African American students. Many young people have scant understanding of his or her past, but collaborations among museums, churches, schools, and homes can improve that. Building self-esteem and enabling people to see and touch their past, historic preservation can be a difference-maker to the good.

What do you see as a future for historic sites and museums like Drayton Hall?

The future? I recommend scholarships in order to get more younger people engaged. Also, if you look at brochures of museums around the country, they are geared to the older person or the educated person. I'd like to see museums open their doors and have their advertising people attract other segments of society. It could be a homeless shelter, which may be the last thing you'd think of, but why not? You do go to schools, and dealing with the young is important, but what about a nice portrait of Drayton Hall in a bar? Many people go there. In the future, maybe you could extend yourself and include the underside of your community. In the future, museums might look outside the box and consider groups of people you've not ever thought about.

Stephanie Meeks:
"A Leader among House and History Museums"

2021 – Telephone Interview

Stephanie Meeks was president and CEO of the National Trust for Historic Preservation 2010 to 2018, and is now president and CEO of the Student Conservation Association.

When you first heard about Drayton Hall, what images came to mind? How did they change?

Stephanie: Since I had not had the opportunity to visit Drayton Hall before I became the president of the National Trust, my first impressions were of a grand Southern plantation with a beautiful building and a place steeped in history. What I learned was that Drayton Hall was so much more. It is the genesis of the notion of "whole place preservation." As I prepared for my first visit, I expected to see a place that was beautiful and engaged in preservation and conservation issues as a leader in our field. I was not disappointed.

I vividly remember my first visit in 2010, just one month into my new position. It was a swelteringly hot August day. The cicadas were loud in the trees. I drove out with you, George, then director of Drayton Hall, and before we visited the mansion, we went down to the river. You explained to me the influence of the river on the site and the importance of the concept of "whole place preservation," an effort that you had led with others to protect the Ashley River landscape, of which Drayton Hall is an important part.

A hallmark of Drayton Hall is the preservation philosophy that has been implemented over many years. Very few historic sites in the country have purposely adopted simple preservation as their guiding philosophy, and it was quite evocative to see it in practice.

Why do you think that Drayton Hall's preservation philosophy is important?

As president of the National Trust, I welcomed the implementation of different treatments at different places. At a Monticello or a Mount Vernon, there is value in trying to recreate the way Jefferson or Washington lived, for example, to draw people to the sites and educate them. At Drayton Hall, which has never had electricity and plumbing, it was courageous to say, "What if we left the building as it is and study the layers of history over time." That's what you get with a preservation application and what is lost with a restoration.

One of my favorite memories about Drayton Hall — one that touched my heart the first time that I went — is the pencil markings on the doorways marking the heights of the Draytons' children, and even one of their dogs, as they had grown up. That's the kind of thing that would be painted over in a restoration. I remember doing the same thing for my children at home. I felt connected to the Draytons who had lived there over time. That's the power of the preservation ethic.

How have your thoughts about Drayton Hall evolved over time?

Because of its commitment to preservation, not restoration, Drayton Hall is a house museum unlike any other I've visited, and it is also a leader among house and history museums in our country in the interaction with the surrounding community. One manifestation is the connection to the descendants of those who had been enslaved at Drayton Hall. George, you did a remarkable job of documenting their oral histories, identifying and memorializing the enslaved people's cemetery, and most powerfully perhaps, connecting with the current generation of descendants — helping them to feel a part of the Drayton Hall family — not as some politically correct part of our history, but as a part of the Drayton Hall story we wanted told. I cherished my memories of getting to know the descendants of the enslaved people at Drayton Hall, to hear them reflect on their families' history, and what Drayton Hall means to them today.

Another facet of Drayton Hall is its conservation leadership and the influence on the landscape on the visitor experience and on our ability to tell that story over time. Drayton Hall has worked hard the past 40 years to ensure that the landscape along the entire corridor has, as much as possible, been placed in permanent protection, that the open space and agricultural values of the Lowcountry will continue to be experienced and contribute to the life of the Ashley River region. These are ways that Drayton Hall has influenced the preservation field that might not, at first blush, be evident, but that have had profound influence.

Why is it important that a site like Drayton Hall get involved with the broader landscape and community beyond its property lines?

There are several reasons. Drayton Hall, situated between historical Ashley River Road and the scenic Ashley River, was located and designed in the 18th century and was shaped by its environs. Today its influence and leadership in conservation of surrounding lands are important locally, but also in laying groundwork for conversation throughout the nation that feature the interplay between historic buildings and the landscape. Drayton Hall has influenced the fields of conservation and preservation and how they interact.

Every historic site can contribute to and facilitate community dialogue about current issues and show how history can inform such dialogues. Managers of each site need to know their community and then create and prioritize strategies to engage the people in them. To be sure, Drayton Hall has a difficult African American history, which must be dealt with forthrightly and with courage. Improving race relations is high on the national agenda. Sites like Drayton Hall can become a platform where people come together in a safe space to talk about race and history and other issues we're dealing with as a country and as a world. All of that takes courage and leadership, which not every site has. But they have an opportunity, plus, I think, an obligation.

What can Drayton Hall and historic sites do to enhance education — K through 12 as well as undergraduate, graduates, adult education, and family education?

I'm reminded of my first visit when a children's camp was underway. As a mother, I was entranced seeing young people who were finishing a two-week camp by learning to be guides at Drayton Hall. They'd learned about history, preservation, and public speaking. Their curriculum required that they guide their parents through Drayton Hall. That's one example of how Drayton Hall is leading the way, reaching out to educate communities in South Carolina and bringing young people in.

It speaks to a larger point about historic sites and why they are important. Studying something and then seeing it and touching it is different than simply reading about it in a book or on a historic marker. Sites can develop programming in different ways to build on specific assets and use their histories to educate. They can partner with state curriculum staff to connect programs to state standards and can educate people about the issues of the day and the role each of us can play as voters, donors, and community leaders. They can teach younger students and adults about the preservation of houses, battlefields, and other specific places and explain the use of preservation tools for economic development and community revitalization. Further, sites can engage communities in conversations about growth, change, and gentrification where preservation of historic buildings is often seen in a negative light.

How might sites mitigate attempts to make people who may be different from us into "the other" or not a part of our common humanity?

To be a leader in the larger national dialogue about race, religion, and economic inequality, our historic sites first should come to terms with its own history. Themes of race, inequality, and religious intolerance have been around throughout our national history and throughout most of humanity. We need to honestly share insights from the healing process that we experience at historic sites then broaden the conversation about the role preservation can play in the healing of communities.

Is historic preservation limited to buildings only?

Preservation is evolving as a field. "Whole place preservation" means managing change in both buildings and nearby environs, as manifested at Drayton Hall by its mansion and rural setting. Another element is "intangible history," i.e., memorializing places where no physical history remains. For example, Sites of Conscience preserve places where no buildings remain yet should be preserved so people will not forget. All of this requires partnerships with other organizations. As we look to preservation's future at places like Drayton Hall, partnerships and intersections of interests will be a ripe area of exploration.

What could Drayton Hall and historic sites in general do to help mainstream preservation as an American ethos?

We have much work to do in developing a full appreciation of preservation. In Europe, the natural inclination is to save a building, while in the United States, it's assumed the building will be torn down. Sites like Drayton Hall have an important role because history is tangible here and people experience it. Sites also offer an opportunity to engage directly with the concept of preservation so first and foremost, we should deliver an exemplary experience that leaves them with a positive impression of preservation and that prompts them to come back.

If specific places or structures at Drayton Hall could speak, which ones would you select, and what questions would you like to ask of that place or structure?

I'd be interested in the basement. What happened downstairs? I'm drawn to the stories about the people doing the laundry and the cooking. What were their lives like? Not just their work, but what happened when they returned to their cabins? It would have been an invaluable experience to sit in the corner of Drayton Hall's basement two hundred years ago and then follow those people about the site.

Another place is the enslaved people's cemetery, which is, to the untrained eye, just forestland. That place is hallowed ground. I'd love to know more about the customs that led to those burials and the stories of the people that are there.

How has Drayton Hall touched your life?

It was the first National Trust historic site I visited after becoming president. It shaped my thoughts in many ways about preservation and the role that historic sites play today and in the future. It touched my heart. I've had remarkable experiences at Drayton Hall and in my interactions with people on the site and elsewhere. I often think about the staff, about members of the Drayton family, and of African American families who continue to be engaged.

Drayton Hall has touched my family as well. I want to tell a personal story that has been very meaningful to me about you, George, and a talk you gave at the National Building Museum about Palladio and his influence in the United States, particularly at Drayton Hall. My third-grade son, John, was upset that I was leaving to meet with you, so I invited him to come along. Our talk was longer than I had expected. But in the year 2011, John Meeks knew more about Palladio's influence in the United States than any other third-grader in the country. He has placed prominently in his room the brick you gave him after that night. He remembers that talk because you gave him something he could hold in his hands, a piece of Drayton Hall's history and a piece of Palladio's architectural history. It has certainly enriched my life. I'm reminded of it every time I walk into my son's room.

In thinking about historic sites and education, what do you think we could be doing to enhance our efforts in the future?

Drayton Hall is a leader in preservation and history education in many ways. But we need to think creatively about better ways to engage young people on their own terms and how to blend digital and real-life education. I would hate to abandon the non-digital touch-it, feel-it, experience-it world because it's part of what we have to offer. But based on my experience of having three children, kids today are digital natives. Their first instinct is to look online. If we want to meet them where they are, we should be concerned about the initial online impression made by our website. Are we providing online the information that they seek and not only what adults need? How do we engage young people? As preservation leaders and history educators, our challenge is to use such tools today in order to keep pace with the audiences of tomorrow.

Looking to the future, what questions would you be asking at sites like Drayton Hall?

Drayton Hall is a leader in many facets of preservation, so I'd ask, "What leadership role can Drayton Hall play going forward? How can it continue to influence preservation, history education, conservation, and facilitation of a dialogue here and elsewhere?" I won't try to answer those questions. I'll just ask them.

ACKNOWLEDGMENTS

Many are they who deserve thanks. At the top of the list must be the interviewees and the Drayton family. Without the interviewees' belief in history and its preservation, you would not be holding this book in your hands. Without the Draytons' belief in preservation and their decision not to sell Drayton Hall to a developer, we would not have a historic site. Supported by Charleston preservationists like Frances Edmunds, theirs was an unusual decision and the product of the family's values. We owe much to Charlotta Drayton and her nephews, Charlie and Frank Drayton, and Charlie's children, Molly, Anne, and Chad, and Frank's children, Frank and Randolph. Subsequent generations also contributed, and the good news is that today the Draytons are still measuring their children on Drayton Hall's growth chart, begun in the 1890s on a door jamb in the "library" room on the first floor, bearing Charlotta's name and on the opposite jamb, Nipper's, her dog. In addition to their stories, the Draytons contributed both financial support and heartfelt guidance.

This book would also not have been possible had not Drayton Hall been built and sustained by the work and talents of its enslaved work force and their descendants. Of these Richmond Bowens was the first that I knew. He helped me and so many others understand Drayton Hall as a place with families whose ways of life and values he respected. He'd grown up at Drayton Hall, and to me and whomever, he declared, "This is home." His grandfather, Caesar Bowens, and Caesar's two siblings, John and Catherine, had been enslaved at Drayton Hall, and their family's oral history was that they came over from Barbados with the Draytons in the 1670s, "before the house was built." Richmond in turn introduced me to his younger cousins Rebecca Campbell and Catherine Braxton and his niece Annie Brown Meyers, all of whom opened up their "trunk" of stories in order to preserve history. Through their "Borough Project," Rebecca and Catherine donated to this project.

The Drayton Hall Preservation Trust has graciously permitted me to edit and publish these interviews and to share with you the photographs that connect the stories to faces and places. Carter C. Hudgins, Drayton Hall's devoted President and CEO; Sarah Stroud Clarke, Director of Museum Affairs and Curator of Collections;

Trish Lowe Smith, Curator of Historic Architectural Resources; and Pamela Brown, Executive Assistant, answered the call and made this book possible in ways both obvious and unseen. My thanks run deep. It was Anthony C. Wood, a nationally respected preservation leader and devoted member of Drayton Hall Preservation Trust's board of trustees, who suggested the idea of this book and donated to it. In addition, he edited drafts, penned the Foreword, and contributed wisdom. I hope this book comes close to realizing his vision for why historical organizations need to preserve their *recent* history.

To produce what you now hold in your hands, I thank the Evening Post Books: John Burbage, Co-Founder; Michael Nolan, Executive Editor; Elizabeth Hollerith, Managing Editor; Gill Guerry, Graphic Designer; and Kathryn Smith, Indexer and Editor. Their expertise, advice, and personal support have shown why I made the right choice in choosing them. The South Carolina Archives and History Foundation served as fiscal agents and more. I wish to recognize and thank Eric Emerson, Director of the SC Department of Archives and History as well as a former member of Drayton Hall's advisory site council, and Donna Foster, Advancement Coordinator, who manages the foundation. This book was a new venture for them, and I hope the product will be worth their efforts.

Historians need all kinds of support, and many stepped forward. Esther Beaumont supported this project in myriad ways, serving as interviewee and donor. In addition to a sharp mind, she lent her sharp eye and edited drafts. Other sharp editors who also contributed financially included Alison Rea, direct descendant of John Drayton and devoted family member, and preservationist Mary Anthony, Executive Director of The 1772 Foundation. Drayton Hall's board member and one of my favorite former students, Hampton Morris, and his wife Carter, contributed, as did my brother and sister-in-law Stuart and Sarah McDaniel and their life-long friend, George Johnson, and the Phifer/Johnson Foundation. Joining the effort were dear friends Mimi Cathcart, Drayton Hall board member; Margaret and Bob Seidler; Jan Waring Woods, CPA; and Rebecca Campbell and Catherine Braxton, descendants of Drayton Hall's African American community.

Once again, Paul Wenker and the Robert and Marian Kennedy Charitable Trust stepped forward and generously donated as they have in the past to aid historic preservation. Lending their editing skills were long-time friends and preservationists Gail Rothrock, Kat Imhoff, Merideth Taylor, Jean Cheney, Jessica Garrett, and Mimi Vickers as well as museum professionals Susan Zwerling and Katie Caljean. Producing the maps was my friend Emily Gibbons, and the family lines of descent, Toni Carrier, Director of the Center for Family History at the International African American Museum in Charleston. Guiding me through this entire process and helping with editing, marketing, and website development has been Kristine Morris, former Director of Communications at Drayton Hall and a skilled hand at such. Donating both dollars and outstanding publicity was Michelle McCollum, President of the SC National Heritage Corridor, who, catching the idea quickly, published a series of beautiful and informative stories in *Southern Edge* magazine, magazine. Also helping to take this book to wider audiences was my friend and Drayton descendant, Charles Waring, publisher of the newspaper, *The Charleston Mercury*. Bob and Margaret Seidler contributed too – in more ways than one.

As all writers know, writing is a long and lonely task because words not only have to be right, they have to sound right. Thus, the writer's isolation and concentration. For their understanding, rock-solid love, and consistently good humor, I thank my two sons, James and George, the latter contributing his careful editing skills. I also thank my grandson Allen, who upon arrival, would walk quietly to my desk as I focused on these pages and greet me with a wonderful smile and strong hug, the kind you feel in your heart. As I began these Acknowledgments, I wrote about the people who made this book possible, and at the very top of that list goes my wife, Mary Sue Nunn McDaniel, whose steadfast understanding, support, and love have made, for me, all the difference in the world.

AN INITIAL GUIDE

Using a Historic Place to Build Understanding and Community

"One place understood helps us understand all places better." [1]
– Eudora Welty

History can be divisive or unifying. We've seen how its use has resulted in each. By itself, history is no panacea, for we have seen how it has been used to disparage, racialize, or stigmatize people seen as "different." It is up to us to choose. Choosing history to build understanding and community does not mean we have to agree on everything. Differences of viewpoints are to be expected, as shown by this book, but respect is the key, as is a vision of our common humanity. With that vision and respect in mind, how might we begin? Might we use our museum or a historic place to help build understanding and community and to ask people to contribute their thoughts about it and move us forward? That is what I have tried to do in this book.

Since we all need help, it may come from a wide range of resources, as my Acknowledgments illustrate. They may include your local historical or preservation organization, museum, library, school or college, business, foundation, or friends. Building bridges, of whatever size, is risky but so too is any venture beyond our comfort zone. Let's take the long view and keep our eyes on the prize. The reward may be deeper understanding, empathy, or as Bryan Stephenson declared, "just mercy," which all of us need if our communities are to be healthy.

If you or your organization wish to undertake such a venture, it is not hard but how to begin? The following is an initial guide. Since answers vary and depend on your situation, I pose questions. Also of assistance may be the many questions and answers in my interviews.

---

1 As quoted by Vernon Orville Burton in his essay, "Stranger Redux", in the book, *Becoming Southern Writers: Essays in Honor of Charles Joyner*, edited by Orville Vernon Burton and Eldred E. Prince, Jr., Columbia, SC: The University of South Carolina Press, 2016.

1. Why do you want to do this project in the face of competing priorities? Since we communicate by words and by "chemistry," you need to be clear and honest about the project for the benefit of yourself and others. Are you at ease?

2. Do you as well as members of your organization and community perceive the need for this project?

3. Who are your allies? Your opponents? Be sure to address the negatives in an affirmative manner.

4. This project should be grounded in respect. The purpose is not to prove that one viewpoint is right and the others wrong. You are all part of the same community, so think of this as a learning or team-building exercise towards higher goals.

5. Planning is critical. What are your organization's mission, vision, and strategic plan and the project's needs in terms of time, funding, facilities, or personnel?

6. What historic place or site engages the minds and hearts of a diversity of people? Examples could be a historic site, museum, town center, road, park, or river.

7. What is the demographic range of your community (gender, age, income, race, long-term or new resident, etc.)? What can you do to ensure such a range participates?

8. This project may serve as a model because its products are a book, a website, public programs, and an audiovisual and documentary archive of recent history. What might your project's products be? Publications, public programs, exhibits, website, walking tours, online applications, videos, or archives? Which serve your mission and meet your budget, time frame, and capability? Perhaps proceed in phases but aim for higher goals.

9. Who are the audiences? Do the products fit their interests and needs?

10. What is the structure of interviews? Write your questions and feel free to share them in advance with the interviewee. Please use or modify any of mine, add your own, and ask others as well as interviewees for questions they'd like you to ask.

11. Ask questions that are brief, easily understood, and that elicit answers that connect to your purpose. Try questions that reveal "both/and" — examples being ones that combine both the professional and the personal, the past and the future, the good times and bad times, the real and the imaginary. Tactfully, explore each. Be mindful of time.

12. Produce a leave-behind, explaining the project, and make sure they feel free to contact you.

13. Send your transcriptions with any edits back to the interviewee and ask them to review and edit them. Remember: their interview is like your first draft in your own writing and just as you edit, so too should the interviewee be respected and given that opportunity.

14. When the product is finished, share it with the interviewees to ensure they see the results of their participation and can share the news with others in a positive manner.

15. Produce occasions to celebrate completion and invite interviewees to them. Ask for evaluations and discuss "next steps" so this project marks the end of one endeavor and the beginning of more in fulfillment of higher goals.

For a more detailed guide with resources, please see my website: www.mcdanielconsulting.net.

NOTES

For more information, the reader is encouraged to visit Drayton Hall, consult its archives, view its website, www.draytonhall.org, or read its numerous blogs, studies, and publications, such as *Drayton Hall: The Creation and Preservation of an American Icon*. All video or audio recordings and complete transcriptions, from which these excerpts are drawn, are located there. For immediate access to complete transcriptions, maps, family lines of descent, blogs, selected photographs, how-to guides, and other resources, the reader may visit www.mcdanielconsulting.net.

ABOUT THE AUTHOR

George W. McDaniel, PhD, is the President of McDaniel Consulting, LLC, a strategy firm that helps organizations and museums build bridges within itself and to its broader constituents. For more than 25 years, he served as the Executive Director of Drayton Hall, a historic site of the National Trust for Historic Preservation in Charleston, South Carolina. A native of Atlanta, he earned a BA from Sewanee, a MAT (history) from Brown University, and PhD (history) from Duke. Interspersed through those years were travels to many places—Europe, Africa, Vietnam—where he saw peace and war and learned by experience about cultural differences and commonalities. Beginning with the Smithsonian Institution, he has built a career in education and history museums, earning awards at local, state, and national levels. A nationally respected museum professional and author, he helps organizations to use history, place, and culture to advance their capacities and enhance community engagement.

INDEX

Note: Page numbers in italics refer to images and captions

A

Affy (enslaved woman of Rebecca Drayton), 179
Aiken-Rhett House, 101, 198
alligators, 44, 72, 269
Alston, Elizabeth "Liz", *285*, 285-89
American Revolution, xii, 61, 172-73, 248
Ashley River, x, 13-14, 15, 23, 36, 41, 46, 51, 63, 64, 69, 70, 74-75, 92, 102, 122-23, 130, 141, 160, 188, 191, 195, 199, 244-45, 248, 249, 287, 292
Ashley River Road, xii, xiii, 33, 34, 51-52, 56, 66, 69, 73, 87, 97, 100, 130, 160, 239, 255, 392. *See also* Drayton Hall: Ashley River viewshed of

B

van Balgooy, Max A., *261*, 261-66
Barbados, xii, 7, 8, 238
Barker, Robert E. "Bob" Lee, *148,* 148-54, 156
Beaumont, Esther, *123*, 123-27
Bennett, Craig M., Jr., *204*, 204-211, 222, 230
Biddle, James, 93, 117, 156
Binah (great-grandmother of Roosevelt Geddis), 28, 39, 80-81, 83
Blunt, Lucille, *38*, 38-42, 239
Boan, George, 154
Boone Hall, 172, 248
Bowens, Anna. *See* Mayes, Anna Bowens
Bowens, Caesar, xiii, xxi, 7, 25, 26, 48, 51, 195
Bowens, Catherine, xiii, xxi, 25, 26, 48, 49. *See also* Johnson, Catherine Bowens.

Bowens, Eloise, 42-44
Bowens, Helen, 7, 8, 9, 10
Bowens, Joseph, 44
Bowens, John, xiii, xx, 48
Bowens, Lillian, 35
Bowens, Lucille. *See* Brown, Lucille Bowens
Bowens, Richmond, Jr. (Hershel), xxi, xiii, xxi, 3-4, 5, *7*, 7-12, *12*, 18-19, 21-22, 24, 26-32, 33, 34, 38, 44, 47, 48-49, 52-53, 55, 59, 78-79, 151, 153, 158-59, 173, 194-95, 249, 287
Bowens, Richmond, Sr., xxi, 7-9, 33, 52, 195
Bowens, Robert, 44
Bowens, Samuel, 9, 35
Bowens, Velma, 11, 18, 27, 47, 53
Braxton, Catherine Brown, xiii, xv, xxi, *1*, 1-6, 27, 30, *48*, 48-56, 60, *85*, 85-87, 243, 287-88
Brown, Lucille Bowens, xxi, 195
Buck, Susan, *197*, 197-204
Bunch, Lonnie III, *145,* 145-48, 191, 243
Burns, Sadie Mayes, 35
Burns, Thomas, 35

C

Campbell, Rebecca Brown, xxi, *1*, 1-6, *25*, 25-32, *48*, 48-56, *85*, 85-87, 243, 287-88
Canaan United Methodist Church, 82, 84
Carrier, Toni, 25-32, 43-47, 66-70, *237*, 237-41, 275
Champagne, Tom, 67-68
Chappell, Edward "Ed", *197*, 197-204, 221-22
Charleston Convention and Visitors Bureau, 134-35

Charleston Heritage Federation, 133, 190, 191, 282
Charleston Museum, The, 74, 102
Civil Rights Movement, 36-37, 240-41, 286. *See also* race relations
Civil War, xiii, 172, 174, 175, 242
Clyburn, James, 192, 286-87
Colbert, Stephen, 95
College of Charleston, 172, 177, 241-42
Colonial Williamsburg, 86, 93, 97, 124, 166, 194, 198, 204, 230, 262
colonoware, 87, 169, 247
Continental Congress, xii, 61

D

DeLaine, Marguerite, 8, 10-11
Dennis, Martha, 12, 41
Drayton, Charles (son of founder John Drayton), xx, xii-xiii, xx, 25-26, 158, 174, 176, 194, 195, 196, 229, 236
Drayton, Charles De Vere, xx, 61-62
Drayton, Charles Henry, xiii, xx
Drayton, Charles H. V, xiii, xx
Drayton, Charles H. "Charlie", xiii, xiv, xv, xx, *1*, 1-6, 11, *13*, 13-19, 21, *25*, 25-32, 53, *56*, 56-60, 70, 71, 73, 76, 77, 78, 79-80, 93, 97, 158, 171, 190-91, 226
Drayton, Charles H. "Chad" Drayton Jr., xx, 1-6, 15, 16, 26, *56*, 56-60, 226
Drayton, Charles (Charlie Drayton's grandson), xx, *1*, 1-6, *56*, 56-60
Drayton, Charlie (Charlie Drayton's great-grandson), *56*, 57
Drayton, Charlotta "Aunt Charley", xiii-xiv, xx, 5, 13-14, 16-19, 21, 24, 56, 57, 72, 74, 92, 96, 106, 149, 159, 167, 171, 190-91, 195, 205
Drayton, Frank B., xiii-xiv, xx, 2, 13, 63, 70, 71, 93, 97, 171, 190, 205
Drayton, Frank B. Jr., xx, *1*, 1-6, *70*, 70-76, 205
Drayton, John (founder of Drayton Hall), x, xii, xxii, xx, 20, 26, 61, 65, 126, 128, 163, 167, 168-69, 179, 194, 216, 232
Drayton, John (founder's grandson), xii, xx, 61

Drayton, John Grimke, 69
Drayton, Marley, 72
Drayton, Mary Jervey, 16, 21
Drayton, Randolph, xx, 63, 205
Drayton, Rebecca, xii, 157, 159, 179
Drayton, Thomas Middleton, xiv, *70*, 70-76
Drayton, Thomas Middleton Jr., *70*, 71
Drayton, William Henry (founder's son), xii, xx, 61, 63
Drayton Hall
  African American cemetery at, 8, 11, 12, 18-19, 22, 26, 27, 30-32, 41, 38, 46, 53, 67, 80, 83-84, 99, 132, 145-48, 191, 238-39, 241, 243, 291, 294
  African American genealogy studies at, 237-41, 275
  African American residents of, xiii, 1-6, 7-12, 17, 25-26, 32-38, 39-42, 45, 48-56, 59-60, 65-70, 80-84, 98, 167, 173, 238-240, 241-46, 248-49, 260, 266, 275. *See also* Drayton Hall: slavery and enslaved people at
  African American visitors to, 173-74, 179, 180-81, 192, 242, 249, 265, 266, 272-73, 276, 277-78,
  American Revolution and, xii, 61, 132, 248
  ancestral spirits at, 3-4-6, 26, 37-38, 49, 53, 55
  archaeology at, 4, 7-12, 63, 102, 134, 166-71, 207, 215, 247
  architecture of, x, 23, 63, 73, 77, 79, 94, 97-98, 106, 121-22, 126, 149, 151, 152, 165, 184, 195, 206, 212, 215, 216, 219-20, 222, 223, 225-27, 229, 232, 251, 262-63
  archives of, xiv, 151, 158, 173, 178, 228, 238
  artifacts of, 7, 9, 73, 86, 128, 162-63, 165, 168-69, 196, 275, 280
  Ashley River viewshed of, 63-64, 74-75, 100, 102, 119, 122-23, 125, 130, 160, 226, 234, 250-55, 281, 290
  Board of Trustees of, ix, xiii, 94, 95, 236
  caretaker cottage at, xiii, 17, 24, 32, 35, 150

challenges and opportunities for, 100, 135, 176, 185-87, 193, 203, 247, 258-59, 260-61, 263-65, 268-69, 275, 277, 280, 281-84, 289, 294-95

children's activities at, 3, 13-14, 16-18, 20-21, 27, 41, 45-46, 56-57, 71-72, 78. *See also* Drayton Hall: educational programming at

Christmas at, 10, 13, 29

Civil War and, xiii

construction of, xii, 52, 98, 106, 168, 205-9, 213-17

cooking and food at, 17, 34, 82, 98-99, 247

daily life at, 9-11, 28-29, 39-40, 52, 98-99, 238-3, 246-49, 294

donors to. *See* Beaumont, Esther; Kennedy, Kennedy, Marian K. and Robert A.; Reahard, Sally

Drayton Family Memorial (cemetery) at, 4, 15-16, 22-23, 76, 224, 226

educational programming at, 6, 24, 63, 67, 81, 98-99, 126, 128, 130-31, 134, 139, 156-59, 179- 80, 203-4, 212, 231, 236, 245, 266, 292-93

emancipation at, 8, 49, 248-49, 266

environmental issues and, 74-75, 100, 122-23, 125, 130, 141, 160, 291-92. *See also* Drayton Hall: Ashley River viewshed of; Drayton Hall: Watson Hill development and

family gatherings at, 3, 20, 21, 26-27, 56, 58, 59, 63, 71, 92, 94, 205

farming at, xiii, 246-49. *See also* rice cultivation

finances of, 24, 129, 156-57

first impressions of, 3-4, 5, 20, 36, 49, 56, 57, 62, 71-72, 77-78, 92, 124-25, 133-34, 149, 150, 155, 172-73, 177, 183-84, 189, 198, 212, 219, 224-25, 228, 233, 238, 241, 251-52, 257, 262, 274, 280, 287, 290

Friends membership program of, 149, 156, 159

furniture at, 18,73

gatehouse at, 149, 151

George W. McDaniel Education Center at, 123, 126

growth chart at, 57, 70-71, 167, 291

hangings at, 46, 51

heritage tourism and, 100, 127, 134-35, 184, 189-93, 281

house servants at, xiii, 33, 36, 46, 52, 202, 244

hunting and fishing at, 14, 27, 41

hurricanes at, 27, 38, 57, 71, 78, 113, 133

lack of amenities at, 14-15, 16-17, 24, 74, 92, 106, 159

landscape architecture at, 100, 165, 225-26, 233-36

Lenhardt Collection at, 162-63

Lendhardt Garden at, 236

live oak tree at, 18, 46, 51, 56, 57, 71, 87, 235, 287

livestock at, 27, 33, 39, 98, 159

masonry at, 52, 168, 190, 206, 209, 213, 215

memory map of, xiii, *12*

museum shop (Richard and Jill Almeida Gallery) at, 17, 26, 28, 29, 35, 55, 148, 150-51, 191

paint at, 197-204

parties at, 3, 30 58, 71, 92, 153, 159, 182

phosphate mining at, xiii, 13, 42, 44, 158, 170, 194, 238, 239-40

ponds at, 63, 72, 164

portico at, 132, 156, 168, 201, 204-11, 220-23, 230-31

preservation vs. restoration of, viii, 5, 14, 59, 64, 73-74, 98, 106, 129-30, 138, 140, 152, 156, 159, 163-65, 187, 201-2, 206-7, 216, 229, 257, 263, 266, 290-91

privy at, 125-26, 194-96

race relations at, 21-22, 27-32, 35, 37-38, 53, 54, 59-60, 78-79, 135-36, 170, 174, 208-9, 244-46

religious life at, 29, 40-41, 50, 67, 81-82, 83, 87

Robert A. Kennedy Memorial Library at, 119, 121-22, 126, 226
sale to National Trust of, 2-6, 15, 18, 24, 26, 58, 73-74, 77, 93-95, 97, 116-17
Sally Reahard Visitor Center at, xiii, 63, 102, 165, 235-36
significance of, 56, 57, 58, 61-63, 72, 75, 77, 79-80, 85, 94, 97-98, 125, 130-33, 134, 170, 209, 243-44, 249, 257-58
singing and music at, 29, 30-31, 51, 82, 83, 84, 159, 243
Site Advisory Council of, 127, 128, 136, 138, 145, 287-88
slavery and enslaved people at, 2-6, 7, 23-24, 28-29, 31, 35, 36, 46, 50-52, 54-55, 59-60, 62, 63, 86-87, 98-99, 100, 131-32, 135-36, 158, 169, 173-75, 177, 217, 238, 246-49, 260, 266, 287, 291
stairways at, 21, 23, 52, 77, 168, 199-200, 202, 244-45, 275
store at, *12*, 67-68
tenant houses at, 8, 11, *12*, 28, 39-40, 41
Thanksgiving at, 13, 20, 21, 59, 72, 76, 78, 79
3D modeling at, 169, 208, 230, 231, 232
tours and tour guides at, 58, 72-73, 131, 148-54, 157, 160, 171-76, 177-82, 202, 203, 205, 242, 243, 266, 272, 287, 292
vandalism of, 3, 23, 71, 73
vision for, 129, 218, 226-27, 231, 273, 264-65, 284, 289
Watson Hill development and, 181, 187-88, 250-55
weddings at, 19, 20-21, 23, 26-27, 72, 76, 94, 153
Drayton Hall Preservation Trust, xiv, 48, 73, 127-29, 132, 136, 161, 295-97
Duell, Charles H.P., xiv, 96-101, *96*, 133, 189, 250, 288
Dulaney, W. Marvin, *246*, 246-49

E

Edmunds, Frances, 91, 92-95, 97, 101, 110, 154, 296
Edwards, George, 162-63
Ellem, Warren, 8, 9
Emanuel AME Church. *See* Mother Emanuel
Emerson, W. Eric, *256*, 256-61

F

Fordham, Damon, *171*, 171-76
Foster, Robin, 25-32, 66-70

G

Galbraith, Letitia. *See* Machado, Letitia "Tish" Galbraith
Gates, Steve, *127*, 127-32, 236
Geddis, Luetta Hopkins, 81, 82
Geddis, Roosevelt, *80*, 80-84
Gibson, Johnnie Mae Leach, 65-70
Goodwyn, Larry, xiv, xv
Green, Jonathan, 98, 192
Gullah language and culture, 35, 40, 45, 81, 246, 247
Guss, Alison, 246-49

H

Halifax, Shawn, 269, 284
Harrell-Roye, Shelia, *177*, 177-82
Haynes, Hattie (Nanny Notes), *12*, 45
Hill, Helen, *189*, 189-93
Historic Charleston Foundation, 15, 92-93, 94, 97, 102, 156, 157
historic preservation, 93, 96, 99-101, 120, 137-42, 160, 183-87, 190-93, 204-11, 212-213, 228, 279-80, 289, 293
History Channel, The, 7, 11, 246
Hopkins, Francis "Frank", 81, 83
Hopkins, Hattie, 80-82. *See also* Haynes, Hattie
Hopkins, James, 80-82
Hopkins, Luetta. *See* Geddis, Luetta Hopkins
Howard, Greg Osteen, xiv, *76*, 76-80
Howard, Jennifer, *250*, 250-55
Howard, Molly, *76*, 79

Hudgins, Carter C., 38-42, 129, *161*, 161-65, 166, 210, 222
Huger, Joann Bowens, *43*, 43-47
Huggins, Nancy Naomi Grant Ryan, *148*, 148-54

I

International African American Museum, 25, 192, 237, 241, 245, 275

J

Jamestown, 161-62, 166
Johnson, Catherine Bowens, xxi, 48, 49, 51, 52
Johnson, Cleveland, 27
Johnson, Frank, 49, 50, 52, 53
Johnson, Friday, 49, 52
Johnson, Willis, Sr., xxi, 26, 48, 49-50, 87
Joyner, Charles, 7-12

K

Kennedy, Marian K. "Madge" and Robert A., 119-123, 226
Keyes, Glenn, *219*, 219-23, 235

L

Lawson, Dennis, 150
Leach, Isaac, *65*, 65-70
Leach, Johnny, 45, *65*, 65-70, 239
Lenhardt, Ben, 95
Lewis, Lynne, 7-12, 79, 150, 166
Lilly, Eli and J.K., 104, 108
Logan, Sandy, 15, 226
Lowe Smith, Trish, 208

M

Machado, Letitia Galbraith "Tish", *155*, 155-60
McCollum, Michelle, *280*, 280-84
McDaniel, George W. *1*, 85. *See also* Drayton Hall: George W. McDaniel Education Center
McGee, Patti and Peter, *91*, 91-96
McGill, Joseph, *274*, 274-80, 284
McKay, Jenny Sanford, *133*, 133-36
McLeod plantation site, 248, 271, 284

Magnolia Plantation and Gardens, xii, 8, 29, 32, 42-45, 65, 68-69, 92, 237-39, 252, 276, 284
Marks, Richard "Moby", 205, 210, *211*, 211-18
Marvin, Robert, 225, 234
Mayes, Anna Bowens, 8-9, 32-33
Mayes, Bud, 33
Mayes, Thompson "Tom", *183*, 183-88
MeadWestvaco. *See* WestRock
Meeks, John, 294
Meeks, Stephanie, *290*, 290-95
Meyers, Annie Brown "Girlie", xxi, *1*, *32*, 32-38, 195
Middleton Place, xii, 29, 32, 35, 91-92, 96, 99, 240, 245, 250, 253, 276
Middleton Place Foundation, 96-101, 133
Millard, Jay, 25-27
Mother Emanuel (Emanuel AME Church), 170, 241, 287, 289
Mount Zion AME Church, 50

N

National Trust for Historic Preservation, viii, x, xi, 2, 5, 14, 15, 19, 22-23, 24, 26, 28, 58, 59, 62, 72-73, 76, 77-78, 85, 91, 93, 94, 97, 101, 116-17, 119, 121-22, 128-29, 130, 136, 137-38, 140, 148, 149, 150, 152, 154, 155-57, 160, 164, 166, 183, 184, 186, 187-88, 190, 201, 212, 216, 260, 262, 263, 266, 274, 279-80, 290-94
Nelson, Anne Drayton, 2, *13*, 13-19
Nelson, Garnett, 16
Nelson, Shelby, xx, *1*, 1-6

O

Olive Branch Baptist Church, 40, 67
Onassis, Jacqueline Kennedy, 137, 152-53
Osteen, Molly Drayton, xx, 15-16, *19*, 19-24, 76, 77, 78, 155
Osteen, Monty, *19*, 19-24, 76

P

Paonessa, Laurie, 7
Parker, Scott, 8, 9, 10

Palladian architecture, x, 63, 79, 94, 97-98, 106, 121, 129, 149, 152, 156, 184, 212, 216, 219, 220, 227, 294
Powers, Bernard, *241*, 241-46
Preservation Society of Charleston, 102, 156, 122
Pringle, Ron, 53

R

race relations, 11, 36-37, 45-54, 60, 75, 82, 87, 98-99, 135-36, 138-39, 203-04, 245-46, 267-68, 278-80, 285-86, 288-89, 292. *See also* civil rights movement; Drayton Hall: race relations at
Rea, Alison, xii, *61*, 61-64
Reahard, Ralph, 107
Reahard, Ralph M. III "Bo", *107*, 107-11
Reahard, Sally, 97, 101-18, 156. *See also* Drayton Hall: Sally Reahard Visitor Center
Reahard, Stanley Smith, *107*, 107-11
Reider, Peggy, 177, 178, 180, 181, 228
rice cultivation, x, 28-29, 50, 86, 98, 99, 145, 149, 157, 164, 170, 192, 246-47, 249, 258, 269, 272, 274, 278-79
Runnymede Plantation, 39, 41, 65, 66, 69

S

St. Phillip's AME Church, 81-82
schools, 22, 34, 37, 39, 41, 42, 43, 45, 82. See also Drayton Hall: educational programming at
Seeger, Ken, *250*, 250-55
Sheppard, Mary, 35
Simmons, Philip, 11, 53
Slave Dwelling Project, 274, 275, 277, 279
slavery and enslaved people, 23, 64, 139, 145-48, 170, 172, 174, 175, 179, 180, 185, 187, 192, 245-49, 260, 266, 267-73, 274-80, 287, 288-89. *See also* Drayton Hall: slavery and enslaved people at
Smith, Catherine Payne, *43*, 43-47
Smithsonian Institution, 145, 146, 147, 191, 243
South Carolina, State of, 93, 97, 98

Department of Archives and History, 2, 256-61
Department of Parks, Recreation and Tourism, 98, 134-35, 189
Springfield Baptist Church, 33, 47, 67
Stokes, Viola, 39, 42
Stroud Clarke, Sarah, *166*, 166-71, 210, 222, 228

T

Taylor, Betty Drayton, 61-62
Thomas, Jim, 15, *224*, 224-27
Toby (enslaved manservant of Charles Drayton), 158
Todd, Tracey, 284
Tuminaro, Craig, 15, 177, 181

V

van Balgooy, Max A., *261*, 261-66

W

Washington, Isaac, 39-42
Washington, Rebecca, 39-42
Watson Hill development. *See under* Drayton Hall.
Webster, Matthew "Matt", 15, 166, *194*, 194-96
Weeks, Bill, *112*, 112-15
Wenker, Paul, *119*, 119-23
Wertimer, Sheila, 15, 226, *233*, 233-36
WestRock, 250-54
White, Graham, 8, 10
White, Lorraine S., *80*, 80-84, 243
Wilkins, Gene, *101*, 101-7
Willing, Donald and Katherine, *115*, 115-18
Wood, Anthony C., *136*, 136-42, 169, 237
Wood Family Fellowship, 142, 161, 162-63, 165, 166, 167, 228, 237, 238
Wood, Peter H., xiv, xv, *267*, 267-73
Wood, Stephen J., ix, 137-38, 141-42, 159

Drayton Hall, Charleston, SC*

61

Middleton Place

Magnolia Plantation

Drayton Hall

Ashley River Road

SC

17

*Not to scale

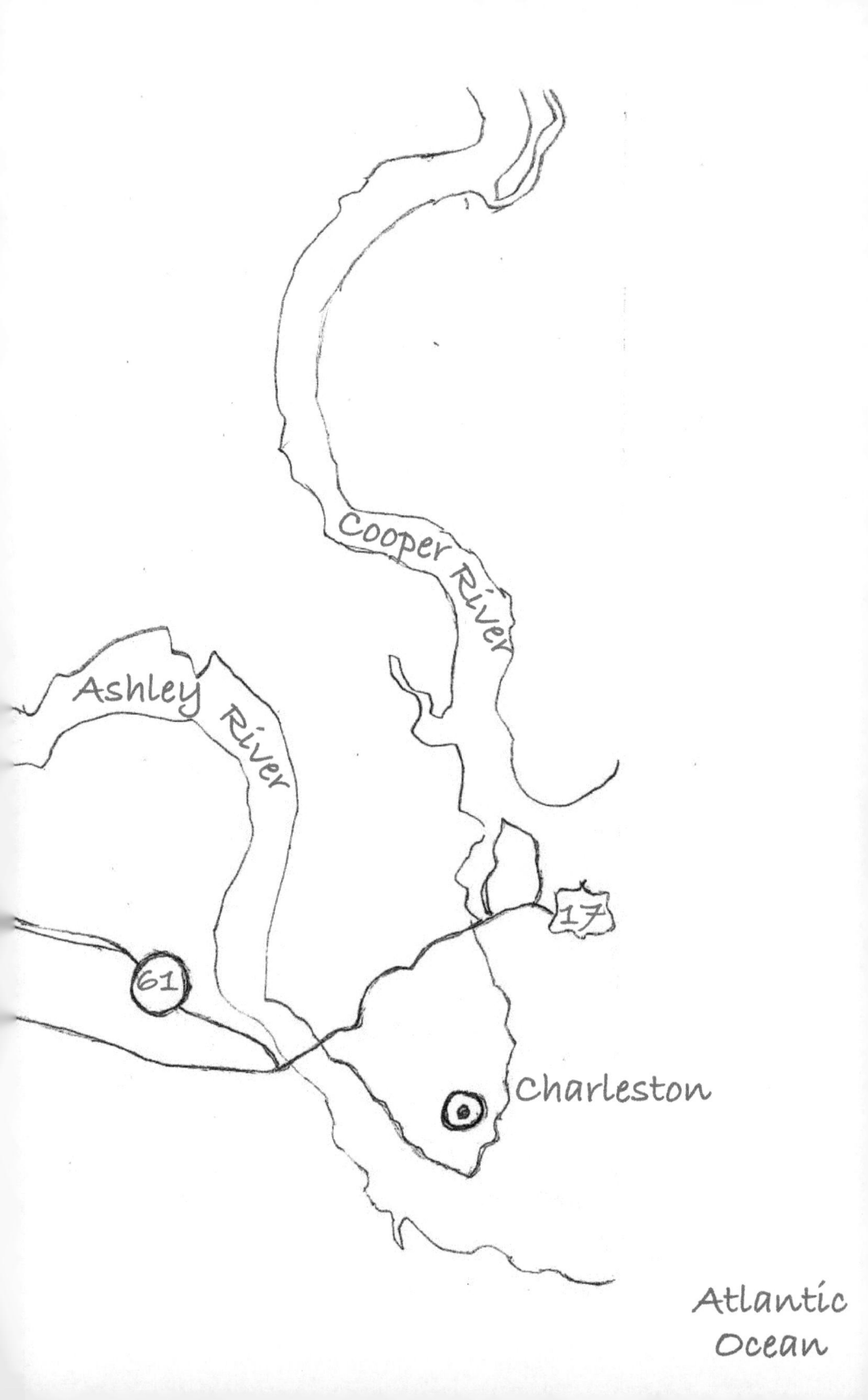

CPSIA information can be obtained
at www.ICGtesting.com
Printed in the USA
BVHW061437160322
631299BV00003B/3